Agnesi to Zeno: Over 100 Vignettes from the History of Math

Sanderson M. Smith

KEY CURRICULUM PRESS
Innovators in Mathematics Education

Agnesi to Zeno: Over 100 Vignettes from the History of Math

Author: Sanderson M. Smith

Editors: Greer Lleuad and Crystal Mills

Copyeditor: Dahlia Armon

Proofreader: Christine Sabooni

Additional writing: Frank Ellis (vignette 54); Leonard Feldman (vignettes 35, 84, 90, 95, and 100); Leon Harkleroad (vignette 96); Tian Zaijin (vignette 48); and Wei Zhang (vignette 96)

Review: Cathy Kessel, University of California, Berkeley, California; Dr. Sidney J. Kolpas, Glendale Community College, Glendale, California; Joe Malkevitch, York College (CUNY), Jamaica, New York; Karen Michalowicz, Mathematics Chair, Langley School, McLean, Virginia; Dr. Charlene Morrow, SummerMath, Mt. Holyoke College, South Hadley, Massachusetts; Claudia Zaslavsky, Author and Mathematics Education Consultant, New York, New York

Editorial support: Romy Fuller and Laura Schattschneider

Solutions: Dudley Brooks and Sarah Block

Production manager: Luis Shein

Cover design and production: Hillary Turner and Terry Lockman

Design: Terry Lockman of Lumina Designworks

Illustrations: J. F. Ptak Science Books of Alexandria, Virginia, and Ellen Hayes

Production and layout: Ann Rothenbuhler and Susan Parini

10 9 8 7 6 5 4 3 2   99 98 97 96

Key Curriculum Press
P.O. Box 2304
Berkeley, CA 94702
510-548-2304
editorial@keypress.com

Limited Reproduction Permission

This book is dedicated to the following programs that have offered support and recognition to me personally and to numerous mathematics teachers.

- Sci-Math Fellowship Program, Council for Basic Education

- National Educator Awards Program, Milken Family Foundation

- Tandy Technology Scholars Program, Tandy Corporation/Texas Christian University

- Presidential Awards for Excellence in Science and Mathematics Teaching, National Science Foundation

- Woodrow Wilson National Fellowship Foundation Summer Programs for Mathematics and Science Teachers

This book is the result of a project supported by a grant from the Council for Basic Education (CBE) in Washington, DC. I am extremely grateful to CBE for providing this fellowship and related funding that allowed me to take time to pursue a project I'd had on the back burner for a number of years.

Contents

Publisher's Preface   v

Author's Preface   vii

Suggested Uses for This Book   ix

1   The Unknown Origin of Counting   1

One-to-one correspondence, tally marks, Mesopotamian cuneiform, Egyptian hieroglyphics, Chinese ideograms, number systems, large number concepts, James Boswell, abacus

2   Ancient References to Pi   3

Approximations for pi, Solomon's palace, molten sea, Archimedes, Liu Hui, Aryabhata, *Aryabhatiya*

3   The Pyramids of Egypt and the Americas   5

Great Pyramid of Gizeh, the mathematics of pyramid construction, Pythagorean theorem, Mayan step pyramids, Temple of the Inscriptions, Temple of the Sun, Pyramid of the Sun, Mesopotamian ziggurats

4   Chinese Mathematical Activities   7

Luo shu, magic squares, Chinese applications of Pythagorean theorem, Yang Hui, Chinese version of Pascal's triangle, Zhu Shijie, *Siyuan yujian* (*Precious mirror of the four elements*)

5   The Rhind Papyrus and the St. Ives Puzzle   9

Rhind Mathematical Papyrus, Henry Rhind, Ahmes, heiratic and hieroglyphic writing, ciphers, unit fractions, Problems 79 and 62 of the *Papyrus,* Moritz Cantor, Fibonacci, *Liber abacci* (*Book of calculations*), St. Ives puzzle.

6   Early Astronomy   11

Astronomy and mathematical invention, importance of solar and lunar cycles, calendars, Egypt, Sirius and Nile floods, Mayan cosmology and calendar, Troth, Yi Xing

7   Cosmologies of the Ancient World   13

Creation myths, Gaia and Themi, Assyrian-Babylonian god Marduk, ancient Egyptian, Indian, and Hebrew cosmologies, Hildegard von Bingen, Galileo Galilei

8   Calendars of the Ancient World   15

Calendrical mathematics, ancient European solar calendar, Babylonian lunisolar calendar, Yoruba farming calendar, Chinese calendar, resonance periods, Greek calendrical computer, Khmer temple calendar, Yasovarman, Stonehenge

9   Thales: A Man of Legend   17

Thales of Miletus, Thales and the Great Pyramid in Egypt, geometric theorem, knowledge exchange in ancient world, King Croesus of Lydia, solar eclipse in sixth century B.C., fundamental geometric concepts proved by Thales

10 The Golden Age of Greece   19

Early Greek mathematicians, development of the deductive system, Christian and Islamic destruction of Greek and Alexandrian academies, Baghdad library and Arabic translations of Greek texts, Aristotle

11 Early Greek Mathematicians   21

Anaximander's astronomical, cosmological, and evolutionary notions, Plato's Academy in Athens, the *Republic,* Plato's views on mathematics and nature's mathematical design, Archimedes' use of physical models and his demonstration of a principle of levers, "Eureka, eureka!" and first law of hydrostatics

12 Ideal and Irrational Numbers   23

Pythagoras, Pythagoreans and their inclusion of women, Pythagorean theorem, *tetractys,* 10 as the ideal number, Pythagorean cosmology, discovery of irrational numbers, legend of Hippasus

13 The Paradoxes of Zeno   25

Greek suspicion of the infinite, Zeno of Elea, the *Dichotomy,* the *Achilles,* Leonhard Euler and infinity, Georg Cantor's work with set theory and the infinite, Eubulides

14 Infinitude of Primes   27

Prime numbers Euclid's proof of the infinitude primes, largest known prime, Anatole Lucas, Christian Goldbach

15 The *Elements* of Euclid   29

Euclidean geometry, deductive system, postulates and theorems, primitive terms, Euclid's geometric assumptions, Pasch's axiom

16 Apollonius and Conic Sections   31

Apollonius, conic sections (circle, ellipse, parabola, hyperbola), use of conics to describe universe, Edmund Halley and Halley's Comet, conic sections in the physical world

17 Eratosthenes' Computation   33

Eratosthenes, library at Alexandria, calculation of circumference of earth, Greek *stadia*

18 Philo, Religion, and Mathematics   35

Philo Judeaus of Alexandria, Neoplatonist and Platonic views about God and mathematics (God controls mathematics or mathematics is an infallible external truth)

19 The Formulas of Heron and Brahmagupta   37

Heron of Alexandria, Heron's formula and the area of a triangle, irrational numbers, Brahmagupta, Brahmagupta's formula and the area of a cyclic quadrilateral, *Brahmasphutasiddhanta (Correct astronomical system of Brahma)*

20 Diophantus of Alexandria   39

Alexandria, Diophantus' *Arithmetica,* solutions for indeterminate equations, Diophantine analysis, riddle of Diophantus

21 African Number Systems and Symbolism   41

African number history, ancient African empires, Yoruba counting words, cowrie shells as currency, taboo against counting living things, one-to-one correspondence, observation versus counting, significant numbers, Kenya finger counting

22 Nine Chapters on Mathematical Art   **43**

Jiuzhang suanshu (*Nine Chapters on the mathematical art*), negative numbers, Wei dynasty, Liu Hui, *Haidao suanjing* (*Sea island mathematic manual*), trigonometric ratios, Liu's estimate of pi, significant early Chinese mathematicians

23 Hypatia of Alexandria   **45**

Theon, education of women in early Greece, Hypatia's commentaries and work with the astrolabe and hydroscope, political tensions that led to Hypatia's murder

24 The Concept of Zero   **47**

Confusion about zero's meanings, seventh-century Hindu developments of concept of zero, Brahmagupta and division by zero, Bhaskara and his *Vija-Ganita,* integration of zero into consistent number system, Mayan developments of concept of zero

25 Mathematics in Play: The Throw Sticks Game   **49**

Probability and game strategy, rules of play for the Apache Throw Sticks Game

26 Mathematicians of the Middle Ages   **51**

Hrotswitha of Gandersheim; medieval convents and the education of women; Hrotswitha's work in literature, history, mathematics, and astronomy; Qin Jiushao and his *Shushu jiuzhang* (*Mathematical treatise in nine sections*), polynomial equations, abstraction of Chinese mathematics; Johannes Müller (Regiomontanus) and trigonometry, *De triangulis omnimodi* (*On triangles of every kind*)

27 Islamic Mathematics   **53**

City of Baghdad established, library of Baghdad, preservation of ancient Greek mathematical texts, *Bayt al-Hikma* (*House of Wisdom*), Muhammad ibn Musa al-Khwarizmi's work with algebra and concept of zero, Abu Ali al-Hasan ibn al-Haytham' work with optics, ibn Yahya al-Samaw'al Islamic astronomy, Muhammad Abu'l Wafa

28 Hindu Mathematicians: Aryabhata and Bhaskara   **55**

Aryabhata's *Aryabhatiya,* Hindu tradition of writing in verse, sine table of *Siddhantas* (*Systems of astronomy*), Ptolemy's table of chords, Bhaskara's work with indeterminate equations and approximations for pi, legend of the *Lilavati*

29 The Long History of Negative Numbers   **57**

Theoretical treatment of negative numbers before 1800 (Brahmagupta, ibn Yahya al-Samaw'al, Bhaskara, Liu Hui, Diophantus, Nicholas Chuquet, Michael Stifel, Girolamo Cardano, François Viète, René Descartes, Antoine Arnauld, Jean le Rond d'Alembert), dual role of minus symbol, Leonhard Euler's work with concept of negative numbers in his *Complete Introduction to Algebra*

30 The Poet Mathematicians   **59**

Omar Khayyam's work cubic equations, parallel postulate, powers of binomial expressions, Persian calendar, the *Rubaiyat,* Henry Wadsworth Longfellow's mathematical poetry

31 The Fibonacci Sequence   **61**

Leonardo of Pisa (Fibonacci), Fibonacci's education in Algiers and his contribution to introducing Hindu-Arabic numerals to Europe, Fibonacci sequence in nature, rabbit problem from *Liber abacci* (*Book of calculation*)

32 The Knotty Records of the Inca   **63**

The rise of the Inca empire, use of the quipu to keep records, quipu construction and method of use, quipu makers

33 Stifel's Number Mysticism   **65**

Algebra and number theory of Michael Stifel's *Arithmetica integra,* Stifel's influence
on John Napier's development of logarithms, Stifel's end-of-world prophecy and
attempt to prove that Pope Leo X was the Antichrist

34 The Golden Ratio and Rectangle   **67**

Pythagoras and the golden ratio, the golden rectangle in art and architecture, Leonardo
da Vinci's *St. Jerome,* Fibonacci sequence

35 Visual Mathematics   **69**

Art and mathematics, mathematics of ancient architectural structures, the Alhambra,
Frank Lloyd Wright and the Solomon R. Guggenheim Museum, mathematical principles
in folk art, modern artists and artistic movements inspired by mathematics, computer
art, fractals

36 The Cardano-Tartaglia Dispute   **71**

Niccolò Tartaglia of Brescia, Girolamo Cardano, Tartaglia's discovery of a method to
solve certain cubic equations, problem-solving contest, Cardano's oath to Tartaglia,
Scipione del Ferro, Cardano's *Ars Magna*

37 The Birth of Complex Numbers   **73**

The square root of –1, early development of complex numbers (Bhaskara,
Giralamo Cardano, René Descartes), imaginary number, properties of real and
complex numbers, multiplication law for radicals, applications of complex numbers, Leonhard Euler and his equation $e^{i\pi} - 1 = 0$, Rafael Bombelli, John-Robert
Argand, Carl Friedrich Gauss

38 Sometime Mathematician: Viète   **75**

François Viète's legal career, developments in algebraic notation, literal coefficient,
Descartes and quadratic equations, negative numbers, Jan Hudde, use of trigonometric
ratios in algebraic equations, *In artem analyticem isagoge*

39 Napier Invents Logarithms   **77**

John Napier, importance of invention of logarithms, today's use of logarithms as exponents, Jobst Bürgi, Napier's attempt to predict the end of the world

40 Ten Days Lost in 1582   **79**

Julius Caesar and the Julian calendar, leap year, inaccuracy of Julian calendar, Christoph
Clavius, Pope Gregory XIII, Gregorian calendar, loss of ten calendar days, calendars
used by different cultures (Julian calendar, Hijra, Hebrew calendar), Maya calendar

41 Changing Universe: Ptolemy, Copernicus, Kepler   **81**

The evolving cosmologies of Claudius Ptolemy, Nicholas Copernicus, and Johannes
Kepler: earth as center of universe, sun as the center of the universe with earth as a
"wanderer," planets moving on an elliptical path with the sun as a common focus for
the planets, Johannes Gutenberg

42 Galileo Relates Experimentation and Theory   **83**

Galileo Galilei's conflict with the Roman Catholic Church over the position of the
earth in the universe, finite and infinite classes of objects, development of the refracting telescope, foundation of the mechanics of freely falling bodies, discovery of four
moons of Jupiter, Giordano Bruno

43 Descartes: A Man Who Sought Change   **85**

René Descartes' attempt to break with ancient thinking, *Discourse on the Method,*
laws of nature as part of predetermined mathematical plan, analytic geometry, Pierre
de Fermat, Cartesian coordinate system, Cartesian plane

44 Pascal's Useful Triangle 87

Blaise Pascal, laws of mathematics as absolute truths, Chinese use of triangle named after Pascal, Pascal's triangle as a probability tool, number relationships of Pascal's triangle

45 The Mystery of Fermat 89

Pythagorean Theorem, Pierre de Fermat, Fermat's Last Theorem, Andrew Wiles and Richard Taylor's proof of Fermat's Last Theorem, Leonhard Euler's equation $a^4 + b^4 + c^4 = d^4$, integers that satisfy Euler's equation

46 Gambling Initiates Probability Study 91

Chevalier de Méré's dice game, Blaise Pascal's analysis of de Méré's game, birth of probability theory, Pierre de Fermat, games of chance

47 The Calculus Controversy 93

Astronomical developments and the invention of calculus, dispute between Isaac Newton and Gottfried Leibniz, Jacob and Johann Bernoulli, Newton's *Principia,* law of gravitation and laws of motion, Leibniz's calculus notation, Leibniz and England's Royal Society, Karl Marx's work in calculus, John Wallis, Isaac Barrow, Christiaan Huygens, René Descartes

48 Mei Wending: Cultural Bridge 95

Mei's role in introducing Western mathematics to China, calendrical mathematics, integration of Chinese application and Western theory, Mei's ability to simply describe complex concepts, Mei Jeu-cheng and the *Mei shi congshu jiyao* (*Collected works of the Mei family*), Mateo Ricci

49 The Bernoulli Family 97

Bernoulli family's eleven mathematicians, Gottfried Leibniz's influence, Jacob I and Johann I contributions to development of calculus, calculus of variations, brachistochrone, contributions of other Bernoullis (Nicholas I, Daniel I, Johann II, Johann III), Marquis de L'Hospital

50 African Patterns and Graphs 99

Real-world application of mathematics, graph theory, Tchokwe *sona* tradition, graph drawings of the Bushoong, geometric patterning in African art, Benin sculpture and carvings, *Oware* board game

51 Perplexing Infinity 101

Ancient Greeks' struggles with infinity, John Wallis and the symbol for infinity, Leonhard Euler's work with infinity, notion of limit and development of calculus, Liu Hui's analysis of infinitesimals, Georg Cantor's examination of the infinite, mathematical concepts that depend on infinity

52 Euler and the Number *e* 103

Leonhard Euler, introduction of notation for the number *e,* use of *e* in finance, compound interest, money growth limited by *e,* the number *e* and growth

53 The Seven Bridges of Königsberg 105

Story of the Königsberg bridge problem, Leonhard Euler's proof that the problem is impossible to solve, graph theory, networks

54 The Mathematics of Music 107

African drumming patterns and rhythms, Pythagoras' connection between musical harmony and whole numbers, Johannes Kepler's connection between harmonic ratios and planets, Joseph Fourier, describing sounds with mathematical expressions, Laurie Anderson and number connotations, binary codes, electronic musical composition, musical scales

55 Maria Agnesi: Linguist, Mathematician, Humanist   **109**

Maria Agnesi's education, ability with languages, interest in Newton's *Principia, Analytical Institutions,* Agnesi's family of curves, religious and charitable work

56 Kant: The Intuitionist   **111**

Immanuel Kant's view that mathematics comes from the human mind, *Metaphysical Foundations of Natural Science,* Isaac Newton's laws of motion, Luitzen Brouwer and the intuitionist school, limitations of Kant's views, David Hume, René Descartes

57 Benjamin Banneker: Problem Solver   **113**

Mathematics in eighteenth-century America, Banneker's mathematical talent and mechanical skill, wooden clock, George Ellicot, self-taught in astronomy and surveying, Banneker's *Almanack* and Thomas Jefferson, Thomas Fuller

58 The Mathematics of Eighteenth-Century France   **115**

Joseph Louis Lagrange, calculus reformation, introduction of notation $f'(x)$ and $f''(x)$, Pierre-Simon Laplace, contributions to celestial mechanics, *Traité de mécanique céleste (Treatise on celestial mechanics),* Adrien-Marie Legendre's work with Euclid's *Elements,* Napoleon Bonaparte's influence on French school curriculum, Napoleon's theorem, Lorenzo Mascheroni, M. Le Blanc

59 Early North American Mathematics   **119**

Anasazi astronomical observatories, Pomo counting and record-keeping methods, geometric patterns in Navajo and Pueblo weaving, role of number 4 in Sioux tradition, Aztec calendars, Ojibwa number pictographs, Hopi basketry

60 Sophie Germain: Courageous Mathematician   **121**

Legend of the death of Archimedes, Germain's struggles to educate herself, pseudonym M. Le Blanc and correspondence with Joseph Louis Lagrange, comments on *Disquisitiones arithmeticae* and correspondence with Carl Friedrich Gauss, work with theories of elastic bodies and surfaces, *Memoir on the Vibrations of Elastic Plates,* Adrien-Marie Legendre, honorary degree from University of Göttingen

61 Carl Friedrich Gauss: Mathematician of Influence   **123**

Childhood mathematical ability, patronage of Duke of Brunswick, use of compass and straightedge to construct polygons with a prime number of sides, fundamental theorem of algebra, director of observatory at Göttingen, Albert Einstein influenced by Gauss, *Disquisitiones arithmeticae* and number theory, contributions to geodesy, contribution to development of the normal distribution curve

62 Mathematics and the Electoral College   **125**

Benjamin Franklin, foundation of electoral college, Twelfth Amendment, modern electoral system, 1979 attempt to abolish electoral college, presidential elections of 1800, 1824, 1888, 1988, and 1992

63 The Parallel Postulate   **127**

Euclid's five postulates, attempts to prove the fifth postulate, Girolamo Saccheri, *Euclid freed of all blemish,* János Bolyai, Nicolai Lobachevsky, non-Euclidean geometry, hyperbolic geometry, Felix Klein's model of a non-Euclidean geometry, John Playfair, Henri Poincaré, G. F. B. Riemann's elliptic geometry, Muhammad ibn Musa al-Khwarizmi

64 Perfect Numbers   **129**

Pythagoreans' number beliefs, Euclid's definition of perfect numbers, Leonhard Euler, question of whether an odd perfect number exists, largest known perfect numbers, Marin Mersenne, Mersenne primes, Thomas Augustus, deficient and abundant numbers

65 Mary Somerville: The Trailblazer   **131**

Somerville's education, number puzzle sparks Somerville's interest in algebra, night-time reading of Euclid's *Elements,* William Somerville, translation of Pierre-Simon Laplace's *Traité de mécanique céleste (Treatise on celestial mechanics),* Caroline Herschel, Royal Astronomical Society, Catherine Beecher, Ada Byron Lovelace

66 Mathematical People of the 1800s   **133**

José Anastácio da Cunha, memoir on ballistics, *Principios Mathematicos* and the notion of convergence, Augustin-Louis Cauchy, Georg Friedrich Bernhard Riemann, Riemann surfaces, topology, non-Euclidean geometry, Mary Everest Boole, how children learn, entrepreneur Maggie Lena Walker, Henri Poincaré and modern topology, Mary Dolciani, Richard Dedekind, Karl Weierstrass

67 Two Who Shocked the World of Mathematics   **135**

William Rowan Hamilton's quaternions and modern abstract algebra, commutative law for multiplication, George Boole and modern symbolic logic, Boolean algebra, Leonhard Euler, Joseph Louis Lagrange

68 De Morgan: Caring Teacher   **137**

Augustus De Morgan's support of education for women and concern for his students, cooperative learning, *Trigonometry and Double Algebra* and modern abstract algebra, *Essay on Probabilities,* De Morgan's Laws, four-color map problem, *A Budget of Paradoxes,* George Peacock, Duncan Farquharson Gregory

69 The Short Career of Galois   **139**

Evariste Galois' foundation of group theory, fifth- and higher degree algebraic equations, troubled life

70 Ada Lovelace: First Computer Programmer   **141**

Friendship with Mary Somerville, William King, collaboration with Charles Babbage, Difference Engine, Analytical Engine, logic program, looping and recursion, computer programming language ADA, Augustus De Morgan, octal and hexadecimal systems

71 Pythagoras and President Garfield   **143**

President James Abram Garfield, 1876 proof of Pythagorean theorem, 1881 assassination, Alexander Graham Bell's attempt to save Garfield's life, Chinese *xian tu*

72 Lewis Carroll: Mathematician of Fantasy   **145**

Charles Lutwidge Dodgson's pseudonym (Lewis Carroll), *Alice's Adventures in Wonderland* and *Through the Looking-Glass,* Carroll's mathematical interests and books, principle of inversion, Cheshire Cat's reversal of premise and conclusion

73 Three Ancient Unsolvable Problems   **149**

Geometric constructions that cannot be accomplished with Euclidean tools, ancient Greeks' attempts to solve these problems, trisection of an angle, construction of the edge of cube having twice the volume of a given cube, construction of a square having an area equal to that of a given circle, Anaxagoras, Hippocrates of Chios

74 Famous Twisted One-Sided Surfaces   **151**

Augustus Ferdinand Möbius, Möbius strip, Felix Klein, Klein bottle, topology

75 Determining Size for Infinite Sets   **153**

Georg Cantor, set theory, theory of the infinite, cardinality, aleph-null, transfinite number, positive rational numbers, David Hilbert, Bertrand Russell, Leopold Kronecker, Henri Poincaré

76 Renaissance Woman: Sofia Kovalevskaya   **155**

Sofia Kovalevskaya's bedroom walls papered with calculus lecture notes, marriage to Vladimir Kovalevsky, move to Heidelberg, Karl Weierstrass, doctorate from Göttingen University, professorship at University of Stockholm, awarded *Prix Bordin* by French Academy of Science, nonmathematical accomplishments, women's movement in Russia, Fyodor Mikhailovich Dostoevsky

77 Schools of Mathematical Thought   **157**

Mathematical philosophy, Intuitionist school, Luitzen Brouwer, Immanuel Kant, mathematics comes from the mind, Logistic school, Bertrand Russell, Alfred North Whitehead, logical construction of the real number system, *Principia Mathematica,* David Hilbert, Formalist school, axiomatic systems, Enrico Fermi, J. Robert Oppenheimer, John von Neumann, David Hume

78 Grace Chisholm Young: Versatile and Prolific   **159**

Grace Chisholm Young's education, marriage to and collaboration with William Young, *The Theory of Sets of Points,* set theory and mathematical analysis, differential calculus

79 An Inconceivable Inn   **161**

One-to-one correspondence between two finite sets of unequal size, puzzle of Hilbert's Hotel, David Hilbert, Georg Cantor, Galileo Galilei, Archimedes

80 Brief Pi Tales   **163**

Approximations for pi (ancient Asia, Rhind Papyrus, Archimedes, Zu Chongzhi, Aryabhata, Bhaskara, William Rutherford), mnemonic devices for remembering pi, Indiana State Legislature's attempts to legislate value for pi, morbus cyclometricus, Ludolph van Cuelen, Comte de Buffon, Gottfried Leibniz, Leonhard Euler

81 Emmy Noether: A Modern Mathematics Pioneer   **165**

Max Noether, University of Erlangen's prejudice against women, axiomatic method, contributions to development of modern algebraic concepts, influence in creation of topology, "the Noether boys," Nazi persecution of Jewish intellectuals, emigration to United States, tributes to Noether (Albert Einstein, Hermann Weyl, Pavel Aleksandrov), Olga Taussky-Todd

82 Ramanujan's Formulas   **167**

Sirnivasa Ramanujan's self-education, voluminous formulas, G. H. Hardy, time in England, Lost Notebook, infinite series, continued fractions, partition theory, statistical mechanics

83 Counting and Computing Devices   **169**

Human fingers and toes, abacus, Greek mechanical computer, quipu, Napier's bones, William Oughtred and slide rule, Pascal's adding machine and Gottfried Leibniz, Charles Babbage's Difference Engine and Ada Byron Lovelace, Herman Hollerith's data processing machine

84 The Computer's Development   **171**

Hand as first computer, ancient Greek mechanical computer, Blaise Pascal's computing machine, Charles Babbage's Difference Engine, Ada Byron Lovelace's programming methods, ENIAC, UNIVAC, microchip, Internet, computer languages BASIC and LOGO

85 Bees as Mathematicians?   **173**

Honeycombs made of hexagons, continuous matrices, most efficient use of space for honey storage

86 von Neumann: Mathematics as Experience   **175**

John von Neumann's belief in mathematics developed through experience, emigration to the United States, contributions to development of many mathematical fields, creation of game theory

87 The Inquisitive Einstein   **177**

Albert Einstein's break with Isaac Newton's laws, theory of relativity, $E = mc^2$, influenced by Carl Friedrich Gauss and G. F. B. Riemann, curved universe of four dimensions (height, width, breadth, and time), Mileva Einstein-Maric

88 Grace Murray Hopper: Ever Confident   **179**

Assigned to intelligence unit of Naval Reserve, Mark I computer, programming abilities, computer programming language COBOL, retired as the only woman admiral in United States Navy

89 Shiing-shen Chern: A Leader in Geometry   **181**

Influential work in differential geometry, education in China, study in Europe, Sino-Japanese War, work at Institute for Advanced Study, organized creation of China's Institute of Mathematics and Nan Kai Mathematical Research Institute

90 M. C. Escher: Artist and Geometer   **183**

Symmetry drawings, influenced by geometric patterns in the Alhambra, tessellations, paradoxes, Penrose triangle

91 Moon Flights   **185**

Neil Alden Armstrong's moon landing, moon stories (Lucian, Ludovico Ariosto, Johannes Kepler, Francis Godwin, Cyrano De Bergerac), Galileo Galilei, Isaac Newton and rocketry, Timothy Ferris, Lewis Thomas

92 Percentages and Statistics: What Do They Tell Us?   **187**

"State-istics," *New York Times'* interpretation of 1977 Bureau of Labor Statistics unemployment figures, confusing percentages with actual counts, influence of statistics

93 When a Loss Could Have Been a Win   **191**

Under certain rules for determining playoff teams in a split baseball season, a team could possible quality for the playoffs by intentionally losing games. The possibility of this situation was present in the major leagues in 1981.

94 Voices from the Well   **193**

Terre Ouwehand's *Voice from the Well,* Caroline Herschel's collaboration with her brother William Herschel, Mary Somerville, Royal Astronomical Society, Albert Einstein and Mileva Einstein-Maric, Charlotte Angas Scott, Mary Francis Winston Newson

95 Gender Equity in Mathematics   **195**

The Ladies Diary, women's access to mathematical education, Dr. Julia Robinson, Association for Women and Mathematics, Dr. Lucy Sells's "critical filter," Math/Science Network, Women in Mathematics Education, International Organization of Women and Mathematics, EQUALS, Family Math at the Lawrence Hill of Science

96 Rózsa Péter and Recursion   **197**

Contributions to theory of recursive function, fractals, *Playing with Infinity,* connections between recursive functions and computer languages, Molly Lynn Watt and LOGO, recursively-defined number processes, Tower of Hanoi, BASIC, PASCAL

97 Triskaidekaphobia   **199**

Fear of the number 13, Friday the 13th, influence on historical figures (Henry Ford, Paul Getty, Elizabeth II), zodiac, genesis of triskaidekaphobia (Hebrew alphabet, Last Supper, London bakers)

98 The Four-Color Problem   **201**

Topology, four-color map problem, Frederick Guthrie and Augustus De Morgan, Kenneth Appel and Wolfgang Haken, first computer-assisted proof, Möbius strip, torus map

99 Problems in Probabilistic Reasoning   **203**

Jack A. Hope and Ivan W. Kelly, ambiguous expressions of probability, "gambler's fallacy," Chevalier de Méré and Blaise Pascal, undue confidence in small samples, confusing unusual events with low-probability events, estimating frequency of memorable events

100 Ethnomathematics   **205**

Cultural experience of mathematics, occupational mathematics, Brazilian street vendors, construction workers, weaving, quiltmaking, language and mathematical understanding, Quechua children in Spanish-speaking schools, International Study Group on Ethnomathematics

101 Fascinating Fractals   **207**

Benoit Mandelbrot, self-similar curves, Waclaw Sierpiński and the Sierpiński gasket, Helge von Koch and the Koch snowflake

102 Reatha Clark King: Woman of Science   **209**

First women scientists, the importance of mathematics in science, Dr. Reatha Clark King, work in colorimetry and education, advocate for minorities and women in higher education, Émilie du Châtelet, Shoemaker-Levy 9, Sputnik

103 How Long Is a Coastline?   **211**

Fractals and chaos theory, Atlantic coastline of United States, scale considerations, Koch snowflake, Peano curve, devil's staircase, self-similarity, space-filling curve.

104 Edna Paisano: Using Statistics to Aid Communities   **213**

Childhood on Nez Percé Indian Reservation, education in family's cultural traditions, mother's career in education, work with Seattle's American Indian community, work with United States Census Bureau, improvement of census accuracy, 1990 census, Fort Lawson, Fanya Montalvo

105 Escalante: Stand and Deliver   **215**

Jaime Escalante's encouragement of calculus students, *Stand and Deliver, ganas,* students' Advanced Placement Calculus Examination, FUTURES with Jaime Escalante, Jackie Joyner-Kersee

106 Chaos in Jurassic Park   **217**

Chaos theory, Michael Crichton's *Jurassic Park,* fictional mathematician Ian Malcolm, DNA cloning of dinosaurs

107 Names in Chaos and Fractals   **221**

Gaston Julia and Julia Sets, Benoit Mandelbrot, self-similarity, Mandelbrot set, Edward Lorenz and chaos theory, butterfly effect, Mitchell Feigenbaum and connections between types of irregularity, Heinz-Otto Peitgen and the beauty of fractals, Robert L. Devaney and dynamical systems, Pythagorean tree

108 Geometric Shapes and Politics   **223**

North Carolina's Twelfth Congressional District, 1993 United States Supreme Court decision regarding 1982 revisions to the 1965 Voting Rights Act, adequate representation for minority candidates, Louisiana's Fourth Congressional District

Appendix: Outstanding Educators I Know   **225**

Selected Answers   **233**

Bibliography   **239**

Index   **261**

Publisher's Preface

From the time at which Sanderson Smith first approached Key Curriculum Press with his preliminary manuscript, *Agnesi to Zeno: Over 100 Vignettes from the History of Math* has interested us for two very important reasons. Not only does the book address the National Council of Teachers of Mathematics (NCTM) *Standards'* recommendation to expose mathematics students to the cultural, historical, and scientific evolution of mathematics, but also many of the writing and research activities accompanying the vignettes are in keeping with the *Standards'* emphasis on communication in mathematics classrooms.

We believe students will be excited by many of the activities that call for class discussion of interesting topics, and we hope that students who are not otherwise motivated in mathematics will enjoy reading about historical personalities, the ways in which mathematics affects our daily lives, and how mathematics is used and developed by many cultures. Additionally, we're certain that mathematics will have a deeper meaning for *all* students when they explore some of the ways in which mathematics has developed through time.

We hope you're now just as interested in *Agnesi to Zeno* as we are! Before you and your students begin your journey through time, we'd like to call your attention to a few issues we feel are important.

As is true of many secondary school materials, the information contained in *Agnesi to Zeno* has been culled primarily from secondary sources—the purpose of this book is not to break any new historical ground, but to synthesize information for students and to hopefully inspire them to further explore topics that interest them. Additionally, please keep in mind that this book is intended to be used as a vehicle for *introducing* students to math history. As such, the author has sometimes simplified complex sequences of events, many of which could fill volumes on their own! Supplement the vignettes by encouraging students to share with the class what they've learned in their research projects or in their reading.

Each vignette contains a Related Reading section that students can refer to for material focusing on the vignette's main theme or on a topic related to the main theme. (The Related Reading section is not necessarily meant to provide students with material they can use as reference material for research projects.) Please note that some of the suggested material may be out of print and unavailable for purchase, but students may possibly find it in the special collections of a public or a university library.

In addition to the author's suggested reading, we'd like to refer you and your students to several other fine publications about the history of mathematics: Victor J. Katz, *A History of Mathematics: An Introduction* (New York: HarperCollins College Publishers, 1993); Frank J. Swetz (ed), *From Five Fingers to Infinity: A Journey through the History of Mathematics.* (Chicago: Open Court Publishing, 1994); J. Baumgart, et al, *Historical Topics for the Mathematics Classroom* (Reston, VA: NCTM, 1989); Ronald Calinger (ed), *Classics of Mathematics* (Oak Park, IL: Moore Publishing, 1982); V. K. Newell, J. H. Gipson, L. W. Rich, and B. Stubblefield (eds), *Black Mathematicians and Their Works* (Ardmore, PA: Dorrance, 1980); the soon-to-be-published book by Nitsa Movshovitz-Hadar and John Webb, *Teaching and Learning Through Mathematical*

Paradoxes (Dedham, MA: Janson Publications); and numerous biographies of individual mathematicians that have been published in recent years.

In the course of your education, you may have found, as we have, that the history of mathematics is often written from a biased perspective. Much of the traditional literature is Eurocentric, focuses on the contributions of male mathematicians, and defines mathematics as solely an academic tradition. In general, this has meant that the influences and contributions of women, people of non-European heritage, and nonacademic mathematicians have been ignored or falsified.

An especially enjoyable aspect of working on this book was uncovering, to the extent we could, the history of the lesser-known people who have shaped mathematics. In this regard, Professor Marty Banks of the University of California, Berkeley's optometry program provided us with one particularly exciting moment. He called our attention to the work of Islamic physicist and mathematician Abu Ali al-Hasan ibn al-Haytham, who in the eleventh century discovered the idea of retinal correspondence, a key concept in binocular vision. Al-Haytham's discovery, recently uncovered by Professor Ian Howard of York University, has traditionally been credited to seventeenth-century Belgian monk Franciscus Aguilonius. (See vignette 27 of this book for more on al-Haytham.) By sharing this information with us, Marty helped us to attain our goal of providing students and teachers with a history that seeks to address more than the traditional math history topics and that is more accurate than previous accounts.

In this same vein, we urge you to ask your students to consider what mathematics is, what situations or contexts allow mathematical ideas to formulate (only in traditional intellectual settings?), who writes history and with what bias, who does mathematics (only those whose professional label is mathematician or philosopher?), and how distinct philosophical and political perspectives generate different answers to these questions. We hope that by looking at these issues, students will begin to discover, for example, that mathematics and history are dynamic entities, and that mathematics developed and used by the "average" person is just as valid as the discoveries and applications attributed to the "great" mathematicians of history. We encourage you and your students to explore the hidden stories—this will only enhance the stories that have already been told.

Key Curriculum Press sincerely hopes that *Agnesi to Zeno: Over 100 Vignettes from the History of Math* will prove to be a valuable addition to your classroom. Enjoy!

Greer Lleuad and Steve Rasmussen

Author's Preface

I t is both sad and ironic that mathematics has frequently been taught as a subject isolated from real life and from other academic disciplines. How else can we account for the number of students who have been turned off from a study of mathematics during the past few decades? How else can we explain the mathematics anxiety that exists in this country among numerous individuals of various ages? *Innumeracy,* a term used by John Allen Paulos to describe an inability to work with basic mathematical concepts, is a disease that ravages our nation. The consequences of mathematical illiteracy can be witnessed in the inefficiency that plagues all aspects of United States society, from our problems in the work force to our dealings with foreign nations. In the words of Carl Sagan: "We live in a society exquisitely dependent on science and mathematics, in which hardly anyone knows anything about science and mathematics. This is a clear prescription for disaster."

> *We can improve. We can keep kids in school longer and achieve a better result. We cannot fail in education. If we fail, we fail our kids, and we fail our future.*
> —Jaime Escalante, *Stand and Deliver*

Fortunately, many organizations and individuals are working to promote quality education and curriculum innovation in the United States. They include the National Association of Mathematicians, International Group for Ethnomathematics, National Council of Teachers of Mathematics (NCTM), Criticalmathematics Educators Group, the Banneker Club of NCTM, the Canadian Mathematics Education Study Group, and the Council of Presidential Awardees in Mathematics. A basic purpose of all these organizations is to promote the realization that the study of mathematics is extremely important and relevant to all students and to the overall welfare of our country. The work of dedicated NCTM members resulted in the NCTM *Curriculum and Evaluation Standards for School Mathematics.* This document provides government-accepted goals and objectives for mathematics education in the United States as we prepare for the challenges of the twenty-first century. However, mathematics educators readily acknowledge that there is still much work to do if we hope to provide quality quantitative education for students in the United States. Among other things, we must establish a belief in what I personally accept as an absolute truth: Mathematics has been, is, and will continue to be, an essential part of human existence.

With this thought in mind, *Agnesi to Zeno: Over 100 Vignettes from the History of Math* presents a series of vignettes that highlight developments in mathematical thought and achievement as they relate to human history. For the most part, the vignettes are chronologically arranged; topics that span long periods of time are placed strategically throughout the book. Each vignette stands alone as a self-contained informational unit and attempts to provide insights that can be easily presented, understood, and appreciated in a classroom setting. Accompanying activities offer students opportunities to research various topics in a more in-depth manner, to discuss ideas and opinions with classmates, and to explore exercises relating to the branches of mathematics featured in the vignettes. Additionally, each vignette contains a list of related reading from an extensive bibliography of over 1,000 references. (I recommend for a school library's mathematics section the references in **bold type**.)

Without question, the most difficult part of writing this book involved deciding what to include and what to leave out of the vignettes. The material in these pages only scratches the surface of the history of mathematics, highlighting events that have shaped the course of human history. As one who gained a knowledge of mathematical history primarily from traditional Eurocentered and male-dominated sources, I have chosen in this book to refer to a number of personalities and events not frequently found in Western mathematics history records.

A number of my teaching colleagues contributed either directly or indirectly to the materials in this book. Members of the Cate School Mathematics Department— Donna Dayton, Dan Goldner, Frank Griffin, the late Allan Gunther, Lola Muldrew, Andy Pearce, Gary Pierce, and Brian Yager—have been sources of information, inspiration, and constructive criticism. Cate librarians Patty Allaback, Betty Benedict, John Wilson, and Betty Woodworth were particularly helpful in digging out resources. Cate teachers in other disciplines who contributed are Charlie Bergman (language), Patrick Collins (art), Jim Durham (English), Frank Ellis (music), David Harbison (history), Jane Maxwell (dramatics), Katie O'Malley (English), and Cheryl Powers (science). Materials were also provided by former Cate students Mia Mitchell and Anthony Sneed. I am fortunate to have a number of dedicated colleagues throughout the country who provided material resources: Mary Jo Aiken, Edina, Minnesota; Willard Blaskopf, Jr., Newark, New Jersey; Pamela Coffield, Columbus, Georgia; Gretchen Davis, Santa Monica, California; Joanne Meldon, Pittsburgh, Pennsylvania; Lucie Refsland, Lewisburg, West Virginia; and Diann Resnick, Houston, Texas. I am grateful to the excellent staff of Key Curriculum Press, specifically Greer Lleuad, Crystal Mills, and Steve Rasmussen for both support and editorial expertise during the publication process. Love and appreciation go to my wife, Barbara, for proofreading and recognizing that this project was of extreme importance to me.

Finally, I wish to express my deepest appreciation to the Council for Basic Education (CBE) for providing me the opportunity to create this book, and, perhaps more importantly, for allowing me the opportunity to be a researcher and a learner in the magnificent discipline of mathematics. Mathematics is exciting in part because there is always more to learn, as recent discoveries in chaos theory have indicated. The CBE experience has endowed me with a greater appreciation of mathematics and history and has increased my desire to work for the betterment of mathematics education in the United States. My genuine wish is that both students and teachers of mathematics will receive future dividends as a result of this book.

Sanderson M. Smith

Suggested Uses for This Book

Mathematics is people-centered, not isolated from reality. It is a discipline that can be used to accurately describe the world and the universe in which we live. The NCTM *Standards* clearly advocates *teaching about* mathematics rather than merely *presenting* the subject as a series of mechanical rules applied to strange-looking expressions. A dedicated mathematics teacher can find numerous ways to make mathematics come alive for students. Visual displays in the classroom, the use of technology and current events materials, field trips, and visiting speakers represent only a small number of sources that can be used to develop knowledge and understanding of the everyday usefulness of mathematics.

There are a number of ways in which this book can serve as a helpful curriculum supplement.

- Include the book on a required reading list. Offer it as a summer reading project or as a reading assignment during the regular school year. Ask students to read books listed in each vignette's Related Reading section.

- Incorporate into lesson plans historical material relating to the mathematics you're teaching in the classroom. Present it as an integral part of mathematics education rather than as "something extra."

- Present, or ask a student to present, a vignette per day. Offer extra credit to students who complete one or more of the research activities. Include material from the vignettes as bonus questions on tests and quizzes. Set aside time on a specific day each week to discuss or report on historical topics.

- Brainstorm with your students to invent alternate activities that may have special relevance for the class (or that we hadn't considered!).

- Ask student teams to research a mathematician of their choosing and present a report to the class—many vignettes serve as an initial source of information. Alternately, ask teams to present to the class research they've done on the vignette activities.

- Ask students to research the struggles and perserverance of those who made names for themselves in the history of mathematics. What allowed mathematicians to overcome prejudices, mistakes, failures, disappointments, limitations, and criticism?

- Develop hands-on activities that simulate the methods used by past mathematicians to obtain or to discover results mentioned in the vignettes (some suggestions appear in the activities). This can alert students to the ingenuity of many historical mathematicians. Alternately, students themselves can research the vignettes and the bibliography to find examples of mathematical creativity. With some teacher guidance, such activities can be a lead-in to the introduction

> *Students should have numerous and varied experiences related to the cultural, historical, and scientific evolution of mathematics so that they can appreciate the role of mathematics in the development of our contemporary society and explore relationships among mathematics and the disciplines it serves: the physical and life sciences, the social sciences, and the humanities.*
> —NCTM *Curriculum and Evaluation Standards for School Mathematics*
>
> *Histories make [us] wise; poets witty; the mathematics, subtile; natural philosophy, deep; moral, grave; logic and rhetoric, able to contend.*
> —Francis Bacon, (1625)

of a new concept, or can serve as reinforcement or enrichment for previously studied ideas.

- Ask students to research some of the many controversies that have developed and continue to develop in mathematics. The vignettes and the bibliography provide insight into some famous controversies between individuals, between schools of mathematical thought, and about mathematics and its relation to other forms of thought.

- Mathematics is a language. Ask students to research the origins of its symbols and words. Some vignettes provide information about this topic, and the bibliography contains numerous sources that can be used for this type of research.

- Use the vignettes to emphasize that we are continually creating mathematics and mathematical ideas. Mathematics is not knowledge that has been and always will be static and unchanging.

- Many mathematics problems were not resolved until hundreds or thousands of years after they were introduced into the realm of human thought. Some have never been resolved. Use the vignettes and the bibliography to explore some of these problems.

Mathematics is rich with history—in fact, mathematics is history. If our educational process deprives mathematics of its history, we will continue to produce citizens who believe that mathematics is a peculiar subject known only to those select few who have "mathematical minds." Hopefully, this book will help teachers convince students that mathematics is important for everyone.

The Unknown Origin of Counting

1

It's unlikely that we will ever know where, when, or how we humans first developed the actual process of counting. We have probably always had some number sense, or at least some way of recognizing more and less when objects were added to or taken from a small group. It's likely that prehistoric humans employed the principle of one-to-one correspondence in their earliest counting methods. For example, to keep a count of sheep, shepherds may have put pebbles into one-to-one correspondence with each member of their flocks.

Any pebbles used for record keeping are lost to us now, but there is speculation that certain twentieth-century archaeological finds represent some of the earliest records of counting. The notches on a 25,000-year-old fossilized bone found in Zaire may have represented phases of the moon, and a centuries-old wolf bone discovered in Eastern Europe contains notches that may have been marks used to tally. Carved in two series—twenty-five in the first, thirty in the second—the notches on the wolf bone are arranged in groups of five, the way we still tally today.

Aside from tally marks, the earliest written evidence of counting comes from ancient Mesopotamian cuneiform, Egyptian hieroglyphics, and Chinese ideograms. The modern decimal system much of the world uses today derives from the early Egyptian and Chinese number systems, which were based on 10. In turn, these systems probably derived from the fact that humans have ten fingers with which to count. By contrast, Babylonia's number system was based on 60, possibly because the number 60 is evenly divisible by many smaller integers. This system is still used all over the world in units of angle measurement and time.

How did early humans deal with *large* number concepts? The oldest tangible evidence we have showing that early societies were familiar with large numbers dates back to 3500 B.C. An Egyptian royal mace records the capture of 120,000 human prisoners, 400,000 oxen, and 1,422,000 goats. These massive numbers suggest that royal tally keepers had methods to count or to estimate large collections of items, such as counting objects in a sample and multiplying by a guessed number of samples.

There is little doubt that numbers and number concepts were important and useful in early societies. However, we don't know whether early humans asked themselves what a number is or speculated how numbers came into being. This will probably forever remain a mystery.

For more on counting and number systems, see vignettes 21, 32, 59, 83, and 84. ★

Egyptian hieroglyphics shown on the funeral papyrus of Queen Makara.

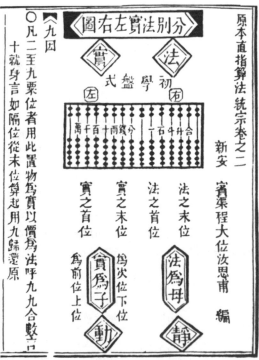

Sixteenth-century illustration of an abacus.

©1996 by Key Curriculum Press

Activities

1. Demonstrate how early people may have used the concept of one-to-one correspondence to account for their possessions. How do you think they counted large quantities of possessions, such as a herd of cattle?

2. Some early societies expressed numbers with various positions of the fingers and the hands. Research how "finger numbers" were represented and how people used them to perform simple computations.

3. Comment on the quote by **James Boswell** (1740–1795) given below.

   Sir, allow me to ask you one question. If the church should say to you, "Two and three make ten," what would you do? "Sir," said he, "I would believe in it, and I would count like this: one, two, three, four, ten." I was now fully satisfied.

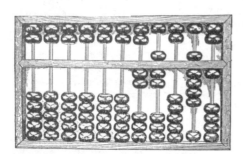

4. The earliest known computing device is the abacus, which is still used in much of Asia. There are many types of abaci, one of which is shown at left. Demonstrate how to perform computations with an abacus.

Related Reading

Bell, E.T. *The Last Problem*. Washington, DC: Mathematical Association of America, 1990.

———. *The Magic of Numbers*. New York: McGraw-Hill, 1946.

Eves, Howard. *An Introduction to the History of Mathematics*. New York: Holt, Rinehart and Winston, 1990.

Friberg, J. "Numbers and Measures in the Earliest Written Records." *Scientific American* (Feb 1984) 78–85.

Joseph, George G. *The Crest of the Peacock: Non-European Roots of Mathematics*. New York: Penguin Books, 1991.

Ore, Oystein. *Number Theory and Its History*. Mineola, NY: Dover, 1988.

Pappas, Theoni. *The Joy of Mathematics*. San Carlos, CA: Wide World/Tetra, 1989.

Room, Adrian. *The Guinness Book of Numbers*. Middlesex, England: Guinness Publishing, 1989.

Struik, Dirk J. *A Concise History of Mathematics*. Mineola, NY: Dover, 1987.

Zaslavsky, Claudia. *Africa Counts: Number and Pattern in African Culture*. New York: Lawrence Hill Books, 1979.

ANCIENT REFERENCES TO PI

2

The Greek letter pi (π) is used as the symbol for the ratio of the circumference of a circle to its diameter, which equals 3.14159 . . . . While many mathematics students probably take this ratio for granted, it wasn't always neatly provided in textbooks. On the contrary, the concept of pi has a long history of development and application.

By 1850 B.C., the ancient Egyptians had squared the circle to get $(\frac{4}{3})^4$, or about 3.1605, as a value for π. According to the Bible, some 900 years later **Solomon** built a palace and a building complex, probably using the mathematics developed by the Egyptians to aid in its construction.

> *And he made the molten sea, ten cubits from one brim to the*
> *other: it was round all about, and its height was five cubits: and*
> *a line of thirty cubits did compass it round about.*
>
> —1 Kings 7:23 (A similar verse appears in 2 Chronicles 4:2.)

The cubit was a unit of measure representing the distance from a man's elbow to the end of his middle finger, about 17 to 22 inches. The molten sea was a high bowl or tank supported by 12 statues of oxen, in which priests washed in preparation for religious ceremonies.

> *Below its brim were ornamental buds encircling it all around,*
> *ten to a cubit, all the way around the sea. The ornamental buds*
> *were cast in two rows when it was cast. It stood on twelve oxen:*
> *three looking toward the north, three looking toward the west,*
> *three looking toward the south, and three looking toward the east;*
> *the sea was set upon them; and all their parts pointed inward. It*
> *was a hand-breadth thick; and its brim was shaped like the brim*
> *of a cup, like a lily blossom. It contained two thousand baths.*
>
> —1 Kings 7:24-26

In ancient Greece, **Archimedes** (ca 287–212 B.C.) found π to be between $\frac{223}{71}$ and $\frac{22}{7}$ by circumscribing and inscribing regular polygons about a circle. Six hundred years later, in a set of Indian manuscripts called *Siddhantas* (*Systems of Astronomy,* A.D. 400), the value for $\pi = 3^{177}/_{1250}$, or 3.1416. It's thought that fifth-century Hindu mathematicians used Archimedes' method to find the value of π, but this isn't known for certain.

Chinese mathematicians, who had always used the decimal system, also searched for values of π. In A.D. 718, one Chinese document shows that $\pi = \frac{92}{29} = 3.1724 \ldots$. **Liu Hui** (ca A.D. 250) definitely used a variation of Archimedes' method, inscribing a polygon of 192 sides to find $3.141024 < \pi \le 3.142704$. Taking it further, he found $\pi = 3.14159$ by inscribing a polygon of 3,072 sides.

For more on pi, see vignette 80. ★

The molten sea.
From A History of π,
©1971 by Petr Beckmann,
St. Martin's Press, Inc.,
New York, NY.

©1996 by Key Curriculum Press

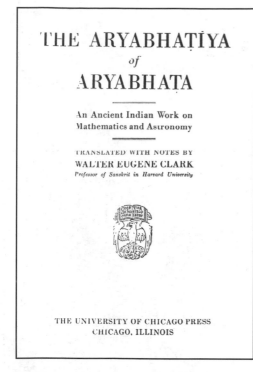

THE ARYABHAṬĪYA
of
ARYABHAṬA

An Ancient Indian Work on
Mathematics and Astronomy

TRANSLATED WITH NOTES BY
WALTER EUGENE CLARK
Professor of Sanskrit in Harvard University

THE UNIVERSITY OF CHICAGO PRESS
CHICAGO, ILLINOIS

An important description of the Hindu numerical system, the Aryabhatiya is one of the earliest known publications to use algebra.

ACTIVITIES

1. Hindu mathematician **Aryabhata** (b A.D. 476) states in his manuscript *Aryabhatiya* (A.D. 499): "Add 4 to 100, multiply by 8, and add 62,000. The result is approximately the circumference of a circle on which the diameter is 20,000." What value of π does this situation yield?

2. The molten sea is described as "round all about," suggesting a circle. What is the length of the circumference of this circle? Of the diameter? Show that these dimensions yield the result $\pi = 3$.

3. A bath was a liquid measure equal to approximately six gallons. How many gallons of water could the molten sea contain? Use the given dimensions to show that priests would have needed ladders or some similar device to bathe in the molten sea. Do your discoveries seem reasonable to you?

4. The ancient Egyptians used the formula $(d - \frac{d}{9})^2$ for the area of a circle with diameter d. What value of π does this formula yield?

5. Modern computers have been used to find π to thousands of decimal places. What algorithms do computers use to compute π?

RELATED READING

Beckmann, Petr. *A History of π*. New York: St. Martin's Press, 1976.

Dunham, William. *The Mathematical Universe: An Alphabetical Journey Through the Great Proofs, Problems, and Personalities*. New York: John Wiley, 1994.

Gillings, Richard J. *Mathematics in the Time of the Pharaohs*. Cambridge, MA: MIT Press, 1972.

Kasner, Edward, and James R. Newman. *Mathematics and the Imagination*. Redmond, WA: Tempus Books, 1989.

Pappas, Theoni. *More Joy of Mathematics*. San Carlos, CA: Wide World/Tetra, 1991.

The Pyramids of Egypt and the Americas

3

The Egyptians had great veneration for their dead ancestors, building permanent tombs and temples to enjoy in the afterlife. These impressive structures have long drawn scholars to Egypt, a rich field for ancient historical and mathematical research.

The construction of the Great Pyramid of Gizeh, built around 2600 B.C., required considerable mathematical and engineering skills. Ancient architects used their knowledge of volume, area, estimation, right angles, and perhaps the geometric relationship we now know as the Pythagorean theorem to compute the size, the shape, the number, and the arrangements of the stones used to build the pyramids.

In addition to Gizeh's famous structure, 35 major pyramids stand near the Nile River in Egypt. Each was built to preserve the mummified body of an Egyptian king, which was placed in a secret chamber filled with gold and precious objects. (Sometimes a smaller pyramid for the body of the queen was constructed next to the king's pyramid.) Some scholars believe that pyramids, rather than structures of a different shape, were used for tombs because the pyramids' sloping sides paralleled the slanting rays of the sun, enabling the soul of the kings to climb to the sky and join the gods.

Many centuries later (A.D. 100–900), Central and South American Indians constructed pyramids equal in size and splendor to those of Egypt. The American pyramids differ from their Egyptian counterparts in that they are not "true" pyramids—they have steps. Because these pyramids were not used as tombs, but rather as platforms for temples, the many steps allowed the priests to access the temples for religious ceremonies and rites. The Mayan Temple of the Inscriptions at Palenque, Mexico, is an exception. It contains an elaborate tomb that was probably constructed prior to the pyramid that sits atop.

Seventeenth-century map of ancient Egypt, engraved by Philippe Cluverio.

Early engraving of Peru's Temple of the Sun.

Notable American pyramids include the Temple of the Sun, constructed on the northern coast of Peru by the Mochica Indians, and the Pyramid of the Sun (A.D. 150) at Teotihuacán in central Mexico. The base of the Pyramid of the Sun is larger than that of Gizeh. ★

Activities

1. In the Yucatan of Mexico, there is a Mayan pyramid called El Castillo that has a platform on the top and a flight of 91 steps on each of the four sides. (Four flights of 91 steps make 364 steps in all. With the top platform adding a level, there are 365 levels to represent the 365 days of the Mayan year.) To the nearest centimeter, what is the height of the top platform if each of the 91 steps is 30 cm deep by 26 cm high? What is the angle of ascent to the nearest degree?

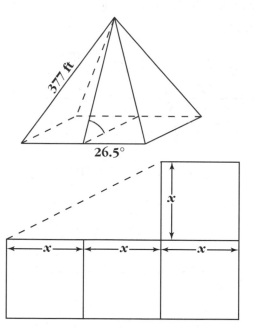

2. With a straightedge and a compass, construct a scale model of a "true" pyramid out of cardboard.

3. Research the ziggurats of Mesopotamia. How and why were they constructed? Do they resemble either the Egyptian or the American pyramids?

4. In 1985, United States Naval Observatory astronomer Richard Walker solved an ancient puzzle. He discovered that the passageway of Egypt's Great Pyramid of Cheops did not descend at an angle of 26.5 degrees to point at the North Star, as was previously thought. Instead, the angle results from placing four stones of equal length in the position shown at left. Show that this construction technique creates an angle that measures 26.5 degrees.

Related Reading

Closs, M.P. (ed). *Native American Mathematics*. Austin, TX: University of Texas Press, 1986.

Eves, Howard. *An Introduction to the History of Mathematics*. New York: Holt, Rinehart and Winston, 1990.

Fakhry, Ahmed. *The Pyramids*. Chicago: University of Chicago Press, 1974.

Gillings, Richard J. *Mathematics in the Time of the Pharaohs*. Mineola, NY: Dover, 1982.

Jacobs, Harold. *Mathematics: A Human Endeavor*. San Francisco: W.H. Freeman, 1987.

Tompkins, Peter. *Secrets of the Great Pyramid*. New York: Harper and Row, 1971.

HISTORY OF MATH

Chinese Mathematical Activities

Chinese legend tells of a giant turtle that emerged from the River Luo and showed itself to Emperor Da Yu around 2000 B.C. On the turtle's back appeared a magic square composed of numbers. The Chinese called this diagram the *luo shu*, believing that it contained magical powers. These magic squares, believed to have had their origin in China 4,000 years ago, are still a source of fascination for many people today.

We don't know who first recognized the famous right triangle relationship we call the Pythagorean theorem ($a^2 + b^2 = c^2$), but it's certain that it has traveled the world! Named after the Greek philosopher Pythagoras (572–497 B.C.), the theorem was known to scholars long before he came across it. He very likely learned of it in Babylonia, where he studied and taught with scholars from all around the world. We see the need for its application in this problem from a twelfth-century Chinese manuscript: "There grows in the middle of a circular pond 10 feet in diameter a reed which projects 1 foot out of the water. When it is drawn down it just reaches the edge of the pond. How deep is the water?" In a thirteenth-century manuscript, mathematician **Yang Hui** challenges: "There is a bamboo 10 feet high, the upper end of which being broken reaches the ground 3 feet from the stem. Find the height of the break."

Some four centuries later, we run into one of the most famous triangles in mathematical history, named after French mathematician Blaise Pascal (1623–1662). However, it has been clearly established that Pascal's triangle was known to the Chinese over 300 years before Pascal was born. The Chinese version of the triangle shown above right appeared in *Siyuan yujian* (*Precious mirror of the four elements,* 1303), written by **Zhu Shijie** (1280–1303).

For more on Chinese mathematics, see vignettes 8, 22, 26, 48, 71, and 89. ★

Fourteenth-century Chinese version of Pascal's triangle.

Activities

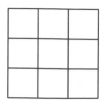

1. What is "magic" about a magic square? Fill in the *luo shu* numbers that form a magic square in the grid at left. Construct some other three-by-three magic squares.

2. The Chinese version of Pascal's triangle (see the illustration in this vignette) displays the binomial coefficients in the expansion of $(a + b)^n$ for $n = 0, 1, 2, 3, 4, 5, 6, 7$, and 8. For instance, $(a + b)^4 = 1a^4 + 4a^3b + 6a^2b^2 + 4ab^3 + 1b^4$. The fifth row of the triangle shows how the Chinese represented 6. Expand $(a + b)^n$ for $n = 5, 6, 7$, and 8 to discover how the Chinese represented other numerical coefficients in the binomial expansion.

3. Use the Pythagorean theorem to solve the problems about the bamboo and the pond referred to in this vignette.

Related Reading

Andrews, William S. *Magic Squares and Cubes.* Mineola, NY: Dover, 1960.

Bennett, Dan. *Pythagoras Plugged In: Proofs and Problems for The Geometer's Sketchpad.* Berkeley, CA: Key Curriculum Press, 1995.

Fults, J.L. *Magic Squares.* La Salle, IL: Open Court Publishing, 1974.

Joseph, George G. **The Crest of the Peacock: Non-European Roots of Mathematics.** New York: Penguin Books, 1991.

Li, Yan, and Du Shiran. **Chinese Mathematics: A Concise History.** New York: Oxford University Press, 1987.

Libbrecht, Ulrich. *Chinese Mathematics in the Thirteenth Century: The Shu-shu Chiu-Chang of Ch'in Chiu-shao.* Cambridge, MA: MIT Press, 1973.

Mikami, Yoshio. *The Development of Mathematics in China and Japan.* New York: Chelsea Publishing, 1961.

Swetz, Frank J. **The Sea Island Mathematical Manual: Surveying and Mathematics in Ancient China.** University Park, PA: Penn State University Press, 1992.

———, and T.I. Kao. *Was Pythagoras Chinese? An Examination of Right Triangle Theory in Ancient China.* Reston, VA: National Council of Teachers of Mathematics, 1977.

THE RHIND PAPYRUS AND THE ST. IVES PUZZLE

The effects of time have destroyed many great works of historical significance, but a few Egyptian papyri have managed to survive over three millennia. The most extensive papyrus of a mathematical nature is the **Rhind Mathematical Papyrus** (ca 1850 B.C.). Purchased in 1858 by Egyptologist **Henry Rhind**, hence its name, it was later willed to the British Museum, where it now rests. (Because it was copied from an earlier work by a scribe named **Ahmes**, it is sometimes called the **Ahmes Papyrus**.) About 1 foot high and 18 feet long, the papyrus contains 85 problems written in hieratic form.*

The *Rhind Mathematical Papyrus* provides us with much information about ancient Egyptian mathematics, particularly in the areas of counting and measuring. Additionally, its use of ciphers represents an important contribution to the development of numerical notation. Because Egyptian arithmetic operations didn't include fractions that contained nonunit numerators, the *Rhind Papyrus* contains a table that allows the reader to represent fractions as a sum of unit fractions (fractions with a numerator of 1). For instance, $2/97 = 1/56 + 1/679 + 1/776$.

Most of the problems in the *Rhind Papyrus* have been deciphered and interpreted, with the exception of Problem 79, which contains a curious set of data.

Houses	7
Cats	49
Mice	343
Heads of wheat	2401
Hekat measures	16807
	19607

Each number is a power of 7, but because the problem in the *Rhind Papyrus* was never accurately interpreted, we don't know what the numbers represent. In 1907, historian Moritz Cantor recognized a possible connection between this data and a problem posed by thirteenth-century mathematician Fibonacci in his *Liber abacci* (*Book of calculation*). A familiar version of Fibonacci's problem is represented in this old English children's rhyme.

> *As I was going to St. Ives I met a man with seven wives;*
> *Every wife had seven sacks; every sack had seven cats; every cat had seven kits.*
> *Kits, cats, sacks, and wives, how many were going to St. Ives?*

This verse, called the St. Ives Puzzle, is part of the world's puzzle lore. One possible answer to the St. Ives Puzzle is 1. As the puzzle states, the speaker was going to St. Ives. If he (or she!) met the man and his wives on a road, they could have been *coming* from St. Ives. ★

Rhind Mathematical Papyrus, Problem 62

- Example of figuring the contents of the bag of various precious metals

A bag containing equal weights of gold, silver, and lead has been bought for 84 *sha'ty* [unit of value]. What is the amount in the bag of each precious metal if a *deben* [unit of weight] of gold costs 12 *sha'ty*, a *deben* of silver costs 6 *sha'ty*, and a *deben* of lead costs 3 *sha'ty*?

- Solution

Add what it costs for a *deben* of each precious metal. The result is 21 *sha'ty*. Multiply 21 by 4 to get 84 (the 84 *sha'ty* it cost to buy the bag). Thus 4 is the number of *deben* of each precious metal.

- Find the value of each metal in this way:

Multiply 12 by 4, getting 48 *sha'ty* for the gold in the bag.
Multiply 6 by 4, getting 24 *sha'ty* for the silver in the bag.
Multiply 3 by 4, getting 12 *sha'ty* for the lead in the bag.
Multiply 21 by 4, getting 84 *sha'ty* altogether.

- **What are some other ways to approach this problem?**

*Ancient Egyptian priests kept their records in the hieratic form, a type of writing consisting of abridged forms of hieroglyphics. Egyptian hieroglyphic writing was a pictographic script whose symbols were often conventionalized pictures of the things they represented.

©1996 by Key Curriculum Press

ACTIVITIES

1. In the *Rhind Mathematical Papyrus,* the area of a circle is described as being equal to the area of a square with a side that is $\frac{8}{9}$ of the diameter. What does this yield as a value for π?

2. Interpret this explanation from the *Rhind Papyrus:* "If you are asked, what is $\frac{2}{3}$ of $\frac{1}{5}$, take the double and the sixfold; that is, $\frac{2}{3}$ of it. One must proceed likewise for any other fraction."

3. Show that $\frac{a}{bc} = \frac{1}{br} + \frac{1}{cr}$, where $r = \frac{(b+c)}{a}$. Use what you discover to represent, in two different ways, $\frac{2}{63}$ as the sum of two unit fractions.

4. The Egyptians invented the paperlike writing material called papyrus. How is papyrus made?

5. The problems in the *Rhind Papyrus* are written in the hieratic form and have been transcribed into hieroglyphics for translation. A hieroglyphic symbol that looks like legs walking to the left indicates addition; legs walking to the right indicates subtraction. What do other hieroglyphic symbols look like? What do they mean?

RELATED READING

Bell, E.T. *The Last Problem*. Washington, DC: Mathematical Association of America, 1990.

Boyer, Carl. *A History of Mathematics,* 2nd ed rev. Uta C. Merzbach. New York: John Wiley, 1991.

Chace, A.B. *The Rhind Mathematical Papyrus*. Reston, VA: National Council of Teachers of Mathematics, 1979.

Ellis, Keith. *Number Power in Nature and in Everyday Life*. New York: St. Martin's Press, 1978.

Eves, Howard. *An Introduction to the History of Mathematics*. New York: Holt, Rinehart and Winston, 1990.

Gillings, Richard J. *Mathematics in the Time of the Pharaohs*. Mineola, NY: Dover, 1982.

Maor, Eli. *To Infinity and Beyond: A Cultural History of the Infinite*. Boston: Birkhauser Boston, 1987.

Resnikoff, H.L., and R.O. Wells. *Mathematics in Civilization*. Mineola, NY: Dover, 1985.

Robins, Gay, and Charles Shute. *The Rhind Mathematical Papyrus*. Mineola, NY: Dover, 1987.

Early Astronomy

For centuries, we humans have looked upward in an effort to understand the universe and our place in it. In the course of our earliest ancestors' celestial searching, the science of astronomy was developed. Not only has this science of the skies paved the way for inventions ranging from the calendar to the space shuttle, but it has always gone hand in hand with the study and development of mathematical concepts and tools.

The patterns of such heavenly bodies as the sun and the moon were vastly important to early peoples. Successful agricultural management depended on an understanding of the sun's seasonal cycles. The phases of the moon determined the occurrence of various ritual practices. Solar and lunar eclipses were especially significant, predicted and used by religious leaders to demonstrate their power, or seen by the populace as messages from the gods.

To keep track of astronomical events over long periods of time, early astronomers created calendars. In ancient Egypt, for example, each year priests observed that the star Sirius first appeared over the horizon just before sunrise on a summer morning. A few days later, the Nile spilled over its banks and people hurried to move their livestock and possessions to higher ground. Over time, the priests noted that the flooding of the river coincided with the appearance of the star, and after about fifty years of observation, it became evident that the rising of the star could be predicted. The time between its first appearance each summer was calculated to be 365 days and a bit more—in four years the "bit more" amounted to a full day. So, the Egyptians produced a value of 365¼ days for the year's length, which is extremely close to what we now use as the true value, 365.2422 days.

The Maya of southern Mexico and Guatemala believed that the sun, the moon, and the planets were gods who conducted their lives in the skies, high above the human realm. In observing the movements of their sky gods, Mayan priests discovered that these heavenly bodies circled the earth in regular cycles. This was important information. By being able to anticipate these cycles, the priests could provide the Mayan government with the correct times to plant crops, celebrate festivals, and otherwise conduct the affairs of the kingdom. Thus they modified their complex number system to create one of history's most accurate and beautiful calendars.

For more on astronomy and calendars, see vignettes 7–9, 11, 23, 26–28, 30, 40–42, 47, 48, 57, 59, 65, and 94. ★

Saturnus

Allegorical representation of Saturn as Cronus, the Greek god of the harvest. In ancient Assyria, Saturn was represented by the hunting god, Nisroch, and in Babylonia by the god Ninib.

©1996 by Key Curriculum Press

Activities

1. How did the Babylonians make their advance predictions of eclipses of the sun and moon? What mathematical principles did they use to do so?

2. Egyptian physician **Troth** (ca 3000 B.C.) devised a solar calendar known as the Calendar of Troth. How was this calendar constructed?

3. How did astronomer **Yi Xing** (A.D. 683–727) contribute to the development of mathematics in China?

4. Identify the numbers and the units associated with the terms *light year, magnitude of a star,* and *astronomical unit.* The star Sirius (Dog Star), in the Canis Major (Big Dog) constellation, is 8.5 light years from earth and 26 times as luminous as our sun. In miles, how far is Sirius from Earth?

Canis Major

Related Reading

Asimov, Isaac. *Guide to Earth and Space.* New York: Ballantine Books, 1991.

Bushwich, N. *Understanding the Jewish Calendar.* Brooklyn, NY: Moznaim, 1989.

Cleminshaw, C.H. *The Beginner's Guide to the Stars.* New York: Thomas Y. Crowell, 1977.

McLeish, John. *The Story of Numbers: How Mathematics Has Shaped Civilization.* New York: Fawcett Columbine, 1991.

Moeschl, Richard. *Exploring the Sky.* Chicago: Independent Publishers Group, 1989.

Newman, James R. *The World of Mathematics.* Redmond, WA: Tempus Books, 1988.

Tauber, Gerald E. *Man's View of the Universe.* New York: Crown Publishers, 1979.

Cosmologies of the Ancient World

7

The mysteries of the universe have intrigued humankind since ancient times. **Cosmology** is the branch of philosophy that deals with the origin and the structure of the universe. Over time, cosmologies have evolved according to the developments we've made in other areas, such as astronomy and mathematics.

Early cosmologies were often based upon the belief that the universe was created by a deity. One of the earliest of these beliefs is that the goddess Gaia and her daughter Themi established order out of chaos and created the earth and its inhabitants. In the ancient empires of Babylonia and Assyria, the god Marduk, shown at right, was believed to have created the world after halving the chaos-monster Tiamet, from whose two halves sprang the earth and the heavens.

Today we know that the sun is a star and that the moon is a satellite, but in ancient times, the technology required to know these things was nonexistent, and the features of the universe were often represented as people or as animals. For example, in ancient Egypt, the earth was seen as a human figure reclining beneath the floating sun, enclosed by the heavens in the form of a starry woman. In ancient India, Akupara, the tortoise, supported elephants that, in turn, supported the earth, as shown below right. All were surrounded by a snake that represented eternal birth and rebirth.

For more on cosmology, see vignettes 6, 11, 12, 16, 26, 41, 42, 59, and 91. ★

The Assyrian-Babylonian god Marduk, as represented on a wall carving from Nineveh, the ancient capital of Assyria (now in Iraq).

Ancient Hebrew cosmology

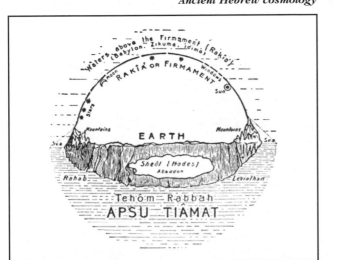

Ancient Hindu cosmology

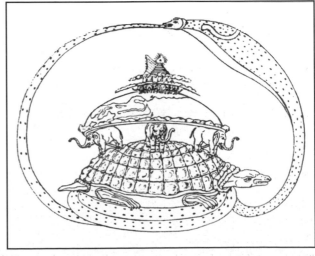

©1996 by Key Curriculum Press

Activities

1. Read about the important contributions the Babylonians and the Assyrians made to the early development of observational astronomy. How did those developments affect the way these early civilizations understood the universe?

2. Compare the cosmological ideas of ancient Egyptian scientists with those of medieval scientist **Hildegard von Bingen** and Renaissance astronomer **Galileo Galilei**. What astronomical and mathematical concepts did each rely upon to come to their understanding of the universe?

3. Explore some of today's theories about the origins of the universe.

Related Reading

Alic, Margaret. *Hypatia's Heritage*. **Boston: Beacon Press, 1986**.

Hawking, Stephen. *A Brief History of Time*. New York: Bantam Books, 1988.

Moeschl, Richard. *Exploring the Sky*. Chicago: Independent Publishers Group, 1989.

Scarre, Chris (ed). *Timelines of the Ancient World*. New York: Dorling Kindersley, 1993.

Tauber, Gerald E. *Man's View of the Universe*. New York: Crown Publishers, 1979.

Calendars of the Ancient World

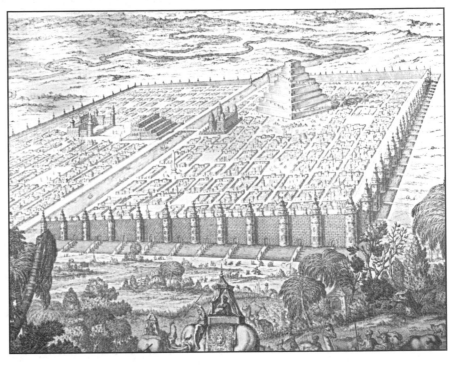

8

Many ancient peoples kept records of astronomical events for agricultural, ceremonial, and administrative purposes. Years of astronomical observation were necessary before accurate calendars could be constructed, and many different systems of calendrical mathematics were developed to conveniently divide units of time.

European bone: A 25,000-year-old piece of bone found in Grotte du Tai, France, may be the oldest known solar calendar. The bone contains more that 1,000 engraved marks whose arrangement suggests that they were grouped into years.

The city of Babylon, capital of Babylonia (ca 1900–539 B.C.). Situated on the Euphrates River, this famous city housed the Hanging Gardens of Babylon, one of the Seven Wonders of the World. From Peter Van der Aa's Le grand theatre historique *(Amsterdam, 1703).*

Babylonian lunisolar calendars: The Babylonian calendar was constructed to accommodate both the solar and the lunar cycles so that it would coincide with important agricultural events. The months of this calendar were alternately twenty-nine and thirty days long, and each month began with the first appearance of the crescent moon. Twelve months equaled 354 days, so the Babylonians created a system of seven leap years every thirteen years—a leap year was thirteen months long.

African farming cycles: To ensure that a community's food supply was sufficient for a given year, Yoruba farmers of Africa learned to understand the growth patterns of their crops and how seasonal changes affected those crops. Over time, farmers related these natural cycles to such astronomical events as the cycling of the moon though the night sky. As a result of this process, the Yoruba determined that a year consisted of thirteen lunar months.

Sacred Chinese cycles: In the ancient Chinese agrarian society, an accurate calendar was a necessity, and calendar makers had to be skilled in coordinating the lunar, solar, and seasonal cycles. Additionally, Chinese calendars were used as instruments for maintaining harmony with heavenly cycles, so they had religious as well as practical meaning. Because people were fascinated by what are called resonance periods—the length of time it takes one cycle to move from agreement with another cycle, though disagreement, and back to agreement—calendars were reformed at the beginning of each new dynasty.

Greek calendrical computer: In the late sixteenth century, an astrological calendar dating back to about 80 B.C. was found near the Greek island of Antikythera. One of the most sophisticated pieces of mechanical engineering from the ancient world, the device contains thirty-one interlocking wheels and was

©1996 by Key Curriculum Press

Engraving of a Roman calendar found incised on a marble cube at Herculaneum, an ancient Italian city buried by the eruption of Mount Vesuvius, A.D. 79. From H. Roux's Herculaneum et Pompeii *(Paris, 1875).*

probably used to compute the changing positions of heavenly bodies.

Khmer temple calendar: An ancient Cambodian temple calendar served as the mausoleum for Yasovarman, king of the Khmer kingdom from A.D. 899 to A.D. 910. On each of its four sides were twenty-seven towers, representing the number of days in the lunar cycle. Twelve towers stood on each of its seven terraces, symbolizing the months of the year in Jupiter's twelve-year cycle.

For more on calendars, see vignettes 6, 30, 40, and 48. ★

Activities

1. Why were lunar calendars used in some ancient societies, solar calendars in others, and seasonal calendars in still others? What benefits did each type of calendar provide?

2. Read about an ancient Chinese calendar. How did Chinese calendar makers reconcile the lunar and solar cycles?

3. Many scholars believe England's prehistoric Stonehenge megalith was constructed to align with certain astronomical events. What were these events? Why would they have been important to prehistoric peoples?

4. Read about a calendar constructed by an ancient culture not mentioned in this vignette. Prepare a visual presentation of what you learn and share it with your class.

Related Reading

Aero, Rita. *Things Chinese.* New York: Doubleday, 1980.

Closs, M.P. (ed). *Native American Mathematics.* Austin: University of Texas Press, 1986.

Francis, Richard L. *Mathematical Look at the Calendar.* Arlington, MA: COMAP, 1988.

Gardner, Martin. *Fractal Music, Hypercards, and More.* New York: W.H. Freeman, 1992.

Scarre, Chris (ed). *Timelines of the Ancient World.* New York: Dorling Kindersley, 1993.

Schiffer, M.M., and L. Bowden. *Role of Mathematics in Science.* Washington, DC: Mathematical Association of America, 1984.

Zaslavsky, Claudia. *Africa Counts: Number and Pattern in African Culture*. New York: Lawrence Hill Books, 1979.

THALES: A MAN OF LEGEND

9

One of the earliest Greek mathematicians we know of is **Thales of Miletus** (ca 580 B.C.). Knowledgeable in many areas, Thales was also considered a statesman, a counselor, an engineer, a businessman, a philosopher, and an astronomer. Despite the fact that none of his original work has survived, he is well remembered.

One story about Thales has him visiting the Great Pyramid in Egypt, which Egyptian priests exhibited to him to demonstrate Egypt's impressive mathematical development. Thales measured both the length of the shadow the pyramid cast over the sand and his own shadow length, and after a few calculations, he told the priests the pyramid's height. Unaware that Thales had written the proof of the geometric theorem stating that corresponding sides of similar triangles are proportional, the priests were surprised that he so quickly calculated the correct height of the pyramid. We know for certain that this sharing of knowledge was mutual—Thales returned home with new geometric knowledge, some of which he'd gained by observing Egyptian surveyors reestablish land boundaries after the annual flooding of the Nile River.

Thales is also remembered as an adept problem solver. Although there was not enough time to build a permanent bridge, King Croesus of Lydia wanted to get his army's equipment across a river quickly to pursue an enemy. At a loss, the king summoned Thales, who solved the problem at a glance. He instructed the troops to dig a canal, diverting the river water into a temporary channel. After the equipment had been moved across the riverbed, the troops filled the canal, and everything was restored to its natural order.

Egypt wasn't the only center of learning Thales traveled to in his search for knowledge. He studied Babylonian astronomical methods, and some say he predicted an eclipse of the sun in Asia Minor in 585 B.C. Whether he actually predicted the event is questionable, but the eclipse occurred! It took place when the nations Media and Lydia were preparing to fight a battle. When the Median and Lydian armies saw the eclipse, they were so frightened by what they perceived to be a bad omen that they hastily called for peace and retreated to their respective homelands. Modern astronomers have calculated backwards and have determined that the eclipse took place on May 28, 585 B.C. The called-off battle is considered to be the first historical event known to the exact day. ★

Thales is credited with proving these fundamental geometric concepts.

1. A circle is bisected by any diameter.

2. The base angles of an isosceles triangle are equal.

3. If two lines intersect, the vertical angles formed are equal.

4. Two triangles are congruent if they have two angles and one side in each respectively equal.

5. An angle inscribed in a semicircle is a right angle. (Records suggest that this fact was known to the Babylonians some 1,400 years before Thales.)

While these are elementary concepts, Thales was the first to support them with logical reasoning as well as experimentation and intuition.

ACTIVITIES

1. Thales devised a geometric method for measuring the distance of a ship from the shore. What was his method?

2. Work out Thales' calculation of the height (*AC* in the figure shown at left) of Egypt's Great Pyramid. Segment *BD* is a pole or a rod of known length.

   a. How did Thales find the length of segment *BE*?

   b. How did he calculate *FC*?

   c. What pair of similar triangles did he use to calculate *AC*?

   d. Use what you discovered in 2c to set up a proportion that allows you to calculate *AC*.

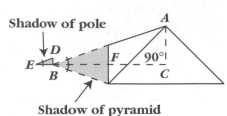

Shadow of pole

Shadow of pyramid

3. Measure the height of a tall object in your neighborhood by using the shadow method Thales used to measure the height of the Great Pyramid.

4. Let *P* be any point other than point *A* or point *B* on the circle shown at left.

   a. What is the measure of angle *APB*?

   b. Find all the possible integer values for *x* and *y*.

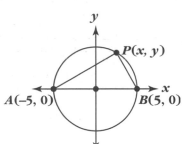

RELATED READING

Bell, E.T. *The Last Problem*. Washington, DC: Mathematical Association of America, 1990.

———. *The Magic of Numbers*. New York: McGraw-Hill, 1946.

Boyer, Carl. *A History of Mathematics,* 2nd ed rev. Uta C. Merzbach. New York: John Wiley, 1991.

———. *The History of Mathematics and Its Conceptual Development*. Mineola, NY: Dover, 1949.

Johnson, Art. *Classical Math: History Topics for the Classroom*. Palo Alto, CA: Dale Seymour, 1994.

Maor, Eli. *To Infinity and Beyond: A Cultural History of the Infinite*. Boston: Birkhauser Boston, 1987.

Pappas, Theoni. *The Joy of Mathematics*. San Carlos, CA: Wide World/Tetra, 1989.

Swetz, Frank. *Learning Activities from the History of Mathematics*. Portland, ME: J. Weston Walch, 1994.

The Golden Age of Greece

10

*Map of ancient Greece, engraved by Petrus Kerius for **A Universal History** (Edinburgh, 1776).*

Many early civilizations believed that the natural phenomena they observed and the mystery of human existence were in the hands of a variety of gods. For a particularly creative period in Greek history (ca 600–200 B.C.), Greek scholars traveled extensively, absorbing a rich variety of ideas and ways of thinking. Building upon both new and established knowledge, they began to expand upon the concept that humans have an intellect that can discover truths through observation and experimentation.

Mathematicians in Greece, including Thales, Pythagoras, Plato, Aristotle, Euclid, Eratosthenes, and Archimedes, developed and promoted the thesis that the world was mathematically designed and that human reasoning powers could comprehend this design. These mathematicians sought to use mathematics as a tool to pursue truth, and they developed a system of thinking that explained the motions of the sun, the moon, and the planets, as well as the general construction of the universe. This system, called deduction, allowed them to show that the truth of a statement was a logical consequence of previously established statements. Because a chain of statements needs a starting point, they established axioms, or postulates, that were accepted as true without proof. All other statements followed logically from them.

In the first century A.D., several forces, such as the Roman conquest of Greece and the rise of Christianity, resulted in the destruction of many Greek accomplishments. The Christians and the Romans burned thousands of "heathen" Greek books, believing that faith, not reason, would lead to truth. Additionally, the Muslims who conquered Egypt in A.D. 640 believed that Greek literature conflicted with the teachings of the Koran, and another destruction of Greek books took place in Alexandria. Fortunately, about a century later the city of Baghdad (the capital of what is now Iraq) became a flourishing intellectual center and established a library. Librarians collected many classic Greek texts from scholars who had fled the destruction of the early Greek and Alexandrian academies and libraries. By the end of the ninth century, the texts had been preserved, translated into Arabic for future study. (For more on Islamic mathematics, see vignettes 27, 29, 30, 31, 35, and 40.)

For more on the mathematics of ancient Greek and Alexandria, see vignettes 9, 11, 12, 13, 15–20, 23, 64, and 73. ★

Activities

1. Pythagoras and his followers were fascinated by number patterns, such as those shown.

   a. Find the fifth and sixth triangular numbers.

   b. Find the fifth and sixth square numbers.

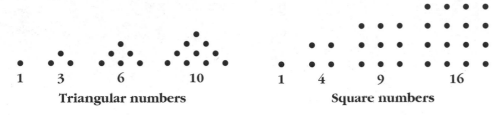

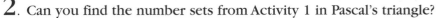

2. Can you find the number sets from Activity 1 in Pascal's triangle?

3. In Plato's dialogue *Meno,* a young slave concludes that a square constructed on the hypotenuse of an isosceles right triangle has twice the area of a square constructed on one of the legs.

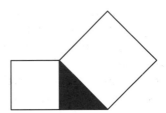

   a. Construct an isosceles right triangle and the squares on both legs. Cut out the two smaller squares, then cut them into pieces that demonstrate that the sum of the areas is the area of the square on the hypotenuse.

   b. Prove that this assertion is true for any isosceles right triangle.

4. What were some of the important mathematical concepts developed by **Aristotle** (384–322 B.C.)?

Related Reading

Aaboe, Asger. *Episodes from the Early History of Mathematics.* Washington, DC: Mathematical Association of America, 1978.

Bell, E.T. *The Last Problem.* Washington, DC: Mathematical Association of America, 1990.

Boyer, Carl. *A History of Mathematics,* 2nd ed rev. Uta C. Merzbach. New York: John Wiley, 1991.

Eves, Howard. *An Introduction to the History of Mathematics*. New York: Holt, Rinehart and Winston, 1990.

Heath, T.L. *History of Greek Mathematics,* Vols I and II. Mineola, NY: Dover, 1981

Hoffman, Paul. *Archimedes Revenge: The Challenge of the Unknown.* New York: W.W. Norton, 1988.

Kline, Morris. *Mathematics in Western Culture.* New York: Oxford University Press, 1964.

Kramer, Edna. *The Nature and Growth of Modern Mathematics.* Princeton: Princeton University Press, 1981.

EARLY GREEK MATHEMATICIANS

11

From about 600 B.C. to 200 B.C., the Greeks rigorously developed systems of mathematical thought in an effort to explain the world around them. Scholars and thinkers traveled far and wide, amassing knowledge and exchanging ideas, and eventually discarded much of the Greek mythology generated by the belief that gods manipulated the physical world according to their whims. The stories of each of the mathematicians listed below could fill a book—and they do!—but they're for you to discover. To get you started, here's a sampling of their contributions.

Give me a place to stand and I shall move the earth.
—Archimedes

I have hardly ever known a mathematician who was capable of reasoning.
—Plato

Anaximander (610-546 B.C.): Anaximander was fascinated by the world he lived in, by the worlds he couldn't reach, and by the origins of all. In addition to creating one of the earliest maps of the world, he was an astronomer who attempted to estimate the size of the sun and who envisioned the planets to be globes of fire and air. Additionally, he fixed the earth at the place where it remained for over 2,000 years, until sixteenth-century astronomer Nicholas Copernicus displaced it from the center of the universe. Not content to simply explore the *existing* world, he also considered its *beginnings,* giving science its first comprehensive—though not very plausible—theory of evolution. In doing so, he helped to shift explanations about nature away from the supernatural. As a mathematician, he produced a formal, if limited, exposition of geometry with theorems arranged in a logical sequence.

Plato (429-347 B.C.): In 385 B.C., Plato founded his Academy in Athens, Greece. A center of learning for hundreds of years, this famous school attracted learned men and women from all over the Mediterranean world. Plato's belief that the study of mathematics was best used for "drawing the soul towards the truth" heavily influenced the Academy's curriculum. In fact, he stated in his *Republic* that "the knowledge at which geometry aims is knowledge of the eternal." This emphasis on mathematics used for training the mind (pure mathematics) rather than for practical purposes (applied mathematics) prepared students for an education in philosophy, Plato's primary interest. Plato's belief system, called Platonism, influenced generations of philosophers after his death. Additionally, Plato espoused the doctrine of nature's mathematical design. Greatly influenced by the Pythagoreans and their theory of numbers, he used triangles to represent spiritual forms of the four material elements: An equilateral triangle represented the spirit of earth; a right triangle, the spirit of water; an isosceles triangle, the spirit of fire; and a scalene triangle, the spirit of air.

Archimedes (ca 287-212 B.C.): The first mathematician we know of to simplify a complicated mathematical problem by creating a physical model of it, Archimedes developed important mathematical principles that are used in the fields of physics and engineering. In one story, he demonstrated a principle of levers by single-handedly pulling a ship out of dock to sea. According to Greek biographer Plutarch (A.D. ca 46-ca 120), "he fixed accordingly upon a ship of burden . . . , which could not be drawn out of the dock without great labor and many men; and . . . , sitting himself the while far off, with no great endeavor, but only holding the head of the pulley in his hand and drawing the cords by degrees, he drew the ship in a straight line, as smoothly and evenly as if [it] had been

ΑΡΧΙΜΗΔΟΥΣ
ΤΟΥ ΣΥΡΑΚΟΥΣΙΟΥ, ΤΑ ΜΕΧΡΙ
νῦν σωζόμενα, ἅπαντα.

ARCHIMEDIS SYRACVSANI
PHILOSOPHI AC GEOMETRAE EX-
cellentissimi Opera, quæ quidem extant, omnia, multis iam seculis desi-
derata, atque à quàm paucissimis hactenus uisa, nuncque
primùm & Græcè & Latinè in lu-
cem edita.

Quorum Catalogum uersa pagina reperies.

Adiecta quoque sunt

EVTOCII ASCALONITAE
IN EOSDEM ARCHIMEDIS LI-
bros Commentaria, item Græcè & Latinè,
nunquam antea excusa.

*Cum Cæs. Maiest. gratia & priuilegio
ad quinquennium.*

Ioannes Bage. Grillingony

BASILEAE,
Ioannes Heruagius excudi fecit.
An. M D XLIIII.

Title page of Archimedes' **Archimedis Syracusani philosophi ac geometrae** *(Basel, 1544).*

©1996 by Key Curriculum Press

in the sea." Archimedes is the mathematician of legend who ran naked through the streets of Syracuse shouting "Eureka, eureka!" ("I have found it!") after having discovered the first law of hydrostatics while taking a bath. (For more on Archimedes, see vignettes 2, 60, and 80.)

For more on the mathematics of ancient Greek and Alexandria, see vignettes 9, 10, 12, 13, 15–20, 23, 64, and 73. ★

ACTIVITIES

1. What is the science of hydrostatics? What is the first law of hydrostatics that Archimedes discovered?

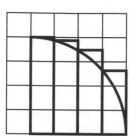

Figure 1

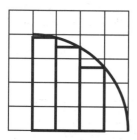

Figure 2

2. Use a compass to draw a quarter-circle in the first quadrant of a coordinate grid. Divide the horizontal radius into four equal segments. Using the left endpoint of each segment, draw rectangles as shown in Figure 1. Then, using the right endpoint of each segment, draw rectangles as shown in Figure 2. Measure to find the sum of the areas of the rectangles in Figure 1; do the same for Figure 2. How do these areas compare with the area of the quarter-circle? How could you use your calculated areas to estimate the circular area? (Archimedes used this approach to calculate areas bounded by complicated curves.) What could you do to produce a more accurate approximation?

3. In Ionia, a Greek settlement in Asia Minor, philosophers attempted to apply reason to human affairs. Why were the Ionians freer to disregard the religious beliefs that dominated the European Greek culture?

RELATED READING

Bell, E.T. *Men of Mathematics*. **New York: Simon and Schuster, 1986.**

Burton, David. *The History of Mathematics: An Introduction.* Boston: Allyn and Bacon, 1985.

Dunham, William. *Journey Through Genius: The Great Theorems of Mathematics.* Somerset, NJ: John Wiley, 1990.

Heath, T.L. *History of Greek Mathematics,* Vols I and II. Mineola, NY: Dover, 1981.

Hoffman, Paul. *Archimedes Revenge: The Challenge of the Unknown.* New York: W.W. Norton, 1988.

Hollingdale, Stuart. *Makers of Mathematics*. **New York: Penguin Books, 1989.**

Lightner, James. "A Chain of Influence in the Development of Geometry." *Mathematics Teacher* (Jan 1991) 15–19.

Vergara, William C. *Mathematics in Everyday Things.* New York: Harper and Brothers, 1959.

Ideal and Irrational Numbers

12

The Pythagoreans were followers of **Pythagoras** (572–497 B.C.), the philosopher and mathematician best known for the famous right triangle theorem named after him ($a^2 + b^2 = c^2$). The Pythagoreans believed that all of nature could be explained by numbers. In fact, their motto stated: "All things are numbers." They especially valued the numbers 1, 2, 3, and 4, which they called the *tetractys*. The Pythagorean oath was: "I swear in the name of the *Tetractys,* which has been bestowed on our soul." They saw fourness in many things, including the four geometric elements (point, line, surface, and solid) and the four material elements (earth, air, fire, and water).

Because the sum of the four numbers of the *tetractys* is 10, the Pythagoreans considered 10 to be the ideal number. They went to great lengths to build an astronomical theory based on number relationships. For example, they maintained that 10 represented the universe, so there must be ten bodies in the heavens. The earth, the sun, the moon, and the five then-known planets made up eight of these bodies. To complete their universe, they introduced a "central fire" and a "counter-earth." Humans couldn't see these two bodies because the portion of the earth where they lived faced away from the bodies.

Pythagoras stressed the importance of both whole numbers and the ratio of whole numbers in the study of nature. After his death, however, his followers used the method of indirect proof to establish that $\sqrt{2}$ cannot be written as the ratio of two whole numbers. In doing so, they discovered irrational numbers—numbers that can't be written as the ratio of two integers.

This discovery caused considerable consternation among the Pythagoreans, because many of Pythagoras' widely accepted conclusions were based on the implicit assumption that all numbers could be written as the ratio of two whole numbers. So as not to discredit him, the Pythagoreans took pains to keep their discovery a secret. Legend has it that a Pythagorean named Hippasus revealed the secret to outsiders. As a result he was tossed overboard by his fellow Pythagoreans while at sea.

For more on irrational numbers, see vignettes 19, 33, and 52. ★

The Women Pythagoreans

During a time when women were considered intellectually inferior to men, the Pythagorean community welcomed women as equals, providing them with opportunities to participate in the fields of science and mathematics. Pythagoras, known as the Feminist Philosopher, encouraged women as students and as teachers. Toward the end of his life, he married one of his more successful students, Theano. An accomplished cosmologist and healer, Theano headed the community after his death, and although she and her daughters faced political persecution, they continued to spread Pythagorean philosophies throughout Greece and Egypt.

Detail from Gregor Reisch's **Margarita philosophica** *(1503), showing Pythagoras working with arithmetic.*

Activities

1. Two of the most interesting numbers in the real number system are π and e. What were the processes used to establish that both of these numbers are irrational?

2. Provide a counterexample to prove that each statement is false.

    a. The sum of two irrational numbers is irrational.

    b. The difference of two irrational numbers is irrational.

    c. The product of two irrational numbers is irrational.

    d. The quotient of two irrational numbers is irrational.

3. A Pythagorean triple is a set of integers a, b, and c that could be the sides of a right triangle. That is, $a^2 + b^2 = c^2$. Show that the following method always generates Pythagorean triples but does not generate *all* Pythagorean triples: Square an odd integer greater than 1. Find the two consecutive integers whose sum is equal to the square of the chosen number. The integer you squared and the consecutive integers you found form a Pythagorean triple.

4. What did the mathematicians of ancient Greece find interesting about the number 8?

5. Prove that if a, b, and c are numbers satisfying the Pythagorean relation $a^2 + b^2 = c^2$, then, for any constant k, the numbers ka, kb, and kc will also satisfy the relation.

Related Reading

Bell, E.T. *The Last Problem*. Washington, DC: Mathematical Association of America, 1990.

Bennett, Dan. *Pythagoras Plugged In: Proofs and Problems for The Geometer's Sketchpad*. Berkeley, CA: Key Curriculum Press, 1995.

Boyer, Carl. *A History of Mathematics*, 2nd ed rev. Uta C. Merzbach. New York: John Wiley, 1991.

Hollingdale, Stuart. *Makers of Mathematics*. New York: Penguin Books, 1989.

Kline, Morris. *Mathematics: The Loss of Certainty*. New York: Oxford University Press, 1980.

Ore, Oystein. *Number Theory and Its History*. Mineola, NY: Dover, 1988.

Room, Adrian. *The Guinness Book of Numbers*. Middlesex, England: Guinness Publishing, 1989.

Smith, Sanderson. *Great Ideas for Teaching Math*. Portland, ME: J. Weston Walch, 1990.

The Paradoxes of Zeno

13

The ancient Greeks were masters of geometry, but they shied away from the concept of the infinite. No one was more influential in promoting a suspicion of the infinite than **Zeno of Elea** (ca 450 B.C.). Little is known of Zeno's life other than that he loved controversy. This trait is evident in his mathematical paradoxes, which assert that motion is impossible and that certain frequently observed events can't happen.

The *Dichotomy*

Before an object can travel a given distance, it first must travel half this distance; but before it can do this, it must travel the first quarter of the distance; and before this, the first eighth of the distance, and so on, ad infinitum. Since it is impossible to exhaust this infinite collection of events, motion cannot happen.

If we'd never perceived an object in motion, this paradox might convince us that it's impossible to hit a target with a bow and arrow—the arrow wouldn't travel any distance.

The *Achilles*

Achilles is racing against a tortoise. Since the tortoise is slower, it is given a head start. Once the race starts, Achilles cannot catch the tortoise because when he reaches the initial position of the tortoise, it will have moved on. Continuing this line of reasoning, whenever Achilles gets to where the tortoise once was, the tortoise has advanced somewhat farther on. Hence, Achilles cannot overtake the tortoise.

The Greeks knew that objects, such as arrows, can travel a certain distance. They knew that a fast runner can overtake a slower runner who may be temporarily ahead in a race. Try as they might, though, they couldn't resolve Zeno's paradoxes. As a result, they developed a deeply rooted suspicion of the infinite and the infinitesimal.

Engraved nineteenth-century illustration of Zeno, based on a bust found in a Roman villa. His deeply furrowed brow no doubt attempts to illustrate his love of paradox.

Zeno's arguments perplexed mathematicians for centuries. The confusion the paradoxes generated was compounded by the fact that infinity was often considered to have the property of a very large number. Swiss mathematician **Leonhard Euler** (1707–1783) did not hesitate to say that $\frac{1}{0}$ is infinite and that $\frac{2}{0}$ is twice as large as $\frac{1}{0}$. It was not until the nineteenth century, when **Georg Cantor** (1845–1918) developed his ideas about set theory and the theory of the infinite, that the mysteries of Zeno's paradoxes were solved.

For more on infinity, see vignettes 14, 51, 75, and 79. ★

©1996 by Key Curriculum Press

Activities

1. Analyze this argument put forth by the Greek philosopher **Eubulides:** One grain of sand does not make a pile, and, if we add another grain of sand to the one, the two grains do not make a pile. When a grain of sand is added to a nonpile, this still doesn't make a pile. Hence, it is impossible to have a pile of sand.

2. Suppose Achilles gave the tortoise a head start of 1,000 meters and that he could run ten times faster than the tortoise. Let the length of the racetrack be x meters. What must be true about the value of x if the following is true?

   a. It is possible for Achilles to win the race.

   b. It is impossible for Achilles to win the race.

   c. The race ends in a tie.

3. In the figure, the tortoise starts D meters ahead of Achilles.

   a. How much faster is Achilles than the tortoise?

   b. How long will it take Achilles to catch the tortoise?

   c. In terms of D, how far will Achilles be from his starting point when he catches up to the tortoise?

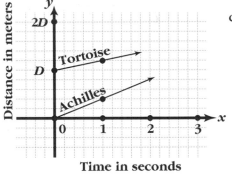

Related Reading

Agostini, Granco. *Math and Logic Games.* New York: Harper & Row, 1980.

Bell, E.T. *Men of Mathematics*. New York: Simon and Schuster, 1986.

Boyd, James N. *Professor Bear's Mathematical World.* Salem, VA: Virginia Council of Teachers of Mathematics, 1987.

Bunch, Bryan H. *Mathematical Fallacies and Paradoxes.* New York: Van Nostrand Reinhold, 1982.

Davies, Paul. *The Edge of Infinity*. New York: Simon and Schuster, 1982.

Maor, Eli. *To Infinity and Beyond: A Cultural History of the Infinite*. Boston: Birkhauser Boston, 1987.

Pappas, Theoni. *The Joy of Mathematics*. San Carlos, CA: Wide World/Tetra, 1989.

Salmon, Wesley (ed). *Zeno's Paradoxes.* New York: Bobbs-Merrill Educational Publishing, 1970.

HISTORY OF MATH

INFINITUDE OF PRIMES

14

Prime numbers—positive integers greater than 1 that are evenly divisible only by themselves and by 1—have been a source of fascination for mathematicians through the ages because they are considered the building blocks from which all integers are made. We credit **Euclid** (ca 300 B.C.) with an elegant proof establishing that the number of prime numbers is infinite. Influenced by the Pythagoreans, he used the method of indirect proof.

Suppose that there are only a finite number of primes,

$$p_1, p_2, p_3, \ldots, p_k,$$

where k is a positive integer representing the number of primes. Construct a number P that is one greater than the product of the numbers in the set of primes. That is,

$$P = p_1 \times p_2 \times p_3 \times \ldots \times p_k + 1.$$

Since P is clearly greater than any of the primes in the list, it must be composite since the list contains all prime numbers. Since every composite number is a product of primes, there must be a prime number that divides P. But division by any of the primes $p_1, p_2, p_3, \ldots, p_k$ results in a remainder of 1, so none of these primes is a factor of P. Hence there must be a prime number that is not one of the finite collection $p_1, p_2, p_3, \ldots, p_k$. This contradicts the assumption that this set contains all of the primes. Hence, the assertion that there is only a finite number of primes is false. We conclude that the number of prime numbers is infinite.

This further is observable in number, that it is that which the mind makes use of in measuring all things that by us are measurable, which principally are expansion and duration; and our idea of infinity, even when applied to those, seems to be nothing but the infinity of number. For what else are our ideas of Eternity and Immensity, but the repeated additions of certain ideas of imagined parts of duration and expansion, with the infinity of number; in which we can come to no end of addition?

—John Locke, An Essay concerning Human Understanding

Because Euclid proved that there is no such thing as the largest prime number, we don't bother to search for it. However, some mathematicians use modern computers to periodically find a number that temporarily holds the title of "the largest known prime number." Before the invention of computers, finding the largest known prime presented quite a challenge. One number that held this distinction for 75 years was discovered by French mathematician **Edouard Anatole Lucas** in 1876. The number is:

$$2^{127} - 1 = 170,141,183,460,469,231,731,687,303,715,884,105,727.$$

For more on infinity, see vignettes 13, 51, 75, and 79. ★

ACTIVITIES

1. **Christian Goldbach** (1690–1764) made a conjecture about prime numbers—it remains unproven to this day. What is Goldbach's conjecture?

2. What is Bertrand's conjecture (made in 1845) about prime numbers?

3. Pairs of primes that differ by two—such as {3, 5}, {5, 7}, and {11, 13}—are called twin primes. What is historically interesting about twin primes?

4. For over 2,000 years, mathematicians have sought to find a polynomial function $f(k)$ which, for values $k = 1, 2, 3, \ldots$, would yield only prime numbers. One function that starts off well is $f(k) = k^2 + k + 41$. Test this function by calculating $f(1), f(2), f(3), f(4),$ and $f(5)$. Can you find a positive integer less than 50 for k such that $f(k)$ is not a prime? (If you approach this problem algebraically, there is one obvious value!)

5. If $f(k) = k^2 - 79k + 1601$, then $f(k)$ is a prime for $k = 1, 2, 3, \ldots, N$. Find the value for N such that $f(N)$ is a prime but $f(N + 1)$ is not.

6. Consider numbers formed by taking the product of consecutive primes and then adding 1. That is, consider the sequence $2 + 1, 2 \times 3 + 1,$ $2 \times 3 \times 5 + 1, 2 \times 3 \times 5 \times 7 + 1, 2 \times 3 \times 5 \times 7 \times 11 + 1, \ldots$. What is the first number in this sequence that is not prime?

RELATED READING

Davis, Philip, and Reuben Hersh. *The Mathematical Experience*. Boston: Birkhauser Boston, 1981.

Dunham, William. "Euclid and the Infinitude of Primes." *Mathematics Teacher* (Jan 1987) 16-17.

Gardner, Martin. "The Remarkable Lore of the Prime Numbers." *Scientific American* (Mar 1964) 120-128.

Hardy, G.H.A. *A Mathematician's Apology*. Cambridge, MA: Cambridge University Press, 1992.

Maor, Eli. *To Infinity and Beyond: A Cultural History of the Infinite*. Boston: Birkhauser Boston, 1987.

Olson, Melfried, and Gerald Goff. "A Divisibility Test for Any Prime." *School Science and Mathematics* (Nov 1986) 578-581.

Shockley, James E. *Introduction to Number Theory*. New York: Holt, Rinehart and Winston, 1967.

Smith, Sanderson. *Great Ideas for Teaching Math*. Portland, ME: J. Weston Walch, 1990.

The Elements of Euclid

15

One of the most famous mathematical works in history, **Euclid's *Elements*** (ca 300 B.C.) is devoted to geometry, to algebra, and to number theory. A compilation of his own work and the knowledge of those before him, Euclid's book is of great significance because its contents are presented in a well-organized, logical manner. In his *Elements,* Euclid attempted to develop an organized form of thinking through deductive reasoning. In a deductive system, we establish a few basic statements (postulates) that are accepted as true. We then establish additional statements (theorems) that reflect the logical consequence of either a postulate or some previously established theorem. This process of reasoning, called Euclidean, has penetrated every branch of mathematics.

Euclid's work does have its flaws, though. For instance, some of his definitions don't really "define," because he doesn't base them on a set of primitive (undefined) terms. We see this in his definitions of the terms given below.

- **Point:** That which has no part

- **Line:** Breadthless length

- **Straight line:** A line which lies evenly with the points on itself

- **Plane angle:** The inclination to one another of two lines in a plane which meet one another and do not lie in a straight line

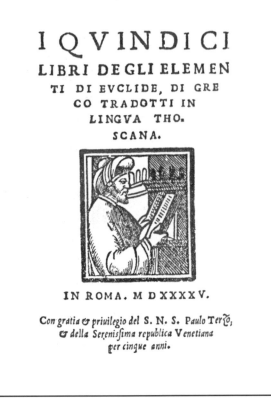

I QVINDICI
LIBRI DEGLI ELEMEN
TI DI EVCLIDE, DI GRE
CO TRADOTTI IN
LINGVA THO.
SCANA.

IN ROMA. M D XXXXV.

*Con gratia & priuilegio del S. N. S. Paulo Ter̃o;
& della Serenissima republica Venetiana
per cinque anni.*

Portrait of Euclid from
I quindici libri degli
elementi di Euclide
(Rome, 1545).

Additionally, in some instances Euclid assumed that certain figures held properties that were not logically justified by postulates or previously established theorems. For instance, he assumed that if a line enters a triangle at a vertex, it intersects the opposite side if extended (see figure at right). Today, this assumption is known as Pasch's axiom.

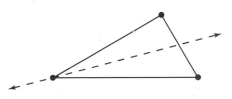

Many of the concepts and ideas in the Elements have been revised and modernized. For example, we now accept *point, line,* and *plane* as primitive terms and use them to create other definitions. Because Euclidean concepts have so heavily influenced the development of geometry, they are still the focus of study in geometry classes around the world. ★

Activities

1. What is logically inconsistent about the idea of defining a point as "the intersection of two lines"?

2. What is Euclid's fifth postulate? Why is it of great historical interest? (For information on Euclid's fifth postulate, see vignette 63.)

3. The Euclidean algorithm, found at the beginning of Book VII of the *Elements,* describes a process for finding the greatest common divisor of two positive integers. Research this algorithm, then use it to find the greatest common divisor of (a) 1,596 and 11,220 and (b) 1,064; 9,338; and 3,003.

4. Show that if p is a prime that divides the product xy, then either p divides x or p divides y.

Related Reading

Adele, Gail. "When Did Euclid Live? An Answer plus a Short History of Geometry." *Mathematics Teacher* (Sept 1989) 460–463.

Bell, E.T. *The Last Problem*. Washington, DC: Mathematical Association of America, 1990.

Boyer, Carl. *A History of Mathematics,* 2nd ed rev. Uta C. Merzbach. New York: John Wiley, 1991.

Eves, Howard. *An Introduction to the History of Mathematics*. **New York: Holt, Rinehart and Winston, 1990.**

Heath, T.L. *History of Greek Mathematics,* Vols I and II. Mineola, NY: Dover, 1981.

———. *13 Books of Euclid's* Elements. Mineola, NY: Dover, 1956.

Knorr, W.R. *The Evolution of the Euclidean Elements*. Boston: D. Reidel Publishing, 1975.

Maor, Eli. *To Infinity and Beyond: A Cultural History of the Infinite*. **Boston: Birkhauser Boston, 1987.**

Apollonius and Conic Sections

16

Greek astronomer **Apollonius** (ca 262 B.C.) is best known for his work *Conic Sections,* in which he describes the series of graceful curves formed when a plane surface intersects a cone. Different figures are formed by this intersection, depending on *where* the plane intersects the cone: parallel to the base (a circle), oblique to the base (an ellipse), such that it intersects the base (a parabola), and parallel to the altitude of the cone (a hyperbola)—in this last case the plane also intersects a mirror image of the cone atop the given cone. The Greeks studied the conics out of interest and curiosity, and used them in problems involving geometric constructions.

The comet of 1066, as pictured in the Bayeaux Tapestry (ca A.D. 1080) by Matilda of Flanders.

Today, we know that conic sections are part of the reality that represents and describes our modern world. They are everywhere! We can see this, for example, when we observe the paths of our galaxy's planets. With their finite knowledge of the universe, early scholars probably didn't envision that seventeenth-century mathematicians and scientists would use the conics to represent the paths that projectiles, satellites, planets, and stars follow under the influence of gravity. **Nicholas Copernicus** (1473–1543) thought that our solar system's planets traveled in circular paths, then **Johannes Kepler** (1571–1630) discovered that the ellipse better represents their journey around the sun. **Galileo Galilei** (1564–1642) found that the parabola describes the motions of trajectiles on the earth. (For more on Nicholas Copernicus, Johannes Kepler, and Galileo Galilei, see vignettes 41 and 42.) In 1704, **Edmond Halley** (1656-1743) used data from comets observed in 1456, 1531, 1607, and 1682 to conclude that they represented a single comet orbiting the sun every 76 years in an elliptical path. (Ancient documents suggest the Chinese observed this comet in 240 B.C.) Halley then correctly predicted that this comet named after him would return in 1758.

There are many other examples of the presence of conic sections in our world. A sonic boom wave has the shape of a cone, which, as it expands, intersects the ground in a hyperbolic curve. At any given instant, people along the curve are hearing the boom at the same time. Satellite dishes and reflecting telescopes are examples of the parabola. On a "no lose" elliptical pool table, a ball shot through one focus always makes it into the pocket at the other focus. ★

Circle   **Ellipse**

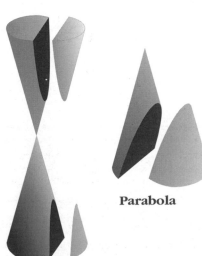

Parabola

Hyperbola

©1996 by Key Curriculum Press

Activities

1. In a plane, a parabola is the set of points equidistant from a line, called the directrix, and a point not on the line, called the focus. The parabola $y = \frac{1}{20} x^2$ with focus $(0, 5)$ and directrix $y = -5$ is shown below. Point $P = (30, 45)$.

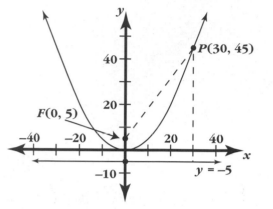

   a. What is the distance from point P to the directrix? What is the distance PF?

   b. Based on what you discovered in 1a, is point P on the parabola?

   c. Do the coordinates of point P satisfy the equation of the parabola? Find two other points that satisfy the equation. In each case, check to see if the points are equidistant from the directrix and the focus.

2. In a plane, an ellipse is the set of points such that the sum of the distances from each point to two fixed points (the foci) is a constant. The ellipse $\frac{x^2}{100} + \frac{y^2}{64} = 1$ with foci at $(-6, 0)$ and $(6, 0)$ is shown at left.

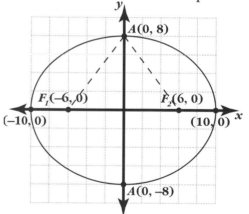

   a. Consider the point $A(0, 8)$. What is the total distance $AF_1 + AF_2$?

   b. Show that the point $P(6, 6.4)$ satisfies the equation of the ellipse.

   c. Calculate $PF_1 + PF_2$ and compare the total to that in 2a.

   d. Find two other points that satisfy the equation of the ellipse. For each point, calculate the sum of its distances from the foci. Compare your results to those in 2a.

3. Research how parabolic surfaces are used in automobile headlights and in French solar furnaces.

Related Reading

Boyer, Carl. *A History of Mathematics*, 2nd ed rev. Uta C. Merzbach. New York: John Wiley, 1991.

Eves, Howard. *An Introduction to the History of Mathematics*. New York: Holt, Rinehart and Winston, 1990.

Jacobs, Harold. *Mathematics: A Human Endeavor*. San Francisco: W.H. Freeman, 1987.

Pappas, Theoni. *The Joy of Mathematics*. San Carlos, CA: Wide World/Tetra, 1989.

HISTORY OF MATH

ERATOSTHENES' COMPUTATION

17

In the third century B.C., Greek mathematician **Eratosthenes** (276–194 B.C.) performed an important function: He was the chief librarian of the library at Alexandria. Established during the fourth century B.C., this famous library was a sort of university where scholars and students could meet to discuss philosophy and literature. By the time it was destroyed in the fourth century A.D., the library had collected and organized over 500,000 Greek works on thousands of topics, making it a center for research and learning in the Egyptian and Greek worlds.

Alexandria, the capital of Egypt, as depicted by nineteenth-century engraver Samuel Walker.

In addition to administering the library, Eratosthenes was an accomplished mathematician who is well known for his attempt to measure the circumference of the earth. Using only simple geometric concepts, his measurement was remarkably accurate. Eratosthenes observed that at the ancient city of Syene (now Aswan) on the Nile, a vertical pole cast no shadow at noon on summer solstice. He knew that during this same time in the city of Alexandria—on the same meridian as Syene—the angle formed by a vertical pole and the segment from its top to the tip of its shadow (point *a* in the figure) was about 7°12′, or about 1/50 of a complete circumference. He also knew that the distance from Syene to Alexandria was 5,000 Greek *stadia*. Assuming that the sun's rays are parallel (making *a* = *b*) and letting *C* represent the center of the earth, he was able to calculate the number of *stadia* in the circumference of the earth.

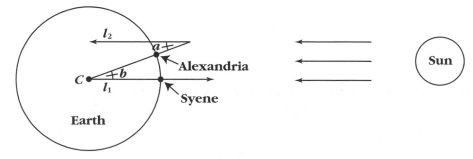

A *stadium* (the singular form of *stadia*) is approximately 516.7 feet. If we convert Eratosthenes' calculations into miles, we can show that the error in his measurement of the earth's circumference was well under two percent. ★

ACTIVITIES

1. Using Eratosthenes' figures, calculate the number of stadia in the circumference of the earth, then convert your answer to miles. Compare your result with what we now know to be the equatorial circumference of the earth (24,901.55 miles).

2. Research the Greek word *stadium*. How does it relate to the English use of the word today?

3. Eratosthenes attempted to calculate the distance from the earth to the moon and the sun. What methods did he use? How accurate were his computations?

4. What is the sieve of Eratosthenes? Demonstrate how it can be used to find prime numbers.

RELATED READING

Bell, E.T. *The Last Problem.* Washington, DC: Mathematical Association of America, 1990.

Boyer, Carl. *A History of Mathematics,* 2nd ed rev. Uta C. Merzbach. New York: John Wiley, 1991.

Eves, Howard. *An Introduction to the History of Mathematics.* New York: Holt, Rinehart and Winston, 1990.

Johnson, Art. *Classical Math: History Topics for the Classroom.* Palo Alto, CA: Dale Seymour, 1994.

Moise, Edwin, and Floyd Downs. *Geometry.* Menlo Park, CA: Addison-Wesley, 1982.

Resnikoff, H.L., and R.O. Wells. *Mathematics in Civilization.* Mineola, NY: Dover, 1985.

Swetz, Frank. *Learning Activities from the History of Mathematics.* Portland, ME: J. Weston Walch, 1994.

Philo, Religion, and Mathematics

18

Philo Judaeus (20 B.C.–A.D. 50) was a Neoplatonist religious philosopher from Alexandria whose views on God disturbed mathematicians of his time. Philo believed that the world is dependent upon God, but that God is independent of the world—a fundamental assumption in Judaism, Christianity, and Islam. He maintained that God is omnipotent, which meant to him four things.

- God created the world out of nothing and implanted in it certain laws of nature by which it is governed.

- Before the creation of the world, God could have chosen not to have created it or to have created another type of world governed by another type of law.

- In the now-existing world, God can override the laws that are implanted in the world and can create what are called miracles.

- God can destroy this world and create in its stead a new world.

This view ran counter to the views of mathematicians who believed that mathematics was a permanent and infallible external truth. The possibility that mathematical law could be abolished by some authority troubled them—and other religious philosophers as well. Opinion was split on whether God's omnipotence included the power to "bring it about that it should not follow from the nature of a triangle that its degrees should be equal to two right angles" (Wolfson, *Religious Philosophy*).

One opinion placed God at the pinnacle of power, able to control the laws of mathematics. The opposing opinion limited God's power, seemingly separating God and mathematics.

The Platonic view of mathematics came close to equating the word *God* with the word *mathematics,* which meant that mathematics was independent of the world. Therefore, mathematics existed prior to and apart from the world, and if the world ever came to an end, mathematics would continue to exist. Because the word *world* has long referred to the whole physical cosmos, those involved with the early development of mathematics took on the task of discovering the mathematics that had always existed. They often found themselves asking: Are the laws of mathematics the laws of God? Even today, some scholars debate this question. ★

The relationship between the spiritual and the secular, illustrated as a discussion between Theologius and Astronomus, the personifications of theology and astronomy. From Alliaco's Concordatia astronomia et theologia *(Augsberg, 1490).*

Activities

1. Who were the Platonists and the Neoplatonists? What was the philosophy of each group?

2. How was the development of mathematics affected by the rise of Christianity? By Islamic beliefs? Do the religious beliefs of today's world affect the current study and development of mathematics? In what ways?

3. What reaction do you think Philo would have had to the discovery of non-Euclidean geometries? What about the early mathematicians who believed that mathematics was a permanent and infallible external truth? (For information on non-Euclidean geometries, see vignettes 63 and 66.)

Related Reading

Barrow, John D. *Pi in the Sky: Counting, Thinking, and Being*. New York: Oxford University Press, 1992.

Davis, Philip, and Reuben Hersh. *Descartes' Dream*. New York: Harcourt Brace Jovanovich, 1986.

Ferris, Timothy. *The Universe and Eye*. San Francisco, CA: Chronicle Books, 1993.

Hawking, Stephen. *A Brief History of Time*. New York: Bantam Books, 1988.

Jaki, Stanley L. *Cosmos and Creator*. Edinburgh: Scottish Academic Press, 1980.

Ross, Hugh. *The Fingerprint of God*. Orange, CA: Promise Publishing, 1989.

Thiel, Rudolf. *And There Was Light: The Discovery of the Universe*. New York: Alfred A. Knopf, 1957.

Wolfson, Harry. *Religious Philosophy*. Cambridge, MA: Harvard University Press, 1961.

The Formulas of Heron and Brahmagupta

19

> *As the sun eclipses the stars by his brilliancy, so the man of knowledge will eclipse the fame of others in assemblies of the people if he proposes algebraic problems, and still more if he solves them.*
>
> —Brahmagupta

Egyptian mathematician **Heron of Alexandria** (ca A.D. 50–100) made considerable contributions to the development of applied mathematics. He is best known for his derivation of a famous formula for the area of a triangle in terms of its three sides: If a, b, and c are the sides of a triangle, and if $s = {}^{(a + b + c)}\!/_2$, then the area of the triangle is $\sqrt{s(s - a)(s - b)(s - c)}$ square units.*

While applying a formula to a sample problem doesn't prove the formula, we can check out whether Heron's formula works with a right triangle. The area of the right triangle shown at right is one half the product of its legs. That is, the area is $\frac{1}{2}(3)(4) = 6$ square units. Using Heron's formula, we see that $s = {}^{(3 + 4 + 5)}\!/_2 = 6$, and the area of the triangle is $\sqrt{6(6 - 3)(6 - 4)(6 - 5)} = \sqrt{36} = 6$ square units.

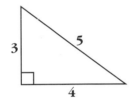

Heron's formula sometimes yields irrational values. For example, if you applied it to a triangle whose sides are 5, 6, and 7 units, then you would find that the triangle's area is $\sqrt{216}$ square units, an irrational result. Heron didn't share the belief of his Greek colleagues that irrational numbers could not exist, and that, in general, the product of more than three numbers was meaningless. In this sense, he was ahead of his time.

About 500 years later, Hindu mathematician **Brahmagupta** (b A.D. 598) discovered a formula similar to Heron's for the area of a cyclic quadrilateral: $\sqrt{(s - a)(s - b)(s - c)(s - d)}$, where $s = {}^{(a + b + c + d)}\!/_2$. (A cyclic quadrilateral is a quadrilateral that can be inscribed within a circle, as shown at right.) Brahmagupta's most important work was *Brahmasphutasiddhanta (Correct astronomical system of Brahma,* A.D. 628). In medieval India, most mathematical works were written as chapters of astronomy books, and the mathematical concepts and techniques were applied to astronomical problems. This was true of the *Brahmasphutasiddhanta*—and it was written completely in verse. (For more on the mathematics of India see vignettes 2, 24, 28, and 82.) ★

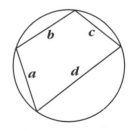

*See the proof for this theorem in the Bernard Oliver article listed in Related Reading.

Activities

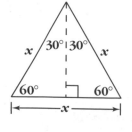

1. Use the properties of basic geometry to derive the formula for the area of an equilateral triangle in terms of a side x. Then use Heron's formula to determine the area in terms of x. Compare the area formulas you obtained by using these different methods.

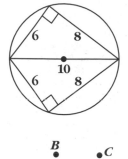

2. The figure at left shows a cyclic quadrilateral inscribed within a circle with a diameter of 10. Calculate the area of the quadrilateral by adding the areas of the two triangles shown and applying Brahmagupta's formula.

B
●   ●*C*

3. Given the three points *A, B,* and *C* shown at left, find the collection of all points, *D,* such that the four points *A, B, C,* and *D* could be joined in some order to form a cyclic quadrilateral.

A●

4. The area of a right triangle with legs of length a and b is $ab/2$. Use Heron's formula to derive this formula.

Related Reading

Datta, B., and A.N. Singh. *History of Hindu Mathematics.* Bombay, India: Asia Publishing House, 1962.

Dunham, William. "An 'Ancient/Modern' Proof of Heron's Formula." *Mathematics Teacher* (Apr 1985) 258–259.

Eves, Howard. *An Introduction to the History of Mathematics*. New York: Holt, Rinehart and Winston, 1990.

Heath, T.L. *History of Greek Mathematics,* Vol II. Mineola, NY: Dover, 1981.

Neugebauer, Otto. *The Exact Sciences in Antiquity.* Mineola, NY: Dover, 1969.

Oliver, Bernard. "Heron's Remarkable Triangle Area Formula." *Mathematics Teacher* (Feb 1993) 161–163.

Pappas, Theoni. *The Joy of Mathematics.* San Carlos, CA: Wide World/Tetra, 1989.

Diophantus of Alexandria

20

From the days of **Euclid** (ca 300 B.C.) to the time of **Hypatia** (A.D. 415), Alexandria, a city in northern Egypt, was the world's center of mathematical activity. Many famous mathematicians studied and lived there, among them **Diophantus** (ca A.D. 250), a heavily influential figure in the development of algebra. His most important work was *Arithmetica,* which contains impressive number theorems and about 130 diverse problems.

An interesting feature of Diophantus' algebra are his solutions for indeterminate equations. An example of an indeterminate equation is $5x + 2y = 20$, where the number of unknowns (two) exceeds the number of equations (one). Because he recognized only positive rational number solutions, some of his solutions are restricted to integers. In his search for ways to find solutions for indeterminate equations, he founded the branch of algebra we call Diophantine analysis.

Although his contributions to mathematics are of great importance, we know little about Diophantus' life other than that he lived in Alexandria—and we are reasonably certain of his age when he died. One of his admirers described Diophantus' life in an algebraic riddle, which legend tells us appeared on his tombstone.

> *Diophantus' youth lasted $^1/_6$ of his life.*
> *He grew a beard after $^1/_{12}$ more of his life.*
> *After $^1/_7$ more of his life, Diophantus married.*
> *Five years later he had a son.*
> *The son lived exactly $^1/_2$ as long as his father.*
> *Diophantus died just four years after his son's death.*
> *All of this totals the years Diophantus lived.*

Can you solve the riddle to determine Diophantus' age at death? ★

A page from the first volume of Diophantus' six-volume Arithmetica, *written in Greek with Latin translation.*

©1996 by Key Curriculum Press

Activities

1. Research some of the algebraic symbols introduced by Diophantus.

2. Solve these problems from *Arithmetica*.

   a. Find four numbers that, taken three at a time, add up to 22, 24, 27, and 20.

   b. In the right triangle *ABC*, right angled at *C*, *AD* bisects angle *A*. Find the set of smallest integers for *AB*, *AD*, *AC*, *BD*, and *DC* such that *DC*:*CA*:*AD* = 3:4:5.

3. When converting temperatures from Fahrenheit to Celsius, we use the formula $C = \frac{5}{9}(F - 32)$. If we substitute integer values for F and round the values of C to the nearest integer, then we are finding (approximate) Diophantine solutions. What other common formulas are used in this way?

Related Reading

Bergamini, David (ed). *Mathematics: Life Science Library*. New York: Time-Life Books, 1972.

Boyer, Carl. *A History of Mathematics,* 2nd ed rev. Uta C. Merzbach. New York: John Wiley, 1991.

Ellis, Keith. *Number Power in Nature and in Everyday Life*. New York: St. Martin's Press, 1978.

Gaughan, Edward D. "An 'Almost' Diophantine Equation." *Mathematics Teacher* (May 1980) 374–376.

Hogben, Lancelot. *Mathematics for the Millions*. New York: W.W. Norton, 1967.

Kline, Morris. *Mathematics for the Nonmathematician*. Mineola, NY: Dover, 1967.

Pappas, Theoni. *The Joy of Mathematics*. San Carlos, CA: Wide World/Tetra, 1989.

Peressini, Anthony, and Donald Sherbert. *Topics in Modern Mathematics*. New York: Holt, Rinehart and Winston, 1971.

AFRICAN NUMBER SYSTEMS AND SYMBOLISM

frica, with its multitude of peoples and languages, is a rich source of number history. Certain cultures followed traditions based on number symbolism, and many ancient African empires required extensive systems of numeration to accommodate their thriving markets. Among these empires were Ghana, which traded in gold; Kush, with its iron-working city of Meroë; and areas of Kenya and South Africa that prospered in cattle herding.

The role economics played in the development of many African number systems is evident in the language of Nigeria's Yoruba culture. In this language, the word for the number 1 is *okan,* for the number 3 is *eta,* and for the number 5 is *arun.* The fact that the Yoruba used cowrie shells as currency is reflected in the counting forms of these words: The word *ookan* represents one object, *eeta* represents three, and *aarun* represents five. In these extended forms, *oo, ee,* and *aa* are the contracted forms of the word *owo,* meaning "cowrie" or "money." Economics also influenced the learning of this number system—Yoruba children learned how to count and figure by observing their parents buying and selling in the marketplace.

Cultural traditions also affected the way Africans used numbers to count, and people often relied upon a variety of intellectual skills to solve number-related problems. For example, in many African cultures, there is a strong taboo against counting living things—doing so can cause harm to what is counted. However, empires needed accurate information about who and what to tax, so they devised innovative, indirect ways to count. Using the concept of one-to-one correspondence, they counted shells that represented livestock or food that represented the number of people in a village. Children were taught to avoid counting by cultivating their powers of observation. Thus, when a boy was taught to watch over his family's cattle, he was required not simply to know their number, but instead to recognize each animal's markings, size, color, and so on. In this way, when he brought the herd home from grazing at the end of the day, he would know by sight if an animal were missing.

As in many other cultures around the world, some numbers have held special significance in Africa. For example, speaking the names of certain numbers was considered taboo among certain groups. In the Ga language of Ghana, 7 was a particularly ominous number and was always represented in the spoken word as 6 + 1. The number 5, however, is still considered a protective number in many parts of North Africa. It appears in the form of a human hand, often woven into banners and painted over doorways to avert evil.

For more on African and African American mathematics, see vignettes 8, 50, 54, 57, 66, and 102. For more on counting, number systems, and significant numbers, see vignettes 1, 12, 21, 31–34, 44, 52, 54, 59, 83, 84, and 97. ★

Finger Counting in Kenya

A variety of number systems have been used in Africa, many based on the numbers 5, 6, 10, and 20. Among certain groups, number systems developed from finger or gesture counting. A gesture system used by the Taita people of Kenya to count cattle or other commodities is shown below.

1 = right hand, forefinger extended

2 = right hand, first two fingers

3 = right hand, three fingers

4 = right hand, four fingers

5 = closed right fist

6 = right fist, left thumb

7 = right fist, left thumb and forefinger

8 = eight fingers (no thumbs)

9 = clasp left fingers in right hand

10 = both fists closed

These gestures were accompanied by words that represented large numbers. For instance, making the gesture for 7 and saying the word for 20 indicated 27.

ACTIVITIES

1. Read about the counting, number, and record-keeping systems that have been used by a particular cultural group in Africa. Prepare a visual presentation of what you learn and share it with your class.

2. Although the number 5 is a protective number in certain areas of North Africa, it has been considered unlucky by the Asante people of Ghana. What is the symbolism that has been associated with other numbers in African cultures? How do these associations compare with those of other cultures around the world?

3. The Yoruba were not the only people in Africa to use cowrie shells as money. Explore the use of this material for currency in other African cultures. How was it used? What other materials have been used for currency in Africa?

RELATED READING

Gay, J., and M. Cole. *The New Mathematics in an Old Culture: A Study of Learning Among the Kpelle of Liberia*. New York: Holt, Rinehart and Winston, 1976.

Gerdes, Paulus. *Lusona: Geometrical Recreations of Africa*. Maputo, Mozambique: African Mathematical Union, 1991.

Nelson, David, et al. *Multicultural Mathematics*. New York: Oxford University Press, 1993.

Schimmel, Annemarie. *The Mystery of Numbers*. New York: Oxford University Press, 1993.

Schwartz, Richard H. *Mathematics and Global Survival*. Needham, MA: Ginn, 1990.

Zaslavsky, Claudia. *Africa Counts: Number and Pattern in African Culture*. New York: Lawrence Hill Books, 1979.

———. *Multicultural Mathematics*. Portland, ME: J. Weston Walch, 1993.

———. "Multicultural Mathematics Education for the Middle Grades." *Arithmetic Teacher* (Feb 1991) 8–13.

HISTORY OF MATH

Nine Chapters on Mathematical Art

22

Math historians in the Western world recognize Euclid's *Elements* as an ancient classic. In the East, the corresponding classic is a Chinese manuscript called the ***Jiuzhang suanshu*** (*Nine chapters on the mathematical art*). We don't know who wrote it, but we believe it was written around 200 B.C. Quite sophisticated, the mathematics in the *Jiuzhang* indicated, for instance, that the Chinese knew how to use negative numbers in computations, a concept their Western counterparts had not yet discovered.

Almost a half a century after the *Jiuzhang* was written, the ruler of the Wei dynasty put officials to work revising literary and scientific classics of the past. Because the dynasty considered the mathematics in the *Jiuzhang* essential for the efficient operation of the community and government, they asked mathematician **Liu Hui** (ca A.D. 250) to revise the text. In addition to copying it, Liu strengthened and expanded the text's contents. For example, he developed and used methods of proof to establish the validity of many assertions that had been stated without proof. His extension of the ninth chapter, in which he laid the foundation for the establishment of trigonometric ratios, was eventually distributed as a separate manuscript called the *Haidao suanjing* (*Sea island mathematical manual*). The *Jiuzhang* and the *Haidao suanjing* set the standard for Asian mathematics for hundreds of years after Liu's death.

Liu is also remembered for producing the most accurate estimate of the number pi (π) known to exist in the ancient world. He obtained his value of 3.141024 by tediously inscribing regular polygons in a circle. His value was produced using a regular polygon of 192 sides.

For more on Chinese mathematics, see vignettes 4, 8, 26, 48, 71, and 89. For more on pi, see vignettes 2 and 80. ★

Other significant early Chinese mathematicians

- **Wang Xiaotong** (ca A.D. 625): Work with cubic equations.
- **Li Ye** (1192–1279): Geometric problems leading to equations of higher degree.
- **Zhu Shijie** (1280–1303): Work with summing series and Pascal's triangle.
- **Guo Shoujing** (1231–1316): Calendar reform and spherical trigonometry.
- **Cheng Dawei** (ca 1590): Wrote oldest surviving work about the *suan pan* (abacus).

This woodblock print from the encyclopedia **Tu Shu Ji Cheng** *(1726) illustrates a sea island problem.*

Activities

1. Research and solve some of the 246 problems that appear in the *Jiuzhang suanshu*.

2. Some maintain that the early Western world borrowed heavily from ancient Chinese mathematics. Why then is Chinese mathematics relatively unknown in the West?

3. The number 8 is highly esteemed in China. Identify the sets of eight objects given below. Why are they significant?

   a. The eight symbols of Buddhism

   b. The eight emblems of Confucianism

   c. The eight symbols of the immortals in Taoism

4. Chinese burial chambers were similar in shape to the frustum of a pyramid. The *Jiuzhang* provides the formula

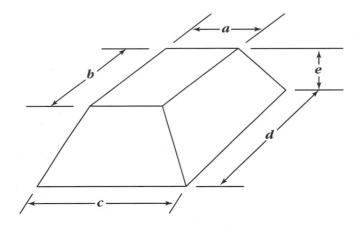

   $V = \frac{1}{6}[(2a + c)b + (2c + a)d]e$ for the volume of a chamber such as that shown at left. Is this formula accurate? To help you answer this question, research the formula developed by the Egyptians for the frustum of a pyramid (the theorem of Pappus).

Related Reading

Dunham, William. *The Mathematical Universe: An Alphabetical Journey Through the Great Proofs, Problems, and Personalities.* New York: John Wiley, 1994.

Joseph, George Gheverghese. *The Crest of the Peacock: Non-European Roots of Mathematics.* London: J.B. Tauris, 1991.

Kline, Morris. *Mathematics: A Cultural Approach.* Reading, MA: Addison-Wesley, 1962.

Li, Yan, and Du Shiran. *Chinese Mathematics: A Concise History*. New York: Clarendon Press, 1987.

Needham, M. *Science and Civilization in China*, Vol III. Cambridge, MA: Cambridge University Press, 1959.

Swetz, Frank. *The Sea Island Mathematical Manual: Surveying and Mathematics in Ancient China.* University Park, PA: Pennsylvania State University Press, 1992.

Temple, Robert. *The Genius of China.* New York: Simon and Schuster, 1986.

Hypatia of Alexandria

23

The first woman mathematician we know about in any detail is **Hypatia of Alexandria** (A.D. 370–415). She learned mathematics from her father, **Theon**, a writer credited with keeping the spirit of Greek mathematics alive during a time when Christian zealots considered mathematics and science to be heresy. Although it was unusual for women of early Greece to receive an education, Hypatia became a highly respected teacher, writer, astronomer, and scientist.

Most of Hypatia's original work has been lost, but it is referred to in numerous texts. During Hypatia's time, teachers often supplied instructional materials to their students by writing commentaries on the pages of already existing scholarly works. In the process, these teachers contributed new material to their fields of study. It is believed that Hypatia authored substantial commentaries on such works as Apollonius' *Conics,* Diophantus' *Arithmetica,* Ptolemy's *Almagest,* and Archimedes' *Measurement of the Circle.* Considered charismatic, knowledgeable, and versatile, she was a popular teacher, in part because she explained complex mathematical ideas clearly and precisely. Reportedly, her eloquent lectures drew scholars from Africa, Asia, and Europe.

An interest in mechanics and the practical applications of mathematics served Hypatia in her roles as astronomer and scientist. It is through correspondence between her and one of her students that we know of her designs for an astrolabe, a tool that determines the altitudes of the stars and the planets. Additionally, she developed the concepts and construction ideas for other scientific devices such as the hydroscope, an instrument used for viewing objects far below the surface of water.

Because her devotion to education and learning countered the Roman Empire's Christian doctrines, Hypatia became a focal point in the political tensions between Christians and non-Christians in Alexandria. Her Neoplatonic views, which were based on the philosophies of such non-Christians as Plato and Aristotle, prompted a mob of zealous Christian monks to murder her in March, A.D. 415. ★

Idealized portrait of Hypatia.

This sixteenth-century woodcut by Hans Holbein II depicts two astronomers observing the phases of the moon. The astronomer on the left holds dividers on a celestial sphere, while the astronomer on the right makes measurements with an astrolabe and a backstaff.

©1996 by Key Curriculum Press

Activities

1. Provide some details on the hydroscope and the astrolabe.

2. Discuss this statement made by Theon to Hypatia: "Reserve your right to think, for even to think wrongly is better than not to think at all."

3. Research the role of women in early Greek society. How did this role compare with that of women in early Egyptian society?

4. How did Hypatia's scientific views and methods conflict with the dominant Christian religion of Alexandria? How were these conflicts magnified when **Cyril** became archbishop of the Alexandrian Church in A.D. 412?

5. Why is the death of Hypatia considered by some to mark the end of the Greek mathematical tradition in Alexandria?

Related Reading

Alic, Margaret. *Hypatia's Heritage*. **Boston: Beacon Press, 1986**.

Bell, E.T. *The Last Problem*. Washington, DC: Mathematical Association of America, 1990.

Carter, Jack. "Discrete Mathematics: Women in Mathematics." *California Mathematics Council ComMuniCator* (Mar 1993) 10-12.

Fabricant, Mona, and Sylvia Svitak. "Why Women Succeed in Mathematics." *Mathematics Teacher* (Feb 1990) 150-154.

Grinstein, Louise S., and Paul Campbell. *Women of Mathematics: A Bibliographic Sourcebook*. Westport, CT: Greenwood Press, 1987.

Kingsley, Charles. *Hypatia, or New Foes with an Old Face*. New York: E. P. Dutton, 1907.

Osen, Lynn. *Women in Mathematics*. Cambridge, MA: MIT Press, 1984.

Perl, Teri. *Women and Numbers: Lives of Women Mathematicians plus Discovery Activities*. **San Carlos, CA: Wide World/Tetra, 1993**.

The Concept of Zero

24

Today we take the number 0 for granted, but did you know that it came into our number system relatively recently? This may have been the result of confusion on the part of early mathematicians about zero's multiple meanings. Even today, the fact that the number 0 must be distinguished from nothing (for example, the temperature 0 degrees is certainly something other than nothing) still confuses some people.

Mathematicians in seventh-century India reasoned that since zero is a number, it follows that number operations can be performed with it. **Brahmagupta** (b A.D. 598), who produced rules for operations with positive and negative numbers, asserted that $0 \div 0 = 1$. He didn't see the logical complications produced by this assertion. However, he did seem aware that the division of a nonzero number by zero was a touchy matter, because he did not offer any comment or possible values for $a \div 0$ when $a \neq 0$.

Many centuries later, **Bhaskara** (1114–1185), the leading Indian mathematician of the twelfth century, was the first to suggest that if $a \neq 0$, then $\frac{a}{0}$ is infinite. The statement below appears in his text *Vija-Ganita* (ca 1150).

> *Statement: Dividend 3. Divisor 0. Quotient the fraction $\frac{3}{0}$. This fraction of which the denominator is cipher, is termed an infinite quantity. In this quantity consisting of that which has cipher for a divisor, there is no alteration, though many be inserted or extracted . . . .*

The statement shows that Bhaskara had a good understanding of this concept, but by asserting that $\frac{a}{0} \times 0 = a$, we can also see that during his time there was still uncertainty about division and multiplication by zero.

Long after early Mayan and Hindu mathematicians initially began working with the concept of zero, our number system has been structured so that zero and negative numbers have joined positive numbers in a consistent and logical structure.

For more on the history of numbers, see vignettes 1, 12, 14, 21, 29, 37, 52, 64, and 67. ★

The Maya and Zero

It has long been believed that India first introduced the number 0. Now, however, it's known that the Maya of southern Mexico and Guatemala (ca 300 B.C.–A.D. 900) discovered and used zero independently of, and possibly before, the mathematicians of India. One of the Mayan symbols for zero was an empty oyster shell, signifying a hollow. Not only did the Maya use the zero to represent "nothingness," but also to define the value of a number's position. For example, a picture of an oyster shell alone represented the number 0, and an oyster shell shown with a dot above it represented the number 20, or 2 and 0. (See Activities.)

A Mayan glyph (pictograph) for the number zero.

Activities

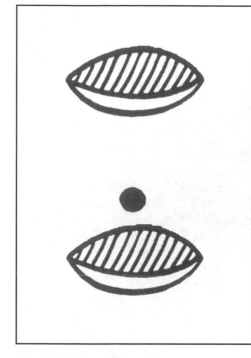

Shown at top is the Mayan "empty oyster shell" zero, called xok, *meaning "hollow." Shown at bottom is the number 20.*

1. What are some of the logical difficulties that arise when you attempt to define $\%$ to be 1 or 0?

2. What is the distinction between a line with a slope of zero and a line with no slope?

3. Research the origin of the word *zero*.

4. The Maya had many symbols for zero. What did some of these symbols look like?

Related Reading

Agostini, Granco. *Math and Logic Games.* New York: Harper and Row, 1980.

Bergamini, David (ed). ***Mathematics: Life Science Library*. New York: Time-Life Books, 1972.**

Boyd, James N. *Professor Bear's Mathematical World.* Salem, VA: Virginia Council of Teachers of Mathematics, 1987.

Boyer, Carl. *A History of Mathematics,* 2nd ed rev. Uta C. Merzbach. New York: John Wiley, 1991.

Contino, Mike. "The Question Box: Watch Out for Zero." *California Mathematics Council ComMuniCator* (June 1993) 22.

Johnson, Art. *Classical Math: History Topics for the Classroom*. Palo Alto, CA: Dale Seymour, 1994.

Pappas, Theoni. *More Joy of Mathematics*. San Carlos, CA: Wide World/Tetra, 1991.

Paulos, John Allen. *Innumeracy: Mathematical Illiteracy and Its Consequences*. New York: Hill and Wang, 1988.

Schimmel, Annemarie. *The Mystery of Numbers*. New York: Oxford University Press, 1993.

Mathematics in Play: The Throw Sticks Game

25

Some think that mathematics is only a course of study in school, but people use mathematical concepts every day in their practical, artistic, and recreational pursuits. For example, in strategizing about their moves in a game, players often consider the likelihood that a certain event in the game will occur. This likelihood, or probability, often determines the accumulation of points or the advancement of a player's position in a game. We can see this in a game known as the **Throw Sticks Game**, created by the Apache tribe of the United States Southwest.

In this game, the playing area is a circle 5 feet in diameter. In its center there is a flat, round rock 8 to 10 inches in diameter, and around its circumference, four sets of ten small stones are arranged, as shown in the Activities. These stones are called counters. Each of the game's four players has three staves, which are about 12 inches long. One half of a stave is shaved flat, and the other half is rounded. The staves are painted yellow, with a green band on their flat sides. The players start the game by positioning themselves where the four sets of counters are arranged. They each place a distinctive marker, usually a colored stick, by their counters. In turn, each player throws his or her staves, on end, one at a time, at the center rock so that they bounce off it. Here's how the game goes.

Stick game. — A common guessing game of the tribes of California and the N. Pacific coast, one that extends entirely across the continent to Canada and the Atlantic The sticks, probably originally arrow shaftments, are shuffled and divided, the object being to guess in which bundle either the odd or a particularly marked stick is concealed. (See *Straw game*, below.)

oTICK GAME

Stick dice game. — A widely distributed game in which several 2-faced lots are

STICK DICE GAME

tossed in the air like dice, the counts being kept on a diagram or with sticks. The number of the dice ranges from 3 upward, 4 being the most common.

Stilts. — Stilt-walking is a children's sport among the Hopi and Shoshoni, and from its existence in Mexico is probably indigenous among the Indians.

Straw, game of. — The name given by early writers to a guessing game played by Huron and other tribes of the Atlantic slope. The implements consisted of fine splints or reeds, and the object of the game was to guess the number, odd or even, when the bundle was divided at random.

Illustrations of some American Indian games. From Ferdinand Hodge's **Handbook of American Indians North of Mexico** *(Washington, DC, 1912).*

- A player earns points according to how the staves land inside the circle.

3 round sides up	= 10 points
3 flat sides up	= 5 points
1 round side up and 2 flat sides up	= 3 points
2 round sides up and 1 flat side up	= 1 point

- If any of the staves misses the rock or bounces outside the circle, the player forfeits his turn and earns no points.

- A player moves her marker around the circle according to the number of points she earns. When she reaches or passes her starting point, she removes one of her counters. If her marker lands at a position containing the marker of another player, that player must move his marker back to his starting position.

- The winner is the first player to get around the circle ten times (the first to remove all of his counting stones).

For more on American Indian mathematics, see vignettes 3, 6, 24, 32, 40, 59, and 104. For more on games and probability, see vignettes 44, 46, 49, 86, 93, and 99. ★

Activities

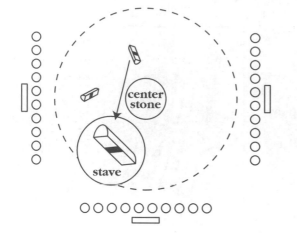

marker
counters

center
stone

stave

1. Construct staves similar to those used in the Throw Sticks Game (see vignette).

   a. As described in the rules of the game, throw the staves one at a time at a rock. Do this several times and record the number of cases in which the round side comes up and the number of cases in which the flat side comes up.

   b. Calculate the empirical probability that the stave will come to rest with the round side up and that the stave will come to rest with the flat side up.

   c. If p represents the probability that the stave comes to rest with the round side up, what is the probability that when three staves are thrown, all three will fall round side up? All three will fall flat side up? One will fall round side up and two will flat side up? Two will fall round side up and one will fall flat side up?

2. A game known as *Ashbii* is played by Navajo women and children. How is it played?

Related Reading

Castillo, Toby T. *Apache Mathematics, Past and Present.* Whiteriver, AZ: Whiteriver Middle School Press, 1994.

Closs, M.P. (ed). *Native American Mathematics*. Austin: University of Texas Press, 1986.

Dobler, Sam. *From Recreation to Computation Around the World.* San Carlos, CA: Math Products Plus, 1980.

Goodwin, Grenville. *The Social Organization of the Western Apache.* Tuscon: University of Arizona Press, 1969.

Grunfeld, Frederic (ed). *Games of the World.* New York: Ballantine Books, 1977.

Joseph, George G. *The Crest of the Peacock: Non-European Roots of Mathematics*. New York: Penguin Books, 1991.

Zaslavsky, Claudia. "Bringing the World into the Math Class." *Curriculum Review* 24 (Jan/Feb 1985) 62–65.

———. *Multicultural Mathematics*. Portland, ME: J. Weston Walch, 1993.

Mathematicians of the Middle Ages

26

T he period from the late fifth century A.D. to the Renaissance is sometimes viewed as a rather dismal period in which there was little intellectual development. However, many scholars around the world made significant and creative contributions to all fields of study, including mathematics.

> *It is not knowledge which is dangerous, but the poor use of it.*
> —Hrotswitha

Hrotswitha of Gandersheim (A.D. 935–1000): The first British woman mathematician of record, Hrotswitha was a Benedictine nun. During her time, the best, and often only, place for a woman to receive an education was a convent. Well-read and creative, she was known for writing original, poetic moral dramas and local history. Additionally, she studied mathematics and science, recording arithmetic and geometry lessons not only for her own studies, but for the education of other women in her convent. Interestingly, it seems that her ideas about astronomy and physics predated those of Nicholas Copernicus and Isaac Newton by about 500 years—she wrote that the sun is the center of the universe and that its gravitational pull "holds in place the stars around it much as the earth attracts the creatures which inhabit it." (For more on Nicholas Copernicus and Isaac Newton, see vignettes 41 and 47.)

Qin Jiushao (1202–1261): In the mid-1230s, the Mongols were in the process of conquering North China. During this time, Chinese mathematician Qin Jiushao studied mathematics in the Board of Astronomy, which happened to be caught in the fighting. To forget his unhappiness at living in a war zone, he devoted himself to the study of, as he put it, "mysterious and vague matters." The result of his studies was his *Shushu jiuzhang* (*Mathematical treatise in nine sections,* 1247). In this influential work, he presented various problems and their solutions, including improved methods for solving polynomial equations of various degrees. Additionally, Qin's work, and that of his contemporaries, represented the beginning of an important development in Chinese mathematics: abstraction. Previously, Chinese mathematicians had focused on problems that had some practical application in everyday life. (For more on Chinese mathematics, see vignettes 4, 8, 22, 48, 71, and 89.)

Johannes Müller (1436–1476): The work of German astronomer Müller, generally known as **Regiomontanus**, greatly contributed to the establishment of trigonometry as a branch of mathematics. Having translated Ptolemy's *Almagest,* he determined that scholars who studied this work would benefit from a systematic approach to the relationships of

Title page of Regiomontanus' De triangulis omnimodi *and* De quadratura circuli *(Nuremberg, 1533).*

sides and angles in triangles, something the *Almagest* lacked. The first half of his *De triangulis omnimodi* (*On triangles of every kind*), written in 1463 and published in 1533, dealt with plane triangles and the second half with spherical triangles. Truly wishing his readers to understand his methods, he provided clear examples of his work, an improvement upon earlier European trigonometry texts. (For more on Ptolemy, see vignette 41.) ★

Activities

1. Read about the life of **Hildegard von Bingen** (A.D. 1098–1179), an abbess in medieval Germany who did considerable work in the fields of science, cosmology, and music.

2. Explore the foundations of the transition in medieval China from an emphasis on applied mathematics to an acceptance of pure mathematics. For what purposes were each of these fields studied?

3. Solve this problems from Regiomontanus' *De triangulis:* In triangle *ABC,* suppose the ratio $\angle A : \angle B = 10 : 7$ and the ratio $\angle B : \angle C = 7 : 3$. Find the three angles and the ratio of the sides.

4. What are some of the contributions of other medieval mathematicians?

Related Reading

Alic, Margaret. *Hypatia's Heritage*. Boston: Beacon Press, 1986.

Calinger, Ronald (ed). *Classics of Mathematics*. Oak Park, IL: Moore Publishing, 1982.

Denson, Philinda Stern. "Mathematics History Time Line." *Mathematics Teacher* (Nov 1987) 640-642.

Johnson, Art. *Classical Math: History Topics for the Classroom*. Palo Alto, CA: Dale Seymour, 1994.

Joseph, George G. *The Crest of the Peacock: Non-European Roots of Mathematics*. New York: Penguin Books, 1991.

Li, Yan, and Du Shiran. *Chinese Mathematics: A Concise History*. New York: Oxford University Press, 1987.

Paulos, John Allen. *Beyond Numeracy: Ruminations of a Numbers Man*. New York: Alfred A. Knopf, 1991.

Swetz, Frank. *Learning Activities from the History of Mathematics*. Portland, ME: J. Weston Walch, 1994.

————. *The Sea Island Mathematical Manual: Surveying and Mathematics in Ancient China*. University Park, PA: Penn State University Press, 1992.

27

Islamic Mathematics

During the Middle Ages, the Islamic world represented fertile ground for both mathematical development and the preservation of ancient mathematical knowledge. An important event that helped shape this era in mathematics history was the establishment in A.D. 766 of the city of Baghdad (the capital of what is now Iraq).

Baghdad's reputation as a flourishing intellectual center was secured during the early ninth century A.D. with the construction of a library and a research center. The library soon began collecting and translating into Arabic manuscripts from all parts of the Islamic world. These manuscripts included many classic Greek texts that Athenian and Alexandrian scholars had brought to the Near East during the first and seventh centuries A.D. By the end of the ninth century A.D., many important works by such Greek mathematicians as Euclid, Apollonius, and Diophantus had been translated into Arabic for study. The research center, called the *Bayt al-Hikma,* or House of Wisdom, drew scholars from all over the Arabian peninsula, who not only contributed to the translation of Baghdad's manuscript collection, but also conducted much original research.

Arabic astronomer seated in a celestial chair whose canopy is decorated with the signs of the zodiac and whose back shows the symbols of the planets. Woodcut by Albrecht Dürer for Stabius's Scientia *(Nuremberg, 1504).*

Mathematician and astronomer **Muhammad ibn Musa al-Khwarizmi** (ca A.D. 780–850) was one of the first scholars to study at the *Bayt al-Hikma.* Around A.D. 825, he wrote *Hisab al-jabr wa'l-muqabala* (roughly, "the science of reunion and reduction"), the first known text in elementary algebra. In fact, the word *algebra* is derived from the word *al-jabr.* Al-Khwarizmi introduced systematic approaches to solving equations, and he wrote about the relatively new concept of the number 0. Influential in bringing algebraic knowledge to Europe, his books were the first Arabic mathematics books translated into Latin.

About a century after al-Khwarizmi's death, scientist and mathematician **Abu Ali al-Hasan ibn al-Haytham** (A.D. 965–1039) was born in Basra (now in Iraq). Ibn al-Haytham spent most of his life in Egypt working in optics, using mathematics and experimental observation to systematically examine the human visual system. He is well known for his work regarding the problem of finding the points or points on some reflecting surface at which the light from one of two points outside that surface is reflected to the other. His attempt to solve this problem on a variety of surfaces was not completely successful, but it did demonstrate his thorough understanding of geometry. Recently, Professor Ian Howard of York University uncovered the fact that ibn al-Haytham discovered the idea of retinal correspondence, a key concept in binocular vision. Traditionally, seventeenth-century Belgian monk Franciscus Aguilonius has been credited with this discovery.

For more on Islamic mathematics, see vignettes 10, 29, 30, 31, 35, and 40. ★

Activities

1. According to legend, al-Khwarizmi's will states that if his wife were to have a son, she would inherit one third of the estate and the son would inherit the remaining two thirds. However, if his wife had a daughter, then his wife would inherit two thirds of the estate and the daughter the remaining one third. As things turned out, shortly after al-Khwarizmi's death, his wife gave birth to twins—a boy and a girl. The legend does not specify what happened to his estate. If al-Khwarizmi's wishes were honored, how was the inheritance divided?

2. Read about the mathematical accomplishments of mathematician and physician **ibn Yahya al-Samaw'al** (1125–1180). How did he contribute to the development of decimal arithmetic and negative numbers?

3. The number system used today in the United States and Europe (0, 1, 2, 3, 4, 5, 6, 7, 8, 9) is called the Hindu-Arabic number system. Trace the development of this system and the circumstances that led to its introduction to Europe.

4. Medieval Islamic mathematicians were expert astronomers and contributed much to the development of spherical trigonometry. Why was spherical trigonometry of particular interest to Islamic mathematicians? In what ways did Persian mathematician **Muhammad Abu'l-Wafa** (A.D. 940–997) further the development of this branch of mathematics?

5. Islamic tiling and mosaic art is known throughout the world for its intricacy and beauty. Why is this art mathematically significant?

Related Reading

Berggren, J. *Episodes in the Mathematics of Medieval Islam.* New York: Springer-Verlag, 1986.

Critchlow, K. *Islamic Patterns: An Analytical Approach.* London: Thames Hudson, 1984.

Joseph, George G. *The Crest of the Peacock: Non-European Roots of Mathematics*. New York: Penguin Books, 1991.

Lawlor, Roger. *Sacred Geometry: Philosophy and Practice.* New York: Thames and Hudson, 1989.

McLeish, John. *Number: The History of Numbers and How They Shape Our Lives.* New York: Ballantine, 1991.

Nasr, S.H. *Science and Civilization in Islam.* Cambridge, MA: Harvard University Press, 1968.

HINDU MATHEMATICIANS: ARYABHATA AND BHASKARA

The *Aryabhatiya* (A.D. 499), the first Hindu mathematics and astronomy text by a known author, was written entirely in verse by **Aryabhata** (b A.D. 476). This poetic approach reflected an ancient tradition. As the caste system developed in India during the first millennium B.C., the brahmins, or priests, became responsible for passing religious knowledge from generation to generation. To prevent the lower castes from learning, the brahmins transferred their knowledge in spoken rather than written form. Many of the important concepts were put into poetic verses to facilitate memorization. This process pertained not only to religious traditions, but also to astronomical and mathematical knowledge.

Aryabhata's text contained a version of the sinc tablc that had appeared about a century earlier in the *Siddhantas* (*Systems of astronomy*), the first Hindu work that included trigonometric material. This table represented a very important step in the development of trigonometry: It replaced the time-consuming table of chords **Claudius Ptolemy** had used in the second century A.D. for astronomical calculations.

Several centuries after Aryabhata, **Bhaskara** (1114–1185) was well known for his astronomical and mathematical skill and spent most of his career as the head of an astronomical observatory. Considered by many to have been the leading Hindu mathematician of the twelfth century, he did significant work with indeterminate equations and produced several approximations for the number π, including the frequently used $\frac{22}{7}$.

Bhaskara's major work, the *Siddantasiromani,* was an astronomy text that contained two chapters on mathematics: the *Vija-Ganita,* on algebra, and the *Lilavati,* on arithmetic. The *Lilavati,* meaning "gracious one," was named after Bhaskara's daughter. It seems that astrologers had predicted Lilavati would never marry. Her father, however, was a skilled astrologer himself, and he was able to ascertain the perfect moment for her marriage. Lilavati kept careful track of the time with a water clock. As she leaned over to gaze at the clock just before the time arrived, a pearl from her headdress dropped into the clock, obstructing the flow of the water. Before she realized what had happened, the time for her marriage had passed! To comfort his unhappy daughter, Bhaskara named his chapter on arithmetic after her.

For more on the mathematics of India, see vignettes 2, 19, 24, and 82. ★

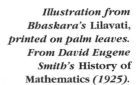

Illustration from Bhaskara's Lilavati, *printed on palm leaves. From David Eugene Smith's* History of Mathematics *(1925).*

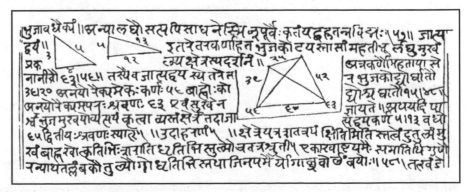

ACTIVITIES

1. Indeterminate equations (equations with many solutions, such as $ax + by = c$) were of great interest to Indian mathematicians. Aryabhata produced a method of solution for first degree indeterminate equations. His method is known as the *kuttaka,* or "pulveriser."

    a. Investigate this solution method.

    b. Find all solutions to this problem: In how many ways can a sum of five dollars be paid in dimes and quarters?

2. Read about Bhaskara's proof of the Pythagorean theorem.

3. In his writings, Bhaskara discussed equations of the form $x^2 = 1 + py^2$, where p is a constant. Equations of this form are called Pell equations. Why was Bhaskara interested in these equations?

RELATED READING

Datta, B., and A.N. Singh. *History of Hindu Mathematics.* Bombay, India: Asia Publishing House, 1962.

Dunham, William. ***The Mathematical Universe: An Alphabetical Journey Through the Great Proofs, Problems, and Personalities*. New York: John Wiley, 1994.**

Katz, J. *A History of Mathematics: An Introduction*. New York: HarperCollins College Publishers, 1993.

Srinvasiengar, C.N. *The History of Ancient Indian Mathematics.* Calcutta, India: The World Press, 1967.

Swetz, Frank J. (ed). *From Five Fingers to Infinity: A Journey Through the History of Mathematics.* Chicago: Open Court Publishing, 1994.

The Long History of Negative Numbers

29

> *Minus times minus is plus,*
> *The reason for this we*
> *need not discuss.*
> —W. H. Auden
>
> *As long as a branch of science offers*
> *an abundance of problems, so long*
> *it is alive; a lack of problems fore-*
> *shadows extinction or the cessation*
> *of independent development.*
> —David Hilbert

It may surprise you to learn that negative numbers troubled mathematicians well into the 1800s—with a few exceptions, mathematicians totally ignored negative numbers! In India, negative numbers were introduced to represent debts, and sixth-century mathematician Brahmagupta even stated rules for adding, subtracting, multiplying, and dividing negative numbers. Similarly, twelfth-century Islamic mathematician ibn yanya al-Samaw'al included rules for adding and subtracting negative numbers in his text *Al-Bahir fi'l-hisab* (*The Shining Book of Calculation,* 1144), yet at the same time in India, Bhaskara deemed negative solutions "inadequate." Earlier, the Chinese used black and red computing rods to manipulate positive and negative numbers. However, as third-century Chinese mathematician Liu Hui was introducing negative numbers for computational use in his revision of the manuscript *Jiuzhang suanshu* (*Nine Chapters on the Mathematical Art,* ca 200 B.C.), Greek mathematician Diophantus was considering equations with negative roots, such as $x + 3 = 0$, unsolvable.

Although European mathematicians eventually acknowledged the negative numbers that appeared in Islamic texts, they continued for centuries to think that negative numbers had no use or meaning. Fifteenth- and sixteenth-century mathematicians Nicolas Chuquet and Michael Stifel both spoke of negative numbers as "absurd numbers." In the 1500s, Girolamo Cardano was willing to accept negative numbers as roots of equations, but considered them impossible solutions, while François Viète simply discarded negative numbers. Seventeenth-century mathematician René Descartes accepted negative numbers to some extent, but he called them "false" because they represented numbers less than nothing.

In the seventeenth century, negative numbers started to come into use more and more, but it took some time to clarify the concept. Some mathematicians continued to be wary of them and to protest their use. An intriguing argument against negative numbers was presented by theologian and mathematician Antoine Arnauld, a friend of Pascal's. He had difficulty accepting that $-1 : 1 = 1 : -1$. Stating that -1 is less than 1, he then asked: "How can a smaller be to a greater as a greater is to a smaller?" Almost a century later, the intellectual Jean le Rond d'Alembert wrote: "A problem leading to a negative solution means that some part of the hypothesis was false but assumed to be true."

The best mathematics texts of the eighteenth century still confused the minus sign (–) used to designate subtraction with the same symbol used to denote a negative number (–6, for example). Finally, however, in his *Complete Introduction to Algebra* (1770), Leonhard Euler successfully compared the process of subtracting $-b$ to the process of adding b by saying, ". . . to cancel a debt signifies the same as giving a gift."

The history of negative numbers demonstrates that mathematical concepts are human-made abstractions, introduced at will and developed if they serve a useful purpose. Today, despite all the historical resistance, negative numbers play a big part in modern society. Have you ever looked at winter temperature charts and maps? You'll see an abundance of negative numbers there!

For more on the history of numbers, see vignettes 1, 12, 14, 21, 24, 37, 52, 64, and 67. ★

Activities

1. Today the minus, or negative, symbol plays a dual role. It indicates both the operation of subtraction and the opposite of a number. Historically, other notations have been used to designate negative numbers. What are some of these notations?

2. If $x < 0$, what can you say about $-x$? Explain why it might be advantageous to read $-x$ as "the additive inverse of x" or "the opposite of x" instead of "negative x."

3. Some believe that an enemy of an enemy is a friend. Statements like this are sometimes used to explain why "a minus times a minus is a plus." Comment on the following proof of the statement.

$$
\begin{aligned}
(-1)(-1) &= (-1)(-1) + (0)(1) \\
&= (-1)(-1) + (-1 + 1)(1) \\
&= (-1)(-1) + (-1)(1) + (1)(1) \\
&= (-1)(-1 + 1) + (1)(1) \\
&= (-1)(0) + (1)(1) \\
&= (1)(1) \\
&= 1
\end{aligned}
$$

Related Reading

Boyer, Carl. *A History of Mathematics,* 2nd ed rev. Uta C. Merzbach. New York: John Wiley, 1991.

Cajori, Florian. *A History of Mathematics.* New York: Chelsea Publishing, 1991.

Crowley, Mary L., and Kenneth Dunn. "On Multiplying Negative Numbers." *Mathematics Teacher* (Apr 1985) 252–256.

Groza, Vivian Shaw. *A Survey of Mathematics: Elementary Concepts and Their Historical Development.* New York: Holt, Rinehart and Winston, 1968.

Kline, Morris. *Mathematics for the Nonmathematician*. Mineola, NY: Dover, 1967.

———. *Why Johnny Can't Add: The Failure of the New Math.* Mineola, NY: Dover, 1967.

Smith, David. E. *History of Mathematics,* Vol 1. Mineola, NY: Dover, 1958.

Struik, Dirk J. *A Concise History of Mathematics*. Mineola, NY: Dover, 1987.

The Poet Mathematicians

30

Known primarily as the author of a collection of poetry titled *Rubaiyat*, Persian-born **Omar Khayyam** (A.D. 1048–1131) was also an astronomer and a mathematician. Below are some of his contributions to mathematics.

- By discovering a geometrical solution for cubic equations, Khayyam was the first to be able to solve every type of cubic equation that possesses a positive root.

- In his critical analysis of Euclid's *Elements,* titled *Discussion of the Difficulties with Euclid,* he considered possible proofs of Euclid's parallel postulate.

- He discovered a rule for determining the fourth, fifth, sixth, and higher powers of a binomial. It is believed that he knew of what is now known as Pascal's triangle to work with powers of binomial expressions.

His most well-known contribution to mathematics is his proposal for the reform of the Persian calendar. He suggested a cycle of 33 years that included 8 years of 366 days. Ever the poet, he wrote a passage in the *Rubaiyat* regarding his reforms.

> *Ah, but my Computations, People say,*
> *Reduced the Year to better reckoning?—*
> *Nay,*
> *'Twas only striking from the Calendar*
> *Unborn Tomorrow, and dead Yesterday.*

(For more about calendars, see vignettes 6, 8, 40, and 48.)

Some seven centuries later, another poet's beautiful, Eastern-influenced verse overshadowed his interest in mathematics. American poet and scholar **Henry Wadsworth Longfellow** (1807–1882) resigned his position as professor of modern languages at Harvard University to find time to write—and his writing included some words about mathematics, a subject for which he had a deep appreciation. Naturally, Longfellow's enjoyment of mathematics found its way into his poetry. (See Activity 5.)

For more on Islamic mathematics, see vignettes 10, 27, 29, 31, 35, and 40. ★

H. M. Burton's rendition of Omar Khayyam reforming the calendar. Courtesy of Culver Pictures, Inc., New York.

Henry Wadsworth Longfellow

©1996 by Key Curriculum Press

> *How dull and prosaic the study of mathematics is made in our schoolbooks; as if the grand science of numbers has been discovered and perfected merely to further the purpose of trade. There is something divine in the science of numbers. Like God, it holds the sea in the hollow of its hand. It measures the earth; it weighs the stars; it illuminates the universe; it is law, it is order, it is beauty. And yet we imagine— that is, most of us—that the highest end and culminating point is bookkeeping by doubly.*
>
> —Longfellow, *Kavanagh: A Tale*

Activities

1. A story about Khayyam says he received a yearly stipend to study mathematics and write poetry because of a pact he'd made with two childhood friends. What was this pact?

2. How did Longfellow develop an appreciation for mathematics?

3. How did Khayyam use geometry to solve the equation $x^3 + b^2x + a^3 = cx^2$?

4. In ancient India, astronomers wrote books in Sanskirt verse, using poetic names for numbers instead of number symbols. Read about these verses and report your findings to your class. What were some of the poetic ways in which numbers were expressed?

5. Solve this problem posed by Longfellow in one of his verses: One-third of a collection of beautiful water lilies is offered to Mahadev, one-fifth to Huri, one-sixth to the Sun, one-fourth to Devi, and six which remain are presented to the spiritual teacher. [Find the number of water lilies.]

Related Reading

Eves, Howard. *An Introduction to the History of Mathematics*. New York: Holt, Rinehart and Winston, 1990.

Fitzgerald, Edward. *The Rubaiyat of Omar Khayyam*. Mineola, NY: Dover, 1990.

Johnson, Art. *Classical Math: History Topics for the Classroom*. Palo Alto, CA: Dale Seymour, 1994.

Kasir, Daoud S. *The Algebra of Omar Khayyam*. New York: Teachers College Press, 1931.

Lamb, Harold. *Omar Khayyam: A Life*. New York: Doubleday, 1936.

Longfellow, Henry Wadsworth. *Kavanagh: A Tale*. New Haven: College and University Press, 1965.

Mitchell, Charles. "Henry Wadsworth Longfellow, Poet Extraordinaire." *Mathematics Teacher* (May 1989) 378–379.

Swetz, Frank. *Learning Activities from the History of Mathematics*. Portland, ME: J. Weston Walch, 1994.

THE FIBONACCI SEQUENCE

31

When he was a boy, **Leonardo of Pisa** (1170–1250)—known since the nineteenth century as **Fibonacci**—often accompanied his merchant father from Italy to what is now Algiers in North Africa. It was there that he studied under Islamic teachers, learning mathematics and the Arabic language. Later, Fibonacci continued his studies, meeting with local scholars and mathematicians as he traveled throughout the Mediterranean. Upon returning to Europe in 1200, he began to write many manuscripts that incorporated and expanded upon the mathematics he had learned from the Islamic world.

One of the first Italian mathematicians to write about algebra, Fibonacci helped introduce the Hindu-Arabic numeral system to Europe. Additionally, he is well known for the sequence that bears his name: 1, 1, 2, 3, 5, 8, 13, 21, 34, 55, 89, 144, ... This sequence starts with two 1's, and each term, beginning with the third, is the sum of the two numbers preceding it.

The **Fibonacci sequence** appears in a number of natural and human-made creations, such as the family tree of a male bee—a male bee has only one parent, his mother; a female bee has both a mother and a father. If you examine the golden pincushion of a daisy, you'll see that it consists of tiny, tightly packed individual flowers, or florets. They are arranged in two sets of curved lines spiraling out from the center. Of these, 21 spiral in a clockwise direction, and the remaining 34 spiral in a counterclockwise direction. Numbers that appear in sequence—Fibonacci numbers—can be seen in the scales of pinecones, the knobbles of pineapples, the leaves of plants, and many other elements of nature.

Can you find the first seven terms of the Fibonacci sequence that appear in the thirteen piano keys shown at right? (The keys show one octave of the chromatic scale.)

For more on Fibonacci and the Fibonacci sequence, see vignettes 5 and 34. ★

The Fibonacci sequence arose from this problem that appeared in Fibonacci's *Liber abacci* (*Book of calculation*, 1202).

"How many pairs of rabbits can be bred in one year from one pair? A certain person places one pair of rabbits in a certain place surrounded on all sides by a wall. We want to know how many pairs can be bred from that pair in one year, assuming it is their nature that each month they give birth to another pair, and in the second month after birth, each new pair can also breed."

Can you solve the problem? (Drawing a diagram will help.) Does the Fibonacci sequence appear in your solution?

ACTIVITIES

1. Generate a Fibonacci sequence, starting with any two numbers. Show that the sum of the first ten numbers is always eleven times the seventh term.

2. Find the Fibonacci sequence in Pascal's triangle. (For information on Pascal's triangle, see vignette 44.)

3. Fibonacci signed his work with the name Blockhead. Why?

4. While it is not known how he did it, Fibonacci found a solution to the cubic equation $x^3 + 2x^2 + 10x = 20$ correct to nine decimal places. Why does this equation have a root between 1 and 2? Write a simple computer program or use spreadsheet mathematics to find this solution.

RELATED READING

Boulger, William. "Pythagoras Meets Fibonacci." *Mathematics Teacher* (Apr 1989) 277–282.

Ellis, Keith. *Number Power in Nature and in Everyday Life*. New York: St. Martin's Press, 1978.

Garland, Trudi H. *Fascinating Fibonaccis: Mystery and Magic in Numbers*. Palo Alto, CA: Dale Seymour, 1987.

Gies, Joseph, and Francis Gies. *Leonardo of Pisa and the New Mathematics of the Middle Ages*. New York: Thomas Y. Crowell, 1969.

Hurd, Stephen. "Egyptian Fractions: Ahmes to Fibonacci to Today." *Mathematics Teacher* (Oct 1991) 561–568.

Jacobs, Harold. *Mathematics: A Human Endeavor*. San Francisco: W.H. Freeman, 1987.

Paulos, John Allen. *Beyond Numeracy: Ruminations of a Numbers Man*. New York: Alfred A. Knopf, 1991.

Schielack, Vincent P. "The Fibonacci Sequence and the Golden Ratio." *Mathematics Teacher* (May 1987) 357–358.

Varnadore, James. "Pascal's Triangle and Fibonacci Numbers." *Mathematics Teacher* (Apr 1991) 314–316, 319.

The Knotty Records of the Inca

32

D uring the fifteenth and sixteenth centuries in South America, the empire of the **Inca** flourished in what is now Peru, Argentina, Bolivia, Chile, and Ecuador. Around 1400, this region was occupied by many different groups of people, and one of these groups, the Inca, began gradually and without violence to gain bureaucratic control of the other groups. A peaceful people, the Inca always left local culture intact and, in fact, often incorporated different aspects of these various cultures into their own. By spreading a common language, Quechua, and by building a strong communication system that utilized a network of highways, the Inca empire became a highly organized civilization comprised of about 4 million people.

With such a large empire to manage and no known system of writing, the Inca required an alternate method for keeping precise, orderly records. By using what is called a **quipu** (pronounced KEE-poo), the Inca were able to record anything that could be counted, such as the population of a village, the amount of food harvested from a crop, the dates of important events, or the composition of work forces.

Seventeenth-century illustration of an Incan treasurer holding a quipu, drawn by Felipe Guáman Poma de Ayala in a letter to the king of Spain. The letter describes Andean life and points out the abuses the Spanish were committing in their rule of the Inca.

Made of cotton or wool, materials easily found in the Inca world, a quipu consisted of a thick cord from which hung many other cords, called pendant cords. Still more cords, called subsidiary cords, hung from the pendant cords. A system of knots on the cords indicated, by their size and position, numbers based on 10. For example, four knots at the top of a cord and six knots near the bottom represented the number 46. Additionally, the cords were dyed many different colors and shades, and the color, the length, and the position of the pendant cords indicated the types of objects being counted. Quipu makers represented a professional class of workers trained at a school in Cuzco, the Inca capital. Their full-time job was to accurately indicate what was happening within the empire by relating the numbers, the colors, and the positions of many sets of cords and knots. These highly portable records were then delivered to and from the empire's many administrators by a series of runners traveling the highways.

Symbols of a sophisticated and complex civilization, most quipus remain undeciphered despite the efforts of modern code breakers.

For more on American Indian mathematics, see vignettes 3, 6, 24, 25, 40, 59, and 104. ★

Activities

1. What other sorts of recording systems require no writing? Can you invent such a system?

2. Study the calendar of the Inca. Present what you learn to your class.

3. In groups of five, devise a construction process for making a quipu. (For ideas on how to make a quipu, see Marcia Ascher and Robert Ascher's *Code of the Quipu,* listed in Related Reading.) Choose a set of data to record, such as the number of compact disks, cassettes, or records you own, the musical artists they feature, and the musical genres they represent. Use a system of knots and differently-colored strings to represent your various data. When your group has completed its quipu, compare it to the quipus the other groups have made. Can your class combine all the quipus to form a set of records?

Related Reading

Alcoze, Thom, et al. *Multiculturalism in Mathematics, Science, and Technology: Reading and Activities.* Menlo Park, CA: Addison-Wesley, 1993.

Ascher, Marcia. *Ethnomathematics: A Multicultural View of Mathematical Ideas*. Pacific Grove, CA: Brooks/Cole Publishing, 1991.

———, and Robert Ascher. *Code of the Quipu: A Study in Media, Mathematics, and Culture.* Ann Arbor, MI: The University of Michigan Press, 1981.

Bocher, Salomon. *Mathematics in Cultural History.* New York: Charles Scribner, 1973.

Closs, M.P. (ed). *Native American Mathematics*. Austin: University of Texas Press, 1986.

Nelson, David, et al. *Multicultural Mathematics.* New York: Oxford University Press, 1993.

Stifel's Number Mysticism

33

Michael Stifel (1486–1567) is considered by many historians to be the most important German algebraist of the sixteenth century. The three parts of his work *Arithmetica integra* (1544) were devoted to rational numbers, irrational numbers, and algebra. Like many mathematicians before him, Stifel worked with the famous triangle named after mathematician Blaise Pascal in the seventeenth century. **John Napier** (1550–1617) studied Stifel's extensive, creative work with irrational numbers, using it to create the most important mathematical development of the Renaissance: logarithms.

In addition to being an influential contributor to mathematics, Stifel certainly qualifies as one of the more eccentric personalities in its history. A priest in his early years, he reacted to corruption he saw in his profession by becoming a zealous religious reformer. Additionally, he developed an interest in number mysticism, studying the Bible and interpreting certain passages in terms of the numbers associated with key words. His studies led him to prophesy that the world would end on October 18, 1533. In preparation for this event, he convinced numerous peasants to abandon work and property to accompany him to heaven. When October 18 came and went—with the world still intact—he had to take refuge in a prison to seek safety from those whose lives he had ruined. Additionally, Stifel tried to "prove" that Pope Leo X was the Antichrist, a satanic figure mentioned in the Bible. From LEO DECIMVS, he removed non-Roman numerals E, O, and S, retaining LDCIMV. He omitted the M—saying that it stood for mystery—and added X, for Leo X, which resulted in the number LDCIVX. Rearranging these letters, he obtained DCLXVI, or 666, the Biblical number associated with the Antichrist.

Over the years, many people who have been fascinated by both mathematics and mysticism have tried to meld these two fields, using numbers to reveal character and to make predictions.

For more on the significance of numbers, see vignettes 12, 21, 31, 34, 44, 52, 54, 59, and 97. ★

> *I've read that things inanimate have moved/And, as with living souls, have been inform'd/ By magic numbers and persuasive sound.*
>
> —Richard Congreve,
> *The Morning Bride*

*An early algebraic use of the plus (+) and minus (−) signs, found in Stifel's **Deutsche Arithmetica** (Johan Petreius, 1545).*

Exempla vom Addiren.

Sum:	+	7.		8	Sum:	—	18.
Sum:	+	11.		3	Sum:	—	6.
Sum:	+	18.		11	Sum:	—	24.

Activities

1. Research Stifel's work with Pascal's triangle. How does his work with this special triangle relate to that done centuries earlier in China?

2. The numbers 4, 7, and 12 are frequently mentioned in the Bible's Book of Revelation, also known as the Apocalypse. Why are these numbers significant? What other numbers in the Bible are considered important? Do other sacred texts contain numbers that have special meaning? Do scholars agree on the significance of these numbers?

3. In the Islamic tradition, many blessings and prayers, such as the blessings for the Prophet Muhammad, are repeated 101 times. In Indo-Pakistan it was customary to give a bride 101 pieces of clothing and 101 trays filled with gifts. What is the significance of the number 101 in these traditions?

4. Many numbers have historical importance. Research the significance of the given numbers in the corresponding religious and cultural traditions.

14 (Babylonia, Islam)	16 (India)	18 (Islam)
19 (Babylonia)	20 (Maya)	27 (Egypt)
28 (Arabic tradition)	36 (China)	40 (Islam, Judaism)
60 (Babylonia)	64 (China, India)	66 (Islam)
72 (China, Islam)	84 (India)	100 (China)
101 (Islam)	108 (Hinduism)	216 (Buddhism)
432 (India)	888 (China)	10,000 (China)

Related Reading

Eves, Howard. *An Introduction to the History of Mathematics*. New York: Holt, Rinehart and Winston, 1990.

Friend, J. Newton. *Numbers: Fun and Facts*. New York: Charles Scribner, 1954.

Hogben, Lancelot. *Mathematics for the Millions*. New York: W.W. Norton, 1967.

Ifrah, Georges. *From One to Zero: A Universal History of Numbers*. New York: Viking Press, 1985.

Kline, Morris. *Mathematics: The Loss of Certainty*. New York: Oxford University Press, 1980.

Pappas, Theoni. *More Joy of Mathematics*. San Carlos, CA: Wide World/Tetra, 1991.

Schimmel, Annemarie. *The Mystery of Numbers*. New York: Oxford University Press, 1993.

The Golden Ratio and Rectangle

34

Leonardo da Vinci's *St. Jerome (ca 1483).*

G reek philosopher Pythagoras (572–497 B.C.), devotee of numbers and their connection to the world, wrote: "The golden proportion exists in the whole of creation. Take the ratio of a length of a man and the height of his navel. The ratio of the sides of the Great Temple. The ratio between the long and short sides of a pentagram. Why is this? Because the ratio of the whole to the greater is the ratio of the greater to the lesser."

What is this "golden proportion," or ratio, that Pythagoras was so enchanted with? The **golden ratio** is created by taking a line segment AB, then selecting a point C on the segment, as shown below right, so that $AC/AB = CB/AC$. If $AB = 1$, then $x/1 = (1-x)/x$. Solving the resulting quadratic equation yields the golden ratio: $x = (1+\sqrt{5})/2 = 1.618033989$, or about 1.6. This ratio is called phi (ø).

The length-to-width ratio of the **golden rectangle**, also called the perfect rectangle, equals the golden ratio. Many believe that the golden rectangle is one of the most visually satisfying of all geometric forms, and it appears in many works of art and architecture. For example, Italian artist, architect, and engineer **Leonardo da Vinci** (1452–1519) was ardently interested in mathematics, and in his unfinished painting *St. Jerome* (ca 1483), shown at right, the saint is loosely enclosed within a golden rectangle. Although as an artist Leonardo was certainly concerned with pleasing proportions, it is not known whether he *deliberately* used the golden ratio in his work.

The Fibonacci sequence, 1, 1, 2, 3, 5, 8, 13, 21, 34, 55, 89, 144, 233, . . . , is also related to the golden ratio. If we form a sequence from the ratio of consecutive terms, $1/1, 2/1, 3/2, 5/3, 8/5, 13/8, 21/13, 34/21, \ldots$, we see that these numbers approach the golden ratio. When we reach the term $233/144$, its ratio is 1.618055556, which is very close to $(1+\sqrt{5})/2$. This ratio can be found in many natural objects, such as nautilus seashells and flowers whose leaves spiral around their stem.

For more on ratios, see vignettes 2, 12, 80, and 92. For more on the Fibonacci sequence, see vignettes 5 and 31. ★

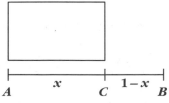

©1996 by Key Curriculum Press

Activities

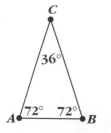

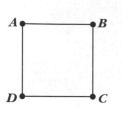

1. An isosceles triangle is called a golden triangle if the ratio of one of its sides to its base is $\frac{(1 + \sqrt{5})}{2}$. Show that triangle *ABC* is a golden triangle.

2. Can you find some examples of art or architecture in which the golden rectangle appears?

3. The figure shown is a square.

   a. Construct the midpoint *M* of segment *CD*.

   b. Construct a point *E* on line *CD* such that *MB = ME*.

   c. From point *E*, construct a perpendicular line intersecting line *AB* at point *F*.

   d. Show that quadrilateral *AFED* is a golden rectangle.

4. In the figure shown, polygon *ABCDE* is a regular pentagon. How many golden triangles can you find in this figure?

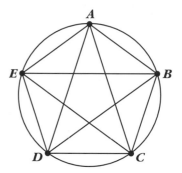

Related Reading

Garland, Trudi H. *Fascinating Fibonaccis: Mystery and Magic in Numbers.* Palo Alto, CA: Dale Seymour, 1987.

Herz-Fischler, Roger. *A Mathematical History of Division in Extreme and Mean Ration.* Waterloo, Ontario: Wilfrid Laurier University Press, 1987.

Lawlor, Roger. *Sacred Geometry: Philosophy and Practice.* New York: Thames and Hudson, 1989.

Linn, Charles. *The Golden Mean.* Garden City, NY: Doubleday, 1963.

Markowsky, George. "Misconceptions About the Golden Ratio." *The College Mathematics Journal* (Jan 1992) 2–19.

Pappas, Theoni. *Mathematics Appreciation.* San Carlos, CA: Wide World/Tetra, 1987.

Rigby, J.F. "Equilateral Triangles and the Golden Ratio." *The Mathematical Gazette* 72 (1988) 27–30.

Runion, Garth E. *The Golden Section and Related Curiosa.* Glenview, IL: Scott Foresman, 1972.

Visual Mathematics

35

A lthough some believe that mathematics and art are diametrically opposed, many beautiful images and objects have resulted from the combination of these two disciplines.

Since ancient times, structures built to honor royalty, for ceremonial purposes, or as mausoleums have reflected the mathematics of architecture and engineering. Such structures include the menhirs at Stonehenge, the Easter Island stone figures in the South Pacific, Africa's "Great Enclosure" at Musawwarat, and the pyramids of Egypt and Central and South America. These constructions were designed with careful attention paid to both calculations that would ensure a solid structure and aesthetics that would inspire awe.

The interiors of many architectural works have been enhanced by the creative use of mathematical forms. A notable example is the Alhambra, a thirteenth-century Moorish palace in Granada, Spain. Because their religious beliefs did not allow them to portray recognizable life forms, Islamic artisans decorated the interior of the palace with elegant symmetric designs. The beauty of mathematics has continued to inspire architects

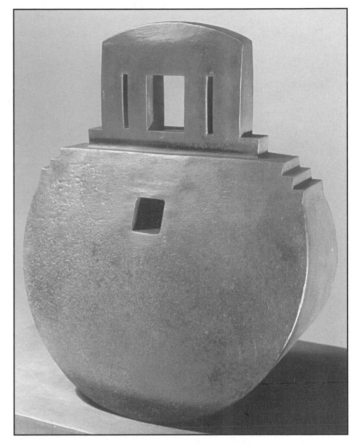

Bella Feldman's **House of Tao** *(1990), contemporary geometric sculpture influenced by Mayan architecture. Photo courtesy of the artist. Reproduced with permission.*

through modern times. New York's Solomon R. Guggenheim Museum, designed by United States architect Frank Lloyd Wright (1857–1959), features a gently sloping helix ramp, more than a quarter mile long and only 100 feet in diameter, from which visitors peruse the museum's collection.

For centuries, mathematical concepts such as symmetry, proportion, and perspective have been inherent in the creative work of people all over the world. Folk art, often created for practical or ceremonial use, continues to represent cultural traditions, history, and perspectives. Handmade clothing, baskets, pottery, and jewelry frequently display geometric forms, often integrated within complex and sophisticated patterns. The traditional art of quilting makes explicit use of the mathematical principles of symmetry and tiling, and many quilt designs are based on the principles of reflection and rotation.

Many modern artists and artistic movements have been inspired by mathematical order and precision. During the early twentieth century, European cubist painters and sculptures, influenced by such African art forms as ceremonial masks, reduced natural forms to their geometric equivalents, then reorganized the object's planar structure. Around the same time, Russian constructivist artists sought to attain a true reality through abstraction, using linear figures and engineering principles to express the power of pure form. In Mexico, constructivist sculptor Mathias Goeritz (b 1915) created massive geometric structures through which people could walk. During the

1960s, American sculptor Louise Nevelson (1900–1988) assembled complex geometric forms within large wooden wall structures called environments.

Today computer technology allows industrial designers and fine and graphic artists to explore new modes of expression. In recent years, computer-generated fractals have come to represent the cutting edge in purely mathematical art. Physicists and mathematicians encountered these fascinating images in the 1960s while investigating the relationship between symmetry and chaos in nature. Now, mathematicians and artists produce beautiful illustrations of fractals, using methods based upon the work of Gaston Julia, Benoit Mandelbrot, and others.

For more on art and mathematics, see vignettes 34, 50, 59, 90, 100, 101, and 107. ★

Activities

1. Explore the folk art of a cultural group that you don't know very much about. Does the artwork of this group use mathematical forms and principles? In what ways? For what purpose is the artwork created? Prepare a visual presentation of what you learn and present it to your class.

2. What are geodesic domes? Investigate the history of these structures, then build your own dome.

3. Read about the ways in which Renaissance artists and builders used mathematical order and harmony in their work. Select a piece of artwork or an architectural construction that interests you. Write an essay that discusses your personal reaction to the work and that describes the work's mathematical qualities.

4. Create a piece of artwork that makes use of a mathematical method or concept.

Related Reading

Blackwell, William. *Geometry in Architecture.* Berkeley, CA: Key Curriculum Press, 1984.

Covarrubias, Miguel. *Indian Art of Mexico and Central America.* New York, NY: Alfred A. Knopf, 1957.

Edwards, Lois, and Kevin Lee. *TesselMania! Math Connection.* Berkeley, CA: Key Curriculum Press, 1995.

Gay, John, and Cole, Michael. *The New Mathematics and an Old Culture: A Study of Learning Among the Kpelle of Liberia.* New York: Holt, Rinehart and Winston, 1967.

Gurther, Edmund B. "Angela Perkins and the Computer as Palette." *International Review of African American Art* (Spring 1992).

Henderson, Linda D. *The Fourth-Dimension and Non-Euclidean Geometry in Modern Art.* Princeton, NJ: Princeton University Press, 1983.

Rucker, Rudy, and James Gleik. *Chaos: The Software.* Sausalito, CA: Autodisk, 1989.

The Cardano-Tartaglia Dispute

36

Portrait of Girolamo Cardano from the title page of **Hieronimi C. Cardani Medici Mediolanensis** *(1553).*

Have you ever seen the movie called *Stand and Deliver,* about calculus teacher Jaime Escalante? While that may be the *only* movie you've ever seen about a figure in mathematics history, there are many other interesting characters who could easily fill the movie screen. Two such characters are Italian mathematicians **Niccolò Tartaglia of Brescia** (1499–1557) and **Girolamo Cardano** (1501–1576). These two became involved in a famous dispute over solution methods for cubic equations.

Students of algebra know that it's easy to obtain the solutions of linear equations ($ax + b = 0$) and quadratic equations ($ax^2 + bx + c = 0$). They also know that there are no easy mechanical methods to solve general equations of the third degree and higher. However, Tartaglia claimed to have discovered a method to solve cubic equations of the form $x^3 + ax^2 = b$. Skeptical mathematicians challenged Tartaglia to a public problem-solving contest, confident that they could prove him wrong. Tartaglia triumphed completely because his discovery really did allow him to solve difficult cubic forms, as he had claimed, while others could solve only simple cubic forms.

Cardano heard about the contest and wrote to Tartaglia, asking for permission to include Tartaglia's discovery, with full credit, in an arithmetic text he was writing. After much initial resistance, Tartaglia presented his solution to Cardano in the form of a riddle but made him promise not to publish it.

Several years later, Cardano worked out his own solutions for various cases of the cubic, and he was anxious to publish them. However, he did not want to break his oath to Tartaglia. Soon after, though, he learned that Italian mathematician **Scipione del Ferro** (1465–1526) had discovered a method for solving cubic equations more than twenty years before Tartaglia. Thus, no longer feeling he needed to keep Tartaglia's discovery a secret, Cardano published the solutions in his *Ars magna, sive de regulis algebraicis* (*The great art, or on the rules of algebra,* 1545), a treatise on cubic and quartic equations. This infuriated Tartaglia, who felt that Cardano should have kept his oath. However, there was nothing he could do about it—it was true that del Ferro had made the original discovery, and in his book, Cardano had been gracious enough to credit Tartaglia's work. ★

Portrait of Niccolò Tartaglia from the title page of **La prima parte del general trattato dinumeri** *(Venice, 1556).*

Activities

1. Show that the cubic equations $ax^3 + bx^2 = c$ and $ax^3 + bx = c$ have easily obtainable solutions if $c = 0$.

2. The general cubic equation has the form $ax^3 + bx^2 + cx + d = 0$, where $a \neq 0$. Explain why an equation of this form must have at least one real number solution.

3. Choose four numbers a, b, c, and d. Use a graphing calculator to find a solution for $ax^3 + bx^2 - cx + d = 0$ by graphing $y = ax^3 + bx^2 + cx + d$.

4. Research the Tartaglia/Cardano method for solving $x^3 + ax = b$. Use the method to solve a specific equation of this form.

5. Read about some of the other contributions Tartaglia and Cardano made to the development of mathematics.

Related Reading

Bergamini, David (ed). *Mathematics: Life Science Library*. **New York: Time-Life Books, 1972.**

David, F.N. *Games, Gods, and Gambling*. New York: Hafner Publishing, 1962.

Eves, Howard. *An Introduction to the History of Mathematics*. **New York: Holt, Rinehart and Winston, 1990.**

Johnson, Art. *Classical Math: History Topics for the Classroom*. Palo Alto, CA: Dale Seymour, 1994.

Ore, Oystein. *Cardano: The Gambling Scholar*. Mineola, NY: Dover, 1965.

Swetz, Frank. *Learning Activities from the History of Mathematics*. **Portland, ME: J. Weston Walch, 1994.**

The Birth of Complex Numbers

37

A lgebra students learn that the real number system can be "extended" by defining $i = \sqrt{-1}$ (thus, $i^2 = -1$), and by defining operations on **complex numbers**, which are numbers of the form $a + bi$, where a and b are real numbers. Like the concept of negative numbers, however, this number idea was slow in coming.

Twelfth-century Hindu mathematician **Bhaskara** (1114–1185) wrote: "The square of a positive number, also that of a negative number, is positive; and the square root of a positive number is two-fold, positive and negative; there is no square root of a negative number, for a negative number is not a square." In his treatise on equations, *Ars magna* (*The great art*), Italian mathematician **Girolamo Cardano** (1501–1576) advanced what he called a "fictitious" quantity. Solving $x + y = 10$ and $xy = 40$, he produced two strange solutions: $5 + \sqrt{-15}$ and $5 - \sqrt{-15}$. He didn't pursue the matter, concluding that his result was "as subtle as it is useless." However, the fact that Cardano wrote down the square root of a negative number at all gave it symbolic existence. Over time, mathematicians began to refer to an expression like $\sqrt{-1}$ as an imaginary number—not a good label, perhaps, but it was introduced by **René Descartes** in the seventeenth century and it stuck. A complex number is formed by adding a real number to an imaginary number.

In many ways, complex numbers behave like real numbers, and many real number properties carry over into the larger set of complex numbers. One property that doesn't carry over is the multiplication law for radicals, $\sqrt{a}\sqrt{b} = \sqrt{ab}$. This property is true in the real number system when neither a nor b is negative, but in the complex number system, $\sqrt{-4}\sqrt{-9}$ does *not* equal $\sqrt{36}$, or 6. Rather, it equals -6 because $(2i)(3i) = 6i^2 = 6(-1) = -6$. This inconsistency may seem strange, but there's no logical reason why laws that hold for a subset of a set should hold for the set itself. In the set of integers, for example, the sum of two members of the set is an integer. However, even though the integers are a subset of the real numbers, we know that the sum of two real numbers is certainly not always an integer.

Later mathematicians established that complex numbers have numerous applications. For instance, complex numbers provide solutions to equations concerning the state of atomic particles in atomic physics. Complex numbers can also be used to model the behavior of vector forces in scientific and engineering situations. Some important numbers in mathematics history besides the imaginary number i include π, e, 0, and 1. In fact, Leonhard Euler produced a formula that contains all of these numbers! It is: $e^{i\pi} + 1 = 0$. ★

Mathematicians who contributed to the development of complex numbers

Rafael Bombelli (1526–1572): Considered complex numbers to be solutions of cubic equations. In his *Algebra* (1572), which contains the first consistent theory of complex numbers, he formulated the four operations (addition, subtraction, multiplication, and division) with complex numbers.

Leonhard Euler (1707–1783): Introduced the symbol $i = \sqrt{-1}$.

Jean-Robert Argand (1768–1822): Applied a geometrical representation of a complex number to show that every algebraic equation has a root in the complex number system. The modern complex number plane (where the y-axis is the imaginary axis) is sometimes referred to as the Argand plane.

Carl Friedrich Gauss (1777–1855): Proved that every nth degree equation has exactly n complex number roots. (Bear in mind that a real number is also a complex number. For example, $5 = 5 + 0i$.)

Activities

1. The product of two complex numbers $a + bi$ and $c + di$ is defined as such: $(a + bi)(c + di) = (ac - bd) + (ad + bc)i$. Keeping in mind that $i^2 = -1$, show that we would obtain this product by ordinary binomial multiplication.

2. In the complex number system, every real number has n distinct n roots. Show that the statements below are true.

    a. The three cube roots of 1 are $1, -\frac{1}{2} + (\frac{\sqrt{3}}{2})i,$ and $-\frac{1}{2} - (\frac{\sqrt{3}}{2})i$.

    b. The four fourth roots of 1 are $1, i, -1,$ and $-i$.

3. The complex number $a - bi$ is defined to be the conjugate of $a + bi$. Show that the product of a complex number and its conjugate is always a real number.

4. How do we define division in the set of complex numbers?

5. Show that for any positive integer n, $i^n = i^{n + 4}$.

Related Reading

Cajori, Florian. *A History of Mathematical Notations,* Vols 1 and 2. Chicago: Open Court Publishing, 1952.

Flegg, Graham. *Numbers: Their History and Meaning.* New York: Schocken Books, 1983.

———. *Numbers Through the Ages.* Dobbs Ferry, NY: Sheridan House, 1989.

Kline, Morris. *Mathematical Thought from Ancient to Modern Times.* New York: Oxford University Press, 1990.

Pólya, George. *Mathematical Discovery.* New York: John Wiley, 1962.

Sondheimer, Ernest, and Alan Rogerson. *Numbers and Infinity—An Historical Account of Mathematical Concepts.* New York: Cambridge University Press, 1981.

Sometime Mathematician: Viète

38

François Viète (1540–1603) is considered to be the most important French mathematician of the sixteenth century, but with the exception of a few years, only Viète's leisure time was devoted to mathematics! As a young man, Viète practiced law, later becoming a member of the Bretagne parliament, then of the king's council. However, in 1584 he managed to anger one of the council's factions and was relieved of his duties. During the six years of his enforced leisure prior to regaining favor and returning to royal service, Viète spent his time on mathematical studies.

His most significant contributions were in algebra. In fact, he introduced or popularized some of the useful notation we still use today: letters representing coefficients, the use of decimal fractions, the signs for addition (+) and subtraction (–), and the fraction bar for division. Half a century later, mathematicians who studied his work, such as Descartes and Fermat, came to appreciate the power of algebra—in Viète's time, algebra was considered a minor appendage to geometry. Viète was the first to introduce the concept of a literal coefficient, a letter that can represent the coefficient of a variable. Prior to this, mathematicians considered two quadratic equations such as $3x^2 + 7x + 5 = 0$ and $4x^2 + 5x + 1 = 0$ as separate entities, even though the same method of solution applied to both. Viète recognized that equations such as these could be written in a general form and that solution formulas could be written in terms of the literal coefficients a, b, and c. Building on this concept, Descartes invented the notation $ax^2 + bx + c = 0$, which is the general form in which quadratic equations are written today.

It is a bit ironic, then, that Viète would not let his literal coefficients represent negative numbers. The rules for operating with negative numbers had been in existence for hundreds of years, but Viète rejected these numbers because he thought they lacked the intuitive and physical meaning of positive numbers. It was not until 1657 that Holland's **Jan Hudde** let literal coefficients represent nega-

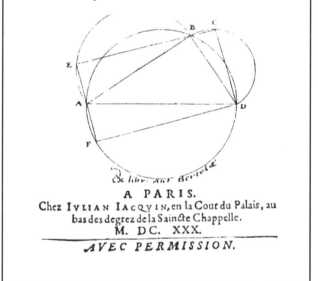

Title page from the first edition of Viète's **Les cinq livres des zetetiques** *(Paris, 1630).*

tive numbers. (For more on negative numbers, see vignette 29.)

Viète's contributions also encompassed the fields of trigonometry and geometry. He realized, for instance, that a trigonometric ratio could be used in an algebraic equation. That is, a series of numbers in a table could represent values taken on by an unknown, as in $y = \sin x$. Additionally, his most important manuscript, *In artem analyticem isagoge* (*Introduction to the analytic art*), published in 1591, helped establish a foundation for logarithms, coordinate and projective geometry, calculus, and many other mathematical developments. ★

Activities

1. Viète outlined a process for approximating a root of an equation. Research this process.

2. Prove these identities that Viète referred to in one of his manuscripts.

    a. $\sin A = \sin(60° + A) - \sin(60° - A)$

    b. $\csc A + \cot A = \cot{}^A\!/_2$

    c. $\csc A - \cot A = \tan{}^A\!/_2$

3. Viète's knowledge of codes was useful to the French in a war against Spain. How did Viète decode Spanish messages?

Related Reading

Bergamini, David (ed). *Mathematics: Life Science Library.* New York: Time-Life Books, 1972.

Boyer, Carl. *A History of Mathematics,* 2nd ed rev. Uta C. Merzbach. New York: John Wiley, 1991.

Dunham, William. *Journey Through Genius: The Great Theorems of Mathematics.* Somerset, NJ: John Wiley, 1990.

Eves, Howard. *An Introduction to the History of Mathematics.* New York: Holt, Rinehart and Winston, 1990.

Hollingdale, Stuart. *Makers of Mathematics.* New York: Penguin Books, 1989.

Kline, Morris. *Mathematics for the Nonmathematician.* Mineola, NY: Dover, 1967.

———. *Mathematics: The Loss of Certainty.* New York: Oxford University Press, 1980.

Swetz, Frank. *Learning Activities from the History of Mathematics.* Portland, ME: J. Weston Walch, 1994.

NAPIER INVENTS LOGARITHMS

39

Scotland-born **John Napier** (1550–1617) invented **logarithms** as a laborsaving device to speed up numerical computation processes. Lacking such modern conveniences as calculators and computers, astronomers in particular were bogged down by figuring out numerical calculations with pencil and paper. Naturally, Napier's invention and book, *A Description of the Wonderful Law of Logarithms* (1614), were enthusiastically accepted throughout Europe. On the three-hundredth anniversary of the book's publication, Lord Moulton wrote:

> *The invention of logarithms came on the world as a bolt from the blue. No previous work had led up to it, nothing had foreshadowed it or heralded its arrival. It stands isolated, breaking in upon human thought abruptly without borrowing from the work of other intellects or following known lines of mathematics thought.*

> —"Inaugural Address: The Invention of Logarithms,"
> *Napier Tercentenary Memorial Volume*

Well into the twentieth century, students all over the world learned how to compute with logarithms. Today we regard logarithms as exponents, a relationship not discovered until long after Napier's death. The modern use of logarithms in high-powered mathematics courses and in computer technology would probably boggle Napier's mind!

Like some other famous mathematicians, Napier's career had its share of controversy. His claim to being the inventor of logarithms was disputed by Swiss instrument maker **Jobst Bürgi** (1552–1632), but it is generally believed that Napier really is the true inventor because he announced his discovery six years before Bürgi published a table of logarithms. Additionally, Napier was fascinated by numbers and, like Michael Stifel before him, attempted to determine the date on which the world would end. (For more on Michael Stifel, see vignette 33.)

For more on computation, see vignettes 70, 83, 84, and 88. ★

Portrait of John Napier from the first edition of **De arte logistica** *(Edinburgh, 1839).*

Title page of the first edition of Napier's **Logarithmorum** *(Edinburgh, 1614).*

©1996 by Key Curriculum Press

ACTIVITIES

1. What exactly are logarithms?

2. What is the story associated with Napier about a thief and a magic rooster?

3. Find some "old-fashioned" logarithm tables and show your class how they were used to perform multiplication and division. This activity will probably make you appreciate modern calculators!

4. Before calculators and computers, slide rules were used for such purposes as solving detailed multiplication and division problems, finding roots, and raising numbers to a power. How was the slide rule operated?

5. The drawing below shows a collection of rods known as Napier's bones, or Napier's rods. Make a set of these rods and show your class how they were used to simplify multiplication.

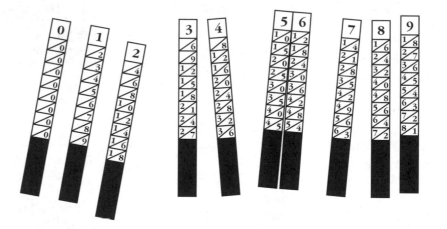

RELATED READING

Cajori, Florian. *A History of the Logarithmic Slide Rule and Allied Instruments.* New York: McGraw-Hill, 1909.

Daintith, John, and R.D. Nelson (eds). *Dictionary of Mathematics.* New York: Penguin Books, 1989.

Jacobs, Harold. *Mathematics: A Human Endeavor*. San Francisco: W.H. Freeman, 1987.

Kasner, Edward, and James R. Newman. *Mathematics and the Imagination.* Redmond, WA: Tempus Books, 1989.

Resnikoff, H.L., and R.O. Wells. *Mathematics in Civilization.* Mineola, NY: Dover, 1985.

Ten Days Lost in 1582

40

I n 46 B.C., Roman ruler **Julius Caesar** put the Julian calendar into effect. Caesar believed 365¼ days was the true length of a year, so he made an ordinary year 365 days long and added an extra day every fourth year. This extra day came to be known as a leap year.

Historical records indicate that in A.D. 730, scientific thinkers concluded a year was actually 11 minutes shorter than Caesar had thought. This mistake of 11 minutes per year threw the calendar off by one day every 128 years. By the year 1582, the Julian calendar was ten days out of line with the seasons. So in that same year, with the advice and assistance of the German mathematician **Christoph Clavius** (1537–1612), Pope Gregory XIII ordered a new calendar to be put into effect. This new calendar was dubbed the **Gregorian calendar**.

These calendar adjustments required some sound mathematical thinking. To keep the Gregorian calendar consistent with the seasons, the first year of each century is a leap year only when that year number can be evenly divided by 400. Hence, the year 1600 was a leap year, but 1700 was not. Additionally, Pope Gregory ordered that ten days be dropped from the year 1582. Thus, when people went to bed on October 5, 1582, they woke up the next morning on October 15, 1582. Some of the world actually lost ten calendar days!

Even today, not all people use the same calendar. Some branches of the Eastern Orthodox Church still determine their holidays according to the Julian calendar, which is now 13 days different from the Gregorian. The Hebrew calendar counts years from the day Judaism considers the day of creation, which some ancient scholars say took place in the year 3761 B.C. As the Gregorian calendar numbers years from the supposed date of Jesus' birth, the Gregorian year 1990 is 5751 in the Hebrew calendar. The Muslim calendar, called the Hijra, numbers its years from A.D. 622, the year the Muslim religion was founded. The Hijra year 1403 is the year 1982 on the Gregorian calendar. An obvious mathematical fact is that 1403 plus 622 does not total 1982—the Hijra year contains only 354 days because it is based on the phases of the moon rather than of the sun.

For more on calendars, see vignettes 6, 8, 30, and 48. ★

Engraving of Augustus Caesar.
From A Universal History **(London, 1776).**

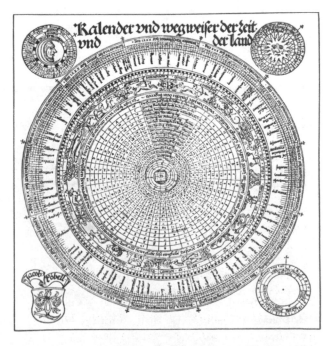

Sixteenth-century wood engraving of the Julian calendar.

Activities

1. What is the Gregorian year 1995 on the Hijra?

2. There are many calendars existing today, each reflecting the needs, cultures, and religions of various people. These include the Balinese, Chinese, Hindu, and New Guinean calendars. Research at least three different calendars. Compare and contrast them with the calendar you use every day.

3. How is the Hebrew calendar similar to the ancient Babylonian calendar?

4. Write a calculator or computer program to convert from the years of one calendar to those of another. Try this with various calendars.

5. *The ancient Maya of southern Mexico and Guatemala devised a reasonably accurate calendar over 2,000 years ago. Their calendar had 18 months, and each day of the month had a different symbol. Some of the symbols are shown below. Read about the Mayan calendar, then prepare a visual presentation of what you learn and present it to your class.

Symbol for day 1

Symbol for day 12

Symbol for day 15

*From Claudia Zaslavsky's *Multicultural Mathematics*. (See Related Reading.)

Related Reading

Bergamini, David (ed). *Mathematics: Life Science Library*. New York: Time-Life Books, 1972.

Boyer, Carl. *A History of Mathematics,* 2nd ed rev. Uta C. Merzbach. New York: John Wiley, 1991.

Bushwich, N. *Understanding the Jewish Calendar.* Brooklyn, NY: Moznaim, 1989.

Eves, Howard. *An Introduction to the History of Mathematics.* New York: Holt, Rinehart and Winston, 1990.

Francis, Richard L. *Mathematical Look at the Calendar.* Arlington, MA: COMAP, 1988.

Pappas, Theoni. *More Joy of Mathematics*. San Carlos, CA: Wide World/Tetra, 1991.

Vogel, Malvina (ed). *The 2nd Big Book of Amazing Facts.* New York: Waldman Publishing, 1982.

Zaslavsky, Claudia. *Multicultural Mathematics*. Portland, ME: J. Weston Walch, 1993.

Changing Universe: Ptolemy, Copernicus, Kepler

41

During the second century A.D., **Claudius Ptolemy** produced a cosmological model based on Aristotle's idea that the earth was the center of the universe. In Ptolemy's model, the earth was surrounded by eight spheres that carried the moon, the sun, the stars, and the five planets known at the time. The larger heavenly bodies moved on smaller circles attached to their respective spheres, while the outermost sphere carried the stars.

Ptolemy's model provided a reasonably accurate system for predicting the positions of the heavenly bodies. Generally accepted by the scientific community, his model was also accepted by Christian thinkers because it provided room outside the spheres for heaven and hell. (For many centuries Christian beliefs heavily influenced Western thinking.)

More than a millennium later, Ptolemy's model had been expanded to include seventy-seven spheres! Intrigued by the fact that some Greek mathematicians had suggested the possibility that the earth revolved around a stationary sun, astronomer **Nicholas Copernicus** (1473–1543) questioned the stationary-earth model. He altered Ptolemy's model, reducing the number of spheres to thirty-four and placing the sun in the center. The earth was then what he called a "wanderer." Copernicus's model was far from what the universe is now known to be, but it certainly prompted constructive critical thinking and provided valuable insight for future astronomers.

One such astronomer was **Johannes Kepler** (1571–1630), whose work was a blend of mystical and fanciful speculation combined with a solid grasp of scientific truths. Breaking with a 2,000-year-old tradition, Kepler discarded the notion that circles and spheres must be used to describe planetary motion. Instead, he proposed that each planet moves on an elliptical path and that the sun is a common focus for all planets. For any planet, the other focus is merely a mathematical

Ptolemy, shown here with quadrant in hand and celestial globe in the foreground. From Nicolo Bascarini's edition of Ptolemy's La Geographica *(Venice, 1547).*

Sixteenth-century woodcut of the Ptolemic celestial spheres. The earth is shown at the center of the universe, surrounded by the planets and the sun, and encompassed by the rest of creation ("Le Firmament").

©1996 by Key Curriculum Press

point at which nothing exists. This discovery represents one of the most important astronomical inductions ever made.

For more on cosmology, see vignettes 6, 7, 11, 12, 16, 26, 42, 59, and 91. ★

Nicholas Copernicus

Activities

1. How did moveable type, invented by **Johannes Gutenberg** in 1456, affect Copernicus before and after he promoted his heliocentric theory?

2. Research Ptolemy's contributions to (a) the construction of a regular polygon, (b) the table of chords, (c) map making, and (d) the theorem relating the diagonals of a cyclic quadrilateral to its sides.

3. Consider a circle made of wire with circumference C. Suppose you cut the circle at one point, then insert into the cut a piece of wire one foot in length, thus increasing the circle's circumference by that length.

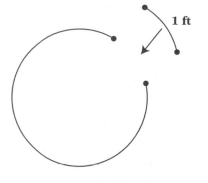

1 ft

   a. If the original circle had a circumference of one foot, what is the difference between its radius and that of the new circle you created?

   b. If the original circle had a circumference of 25,000 miles (the earth's approximate circumference), what is the difference between its radius and that of the new circle you created?

   c. Make a generalization about what you've discovered.

Related Reading

Adamczeivski, Jan. *Nicholas Copernicus and His Epoch.* Philadelphia: Copernicus Society of America, 1973.

Davies, Paul. *The Edge of Infinity*. New York: Simon and Schuster, 1982.

Ekeland, Ivar. *Mathematics and the Unexpected.* Chicago: University of Chicago Press, 1988.

Ellis, Keith. *Number Power in Nature and in Everyday Life*. New York: St. Martin's Press, 1978.

Hawking, Stephen. *A Brief History of Time.* New York: Bantam Books, 1988.

Koestler, Arthur. *The Watershed: A Life of Kepler.* New York: Doubleday, 1960.

Maor, Eli. *To Infinity and Beyond: A Cultural History of the Infinite*. Boston: Birkhauser Boston, 1987.

Resnikoff, H.L., and R.O. Wells. *Mathematics in Civilization.* Mineola, NY: Dover, 1985.

©1996 by Key Curriculum Press HISTORY OF MATH

GALILEO RELATES EXPERIMENTATION AND THEORY

42

Many people know of the conflict **Galileo Galilei** (1564–1642) had with the Roman Catholic Church over the earth's position in the solar system. During his time, the church viewed the earth as stationary, with all the heavenly bodies revolving around it. Galileo, however, supported the Copernican theory, which stated that the sun, not the earth, was the center of the universe. (For more on the Copernican theory, see vignette 41.) Additionally, he recognized that the earth spins daily on its axis, taking a year to journey around the sun. Because his discoveries roused church opposition, Galileo was summoned to appear before the Inquisition. He was forced to recant many of his scientific findings, and legend has him concluding his "confession" by muttering under his breath, "Nevertheless, it does move." In 1992, Pope John Paul II admitted that the church had erred in its condemnation of Galileo almost four centuries before.

In addition to being an important astronomer, Galileo was an accomplished mathematician. In his *Dialogue on the Great World Systems* (1632), he asserted that in mathematics man reaches the pinnacle of all possible knowledge—a knowledge not inferior to that possessed by the divine intellect. One of his mathematical contributions was his recognition of the fundamental distinctions between finite and infinite classes of objects. For example, he noted that it is sometimes possible to create a one-to-one correspondence between the objects in an infinite set (the positive integers: 1, 2, 3, 4, . . .) and a proper subset of the set (the squares of the positive integers: 1, 4, 9, 16, . . .). This one-to-one correspondence is evidenced in the two sequences shown below.

$1, 2, 3, 4, 5, 6, \ldots$

$1^2, 2^2, 3^2, 4^2, 5^2, 6^2, \ldots$

(For more on infinite sets, see vignettes 51, 75, and 79.)

Galileo's experimental methods and discoveries were among those that eventually promoted the development of modern physical science and its applications to technology. In fact, it is Galileo we credit with establishing the modern spirit of science as a combination of both experimentation and theory. ★

Here are a few of the many contributions Galileo made to mathematics and science.

- Developer of the refracting telescope, Galileo also produced the precursor to the modern microscope.

- Seeking mathematical descriptions to describe falling bodies, Galileo produced the formula $s = \frac{1}{2}gt^2$. This formula states that the distance a body falls is proportional to the square of the time of falling.

- He founded the mechanics of freely falling bodies and laid the foundations for the science of dynamics.

- In addition to corroborating the Copernican theory of the solar system, he discovered four of Jupiter's moons.

This whimsical engraving by Francesco Villamoena is the earliest published portrait of Galileo Galilei. It appears in Istoria e dimonstrazioni *(Torino, 1613).*

In his Dissertatio *(Prague, 1610), German astronomer Johannes Kepler congratulates Galileo's observations of celestial objects.*

ACTIVITIES

1. Galileo studied a curve called the cycloid. What is this interesting curve? What did Galileo discover about it?

2. What properties of a pendulum did Galileo discover?

3. In Galileo's time, the Roman Catholic Church tolerated no deviation from the literal word of the Bible. Find a copy of the statement Galileo was forced to make to save his life. In small groups, discuss other historical conflicts between theories and beliefs.

4. What was the fate of **Giordano Bruno** (1548–1600), who asserted that the earth moves around the sun?

5. Comment on the quote by Galileo, given below.

> *Philosophy is written in the grand book—I mean the universe—which stands continually open to our gaze, but it cannot be understood unless one first learns to comprehend the language and interpret the characters in which it is written. It is written in the language of mathematics, and its characters are triangles, circles, and other geometrical figures, without which it is humanly impossible to understand a single word of it; without these, one is wandering about in a dark labyrinth.*

RELATED READING

Dunham, William. *Journey Through Genius: The Great Theorems of Mathematics.* Somerset, NJ: John Wiley, 1990.

Drake, Stillman. *Discoveries and Opinions of Galileo.* Garden City, NY: Doubleday, 1957.

Drake, Stillman. *Galileo at Work: His Scientific Biography.* Chicago: University of Chicago, 1978.

Ferris, Timothy. *The Universe and Eye.* **San Francisco: Chronicle Books, 1993.**

Hollingdale, Stuart. *Makers of Mathematics.* **New York: Penguin Books, 1989.**

Ross, Hugh. *The Fingerprint of God.* Orange, CA: Promise Publishing, 1989.

Struik, Dirk J. *A Concise History of Mathematics.* **Mineola, NY: Dover, 1987.**

HISTORY OF MATH

DESCARTES: A MAN WHO SOUGHT CHANGE

43

Not in the best of health during the early years of his life, French philosopher **René Descartes** (1596–1650) developed the habit of lying in bed until late in the morning. Later in his life, he remembered those meditative hours as being extremely productive periods of thought. They must have indeed been productive: Descartes is considered to be one of the more influential contributors to seventeenth-century mathematical thought.

In 1616, Descartes graduated from the University of Poitiers with a law degree. Deeply dissatisfied with what he had learned, he thought that academicians were much too influenced by the thinkers of antiquity and the philosophy of the ancients. In response, he set out to create a new philosophy of science. Seeking established truths, he constructed his philosophy by accepting as true only those facts that he considered beyond doubt.

Descartes believed that the world was created with a divine mathematical design. In his *Discourse on the Method* (1637), he maintained that the laws of nature were invariable, because they are simply part of a predetermined mathematical plan. Insisting that the most fundamental and reliable properties of matter are shape, extension, and motion in time and space, he asserted that all these properties are mathematically describable.

In his attempts to abandon ancient thinking, he wrote many new works relating to numerous branches of mathematics. His most famous contribution to mathematics may be his technique for studying geometry by analyzing coordinates of points and equations of figures. In developing this technique, he, along with **Pierre de Fermat** (1601–1665), founded the branch of mathematics we call analytic geometry. If you're familiar with the Cartesian coordinate system and the Cartesian plane, you may also know that these geometric concepts were named for Descartes. ★

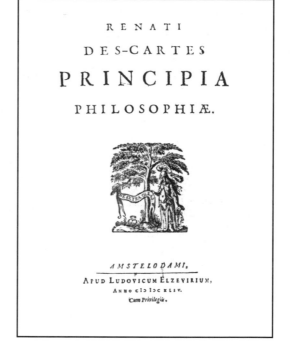

First edition of **Principia Philosophiae** *(Amsterdam, 1649), a classic in the fields of mathematics, optics, and meteors. This work contains the first scientific theory of magnetism as well as the vortex theory of planetary motions.*

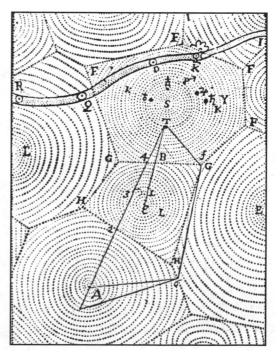

Descartes's representation of the universe, where L, S, A, and E are stars with planetary "systems" revolving around them. From Oeuvres de Descartes *(Paris, 1897–1910).*

ACTIVITIES

1. The family of curves defined by $x^3 + y^3 = 3axy$ is known as the folium of Descartes. Choose different values of a and on a graphing calculator, graph some of the members of this family.

2. Research Descartes's theory of planetary motion in our solar system.

3. Descartes established a rule for determining the upper limits for the number of positive real number roots and the number of negative real number roots of a polynomial equation.

   a. What is this rule, known as Descartes's rule of signs?

   b. Use the rule to show that $x^n - 1 = 0$ has exactly two real roots if n is even and has one real root if n is odd.

   c. Use the rule to show that $x^7 + x^4 + 1 = 0$ has six complex roots.

4. Investigate Descartes's work with polyhedra.

RELATED READING

Davis, Philip, and Reuben Hersh. *Descartes' Dream.* New York: Harcourt Brace Jovanovich, 1986.

Haldane, Elizabeth. *Descartes: His Life and Times.* New York: American Scholar Publications, 1966.

Martain, Jacques. *The Dream of Descartes.* New York: Philosophical Library, 1944.

Reimer, Luetta, and Wilbert Reimer. *Mathematicians Are People, Too,* Vol 2. Palo Alto, CA: Dale Seymour, 1994.

Smith, David E. *The Geometry of René Descartes.* Macia L. Latham (trans). Mineola, NY: Dover, 1954.

Struik, Dirk J. *A Source Book in Mathematics 1200–1800.* Princeton: Princeton University Press, 1969.

Swetz, Frank. *Learning Activities from the History of Mathematics.* Portland, ME: J. Weston Walch, 1994.

Tymoczko, Thomas. *Making Room for Mathematicians in the Philosophy of Mathematics.* Northampton, MA: Smith College, 1981.

Vrooman, J.R. *René Descartes: A Biography.* New York: Putnam, 1970.

Pascal's Useful Triangle

44

French philosopher and mathematician **Blaise Pascal** (1623–1662) believed that the laws of mathematics represented absolute truths. Although the famous triangle named after him was known to the Chinese around 1300, Pascal was the first to record many of its interesting properties. In Pascal's triangle, shown in the top figure at right, each interior number is generated by adding the pair of numbers to its left and to its right in the row above it. For example, in the bottom row, the number 20 is generated by adding the two 10's in the sixth row (the 10's are positioned at the left and right of the 20). The relation of the triangle to the coefficients in the expansion of the binomial $a + b$ is shown in the bottom figure at right.

Pascal was one of the founders of probability theory, and Pascal's triangle is a very useful probability tool. Consider, for example, a family with four children. Let G represent a girl and B represent a boy. From oldest to youngest, the possible boy/girl combinations are as shown below.

		GGBB		
		GBGB		
	GBBB	GBBG	GGGB	
	BGBB	BGGB	GGBG	
	BBGB	BGBG	GBGG	
BBBB	BBBG	BBGG	BGGG	GGGG

The number of combinations in each column is a row in Pascal's triangle. If we know only that a family has four children and we assume that boys and girls are equally likely, then the probability that two are girls and two are boys is ⁶⁄₁₆, or 37.5 percent.

The triangle is also a source of study and fun for people interested in number relationships. One of the triangle's properties is that the sums of the numbers in the rows are, respectively, 1, 2, 4, 8, 16, 32, 64, ... In other words, the sum of the numbers in any row is a power of 2.

For more on Blaise Pascal and Pascal's triangle, see vignettes 4, 31, 46, and 83. ★

A sixteenth-century representation of Pascal's triangle.

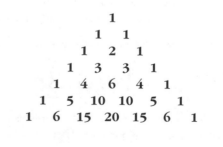

$$(a + b)^0 = 1$$
$$(a + b)^1 = 1a + 1b$$
$$(a + b)^2 = 1a^2 + 2ab + 1b^2$$
$$(a + b)^3 = 1a^3 + 3a^2b + 3ab^2 + 1b^3$$
$$(a + b)^4 = 1a^4 + 4a^3b + 6a^2b^2 + 4ab^3 + 1b^4$$
$$(a + b)^5 = 1a^5 + 5a^4b + 10a^3b^2 + 10a^2b^3 + 5ab^4 + 1b^5$$

Activities

1. Use Pascal's triangle to determine the probability that a family with five children has (a) five girls, (b) four girls and one boy, (c) three girls and two boys, (d) two girls and three boys, (e) one girl and four boys, or (f) five boys.

2. Find some of the number relationships that exist in Pascal's triangle. (For information on this topic, see the Dale Seymour book listed in Related Reading.)

3. The symbol $_nC_r$ is used to represent the number of combinations of n objects taken r at a time—this symbol is found on many calculators. For instance, $_5C_2 = 10$ represents the number of committees of two people that could be determined from a set of five people. How do these combination symbols relate to the numbers in Pascal's triangle?

4. Research some of Pascal's other contributions to mathematics.

5. In the grid shown, the lines represent roads. Ian (point A) wants to visit Nadja at her home (point B). Assuming Ian travels only north or east on the existing roads, how many different routes can he take to reach Nadja's house? Can you find portions of Pascal's triangle in this exercise?

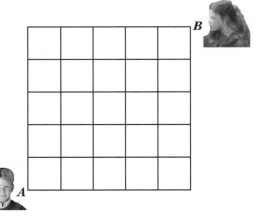

Related Reading

Bishop, Morris. *Pascal: The Life of a Genius*. New York: Reynal and Hitchcock, 1936.

Dunham, William. *Journey Through Genius: The Great Theorems of Mathematics*. Somerset, NJ: John Wiley, 1990.

Green, Thomas M., and Charles Hamberg. *Pascal's Triangle*. **Palo Alto, CA: Dale Seymour, 1986**.

Hollingdale, Stuart. *Makers of Mathematics*. **New York: Penguin Books, 1989.**

Kline, Morris. *Mathematics in Western Culture*. New York: Oxford University Press, 1964.

Seymour, Dale. *Visual Patterns in Pascal's Triangle*. Palo Alto, CA: Dale Seymour, 1986.

Varnadore, James. "Pascal's Triangle and Fibonacci Numbers." *Mathematics Teacher* (Apr 1991) 314–316, 319.

The Mystery of Fermat

45

I f you've studied geometry, you are no doubt familiar with the Pythagorean theorem, which states that if a and b are the lengths of the legs of a right triangle with hypotenuse of length c, then $a^2 + b^2 = c^2$. You probably also know that there are an infinite number of positive integer triples a, b, and c that satisfy this equation, including 3, 4, and 5 and 5, 12, and 13. Have you ever wondered what positive integers would satisfy this equation if a, b, and c were, say, cubed? French mathematician **Pierre de Fermat** (1601–1665) certainly did, and he concluded: There do not exist positive integers x, y, z, and n such that $x^n + y^n = z^n$ when $n > 2$.

In the margins of one of his books, Fermat wrote that he had proved his theorem, known as **Fermat's Last Theorem**. However, he died without leaving a trace of the proof for posterity! As a result, this theorem had long puzzled mathematicians. Until recently,

- No one had ever found positive integers x, y, z, and n that satisfy the conditions stated in the theorem, and

- No one had ever been able to prove that there are no positive integers x, y, z, and n that satisfy the equation when n is greater than 2.

> *I have assuredly found an admirable proof of this, but the margin is too narrow to contain it.*
> —Pierre de Fermat

Over the years, some people thought they had solved this mystery, but their work was found to be flawed. In 1993, Professor Andrew Wiles of Princeton University claimed to have constructed a proof of the theorem. His 200-page document created a major stir in the mathematical world, and it was subjected to careful checking for possible errors. After correcting one serious flaw in his original proof, Professor Wiles, along with colleague Richard Taylor, released a new proof in 1994. This proof is now generally accepted.

Swiss mathematician **Leonhard Euler** (1707–1783) took Fermat's Last Theorem a bit further by hypothesizing that the equation $a^4 + b^4 + c^4 = d^4$ had no positive integer solutions. However, 200 years later, mathematicians used computers to find integers that satisfy Euler's equation. Noam D. Elkins of Harvard University found the first set: $a = 2,682,440$, $b = 15,365,639$, $c = 18,796,760$, and $d = 20,516,673$. The smallest set that satisfies Euler's equation is $a = 95,800$, $b = 217,519$, $c = 414,560$, and $d = 422,481$, discovered by Roger Frye of Massachusetts. ★

Pierre de Fermat

Activities

1. The premise of Fermat's Last Theorem restricts x, y, and z so that they are positive integers. Show that the statements below are true.

    a. If x, y, and z can be integers, then $x^3 + y^3 = z^3$ has infinitely many solutions.

    b. If x, y, and z can be nonnegative integers, then $x^4 + y^4 = z^4$ has infinitely many solutions.

2. Fermat laid the foundation for what we know today as number theory. List some of the conjectures Fermat made in this branch of mathematics.

3. Fermat believed—although he couldn't prove it—that any number of the form $2^{2^n} + 1$ is prime for $n = 0, 1, 2, 3, \ldots$. Read about Euler's work that proved this conjecture false.

Related Reading

Bell, E.T. *The Last Problem*. Washington, DC: Mathematical Association of America, 1990.

Dembart, Lee. "Scientists Buzzing—Fermat's Last Theorem May Have Been Proved." *Los Angeles Times* (8 Mar 1988) 3, 23.

Edwards, Harold. *Fermat's Last Theorem*. New York: Springer-Verlag, 1977.

Hoffman, Paul. "Fermat Still Has Last Laugh." *Discover* (Jan 1989) 48–50.

Kolata, Gina. "Progress on Fermat's Famous Math Problem." *Science* (Mar 1987) 1572–1573.

Marks, Robert. *The Growth of Mathematics: From Counting to Calculus*. New York: Bantam Books, 1964.

Pappas, Theoni. *More Joy of Mathematics*. San Carlos, CA: Wide World/Tetra, 1991.

Shockley, James E. *Introduction to Number Theory*. New York: Holt, Rinehart and Winston, 1967.

Vanden Eynden, Charles. "Fermat's Last Theorem: 1637–1988." *Mathematics Teacher* (Nov 1989) 637–640.

HISTORY OF MATH

Gambling Initiates Probability Study

46

I n the mid-seventeenth century, the **Chevalier de Méré**, a high-living nobleman, was making money by betting that he could get at least one 6 on four rolls of one die. This bet was profitable for him until people started to realize that it was unwise to play his game! It was through experience that de Méré knew he would win more times than he would lose. What he didn't know was that the probability of getting at least one 6 in four rolls of one die is $1 - (\frac{5}{6})^4$, or 51.8 percent.

A compulsive gambler, de Méré thought he would try a different approach. He began to bet he would get a total of 12 (or a double 6) on twenty-four rolls of two dice. This seemed like a good bet, but he began losing money with it. He asked his good friend **Blaise Pascal** to analyze his game—and probability theory was born. On a roll of two dice, there are 36 possible outcomes, as the chart at right shows. Working de Méré's problem "backwards," Pascal calculated the probability that a total of 12 is *not* rolled on twenty-four tosses of two dice. Realizing that this is a multiplication process, he calculated this probability to be $(\frac{35}{36})^{24}$, or 50.9 percent. Therefore, de Méré could expect to lose his bet about 51 percent of the time. As Pascal became more interested in probability, he began to involve his mathematician friend **Pierre de Fermat** in analyzing other gambling situations. (Not surprisingly, Pascal's triangle is a useful tool in the study of probability.) Does it surprise you to learn that a formal study of probability was launched by two mathematicians and a gambler?

Even today, it isn't hard to be fooled by a probability that sounds good. For instance, many people who play games of chance know that in rolling two dice, a total of 7 is more likely than a total of 8. (The dice chart shows that there are six ways to obtain 7 and five ways to obtain 8.) Additionally, a total of 7 is more likely than a total of 6. What would you do if a modern-day de Méré challenged you by stating: I can get an 8 and a 6 rolling two dice before you can get two 7's. Would you accept the challenge? Your challenger would love it if you did. The catch is that your de Méré didn't specify an order for the 8 and the 6. Therefore, there are ten possible ways for him or her to get a favorable first result—and only six for you. The probability that you would lose the challenge can be calculated to be 54.6 percent.

For more on probability, see vignettes 44, 49, 68, and 99. ★

> *The [theory of probability] ... enters into the regulation of some of the most important practical concerns of modern life.*
>
> —George Chrystal
>
> *It is a truth very certain that, when it is not in our power to determine what is true, we ought to follow what is most probable.*
>
> —René Descartes

Green die

	1	2	3	4	5	6
1	2	3	4	5	6	7
2	3	4	5	6	7	8
3	4	5	6	7	8	9
4	5	6	7	8	9	10
5	6	7	8	9	10	11
6	7	8	9	10	11	12

Red die

Activities

1. Pick two different outcomes for sums obtained from rolling two dice. Find the probability that one of the sums will be rolled before the other. For instance, what is the probability that a sum of 5 will be rolled before a sum of 11?

2. Roll two dice to show that the experimental probability of rolling a sum of 8 and a sum of 6 before rolling two sums of 7 is approximately 55 percent. If you're familiar with probability theory, prove that the theoretical probability is 54.6 percent.

3. Assume that 40 percent of the population in a certain city have type O blood. If two blood donors appear at a local blood bank, what is the probability that the given situations are true?

    a. Both have type O blood.

    b. Neither has type O blood.

    c. One has type O blood and the other does not.

Related Reading

David, F.N. *Games, Gods and Gambling*. New York: Hafner, 1962.

Hald, Anders. *A History of Probability and Statistics and Their Applications Before 1750*. Somerset, NJ: John Wiley, 1990.

Lightner, James. "A Brief Look at the History of Probability and Statistics." *Mathematics Teacher* (Nov 1991) 623–630.

McGervey, John D. *Probabilities in Everyday Life*. New York: Ballantine Books, 1986.

Moore, David S. *Statistics: Concepts and Controversies*. New York: W.H. Freeman, 1991.

Paulos, John Allen. *Beyond Numeracy: Ruminations of a Numbers Man*. New York: Alfred A. Knopf, 1991.

Stigler, Stephen M. *History of Statistics: The Measurement of Uncertainty Before 1900*. Cambridge, MA: Harvard University Press, 1986.

Todhunter, Isaac. *A History of the Mathematical Theory of Probability, from the Time of Pascal to That of Laplace*. New York: Chelsea Publishing, 1949.

The Calculus Controversy

47

When astronomers in Europe provided evidence that the earth is not the center of the universe and that the orbits of planets are not circular, new mathematics was needed to explain natural events and the motion of heavenly bodies. Thus, astronomical discoveries led to the development of calculus, an important branch of mathematics that allows us to explore the fleeting mysteries of movement and change.

Mathematicians **Isaac Newton** (1642–1727) and **Gottfried Leibniz** (1646–1716), considered by many to be the cofounders of calculus, became embroiled in a dispute over who had discovered what first. The conflict created quite a rift in the European mathematical community. Swiss mathematicians Jacob and Johann Bernoulli were extremely loyal to Leibniz and hated Newton, while English mathematicians backed Newton and cut themselves off from the developments of continental Europe, which were superior to England's. As a result, mathematical progress in England lagged behind that of the rest of Europe for many years. We can only wonder what progress these highly talented individuals would have made had they put forth a cooperative effort.

Perhaps most famous for establishing the law of gravitation, Newton's ability to treat physical problems mathematically was excellent. His most important work, the *Philosophiae naturalis principia mathematica* (*Mathematical principles of natural philosophy,* 1687), contains a complete system of dynamics and mathematical formulations of motion. His work reinforced the laws of motion developed through years of experimentation by Johannes Kepler and Galileo Galilei. (For more on Johannes Kepler and Galileo Galilei, see vignettes 41 and 42).

The symbolism Leibniz introduced for calculus is still used today. Interested and able in a number of different disciplines, he received degrees of honor in law, religion, statecraft, history, logic, metaphysics, and speculative history. Additionally, he founded the Berlin Academy of Science in 1700. Unfortunately, his conflict with Newton plagued Leibniz in his later years. To get help in resolving their dispute, he appealed to England's Royal Society, which proved to be a fateful mistake. The president of the Royal Society at the time happened to be Isaac Newton! A report prepared by a Newton-appointed commission officially accused Leibniz of plagiarism, effectively ostracizing him from his academic circles before he died in 1716. ★

Calculus and Karl Marx

Calculus has generated controversy about more than just its foundations. During the 200 years after calculus was invented, mathematicians debated the issue of the nature of differentials and the methods used to find the derivative of a function. In the late nineteenth century, German economist, philosopher, and socialist **Karl Marx** (1818–1883) began studying differential calculus in order to broaden his economic theories. After studying several textbooks based on the philosophies of Newton, Leibniz, and others, he, too, joined the debate. In his opinion, certain key information about finding the derivative of a function was accepted without sufficient mathematical justification. In response, he developed a method that approaches this issue from a different perspective and arrives at a conclusion through a set of logical arguments.

©1996 by Key Curriculum Press

Activities

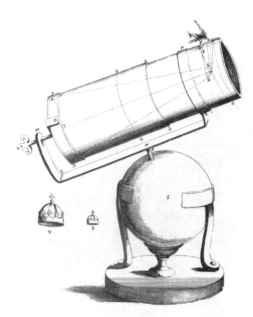

In addition to his work in calculus, Newton invented the reflecting telescope in 1688.

1. Many people consider calculus to be one of the crowning achievements of the human intellect. Why is this so?

2. Read more about some of the other controversies about the development and teaching of calculus.

3. Newton was greatly influenced by the work of English mathematicians **John Wallis** (1616–1703) and **Isaac Barrow** (1630–1677). In what ways did these men contribute to the development of calculus? Research the contributions of **Christiaan Huygens** (1629–1695), a Dutch mathematician and scientist who had considerable influence on Leibniz. How did the philosophy and mathematics of **René Descartes** (1596–1650) influence the development of calculus?

4. Leibniz produced a rule for calculating the nth derivative of $y = uv$, where u and v are functions of x. What is this rule, known as Leibniz's rule?

Related Reading

Christianson, Gale E. *In the Presence of the Creator: Isaac Newton and His Times.* New York: Cambridge University Press, 1984.

Edwards, Charles H. *The Historical Development of the Calculus.* New York: Springer-Verlag, 1979.

Eves, Howard. *Great Moments in Mathematics After 1650.* Washington, DC: Mathematical Association of America, 1982.

Gerdes, Paulus. *Marx Demystifies Calculus,* trans. Beatrice Lumpkin. Minneapolis, MN: Marxist Educational Press, 1985.

Goldberg, Dorothy. "In Celebration: Newton's *Principia,* 1687–1987." *Mathematics Teacher* (Dec 1987) 711–714.

Hall, A.R. *Philosophers at War: The Quarrel Between Newton and Leibniz.* Cambridge, MA: Cambridge University Press, 1980.

Hogben, Lancelot. *Mathematics for the Millions*. New York: W.W. Norton, 1967.

Kline, Morris. *Mathematics: The Loss of Certainty*. New York: Oxford University Press, 1980.

Schimmel, Judith. "A Celebration in Honor of Isaac Newton." *Mathematics Teacher* (Dec 1991) 727–730.

Mei Wending: Cultural Bridge

Chinese mathematician and astronomer **Mei Wending** (1633–1721) was born at the end of the Ming dynasty, not long after Western mathematics were first introduced to China (see sidebar). Years later, he played a key role in bringing these cultures together mathematically.

When he was twenty-seven, Mei began his mathematical education by studying calendrical computation. Over the next several years, he purchased and studied many technical books, including *Chong Zhen li shu* (*Chong Zhen reign treatise on calendrical science,* 1631), a compilation of texts on such subjects as surveying, geometry, and trigonometry. Influential members of the Chinese mathematical community began to notice his talents, and in 1675, a friend recommended that he help write the *Book of the calendar* in the *Ming shi, li zhi* (*History of the Ming dynasty,* ca 1680). He went on to write more than eighty works during his lifetime, becoming an influential mathematician himself.

In much of his work, Mei integrated Chinese and Western mathematical thought, retaining the traditional Chinese emphasis on theory as it concerned practice while allowing for the European emphasis on pure theory. He introduced and expanded concepts relating to a multitude of topics, including practical geometry, problems in Euclid's *Elements,* plane and spherical trigonometry, higher degree roots, and Napier's bones. One of Mei's most important contributions to mathematics was his ability to simply describe complex concepts. Chinese biographer Ruan Yuan (1764–1848) wrote of him: "In his presentation of mathematical theories his aim was clarity, his sentences are neither clumsy nor wordy, he usually used simple language to make the deepest reasoning accessible . . . all these were good intentions."

Mei's work earned him so much respect that he was among the mathematicians regularly summoned by Emperor Kang Xi to discuss mathematical problems. Kang Xi was so impressed by the talent in the Mei family, he later invited Mei's grandson Mei Jeu-cheng to teach mathematics in his court. In 1761, Jeu-cheng compiled many of Wending's important works into *Mei shi congshu jiyao* (*Collected works of the Mei family*).

For more on Chinese mathematics, see vignettes 4, 8, 22, 26, 71, and 89. ★

The Introduction of Western Mathematics

During the Ming dynasty (1368–1644), China experienced great economic growth, which manifested itself in increased foreign trade and artistic development. Roughly around the same time, Europe's economic system had been moving from feudalism to capitalism. As traders and missionaries began traveling to China at the end of the sixteenth century in search of resources, they brought with them the mathematical ideas of the West. This European expansion coincided with Ming government corruption and warfare with neighboring Manchuria, two factors that had all but brought Chinese economic progress to a halt. Anxious to defend its borders against the Manchurian conquest and to regain its economic strength, China expressed an interest in Western science and technology.

In the mathematical arena, development initially centered around the mathematics used to compute an accurate calendar. Over the next 150 years, logarithms and the Western principles of plane and spherical trigonometry were introduced, and Euclid's *Elements* were translated into Chinese.

Activities

1. Before the abacus was invented, counting rods and rhymed verses were used in China for calculation. Mei Wending observed: "The 'verses on division' are very neat and clearly made; they foster the popularization of the abacus." How were counting rods and rhymed verses used? Why did the abacus replace this method of calculation?

2. The introduction of European mathematical ideas in the sixteenth century is known as the first entry of Western mathematics into China. What events in China's socio-political history affected the subsequent exchange of mathematical ideas between China and the Western world?

3. What role did **Mateo Ricci** (1552–1610) play in introducing Western mathematics to China?

Related Reading

Joseph, George G. *The Crest of the Peacock: Non-European Roots of Mathematics*. **New York: Penguin Books, 1991.**

Li, Yan, and Du Shiran. *Chinese Mathematics: A Concise History*. **New York: Oxford University Press, 1987.**

Libbrecht, Ulrich. *Chinese Mathematics in the Thirteenth Century: The Shu-shu Chiu-Chang of Ch'in Chiu-shao*. Cambridge, MA: MIT Press, 1973.

Mikami, Yoshio. *The Development of Mathematics in China and Japan*. New York: Chelsea Publishing, 1961.

Nelson, David, et al. *Multicultural Mathematics*. New York: Oxford University Press, 1993.

Temple, Robert. *The Genius of China*. New York: Simon and Schuster, 1986.

THE BERNOULLI FAMILY

The Bernoulli family was, without doubt, quite capable mathematically! Beginning with brothers Jacob and Johann, no fewer than eleven members made significant contributions to the development of mathematics.

Greatly influenced by **Gottfried Leibniz** (1646–1716), one of the founders of calculus, Jacob I and Johann I realized the power and beauty of this branch of mathematics and developed much of what is now taught in undergraduate calculus classes. (For more on calculus, see vignettes 47, 52, 78, and 105.) They are often considered the inventors of the calculus of variations because of their contributions to the problem of the brachistochrone. No, this is not a dinosaur, but the curve of quickest descent for a mass point moving between two points in a gravitational field. Often bitter rivals, as brothers can sometimes be, they managed to maintain a constant exchange of ideas between themselves and Leibniz.

The Bernoullis were also prolific writers, committing their ideas to the pages of many books. Here are a few of the many contributions this unique family made to the study of mathematics.

- **Nicholas I** developed properties of curves, differential equations, and calculus.

- **Daniel I** wrote books about probability, astronomy, physics, and hydrodynamics.

- **Johann II** began his studies with law, but turned to mathematics and wrote about the mathematical theory of heat and light.

- **Johann III** also studied law and wrote many papers on astronomy, the doctrine of chance, recurring decimals, and indeterminate equations. ★

JACOBI BERNOULLI,
Profeſſ. Baſil. & utriuſque Societ. Reg. Scientiar.
Gall. & Pruſſ. Sodal.
MATHEMATICI CELEBERRIMI,

ARS CONJECTANDI,
OPUS POSTHUMUM

Accedit

TRACTATUS
DE SERIEBUS INFINITIS,

Et EPISTOLA Gallicè ſcripta

DE LUDO PILÆ
RETICULARIS.

BASILEÆ,
Impenſis THURNISIORUM, Fratrum.
cIɔ Iɔcc XIII.

Jacob Bernoulli's Ars Conjectandi (Basel, 1713) contains the first systematic approach to the theory of probability.

ACTIVITIES

1. Calculus students are familiar with L'Hospital's rule, named after French nobleman and amateur mathematician **Marquis de L'Hospital** (1661–1704). How was L'Hospital associated with the Bernoulli family?

2. The curve $(x^2 + y^2)^2 = a^2(x^2 - y^2)$ is known as the Lemniscate of Bernoulli. Substitute a value for a and graph the resulting equation.

3. Research the mathematical achievements and contributions of a few Bernoulli family members.

4. The numbers $B_1 = -\frac{1}{2}$, $B_2 = \frac{1}{6}$, $B_3 = 0$, $B_4 = -\frac{1}{30}$, $B_5 = 0$, and $B_6 = \frac{1}{42}$ represent the first six numbers in a sequence known as the set of Bernoulli numbers. Read about the source of the Bernoulli numbers. How are they generated?

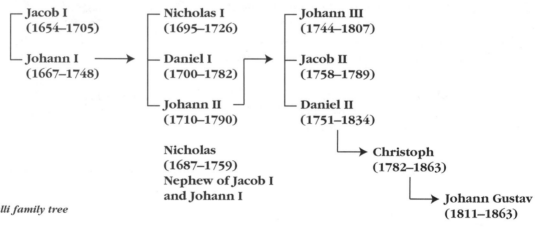

The Bernoulli family tree

RELATED READING

Bell, E.T. *Men of Mathematics.* New York: Simon and Schuster, 1986.

Bergamini, David (ed). *Mathematics: Life Science Library.* New York: Time-Life Books, 1972.

Daintith, John, and R.D. Nelson (eds). *Dictionary of Mathematics.* New York: Penguin Books, 1989.

Dunham, William. "The Bernoullis and the Harmonic Series." *The College Mathematics Journal* (Jan 1987) 18–23.

Eves, Howard. *An Introduction to the History of Mathematics.* New York: Holt, Rinehart and Winston, 1990.

Johnson, Art. *Classical Math: History Topics for the Classroom.* Palo Alto, CA: Dale Seymour, 1994.

Newman, James R. *The World of Mathematics,* Vol II. New York: Simon and Schuster, 1956.

African Patterns and Graphs

50

Occasionally, students in mathematics classes ask: "When am I ever going to use math in the real world?" It can sometimes seem that mathematical subjects have very little application in real life. However, as the activities of many African cultural groups demonstrate, mathematics is not only a subject studied in a classroom, it is an inherent part of life.

The Tchokwe of northeastern Angola use sand drawings called *lusona* (singular) or *sona* (plural) to relate proverbs, tell stories, depict animals, and the like. These drawings utilize concepts from graph theory. (For more on graph theory, see vignette 53.) *Sona* play an important role in passing knowledge from generation to generation. The *akwa kuta sona,* or "those who know how to draw," are responsible for the transmission of this knowledge. A storyteller makes a *lusona* by first drawing a rectangular grid of equally spaced dots, like dots drawn on a piece of graph paper. Then, without lifting his finger from the sand, he quickly traces out figures in one continuous curve.

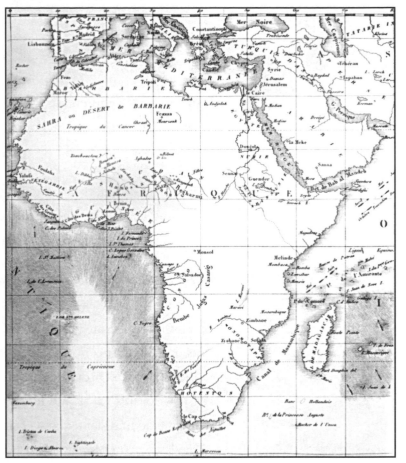

Nineteenth-century map of Africa

Graph drawings have also played a part in the cultural tradition of Zaire's Bushoong. In the early twentieth century, one European ethnologist wrote about the drawings that some Bushoong children showed to him. Although the children did not consider the mathematics of their graphs in a formal sense, they were aware of both the conditions necessary to draw the graph continuously and the procedure used to draw the graph most efficiently.

Geometric patterning is another mathematical idea utilized in much of Africa. For centuries, art has played an important part in the daily and ritual activities of many African cultures. Geometric patterns appear in several artistic media, such as weaving, decorative metal work, and sculpture—one pattern may have several different meanings when it is used in more than one medium. These patterns symbolize natural forms and often stress certain important characteristics of those forms.

Interesting examples of patterned art are found throughout Africa. The red-earth houses of the Igbo in Nigeria are decorated with geometric patterns painted in red, black, green, and white.

A Tchokwe lusona

©1996 by Key Curriculum Press

Wooden shields used by the Kikuyu of Kenya are painted in patterns that reveal their owners' clan. The interlacing patterns found so frequently in the art of Zaire's Kuba culture are based on weaving techniques and fishnets made of knotted string.

For more on African and African American mathematics, see vignettes 8, 21, 54, 57, 66, and 102. For more on nonacademic mathematics, see vignettes 25, 35, 54, 59, and 100. ★

Activities

1. Invent a story and create a *lusona* to help you tell the story to your class. What mathematical concepts will you need to consider in order to do this activity?

2. The Benin of Nigeria are famous for their bronze castings and ivory carvings. Read about the history of this art form in the Benin culture and mathematically analyze the patterns Benin artisans used for decoration.

3. In addition to providing entertainment, recreational activities are often used in Africa to teach children various mathematical concepts, such as counting and strategy. In Ghana, a board game called *Oware* has long been used for this purpose. (Today, an egg carton would serve as a *Oware* board.) Throughout Africa, there have been different versions of play for this game, and it has been called many different names. Investigate this game and its rules. How would you analyze *Oware* mathematically? (An *Oware* board is pictured on the cover of this book.)

Related Reading

Ascher, Marcia. *Ethnomathematics: A Multicultural View of Mathematical Ideas*. **Pacific Grove, CA: Brooks/Cole Publishing, 1991.**

Crowe, Donald. *Symmetry, Rigid Motions, and Patterns.* Alington, MA: COMAP, 1989.

Gay, J., and M. Cole. *The New Mathematics in an Old Culture: A Study of Learning Among the Kpelle of Liberia.* New York: Holt, Rinehart and Winston, 1976.

Gerdes, Paulus. *Lusona: Geometrical Recreations of Africa.* Maputo, Mozambique: African Mathematical Union, 1991.

Nelson, David, et al. *Multicultural Mathematics.* New York: Oxford University Press, 1993.

Schwartz, Richard H. *Mathematics and Global Survival.* Needham, MA: Ginn, 1990.

Zaslavsky, Claudia. *Africa Counts: Number and Pattern in African Culture*. **New York: Lawrence Hill Books, 1979.**

————. *Multicultural Mathematics*. **Portland, ME: J. Weston Walch, 1993.**

Perplexing Infinity 51

hroughout the long history of mathematics, the concept of infinity has seemed to reside in the "twilight zone." The ancient Greeks struggled with the notion of infinite sets and generally regarded infinity as an inadmissible concept. It wasn't until the seventeenth century that mathematician **John Wallis** (1616–1703) created the symbol for infinity (∞), and as recently as the eighteenth century, mathematicians weren't sure exactly what infinity represented. **Leonhard Euler** (1707–1783) is one mathematician who spoke of infinity as a number but never clarified the concept or established its properties. In his *Algebra* (1770), Euler incorrectly stated that $\frac{1}{0}$ equals infinity, then went on to state, also incorrectly and without any clarification, that $\frac{2}{0}$ is twice as large as $\frac{1}{0}$.

We know today that many mathematical ideas would not have been developed if we had not grasped the concept of infinity. For example, the development of calculus and the notion of a limit are inextricably tied to the notion of infinity. Although Chinese mathematician **Liu Hui** (ca A.D. 250) used some notion of limit to analyze infinitesimals, **Georg Cantor** (1845–1918) was the first modern mathematician to seriously examine the infinite. Although many considered some of his ideas to be controversial, he is considered a founder of theories of the infinite.

A number of fundamental mathematical concepts depend on infinity.

> *There is no smallest among the small and no largest among the large; but always something still smaller and something still larger.*
> —Anaxagoras
>
> *Infinity is where things happen that don't.*
> —Anonymous student
>
> *We admit, in geometry, not only infinite magnitudes, that is to say, magnitudes greater than any assignable magnitude, but infinite magnitudes infinitely greater, the one than the other. This astonishes our dimensions of brains, which is only about six inches long, five broad, and six in depth, in the largest heads.*
> —François Voltaire

- Properties that are true for finite sets may not necessarily be true for infinite sets.

- An infinite amount does not necessarily take up an infinite amount of space. For example, a segment that is one inch long contains an infinite number of points.

- An infinite set and a proper subset of the infinite set can have the same number of elements to establish a one-to-one correspondence between set members. For example, the elements in the set $\{1, 2, 3, 4, 5, \ldots\}$ are easily matched with the elements in the "smaller" set $\{1^2, 2^2, 3^2, 4^2, 5^2, \ldots\}$.

- The sum of an infinite set of numbers doesn't need to be an infinite amount. For example, the sum $\frac{1}{2} + \frac{1}{4} + \frac{1}{8} + \frac{1}{16} + \frac{1}{32} + \frac{1}{64} + \ldots$ never exceeds 1, no matter how many terms are used for the sum.

- An object of finite length can be matched with an object of infinite length. In the figure shown at right, the points on the semicircle—which has finite length—are put into a one-to-one correspondence with the points on the line—which has infinite length.

For more on infinity, see vignettes 13, 14, 75, and 79. ★

Activities

1. Comment on these statements.

   a. Parallel lines are sometimes said to intersect at a point at infinity.

   b. The asymptote to a curve intersects the curve at infinity.

   c. A parabola is an ellipse or a hyperbola with one focus at infinity.

2. Draw a line segment one foot long and a second segment one inch long. Demonstrate how you can establish a one-to-one correspondence between points on the shorter segment and points on the longer segment.

3. Show that the integers can be put into a one-to-one correspondence with the set of multiples of ten. Show that the positive integers can be put into one-to-one correspondence with the positive rational fractions. (Read about how Cantor solved the second problem.)

4. How did Cantor establish that there cannot be a one-to-one correspondence between the set of integers and the set of real numbers?

Related Reading

Barrow, John D. *Pi in the Sky: Counting, Thinking, and Being.* New York: Oxford University Press, 1992.

Dauben, Joseph W. *Georg Cantor: His Mathematics and Philosophy of the Infinite.* Cambridge, MA: Harvard University Press, 1979.

Davies, Paul. *The Edge of Infinity.* New York: Simon and Schuster, 1982.

Francis, Richard L. "From None to Infinity." *College Mathematics Journal* (May 1986) 226–230.

Kanigel, Robert. *The Man Who Knew Infinity: A Life of the Genius Ramanujan.* New York: Macmillan Publishing, 1991.

Love, William P. "Infinity: The Twilight Zone of Mathematics." *Mathematics Teacher* (Apr 1989) 284–292.

Maor, Eli. *To Infinity and Beyond: A Cultural History of the Infinite.* Boston: Birkhauser Boston, 1987.

Pappas, Theoni. *More Joy of Mathematics.* San Carlos, CA: Wide World/Tetra, 1991.

Ziman, J. *Puzzles, Problems and Enigmas.* Cambridge, MA: Cambridge University Press, 1981.

Euler and the Number *e*

This German stamp depicts
Leonhard Euler with his
famous equation.

T he name of Swiss mathematician **Leonhard Euler** (1707–1783) is associated with virtually every branch of mathematics. A prolific writer, his works dealt with many subjects, including astronomy, geometry, graph theory, artillery, mapmaking, optics, musical instruments, the design of ships and sails, and the motions of fluids.

Among the many contributions Euler made to mathematics are the introduction of useful notation for functions and the irrational number *e*. The number *e* can be approximated by evaluating the expression $(1 + \frac{1}{x})^x$ for a large value of *x*. In formal mathematical terms, $e = \lim_{x \to \infty} (1 + \frac{1}{x})^x$, or approximately 2.718281828459.

The number *e* is an important number that can be used in many ways. Let's look at how it's used in matters of finance. Pretend you live in a perfect world and you want to invest $10,000 at an annual interest rate of 100 percent. Now, you ask yourself, is the rate compounded yearly, monthly, or by the minute? You want to know this because it will affect how much interest you'll earn. Let's look at a number of possibilities. In the table at right, *N* is the number of times the rate is compounded per year. In one year there are 8,760 hours and 525,600 minutes.

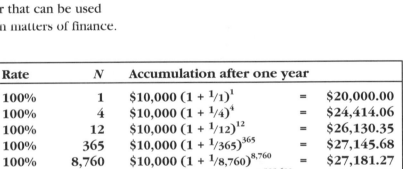

Rate	N	Accumulation after one year		
100%	1	$10,000 $(1 + \frac{1}{1})^1$	=	$20,000.00
100%	4	$10,000 $(1 + \frac{1}{4})^4$	=	$24,414.06
100%	12	$10,000 $(1 + \frac{1}{12})^{12}$	=	$26,130.35
100%	365	$10,000 $(1 + \frac{1}{365})^{365}$	=	$27,145.68
100%	8,760	$10,000 $(1 + \frac{1}{8,760})^{8,760}$	=	$27,181.27
100%	525,600	$10,000 $(1 + \frac{1}{525,600})^{525,600}$	=	$27,182.79

You may think that 100 percent interest compounded a large number of times per year would yield astronomical values for the accumulation of your $10,000 investment. However, regardless of how many times your investment is compounded, it will never grow to be more than $10,000*e*, or $27,182.82, in one year. In general, if an amount *P* is invested at a rate *r* that is compounded continuously, then after one year the accumulated amount $A = Pe^r$.

The number *e*, although unfamiliar to many people, is very much a part of our existence and has great influence on the daily events of our lives. As Edward Kasner and James Newman note in their *Mathematics and the Imagination,* "[The number *e*] has played an integral part in helping mathematicians describe and predict what is for man the most important of all natural phenomena—that of growth."

For more on irrational numbers, see vignettes 12, 19, and 33. ★

Activities

1. Tashi deposits $10,000 into a retirement account and leaves it to accumulate for 25 years. Find the accumulated amount if the interest rate is (a) a true annual rate of 8 percent, (b) 8 percent compounded monthly, (c) 8 percent compounded daily, and (d) 8 percent compounded continuously.

2. Advanced calculus students know that e^x can be expanded in a Maclaurin series to obtain $e^x = 1 + x + \frac{x^2}{2!} + \frac{x^3}{3!} + \frac{x^4}{4!} + \ldots$. Let $x = 1$ and obtain an approximation for e. How many terms of this series are needed to determine e accurate to two decimal places? To three decimal places?

3. Show that $(1 + \frac{r}{N})^N = \left[\left(1 + \frac{1}{\frac{N/r}{r}}\right)^{N/r}\right]^r$. (Hint: Simplify the right side.) Note that $N \to \infty$, $\frac{N}{r} \to \infty$ for a constant, r. If you've worked with limits, can you convince yourself that $\lim_{N \to \infty}(1 + \frac{r}{N})^N = e^r$?

Related Reading

Dunham, William. *Journey Through Genius: The Great Theorems of Mathematics*. Somerset, NJ: John Wiley, 1990.

Hollingdale, Stuart. *Makers of Mathematics*. New York: Penguin Books, 1989.

Kasner, Edward, and James R. Newman. *Mathematics and the Imagination*. Redmond, WA: Tempus Books, 1989.

Pappas, Theoni. *More Joy of Mathematics*. San Carlos, CA: Wide World/Tetra, 1991.

Paulos, John Allen. *Beyond Numeracy: Ruminations of a Numbers Man*. New York: Alfred A. Knopf, 1991.

Smith, Sanderson. *An Introduction to Investment Mathematics*. Englewood, NJ: Franklin Publishing, 1968.

THE SEVEN BRIDGES OF KÖNIGSBERG

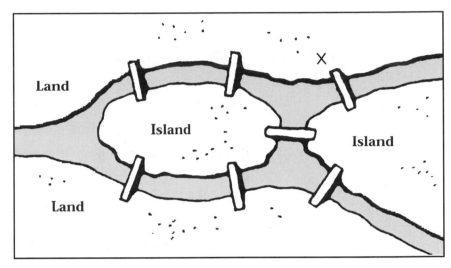

53

The seven bridges of Königsberg.

The city of Königsberg, now called Kaliningrad, is on the coast of the Baltic Sea, at the mouth of what is now called the Pregolya River. There are two islands in the river, linked to the mainland and to each other by seven bridges, as shown at right.

The citizens of Königsberg wondered whether it was possible to make a special type of journey across all the bridges. The traveler had to start at a certain location, cross each bridge exactly once, and end up at the starting point of the journey. For many years, people tried to see if this was possible, but everyone who made the attempt either skipped or recrossed at least one bridge. The town concluded that it couldn't be done, but no one knew why. In 1736, Swiss mathematician **Leonhard Euler** (1707–1783) took an interest in the problem, and he proved that it was impossible to achieve the goal the citizens had proposed. In the process, he established the groundwork for a branch of mathematics now known as graph theory.

Let's take a look at Euler's analysis of the problem. Assume that you start at the location of the ✕ in the drawing. In this case, you are starting on the mainland. Since there are three bridges leading to the east island, you would end up on the east island if you crossed each bridge exactly once. That is, one bridge takes you onto the island, a second bridge takes you off, and the third bridge takes you on. Similarly, there are five bridges leading to the west island, so if you started on the mainland again, you would end up on the west island if you crossed each bridge exactly once.

So, to accomplish the goal of crossing each bridge exactly once, you would have to end up both on the east island and on the west island. This, of course, is impossible, because you can't end up in two places at once. You would face a similar predicament if you started your walk on either island.

Euler reduced the Königsberg bridge problem to what is called a network. A network consists of vertices and arcs, as shown at right. In the figure, I_1 and I_2 are the islands, S_1 and S_2 are the two shores, and the arcs are the bridges. A network is traced by passing over all the arcs exactly once. A vertex can be crossed any number of times—it is even if it has an even number of arcs passing through it, odd if it has an odd number of arcs passing through it. Euler discovered that if a vertex is odd, you would have to begin or end a traceable journey at that vertex. He concluded that a traceable network could have only two odd vertices.

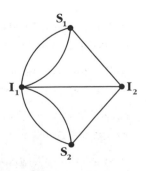

For more on Leonhard Euler, see vignettes 13, 29, 37, 45, 51, 52, and 64. ★

ACTIVITIES

1. How is graph theory applied to problems today?

2. a. How many odd vertices appear in the Königsberg network? Is it traceable?

   b. Draw a picture of the Königsberg network. Add one arc to it so that it becomes traceable.

   c. Construct some traceable networks and some networks that are not traceable.

3. *Draw a network showing eight people, each connected to every other person by a telephone line. Then draw a network in which each person can be directly reached by only two others, but can be indirectly reached by all others.

4. *If each person in the network you created in Activity 3 wishes to speak to every other person separately, how many phone calls would be needed? Draw network diagrams and count the connecting lines for groups of three, four, five, six, seven, and eight people. What method would describe how to answer this question for groups of 10, 100, and 1,000 people?

*Contributed by Leonard Feldman.

RELATED READING

Bell, E.T. *Men of Mathematics*. New York: Simon and Schuster, 1986.

Biggs, N.C., E.K. Lloyd, and R.J. Wilson. *Graph Theory 1736-1936*. New York: Clarendon Press, 1986.

Davies, Paul. *The Edge of Infinity*. New York: Simon and Schuster, 1982.

Jacobs, Harold. *Mathematics: A Human Endeavor*. San Francisco: W.H. Freeman, 1987.

Kasner, Edward, and James R. Newman. *Mathematics and the Imagination*. Redmond, WA: Tempus Books, 1989.

Moise, Edwin, and Floyd Downs. *Geometry*. Menlo Park, CA: Addison-Wesley, 1982.

Pappas, Theoni. *The Joy of Mathematics*. San Carlos, CA: Wide World/Tetra, 1989.

Sacco, William, et al. *Graph Theory: Euler's Rich Legacy*. Providence, RI: Janson Publications, 1987.

The Mathematics of Music

54

Music is essential to every culture. Performed as a means of communication, to accompany work or play, for ritual purposes, or simply for entertainment, music has always been a part of people's daily existence—and so has the mathematics inherent in that music.

The highly complex rhythmic patterns of **African drumming** have long influenced music all over the world. For example, in African group drumming, a lead drummer initiates a theme and the other drummers elaborate on it. Thus, everyone is playing a different rhythm, all at the same time. Many of today's musical forms are based on this unification of individual rhythms.

The ancient Pythagoreans, to whom "all things are numbers," believed that music was simply audible numbers. In the sixth century B.C., **Pythagoras** found a marvelous connection between musical harmony and whole numbers. By testing the connections between ratio and harmony on strings, bells, and glasses of water, he discovered what so many musicians know: pluck any string, sound any pipe, open your mouth to speak, and four-, five-, even six-part harmony pours forth.

The comparison of mathematics and music is often particularly apt. The most attractive music is spoiled by a bad performance. So it is that many an admirable mathematical thought languishes amid the colorless rigor of a formal exposition.

—Ross Honsberger

I think there certainly is a link [between mathematics and music], for various reasons. One is that they are both creative arts. When you're sitting with a bit of paper creating mathematics, it is very like sitting with a sheet of music paper creating music.

—Robin Wilson

In his *Harmonices mundi* (*Harmonies of the world*, 1619), German astronomer **Johannes Kepler** connected harmonic ratios to different planets. When he compared these ratios to the planets' daily angular movements around the sun, he found some interesting correspondences. For example, the daily movement of Saturn at the point on its orbit farthest from the sun is 1'46", and its daily movement at the point closest to the sun is 2'15". The ratio between 1'46" and 2'15" is approximately 4 : 5, or a major third. For Mars, the ratio is 26'14" : 38'1", or approximately 2 : 3, a fifth. Of these correspondences, Kepler wrote, "Accordingly the movements of the heavens are nothing except a certain everlasting polyphony . . . ."

About 200 years later, French mathematician **Joseph Fourier** proved that both instrumental and vocal musical sounds can be described by mathematical expressions that are the sums of periodic sine functions. Each distinct musical sound has a quality that can be obtained by plucking a string at different points. Sound waves produced in this way, display the sine and cosine curves as shown at right. Additional mathematics is found in harps and in organ pipes—the shapes of these instruments reflect the exponential curve $y = k^x$, where $k > 0$.

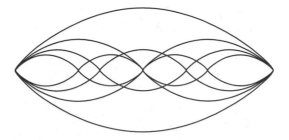

Today, many musical artists use computers to both compose and play music. In her innovative concert film, *Home of the Brave* (1986), **Laurie Anderson** begins her performance with a monologue about the merits and drawbacks of the numbers 1 and 0. She says:" . . . we need to get rid of the value judgments attached to these two numbers and realize that to be a zero is no better, no worse than to be number one, because what we are actually looking at here are the building blocks of the modern computer age." She then displays portions of the binary codes representing the Gettysburg Address and a song she composed on her computer. ★

Activities

1. Just as there exists a rational number between any two distinct rational numbers, there exists a tone that is between any two tones. Because it isn't practical to compose music from an infinite choice of tones, musical scales have been developed that classify a small number of tones. When sounded together in a number of different combinations, these tones produce pleasant auditory sensations. Compare scales from different cultures. For instance, how do scales used in the United States differ from those used in the Middle East or in Asia?

2. Investigate scales used in the just intonation system and the equal-temperament system.

3. In groups of four, explore the work of a musical artist or a band whose music makes use of computers or other electronic devices. (Each group should pick a different artist.) Prepare a short presentation that includes the history of the artist or the band, the ways in which technology is used in their work, and a sample of their music. Here are some suggested musicians: Jimi Hendrix, Yoko Ono, Klaus Schulze, Talking Heads, the Beatles, Laurie Spiegel, David Bowie, Brian Eno, Père Ubu, and Laurie Anderson.

Related Reading

Boulez, Piene, and Andrew Gerzso. "Computers in Music." *Scientific American* (Apr 1988) 44–51.

Dalton, LeRoy. *Algebra in the Real World.* Palo Alto, CA: Dale Seymour, 1983.

Gardner, Martin. *Fractal Music, Hypercards, and More.* New York: W.H. Freeman, 1992.

Garland, Trudi, and Charity Kahn. *Math and Music: Harmonic Connections.* Palo Alto, CA: Dale Seymour, 1994.

Holmes, Thomas B. *Electronic and Experimental Music.* New York: Charles Scribner, 1985.

Howell, John. *Laurie Anderson.* New York: Thunder's Mouth Press, 1992.

Maria Agnesi: Linguist, Mathematician, Humanist

55

Born into a wealthy family, **Maria Gaetana Agnesi** (1718–1799) was able to receive something of great value: an excellent private education. Generally, access to any educational opportunity was difficult for women and girls of Agnesi's time. She demonstrated a special ability for languages. At the age of nine she wrote—in Latin—an elaborate address maintaining that it was entirely appropriate for women to be educated in the liberal arts. A few years later, she was fluent in Italian, Latin, Greek, Hebrew, French, Spanish, and German, earning her the appelation "Oracle of Seven Languages."

Agnesi's father, a professor of mathematics at the University of Bologna, frequently assembled in his home some of the most distinguished scholars of the time for discussions. Agnesi participated in many of these discussions, holding forth on complex philosophical issues. She was especially interested in the philosophy of Isaac Newton as he had presented it in his *Principia* (1687).

In her teens, Agnesi planned to become a nun, but her father insisted that she instead pursue her mathematical and scientific interests. Thus she spent the next twenty years educating her younger brothers and concentrating on her own work. While in her twenties, she published her most important mathematical work, *Analytical Institutions* (1748), written as a textbook for her brothers. In it she presented a variety of mathematical subjects ranging from algebra and geometry to differential and integral calculus. Considered to be very well written and clear, *Analytical Institutions* was translated into French and English and widely used as a textbook. In addition to expanding upon the concepts and ideas of Newton and Gottfried Leibniz, the book includes an extensive discussion of Agnesi's work with the family of curves generated by the equation $x^2y = 4a^2(2a - y)$.

When Agnesi's father became ill in 1748, she began to lecture in his stead, and two years later she was appointed to the position of mathematics chair at the University of Bologna. However, she soon relinquished her position and devoted the rest of her life to religious studies and charitable works. ★

Maria Gaetana Agnesi

Activities

1. Agnesi's family of curves is known as the Witch of Agnesi. The curve is not meant to depict a witch, but was titled due to a mistranslation of a term used to describe cubic equations. How did this happen?

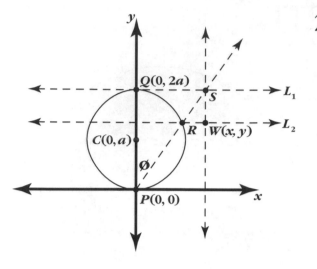

2. Consider the circle with diameter PQ and center at $(0, a)$, as shown. A tangent line L_1 is constructed to the circle at point Q. A line from point P is drawn to intersect the circle at point R and extended to intersect line L_1 at point S. From point R, a line L_2 is drawn parallel to line L_1. From point S a line is drawn parallel to the y-axis, intersecting L_2 at point W. Agnesi's curve is the set of points W generated by points R on the circle.

   a. Using the labels in the diagram, show that $x = 2a \tan \emptyset$ and $y = 2a \cos^2 \emptyset$.

   b. Using trigonometric identities, eliminate $\emptyset$ and obtain an equation relating x to y.

   c. Show that the equation in 2b can be written in the form $4a^2(2a - y) = x^2 y$.

3. Choose some numerical values for a and graph some members of Agnesi's curve's family.

Related Reading

Alic, Margaret. *Hypatia's Heritage*. Boston: Beacon Press, 1986.

Carter, Jack. "Discrete Mathematics: Women in Mathematics." *California Mathematics Council ComMuniCator* (Mar 1993) 10-12.

Grinstein, Louise S., and Paul Campbell. *Women of Mathematics: A Bibliographic Sourcebook*. Westport, CT: Greenwood Press, 1987.

Osen, Lynn. *Women in Mathematics*. Cambridge, MA: MIT Press, 1984.

Perl, Teri. *Math Equals: Biographies of Women Mathematicians and Related Activities*. Menlo Park, CA: Addison-Wesley, 1978.

———. *Women and Numbers: Lives of Women Mathematicians plus Discovery Activities*. San Carlos, CA: Wide World/Tetra, 1993.

HISTORY OF MATH

Kant: The Intuitionist

56

T hough **Immanuel Kant** (1724–1804) was primarily a philosopher, he taught mathematics and physics at the University of Königsberg in East Prussia from 1755 to 1770. (East Prussia was in what is now Estonia.) His views on the nature of mathematical laws differed considerably from those of his colleagues, most of whom believed in a universe subject to laws independent of the human mind. It was commonly held that the world was mathematically designed. Humans strove to uncover that design and to use it to predict what would happen in their everyday lives.

Kant, however, believed that mathematics was *not* inherent in the physical world, but came from the human mind. He asserted that our minds possess the forms of space and time, which he considered modes of perception, or intuition. Because the intuition of space originated in the mind, the mind automatically accepted certain properties of this space. So, for example, the laws of Euclidean geometry were not inherent in the universe, but instead were human mechanisms used to organize and rationalize sensations. Additionally, as Kant claimed in his *Metaphysical Foundations of Natural Science* (1786), the laws of motion developed by **Isaac Newton** (1642–1727) were self-evident and could be derived from pure reason. In a general sense, Kant claimed that the world of science was a world of sense impressions arranged and controlled by the mind.

Having added an element of confusion to the existing mathematical thought, Kant's beliefs also temporarily restricted some mathematical exploration. Mathematicians had been studying nature to uncover the laws of mathematics, but Kant argued that these laws would be found in the recesses of the human mind. For a time, his intriguing ideas hindered the acceptance of contrary views. More than a century after his death, Kant's philosophies still influenced mathematicians, and headed by Dutch mathematician **Luitzen Brouwer** (1881–1966), the intuitionist school of mathematical thought was founded. (For more on the intuitionist school, see vignette 77.)

Modern developments have clouded Kant's doctrine that our minds create what we view in nature. Do airplanes, television sets, or computers exist because our minds organize sensations that allow us to experience them? Additionally, his intuitionist views don't offer us any insight into *why* mathematics works. However, despite the fact that some of Kant's ideas were at odds with the obvious successes of mathematics and science, he remains a highly respected philosopher. ★

> These examples [taken from the geometry of the circle] indicate what a countless number of other such harmonic relations obtain in the properties of space, many of which are manifested in the relations of the various classes of curves in higher geometry, all of which, besides exercising the understanding through intellectual insight, affect the emotion in a similar or even greater degree than the occasional beauties of nature.
>
> —Immanuel Kant

Activities

1. Kant asserted that mathematics was knowable *a priori*. What is *a priori* knowledge?

2. Historian John D. Barrow asserted that the discovery of non-Euclidean geometries made Kant's view of *a priori* knowledge "look a little silly." Elaborate on Barrow's statement.

3. How did the views of Scottish philosopher **David Hume** (1711–1776) on mathematics and its relation to the universe compare with those of Kant?

4. **René Descarte**'s views on mathematics differed considerably from those of Kant. Contrast these opposing views.

Related Reading

Barker, Stephen F. *Philosophy of Mathematics.* Englewood Cliffs, NJ: Prentice-Hall, 1964.

Barrow, John D. *Pi in the Sky: Counting, Thinking, and Being*. New York: Oxford University Press, 1992.

Bell, E.T. *The Magic of Numbers.* New York: McGraw-Hill, 1946.

Dummett, Michael. *Elements of Intuitionism.* New York: Clarendon Press, 1977.

Kline, Morris. *Mathematics: The Loss of Certainty*. New York: Oxford University Press, 1980.

Maor, Eli. *To Infinity and Beyond: A Cultural History of the Infinite*. Boston: Birkhauser Boston, 1987.

Marks, Robert. *The Growth of Mathematics: From Counting to Calculus.* New York: Bantam Books, 1964.

Ross, Hugh. *The Fingerprint of God.* Orange, CA: Promise Publishing, 1989.

BENJAMIN BANNEKER: PROBLEM SOLVER

57

The first African American to be recognized for his mathematical abilities, **Benjamin Banneker** (1731–1806) lived during a period of United States history when there was little interest in the scholarly pursuit of mathematics. Rather, this field of study was valued as it applied to such endeavors as engineering, carpentry, and quiltmaking. Banneker's abilities and interests suited his times: He was a problem solver.

Banneker was born in Maryland to a former slave and the daughter of a former indentured servant from England who had married her own slave. His grandmother taught the young Banneker how to read and write, and during the winter months, he attended a Quaker school. His mathematical talent was apparent to his teachers, but as the son of a farmer, he was unable to devote his full energies to his studies. Nevertheless, while he worked on the farm, he spent what little spare time he had applying the rules of arithmetic to a variety of practical areas. His mechanical skills were such that at the age of twenty-two he built a striking clock out of hardwood, which brought him much acclaim. The clock kept accurate time until it was destroyed in a fire fifty-three years later.

In the late 1780s, Banneker became interested in the skies. Having borrowed a variety of technical books and a telescope from his friend and neighbor, **George Ellicot**, he began to teach himself the principles of astronomy and surveying. Several years later, Banneker predicted a solar eclipse with considerable accuracy, and in 1792, he published his first *Almanack,* which contained detailed observations of the evening sky and many astronomical calculations. He sent a copy to Secretary of State Thomas Jefferson, who was so impressed that he sent it to the French Academy of Science. In eighteenth-century America, almanacs were an indispensable source of weather information, planting advice, entertainment, and literary and historical knowledge. Banneker's almanacs were so popular that he continued to publish them until 1797.

For more on African and African American mathematics, see vignettes 8, 21, 50, 54, 66, and 102. ★

Title page of Benjamin Banneker's 1795 Almanac (Baltimore, 1795).

ACTIVITIES

1. *When Banneker sent his first *Almanack* to Jefferson, he included a letter criticizing Jefferson for owning slaves. Research the effect of this letter and identify the specific topics that were referenced in the *Almanack*.

2. Research the mathematical accomplishments and abilities of **Thomas Fuller** (1710–1790), who was brought to the United States from Africa when he was fourteen years old and sold into slavery. Why were abolitionists interested in Fuller's calculating abilities?

3. Banneker liked to invent and solve mathematical puzzles, recording them in his notebook. Solve his version of the well-known hundred fowls puzzle: A gentleman sent his servant with £100 to buy 100 cattle, with orders to give £5 for each bullock, 20 shillings for each cow, and one shilling for each sheep. (Recall that 20 shillings equals £1.) What number of each sort of animal did he bring back to his master?

4. To the present day, the United States has produced relatively few African American mathematicians and scientists. With your class, discuss why you think this is so.

5. Read about Banneker's work with the commission appointed by President George Washington to survey the boundaries of what is now the District of Columbia.

*From Claudia Zaslavsky's *Multicultural Mathematics*. (See Related Reading.)

RELATED READING

Bedini, Silvio. *Life of Benjamin Banneker.* New York: Charles Scribner, 1972.

Benjamin Banneker (poster). Burlington, NC: Cabisco Mathematics, Carolina Biological Supply, 1991.

Conley, Kevin. *Benjamin Banneker.* New York: Chelsea Publishing, 1989.

Johnson, Art. *Classical Math: History Topics for the Classroom.* Palo Alto, CA: Dale Seymour, 1994.

Newell, Virginia K., and Joella Gipson. *Black Mathematicians and Their Works.* Ardmore, PA: Dorrance, 1980.

Fauvel, John, and Paulus Gerdes. "African Slave and Calculating Prodigy: Bicentenary of the Death of Thomas Fuller." *Historia Mathematica* 17(2) (1990) 141–151.

Zaslavsky, Claudia. *Multicultural Mathematics.* Portland, ME: J. Weston Walch, 1993.

The Mathematics of Eighteenth-Century France

58

A number of eighteenth-century mathematicians in France made significant contributions to the field of mathematics and mathematics education. However, they didn't teach in universities as many earlier mathematicians did, but applied their skills in the military or for the state. In fact, some are remembered not for their mathematics, but for their other endeavors.

Joseph Louis Lagrange (1736–1813)

Born in Turin, Italy, Lagrange taught mathematics at the military academy of Turin and later found a royal patron in Louis XVI of France. Recognizing the unsatisfactory state of the foundations of analysis, he attempted to make the study of calculus more rigorous. These attempts had a deep influence on future mathematical research. In the process of his reform, he took a critical look at the works of Newton, Euler, and Leibniz, and he created the calculus notation $f'(x)$ and $f''(x)$, which we still use today. Additionally, Lagrange contributed to the study of astronomy and to the development of the theory of finite groups.

Pierre-Simon Laplace (1749–1827)

Born of poor parents, Laplace's mathematical ability allowed him to obtain good teaching posts during the uncertain times dictated by the French Revolution. In fact, he taught mathematics at the Military School of Paris, the school where Napoleon studied. Laplace was devoted to the study of astronomy, and in developing mathematics for applications in this science, he made significant contributions to celestial mechanics, probability, differential equations, and geodesy. His work *Traité de mécanique céleste (Treatise on celestial mechanics)*, an analysis of the solar system, earned him the title "The Newton of France."

Adrien-Marie Legendre (1752–1833)

Legendre also taught at the Military School of Paris. His most influential work, *Éléments de géométrie (Elements of geometry)*, represented a rearrangement and simplification of many propositions in Euclid's *Elements*. (For more on Euclid's *Elements*, see vignette 15.) Very well received in the

Nineteenth-century engraving of Joseph Louis Lagrange.

Early portrait of Adrien-Marie Legendre.

©1996 by Key Curriculum Press

Napoleon's Theorem

Little known to geometry students today is a seldom used, but interesting, theorem often attributed to Napoleon.

Given any triangle *ABC,* if equilateral triangles are constructed on the sides of triangle *ABC,* as shown, and if *P, Q,* and *R* are the centroids of these triangles, then triangle *PQR* (shaded) is an equilateral triangle.

A proof of this theorem can be found in H. S. M. Coxeter and Samuel L. Greitzer's *Geometry Revisited*—see Related Reading.

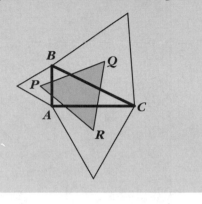

United States, his work became the prototype of United States geometry books. Additionally, Legendre's work significantly contributed to such higher mathematics as number theory, elliptic functions, integrals, and the method of least squares.

Napoleon Bonaparte (1769–1821)

You may be familiar with Napoleon's famous portrait—the general with a hand in his jacket—but did you know that Napoleon excelled only in mathematics during his nine years as a boarding school student? He readily absorbed algebra, trigonometry, geometry, and the properties of the conic sections. As a young man, he completed his studies at the Military School of Paris with superior grades in mathematics, earning him the commission of second lieutenant of the Royal Artillery. Recognized for his excellence in mathematics, he was also appointed to the mathematics section of the French National Institute. Throughout his lifetime, Napoleon was a strong advocate of education, and his efforts ensured that mathematics became a permanent part of the French school curriculum. Prior to his time, French schools concentrated mostly on literature and languages. ★

> *The advancement and perfection of mathematics are intimately connected with the prosperity of the state.*
> —Napoleon Bonaparte

Activities

1. Research the mathematical contributions of **Lorenzo Mascheroni** (1750-1800), a poet and a mathematician who had considerable influence on Napoleon.

2. History associates Lagrange with a person named **M. Le Blanc**. Who was Le Blanc?

3. What were Laplace's contributions to probability theory and to what we know about the number π?

4. Use interactive geometry software to make a model of Napolean's theorem.

5. One of Lagrange's theorems states that every natural number can be written as the sum of the squares of four integers. For instance, $23 = 3^2 + 3^2 + 2^2 + 1^2$ and $59 = 7^2 + 3^2 + 1^2 + 0^2$.

   a. Choose some other whole numbers and write them as the sum of four squares.

   b. Show that 59 can be written as the sum of the squares of four nonzero numbers.

6. In the summer of 1799, one of Napoleon's army engineers found the Rosetta Stone. Why was this discovery significant?

Related Reading

Connelly, Owen (ed). *The Historical Dictionary of Napoleonic France, 1799-1815.* Westport, CT: Greenwood Press, 1985.

Courant, Richard, and Herbert Robins. *What Is Mathematics?* New York: Oxford University Press, 1948.

Coxeter, H.S.M., and Samuel L. Greitzer. *Geometry Revisited.* Washington, DC: Mathematical Association of America, 1967.

Gillespie, Charles C. "The Scientific Importance of Napolean's Egyptian Campaign." *Scientific American* (Sept 1994).

Herold, J. Cristopher. *Bonaparte in Egypt.* New York: Harper and Row, 1962.

Hollingdale, Stuart. *Makers of Mathematics.* New York: Penguin Books, 1989.

Jacobs, Harold. *Mathematics: A Human Endeavor.* San Francisco: W.H. Freeman, 1987.

Maynard, Jacquelyn. "Napoleon's Waterloo Wasn't Mathematics." *Mathematics Teacher* (Nov 1989) 648-653.

Early North American Mathematics

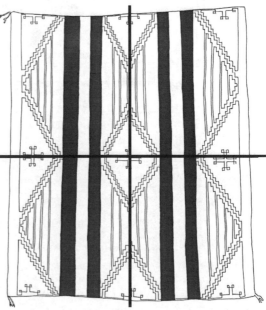

59

Many early North American Indian societies had no written language and thus left no written records of their mathematical knowledge. As a result, what we now know of early American mathematics has come from studying artifacts, exploring modern applications of traditional mathematical knowledge, and reading the accounts of ethnologists. Because the mathematical accomplishments of these early societies are as varied as the cultures themselves, it isn't possible to fully describe them in one vignette. Here's some history to get you started on your own exploration of this rich topic.

In the Hopi cosmology, **Hahaiwugti** *is the earth woman, mother goddess of growing.*

Anasazi astronomy

Some 1,500 years ago, an American Indian people called the Anasazi lived in what is now the southwestern United States. It is believed that the elaborate Anasazi ceremonial structures at Chaco Canyon in northwestern New Mexico and at Mesa Verde in southwestern Colorado were used in part for astronomical purposes. Many of the structures seem to contain areas from which to observe significant astronomical events such as the summer and winter solstices.

Pomo counting methods

In the early twentieth century, the Pomo of California were known to be skilled counters. In one of many counting systems used by the Pomo, large amounts were represented by sticks and beads. A small stick represented every eighty beads. When five of these small sticks had been counted, they were replaced by a larger stick that represented four hundred, the largest Pomo unit for this particular system. When traveling, the Pomo kept track of the days by using a string system similar to the Peruvian Inca's quipu. Each night, a knot was tied to represent that day's travel. These records were called *kamalduyi*, meaning "day count."

Navajo and Pueblo symmetry

The Navajo and Pueblo of the southwestern United States have long been experts at weaving blankets and rugs on looms, creating beautiful, sophisticated geometric designs. If you were to rotate the blanket shown at right 180 degrees, its pattern would remain unchanged because this pattern has rotational symmetry. If you were to fold the blanket horizontally and then vertically, you would end up with four identically patterned layers. This type of design is creat-

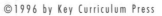

ed by filling one quadrant of a coordinate system with a pattern, then creating mirror images of the pattern in the other three quadrants.

Sioux number symbolism

The number 4 has played an important role in many American Indian cultures. The Sioux have considered 4 the perfect number and it has often been associated with their sacred symbol, the circle. In Sioux mythology, Skan, the sky, created the world in groups of four: sun, moon, earth, and sky; day night, month, and year. The world is filled with four species of animals who creep, fly, walk on two legs or four, and human beings live through four ages: infancy, childhood, maturity, and old age.

For more on American Indian mathematics, see vignettes 3, 6, 8, 24, 25, 32, and 104. ★

Chap-Pek, *Aztec symbol of the earth.*

Activities

1. About 500 years ago, the Aztecs of central and southern Mexico used two calendars: an annual calendar and a ritual calendar called the *tonalpohualli*. What was the significance of each calendar? How was each calendar computed?

2. Read about the number pictographs of the Ojibwa, an American Indian society that has historically occupied the Lake Superior region of Canada and the United States. Prepare a visual presentation of what you learn and share it with your class.

3. *The Anasazi wove flat, coiled baskets. Their descendants, the Hopi of northern Arizona, have continued this tradition. Investigate some Hopi patterns and the methods used to create them.

*From Claudia Zaslavsky's *Multicultural Mathematics*. (See Related Reading.)

Related Reading

Bolz, Diane M. "The Enduring Art of Navajo Weaving." *Smithsonian* (Aug 1994) 20.

Castillo, Toby T. *Apache Mathematics, Past and Present.* Whiteriver, AZ: Whiteriver Middle School Press, 1994.

Closs, M.P. (ed). *Native American Mathematics*. **Austin: University of Texas Press, 1986**.

Crowe, Donald. *Symmetry, Rigid Motions, and Patterns.* Arlington, MA: COMAP, 1989.

Ferguson, William, and Arthur Rohn. *Anasazi Ruins of the Southwest in Color.* Albuquerque, NM: The University of New Mexico Press, 1986.

Goodwin, Grenville. *The Social Organization of the Western Apache.* Tucson: University of Arizona Press, 1969.

Zaslavsky, Claudia. *Multicultural Mathematics*. **Portland, ME: J. Weston Walch, 1993**.

Sophie Germain: Courageous Mathematician

60

During ten years of French revolutionary violence, Paris-born **Sophie Germain** (1776–1831) spent much of her time confined to her house, reading in her father's library. According to one story, at age thirteen she came upon the famous legend of the death of **Archimedes** in Montucla's *History of Mathematics*. In the legend, Archimedes was designing a machine to repel the Romans who were attacking the Greek city-state of Syracuse. So engrossed was he in the study of a mathematical figure in the sand that he paid no heed to a Roman soldier ordering him to stop. Consequently, he was speared to death. (For more on Archimedes, see vignette 11.) This legend so impressed Germain that she resolved to study mathematics.

Her desire was opposed by her family, who contended that it was improper for women and girls to study mathematics. Undaunted, Germain studied differential calculus at night while her family slept. In fact, she studied so much and slept so little that her parents began to fear for her health. To force her to get the rest she needed, they made sure her bedroom was without a light or a fire. They even took her clothes from her after she had retired for the night so that she would have to stay in bed to keep warm! She pretended to cede to her parents' wishes, but when she was sure they were asleep she wrapped herself in her bedding and

> *...without a doubt she must have the noblest courage, quite extraordinary talents, and a superior genius.*
>
> —Carl Friedrich Gauss of Sophie Germain

> *Algebra is but written geometry, and geometry is but figured algebra.*
>
> —Sophie Germain

devoted herself to her studies, even when it was so cold that the ink in her inkwell froze. Realizing that their daughter was bound and determined to follow her passion, Germain's parents allowed her to study during the day.

A few years later, despite the fact that the École Polytechnique didn't accept women and she was unable to attend, Germain obtained various professors' lecture notes. Having become fascinated with the new field of mathematical analysis being developed by French mathematician **Joseph Louis Lagrange** (1736–1813), she wrote to him with comments about his work, using the pseudonym **M. Le Blanc**. Lagrange was extremely impressed with her comments, and upon learning Germain's true identity, he commended her perceptions. (For more on Joseph Louis Lagrange, see vignette 58.)

In 1801, Germain once more took up pen and paper and wrote to German mathematician **Carl Friedrich Gauss** (1777–1855), offering insights related to his publication *Disquisitiones arithmeticae (Investigations in arithmetic)*. Concerned that Gauss might be prejudiced against a woman mathematician, she again used the pseudonym M. Le Blanc. As did Lagrange before him, Gauss found her comments valuable, and he initiated a correspondence with "Mr. Le Blanc." After several letters, he discovered Germain's true identity. Gauss developed such high esteem for Germain that he recommended, and

Sophie Germain, "philosophe et mathematicienne."
Photo courtesy of Stock Montage, Chicago, Illinois.

©1996 by Key Curriculum Press

was successful in obtaining, an honorary degree for her from the University of Göttingen. (For more on Carl Friedrich Gauss, see vignette 61.)

Germain made valuable contributions in many fields, including chemistry, physics, geography, history, number theory, and philosophy. She worked on mathematical theories involving the study of internal forces occurring in an elastic body subjected to the action of external forces, and published many papers dealing with the nature, bounds, and extent of elastic surfaces. Additionally, the Institut de France awarded her a prize for one of her memoirs, *Memoir on the Vibrations of Elastic Plates,* and several of her theorems were published in works of another French mathematician, **Adrien-Marie Legendre** (1752–1833). ★

Activities

1. Germain intially contacted Gauss because she was interested by the work he was doing in number theory. What is number theory? Choose an era in history in which significant work was accomplished in this branch of mathematics, and research that work.

2. Germain created a theorem that was used in attempts to prove Fermat's Last Theorem. What was Germain's theorem?

3. Why were women discouraged from studying mathematics and science during Sophie Germain's time?

Related Reading

Alic, Margaret. *Hypatia's Heritage*. Boston: Beacon Press, 1986.

Carter, Jack. "Discrete Mathematics: Women in Mathematics." *California Mathematics Council ComMuniCator* (Mar 1993) 10–12.

Edeen, J., S. Edeen, and V. Slachman. *Portraits for Classroom Bulletin Boards—Women Mathematicians.* Palo Alto, CA: Dale Seymour, 1990.

Grinstein, Louise S., and Paul Campbell. *Women of Mathematics: A Bibliographic Sourcebook.* Westport, CT: Greenwood Press, 1987.

Mozans, H.J. *Woman in Science.* Cambridge, MA: MIT Press, 1974.

Phillips, Patricia. *The Scientific Lady: A Social History of Women's Scientific Interests 1520–1918.* New York: St. Martin's Press, 1990.

Spender, Dale. *Women of Ideas and What Men Have Done To Them.* London: HarperCollins, 1990.

Swetz, Frank. *Learning Activities from the History of Mathematics.* Portland, ME: J. Weston Walch, 1994.

Carl Friedrich Gauss: Mathematician of Influence

61

Some of Gauss's accomplishments

- His publication *Disquisitiones arithmeticae* (*Investigations in arithmetic*) is of fundamental importance in the modern theory of numbers.

- A productive inventor, Gauss designed many scientific instruments, including some used in geodesy, the study of the curvature, shape, and dimensions of the earth.

- He further developed the normal distribution curve, now often referred to as the Gaussian curve, first recognized by French mathematician **Abraham De Moivre** (1667–1754).

When German-born **Carl Friedrich Gauss** (1777–1855) was attending primary school, his teacher, J. G. Büttner, asked the class to produce the sum of the first one hundred natural numbers: $1 + 2 + 3 + 4 + \ldots + 97 + 98 + 99 + 100$. Büttner thought this project would keep the class occupied for a good period of time, but the nine-year-old Gauss came up with the solution in a matter of seconds. He realized that there were fifty pairs of numbers $(1 + 100, 2 + 99, 3 + 98, 4 + 97,$ and so on) and that the sum of each pair was 101. Hence, the sum requested by Büttner was simply 50×101, or 5050. Impressed, Büttner not only arranged for Gauss's admittance to a secondary school so that he could study a higher-level curriculum, but he also secured a tutor and advanced textbooks for the young student.

Upon completing his secondary studies at the age of fourteen, Gauss received a stipend from the Duke of Brunswick to attend the newly established Collegium Carolinium, a science academy intended to train local government and military personnel, then the University of Göttingen, and finally the University of Helmstedt. During his years as a student, Gauss made many discoveries and solved many problems that had eluded mathematicians before him. For example, although it had long been known how to construct an equilateral triangle and a regular pentagon with a compass and a straightedge, it was not known how to use these tools to construct other polygons with a prime number of sides. Gauss demonstrated that a regular polygon with seventeen sides could also be constructed with a compass and a straightedge. Additionally, at the age of twenty, in his doctoral dissertation dedicated to his patron the duke, he proved what is called

Carl Friedrich Gauss

©1996 by Key Curriculum Press

the fundamental theorem of algebra (every polynomial equation has a number of solutions equal to its degree).

Among Gauss's many other achievements are his significant contributions to complex number theory, vector analysis, and differential geometry. Much of his work has been influential in the scientific fields. He was the first director of the famous observatory built at Göttingen, and he set a standard of rigorous thinking for future astronomers and scientists—**Albert Einstein** (1879–1955) used Gauss's ideas in works relating to relativity and atomic energy.

For more on Carl Friedrich Gauss, see vignette 60. ★

Activities

1. Use Gauss's technique for adding up consecutive integers to find the given sums.

   a. $1 + 2 + 3 + \ldots + 99{,}999 + 100{,}000$

   b. $762 + 763 + 764 + \ldots + 999 + 1{,}000$

   c. $1 + 2 + 3 + \ldots + (n - 1) + n$, where n is a positive integer

2. Some of Gauss's work involved the triangular numbers: 1, 3, 6, 10, 15, 21, 28, ...

   a. Why are these numbers called triangular numbers?

   b. Gauss asserted that any positive can be written as the sum of, at most, three triangular numbers. Choose some positive integers and check this assertion.

3. What were Gauss's contributions to the field of non-Euclidean geometry?

Related Reading

Bühler, W.K. *Gauss: A Biographical Study.* New York: Springer-Verlag, 1981.

Dunham, William. *Journey Through Genius: The Great Theorems of Mathematics.* Somerset, NJ: John Wiley, 1990.

Dunningham, G.W. *Carl Friedrich Gauss: Titan of Science.* New York: Hafner Publications, 1955.

Hooper, Alfred. *Makers of Mathematics.* New York: Vintage Books, 1948.

Kline, Morris. *Mathematics: An Introduction to Its Spirit and Use.* San Francisco: W.H. Freeman, 1979.

Kramer, Edna. *The Nature and Growth of Modern Mathematics.* Princeton, NJ: Princeton University Press, 1981.

Pappas, Theoni. *More Joy of Mathematics*. San Carlos, CA: Wide World/Tetra, 1991.

Schaaf, William L. *Carl Friedrich Gauss: Prince of Mathematics.* New York: Franklin Watts, 1964.

Wolfe, Harold. *Introduction to Non-Euclidean Geometry.* New York: Holt, Rinehart and Winston, 1945.

MATHEMATICS AND THE ELECTORAL COLLEGE

62

There has not been any science so much esteemed and honored as this of mathematics, nor with so much industry and vigilance become the care of great [people], and labored in by the potentates of the world ....

—Benjamin Franklin

Why aren't United States presidents elected directly by the people? As much as they valued democracy, our country's founders feared that *too much* democracy might be a dangerous thing! They had already decided that George Washington would be the first president, but Benjamin Franklin warned them: "The first man at the helm will be a good one. Nobody knows what sort may come afterwards."

To maintain control over the election process, the founders came up with the idea of the **electoral college**. In this system, each state chose presidential "electors" who voted for two candidates. The number of electors in a state equaled the number of senators and representatives that state had in Congress. The candidate who won a majority of electoral votes would be president, and the second-place finisher would be vice-president. However, if neither candidate received a majority of the electoral votes, the election would be determined in the House of Representatives, where each state had a single vote. When this system was created, the founders believed that no one could win a majority of the electoral votes because there would most likely always be more than two candidates competing. Therefore, the important decisions would always be made by the enlightened Congress!

It wasn't long before the situation anticipated by our founders came about and political parties had more than one presidential candidate. In 1800, Thomas Jefferson and Aaron Burr (Democratic-Republicans) each received 73 electoral votes, John Adams (Federalist) had 65, and Charles C. Pinckney (Federalist) had 64. The House chose Jefferson for president. After the presidential election of 1800, voting for the offices of president and vice-president was separated under the Twelfth Amendment. In 1824, there were four candidates: John Quincy Adams, Andrew Jackson, Henry Clay, and William H. Crawford. Jackson led in the popular vote but failed to win a majority of electoral votes, so the House chose Adams for president.

Today, the candidate who wins the popular vote in a state gets all of that state's electoral votes. In 1988 and 1992, there were 538 electoral votes (435 members of the House, 100 members of the Senate, and 3 electoral votes for the District of Columbia). Electors, who cannot be members of Congress, are chosen for the ceremonial task of casting their state and party's electoral votes on election day—but there is no law that says an elector must vote for his or her party's popularly elected candidate. So, sometimes symbolic protest votes are cast. In 1988, for instance, an elector from West Virginia voted for Lloyd Bentsen rather than his party's choice, Michael Dukakis.

Under the electoral college system, it's possible to win the popular vote and lose an election that is not decided by the House. For example, in 1888, Grover Cleveland won the popular vote, but lost the presidency to Benjamin Harrison in the electoral vote.

In 1979, an attempt to abolish the electoral college and replace it with a simple election was defeated in the Senate. However, every four years many citizens wonder why we keep a voting process that was originally created to deprive the electorate of its voting power. ★

ACTIVITIES

1. A system of voting known as approval voting replaces the "one person, one vote" principle with the "one candidate, one vote" principle. What is approval voting and when might it be effectively used?

2. In what other ways does mathematics play a role in modern elections?

3. *Voting in a democratic society does not always yield conclusive results. Suppose a club has fifty-five voting members and five members running for president: Chin, Vallejo, Pak, Ionesco, and Yager. Members are asked to rank the five candidates from 1 to 5, with 1 being first choice, 2 being second choice, and so on. The results of the ranking are given below.

	1	2	3	4	5
18 members	Chin	Ionesco	Yager	Pak	Vallejo
12 members	Vallejo	Yager	Ionesco	Pak	Chin
10 members	Pak	Vallejo	Yager	Ionesco	Chin
9 members	Ionesco	Pak	Yager	Vallejo	Chin
4 members	Yager	Vallejo	Ionesco	Pak	Chin
2 members	Yager	Pak	Ionesco	Vallejo	Chin

Who wins the election in each case given below?

a. The winner is the candidate with the most first-place votes.

b. There is a run-off between the two candidates receiving the most first-place votes.

c. Five points are given for a first-place vote, four points for a second-place vote, three points for a third-place vote, two points for a fourth-place vote, and one point for a last-place vote.

d. The winner is the person who beats each candidate in a two-person contest.

*Activity invented by Joseph Malkevitch.

RELATED READING

Davis, Kenneth C. *Don't Know Much About History.* New York: Avon Books, 1990.

Paulos, John Allen. *Beyond Numeracy: Ruminations of a Numbers Man.* New York: Alfred A. Knopf, 1991.

The Parallel Postulate

63

For 2,000 years, the five postulates about the physical world that **Euclid** (ca 300 B.C.) established in his *Elements* were accepted as truths. (Postulates are statements accepted as true without proof.) One of these was the famous **parallel postulate**: Given a line *L* and a point *P* not on line *L,* there exists exactly one line in the plane of point *P* and line *L* that contains point *P* and is parallel to line *L.* * For centuries, mathematicians believed that the parallel postulate could be proved using Euclid's other postulates—if so, this would make it a theorem, not a postulate. Many people have made a variety of attempts to show that the parallel postulate is a logical consequence of the other postulates. However, all their attempts failed.

One notable effort was made by Italian Jesuit priest and mathematician **Girolamo Saccheri** (1667–1733), who in 1733 published a book entitled *Euclides ab omni naevo vindicatus* (*Euclid freed of all blemish*). This attempt to free Euclid of flaws was itself flawed, but the book earned Saccheri a place in the history of mathematics—he developed many results that are theorems in Bolyai-Lobachevsky geometry.

Hungarian-born **János Bolyai** (1802–1860) was so absorbed by the parallel line dilemma that his father, fearful for the health of his son, wrote: "For God's sake, I beseech you, give it up. Fear it no less than sensual passions because it, too, may take all your time, and deprive you of your health, peace of mind, and happiness in life."

Bolyai was not dissuaded. He, along with Russian mathematician **Nikolai Lobachevsky** (1792–1856), now shares the credit for creating non-Euclidean geometry. They demonstrated that there are other geometric systems that conform to Euclid's first four postulates, but they are systems in which the parallel postulate is not true. The discovery of non-Euclidean geometries thus established that the parallel postulate is not a logical consequence of the other postulates.

The non-Euclidean geometry of Bolyai and Lobachevsky is called hyperbolic geometry. A much simpler non-Euclidean geometry was created by **Felix Klein** (1849–1925). In the Klein model, the entire universe is confined to the interior of a circle. For example, a line is a chord joining two points on the circle, as shown above right. (The line does not contain the endpoints of the segment because they

Portrait of the young Nikolai Lobachevsky.

*Over the years, many substitutes have been devised to replace Euclid's parallel postulate. The substitute most commonly used in modern United States geometry books was made famous by Scottish physicist and mathematician John Playfair in his *Elements of Geometry* (1795): "Through a given point not on a given line can be drawn only one line parallel to the given line."

©1996 by Key Curriculum Press

are not within the interior of the circle.) Many Euclidean properties are satisfied in the Klein model, but there are some interesting exceptions. Using the definition of parallel lines—two distinct lines in a plane that do not intersect—there are infinitely many lines through a point *P* parallel to a line that does not contain point *P*, as shown below right. (For more on Felix Klein, see vignette 74.)

The discovery of non-Euclidean geometries defied existing human intuition, common sense, and experience—and demonstrated the heights to which our minds can reach.

For more on Euclid and the Elements, *see vignette 15. For more on non-Euclidean geometry, see vignette 66.* ★

Activities

1. Read about the mathematical contributions of French mathematician **Henri Poincaré**. Describe the non-Euclidean "world" he created.

2. Research the Saccheri quadrilateral. How has it been used in attempts to establish a proof of Euclid's parallel postulate?

3. What are some of the features of elliptic geometry, the non-Euclidean geometry of German mathematician **G. F. B. Riemann**? (For information on G. F. B. Riemann, see vignette 66.)

4. Use a plane and a sphere (a sheet of cardboard and a large ball will work) to demonstrate for the class how the geometry of the sphere is different from the geometry of the plane.

5. Read about **Muhammad ibn Musa al-Khwarizmi**'s attempt to prove the parallel postulate. (For information on al-Khwarizmi, see vignette 27.)

Related Reading

Cajori, Florian. *A History of Mathematics.* New York: Chelsea Publishing, 1991.

Fokio, Catherine. "Bring Non-Euclidean Geometry Down to Earth." *Mathematics Teacher* (Sept 1985) 430–431.

Gans, David. *An Introduction to Non-Euclidean Geometry.* New York: Academic Press, 1973.

Henderson, Linda D. *The Fourth-Dimension and Non-Euclidean Geometry in Modern Art.* Princeton, NJ: Princeton University Press, 1983.

Lénárt, István. *Non-Euclidean Adventures on the Lénárt Sphere.* Berkeley, CA: Key Curriculum Press, 1996.

Lockwood, James R., and Garth E. Runion. *Deductive Systems: Finite and Non-Euclidean Geometries.* Reston, VA: National Council of Teachers of Mathematics, 1978.

Miller, Charles, and Vern E. Heeren. *Mathematical Ideas.* Oakland, NJ: Scott Foresman, 1982.

Rosenfeld, B.A. *A History of Non-Euclidean Geometry: Evolution of the Concept of a Geometric Space.* New York: Springer-Verlag, 1988.

Perfect Numbers

64

Pythagoras (572-497 B.C.) and the Pythagoreans promoted the doctrine that all of nature could be explained by numbers, and the Greeks were fascinated with whole numbers and ratios of whole numbers. More than 200 years after Pythagoras, **Euclid** (ca 300 B.C.) defined a perfect number to be a number that is equal to "the sum of its parts." That is, a number is perfect if it is the sum of its proper divisors (all divisors except the number itself). The smallest perfect number is 6. Its proper divisors are 1, 2, and 3, and $1 + 2 + 3 = 6$. The number 16 is not perfect because $1 + 2 + 4 + 8 \neq 16$. The next perfect number after 6 is 28, which equals $1 + 2 + 4 + 7 + 14$.

The search for perfect numbers has long occupied mathematicians. Euclid proved that any number having the form $2^{n-1}(2^n - 1)$, where n is 2 or larger, is a perfect number if the number in parentheses, $2^n - 1$, is a prime. He did not claim that every perfect number had to have this form. **Leonhard Euler** (1707-1783) took this further by proving that every *even* perfect number must have this form. However, to this day no one has found any odd perfect numbers—and no one has been able to prove that there are none! Modern computers searching far into the reaches of our infinite number system have come up empty so far, but this doesn't mean that extremely large odd perfect numbers don't exist. This problem continues to be one of the great unsolved issues in mathematics.

Numbers related to perfect numbers have also long posed a challenge for mathematicians. One number with an interesting story is $2^{67} - 1$, a number once considered to be a Mersenne prime (see sidebar). That this number is, in fact, not a prime was demonstrated by mathematician **Edouard Anatole Lucas** in 1876, but he was unable to provide the factors. In 1903, **Frank Nelson Cole** of Columbia University was slated to speak at a meeting of the American Mathematical Society. However, rather than speak, he worked silently at the blackboard. By multiplying 2 by itself 67 times, then subtracting 1, he came up with the number 147,573,952,588,676,412,927. He then wrote $193,707,721 \times 761,838,257,287$, which again resulted in the number 147,573,952,588,676,412,927. Without the aid of a computer, he'd found the factors for the number $2^{67} - 1$, a feat which had taken him twenty years to accomplish!

For more on the history of numbers, see vignettes 1, 12, 14, 21, 24, 29, 37, 52, and 67. ★

Number Facts

- As of 1990, the largest known perfect number is $2^{19936}(2^{19937} - 1)$, which has 12,003 digits.

- A prime number of the form $2^n - 1$ is called a Mersenne prime, named for French Minimite friar **Marin Mersenne** (1588-1648). Euclid's formula shows that Mersenne primes are factors of even perfect numbers. In January 1994, Cray Research found the latest Mersenne prime: $2^{859433} - 1$. It has 258,716 digits!

- Of the eight smallest perfect numbers, the largest is 2,305,843,008,139,952,128.

Activities

1. What are some perfect numbers other than 6 and 28?

2. Comment on this quote by **Thomas Augustus**, also known as St. Augustine.

   Six is a number perfect in itself, and not because God created all things in six days; rather the inverse is true, that God created all things in six days because this number is perfect, and it would remain perfect, even if the work of the six days did not exist.

3. If n is a perfect number, show that the sum of all its divisors, including the number itself, is $2n$.

4. A number is said to be deficient if the sum of its proper divisors is less than the number itself. A number is said to be abundant if the sum of its proper divisors is greater than the number itself. Write a program on a computer or on a graphing calculator that determines whether a number is perfect, deficient, or abundant.

Related Reading

Bezuszka, Stanley, and Margaret Kenney. *Number Treasury*. Palo Alto, CA: Dale Seymour, 1982.

———. Mary Farrey, and Margaret Kenney. *Contemporary Motivated Mathematics*, Book 3. Chestnut Hill, MA: Boston College Press, 1980.

Dunham, William. *The Mathematical Universe: An Alphabetical Journey Through the Great Proofs, Problems, and Personalities*. New York: John Wiley, 1994.

Ellis, Keith. *Number Power in Nature and in Everyday Life*. New York: St. Martin's Press, 1978.

Shoemaker, Richard W. *Perfect Numbers*. Reston, VA: National Council of Teachers of Mathematics, 1973.

Mary Somerville: The Trailblazer

65

Scottish-born mathematician **Mary Fairfax Somerville** (1780–1872) was ten years old when her father sent her to a boarding school so she could learn social graces and become educated. However, Somerville had little interest in the memorization type of education provided at that school. Not only was she unhappy, but after one year, she was also a poor writer and speller. Her parents let her come home, and when she was thirteen years old, she attended another school. There she discovered that she liked working with numbers, and she developed an interest in the night sky, reflecting her keen interest in nature. As she read books on astronomy and elementary mathematics, she realized she would have to study higher mathematics to understand more of what she was observing. Somerville's relatives, though, were concerned about her constant desire to read. In those days, some feared that girls and women were too frail to withstand much book study!

It was a number puzzle in a fashion magazine that really sparked Somerville's interest in pursuing a quality mathematics education. In addition to numbers, the puzzle contained the letters x and y. This interested Somerville, and she learned that the puzzle involved a branch of mathematics known as algebra. Despite her relatives' concerns about her mental health, she eagerly read mathematics books secretly supplied by her younger brother's tutor. While her family slept, she studied algebra and Euclid's *Elements* by candlelight at night. (For more on Euclid's *Elements,* see vignette 15.) When her parents became aware of her nocturnal reading and removed her candles, she worked the problems out in her head.

> *She took the liveliest interest in all that has been done of late years to extend high education to women both classical and scientific and hailed the establishment of the Ladies' College at Girton as a great step in the true direction and one which could not fail to obtain most important results.*
> —Martha Somerville, daughter of Mary Somerville

After her first husband died, Somerville and her children moved in with her parents, and she resolved to devote her life to the study of mathematics. As a grown woman, she could openly study the subjects she loved, and she was encouraged to do so by the Edinburgh intellectual community. She eventually remarried. Her second husband, William Somerville, was extremely supportive of her mathematical interests and even studied with her at times.

Lack of a formal education was only a minor handicap for Somerville. She created her own personal library with books on algebra, geometry, logarithms, calculus, physics, astronomy, and probability theory. In addition to publishing many articles and papers, she translated into English **Pierre-Simon Laplace**'s *Traité de mécanique céleste (Treatise on celestial mechanics),* a discussion of the mathematics of contemporary astronomy. Laplace's manuscript contained only a few solutions to the many complex problems he presented. In answer to this, Somerville included in her first book, *The Mechanism of the Heavens* (1831), the solutions to his problems. Her book was an instant success and she received much praise throughout England. Somerville went on to publish three more books, and she received many honors and honorary degrees. In 1835, both she and **Caroline Herschel** were named as the first honorary female members of the Royal Astronomical Society. (For more on Caroline Herschel, see vignette 94.)

Engraved portrait of Mary Fairfax Somerville.
Illustration courtesy of Stock Montage, Chicago, Illinois.

In addition to her mathematical work, Somerville was an active promoter of equal rights for women in education. She will no doubt long be remembered for her efforts in opening the doors of opportunity in mathematics and science for all women. ★

Activities

1. Research the life and contributions of **Catherine Beecher** (1800–1878), a pioneer in American mathematics education.

2. Somerville was a source of inspiration for **Ada Byron Lovelace**. How did these two women meet? How did Somerville encourage Lovelace in mathematics? (For information on Ada Byron Lovelace, see vignette 70.)

3. Construct an epicycloid, a curve generated by a point on the circumference of a circle that rolls on the outside of a fixed circle. How is this curve similar to and different from Agnesi's curve? (For information on Maria Agnesi and Agnesi's curve, see vignette 55.)

Engraved plate from Somerville's **On the Connexion of the Physical Sciences** *(London, 1834).*

Related Reading

Alic, Margaret. *Hypatia's Heritage*. **Boston: Beacon Press, 1986.**

Baum, Joan. *The Calculating Passion of Ada Byron*. Hamden, CT: Archon Books, 1987.

Goodsell, Willystine. *Pioneers of Women's Education in the United States*. New York: McGraw Hill, 1931.

Gornick, Vivian. *Women in Science: Portraits from a World in Transition*. New York: Simon and Schuster, 1983.

Grinstein, Louise S., and Paul Campbell. *Women of Mathematics: A Bibliographic Sourcebook*. Westport, CT: Greenwood Press, 1987.

Johnson, Art. *Classical Math: History Topics for the Classroom*. **Palo Alto, CA: Dale Seymour, 1994.**

Kenshaft, Patricia (ed). *Winning Women into Mathematics*. Washington, DC: Mathematical Association of America, 1991.

Perl, Teri. *Women and Numbers: Lives of Women Mathematicians plus Discovery Activities*. **San Carlos, CA: Wide World/Tetra, 1993.**

Phillips, Patricia. *The Scientific Lady: A Social History of Women's Scientific Interests 1520–1918*. New York: St. Martin's Press, 1990.

HISTORY OF MATH

Mathematical People of the 1800s

66

T he discovery of non-Euclidean geometries and other mathematical "oddities," such as quaternions, made the 1800s an age of uncertainty for mathematicians. The realization that mathematical laws established in the past were not universal truths caused mathematicians and educators to examine what they now saw to be shaky foundations. During this time, many people took advantage of these and other uncertainties, moving beyond traditional roles and ways of thinking.

José Anastácio da Cunha (1744–1787): After Portuguese mathematician da Cunha served as an officer during the French and Spanish invasion of Portugal in 1762, he wrote a memoir on ballistics, the study of projectiles such as bullets or bombs. As a result of his work, he was appointed to the chair of geometry at the University of Coimbra in 1773. A decade later, he introduced in his *Principios Mathematicos (Mathematical Principles,* 1782) the notion of convergence, an important concept in calculus. Although *Principios* was translated into French in 1811, it was not noticed in the faraway French and German mathematical communities. Thus, when French mathematical physicist **Augustin-Louis Cauchy** (1789–1857) developed the concept of convergence independently in 1821, his work, not da Cunha's, was used in the modern development of calculus.

Georg Friedrich Bernhard Riemann (1826–1866): The 1851 doctoral dissertation of this German mathematician led to the concept of Riemann surfaces. In turn, these aided the development of the branch of mathematics known as topology, the study of properties of geometric forms that do not change under transformations such as bending or stretching. Riemann is also the creator of a non-Euclidean geometry that fits physical space. A theorem from his geometry states: All lines perpendicular to a straight line meet in a point. In Euclidean geometry, such lines would be parallel. If Riemann's theorem seems unreasonable to you, think of all the lines on the earth's surface that are perpendicular to the equator—they are called great circles. (For more on non-Euclidean geometry, see vignette 63.)

Mary Everest Boole (1832–1916): Boole taught herself calculus, but she is probably better known for her innovative realization that students can learn mathematics and science through hands-on activities, as contrasted to rote memorization. By developing successful teaching methods that took advantage of natural materials and children's imagination, Boole made educators think about *how* children learn.

French mathematician Henri Poincaré (1854–1912) firmly believed that mathematics could be used to describe physical reality. Heavily influenced by the work of Riemann, he was the first to use topological methods in algebraic geometry and is credited with being the founder of modern topology.

Maggie Lena Walker. Photo courtesy of the United States Department of the Interior.

©1996 by Key Curriculum Press

Maggie Lena Walker (1867-1934): United States entrepreneur Walker applied her mathematics education in business to become a nationally prominent community leader. When she was fourteen years old, she joined the Independent Order of St. Luke, a burial society that promoted humanitarian causes and cared for the sick and aged. A member of the organization for over fifty years, her business acumen and public relations skills were instrumental to the organization's success. In 1903, she founded the St. Luke Penny Savings Bank, serving as its first president. In doing so, she became the first woman bank president in the United States. Now called The Consolidated Bank and Trust Company, the bank continues to thrive as the oldest African American–operated financial institution in the United States. ★

Cauchy's 789 publications put him second only to Leonhard Euler in written output. Calculus students frequently find his name in textbooks—there is the Cauchy root test, the Cauchy ratio test, the Cauchy inequality, Cauchy's integral formula, and Cauchy-Riemann differential equations.

Activities

1. Read about the considerable impact **Mary Dolciani** (1923-1985) had on modern mathematics education. Why were some of her ideas considered controversial?

2. Read about the work of German mathematician **Richard Dedekind** (1831-1916) and its relation to the logical development of the real number system. What is a Dedekind cut?

3. What were some of the contributions Augustin-Louis Cauchy made to the study of complex numbers? (For information on complex numbers, see vignette 37.)

4. Why is German mathematician **Karl Weierstrass** (1815-1897) considered by some to have been one of the world's greatest mathematics teachers?

Related Reading

Burton, David. *The History of Mathematics: An Introduction*. Boston: Allyn and Bacon, 1985.

Dauben, J.W. (ed). *The History of Mathematics from Antiquity to the Present. A Selected Bibliography*. New York: Garland, 1985.

Dedron, P., and J. Itard. *Mathematics and Mathematicians*, Vols I and II. London: Transworld Publications, 1973.

Eves, Howard. *Great Moments in Mathematics After 1650*. Washington, DC: Mathematical Association of America, 1982.

Fauvel, John, and Jeremy Gray. *The History of Mathematics, A Reader*. Dobbs Ferry, NY: Sheridan House, 1987.

Vare, Ethlie Ann, and Greg Ptacek. *Mothers of Invention, from the Bra to the Bomb: Forgotten Women and Their Unforgettable Ideas*. New York: Morrow, 1988.

©1996 by Key Curriculum Press

Two Who Shocked the World of Mathematics

The modern age of mathematics began in 1800. Prior to this time, mathematicians had thought the study of mathematics was a search for truth. However, with the discovery of such "new" mathematics as non-Euclidean geometries, intellectuals began to seriously question whether the laws of mathematics were really of divine origin rather than of human creation.

Nineteenth-century mathematicians were dealt an additional shock by Irish mathematician **William Rowan Hamilton** (1805–1865). During his time, it seemed inconceivable to mathematical thinkers that there could be a consistent and logical algebra with a structure contrary to that of the common algebra of arithmetic—that's the algebra taught in schools today. However, Hamilton invented a new type of number, a vectorlike quantity called a quaternion. The laws of operation in quaternion algebra are the same as those of ordinary algebra—except that the commutative law for multiplication that we take for granted doesn't hold. That is, if a and b are quaternions, then it doesn't follow that $a \times b = b \times a$. In fact, in this system, $a \times b = -b \times a$. With Hamilton's creation, mathematicians realized that the basic laws of common algebra are not universal truths. His work led to the invention of other useful algebras and paved the way for modern abstract algebra.

Englishman **George Boole** (1815–1864), while a professor of mathematics in Ireland, began to concentrate on the logic used in the construction of algebraic systems. In his book *An Investigation of the Laws of Thought* (1854), Boole established the foundations for modern symbolic logic, and in the process he created a new algebra, now called Boolean algebra. He demonstrated that the process of logical reasoning can be carried out using algebraic symbols. (For more on logic, see vignettes 13, 68, 72, and 77.) An example of Boolean algebra is shown in the sidebar.

William Rowan Hamilton has been described as an eighteenth-century man living in the nineteenth century and speaking to the twentieth.

One of the mathematical innovators of his century, Boole's ideas are applied in many of today's fields, including circuit design, probability, insurance, and information theory. ★

Activities

1. Consider the set of two-by-two matrices. Show that addition of matrices is commutative, but multiplication of matrices is not.

2. What is the principle of least action, developed by **Leonhard Euler** and **Joseph Louis Lagrange** and later generalized by Hamilton?

3. The equation $x + (1 - x) = 1$ is a representation of the law of the excluded middle, developed by Boole. What is this law?

Related Reading

Bochenski, I.M. *A History of Formal Logic*. South Bend, IN: Notre Dame University Press, 1961.

Hankins, T.L. *Sir William Rowan Hamilton*. Baltimore: Johns Hopkins University Press, 1980.

Johnson, Art. *Classical Math: History Topics for the Classroom*. Palo Alto, CA: Dale Seymour, 1994.

MacHale, Desmond. *George Boole: His Life and Work*. Dublin, Ireland: Boole Press, 1985.

Papert, Seymour. *Mindstorms*. New York: Basic Books, 1980.

Resnikoff, H.L., and R.O. Wells. *Mathematics in Civilization*. Mineola, NY: Dover, 1985.

Swetz, Frank. *Learning Activities from the History of Mathematics*. Portland, ME: J. Weston Walch, 1994.

Wilder, Raymond. *The Evolution of Mathematical Concepts*. New York: John Wiley, 1968.

De Morgan: Caring Teacher

A teacher for many years at London University, **Augustus De Morgan** (1806–1871), was an outstanding mathematics teacher and contributed much to this academic discipline. It is not only his academic accomplishments that make him a legend in mathematics history, but also his generous spirit.

De Morgan was a kind man with strong convictions. He was an outspoken advocate of women's rights and encouraged women to study mathematics during a time when women's education was considered to be of low priority. So committed was he to this, he provided mathematical lectures to women's classes without charge. He argued against religious affectations and failed to qualify for his graduate degree at Cambridge University because he objected to the required religious tests. Nevertheless, his academic ability earned him a teaching position at London University. He genuinely cared about his students, and he gained their affection with his insight, creativity, and sense of humor. It was important to him that his students learn the material he taught, so he encouraged cooperative learning and the use of take-home exams. Shunning honorary degrees and a membership in England's Royal Society, he instead devoted his life to his family, his students, and his friends.

As a mathematician, De Morgan wrote texts on algebra, trigonometry, differential and integral calculus, the calculus of variations, and probability. His book *Trigonometry and Double Algebra* (1849) established some of the foundations for modern abstract algebra, and he developed many laws of probability in his *Essay on Probabilities* (1838). Perhaps his best remembered mathematical contributions are two laws of symbolic logic known as De Morgan's laws. One of these laws states that the negation of the statement *"P and Q"* is equivalent to the statement *"not P or not Q."* The second law states that the negation of the statement *"P or Q"* is equivalent to the statement *"not P and not Q."* Additionally, De Morgan worked on the famous four-color map problem. He tried to prove that four colors are sufficient to color any map on a plane so that areas with common boundaries are colored differently—this assertion was not actually proved until 1976. A lover of puzzles and paradoxes, his famous book *A Budget of Paradoxes* (1872) remained in print for much of the twentieth century.

For more on logic, see vignettes 13, 67, 72, and 77. For more on the four-color map problem, see vignette 98. ★

> *Great fleas have little fleas upon their backs to bite 'em,*
> *And little fleas have lesser fleas, and so ad infinitum.*
> *And the great fleas themselves, in turn, have greater fleas to go on;*
> *While these again have greater still, and greater still, and so on.*
>
> —Augustus De Morgan

Activities

1. Born in 1806, De Morgan once made this true statement: "I was x years old in the year x^2." What is the value of x?

2. De Morgan, along with British algebraists **George Peacock** (1791–1858) and **Duncan Farquharson Gregory** (1813–1844), was among the first to notice the presence of structure in algebra. Elaborate on this discovery.

3. De Morgan's laws, stated in terms of sets, are shown below. Use the Venn diagrams given below to demonstrate the equivalency of the indicated sets. (The notation A' refers to the complement of A; that is, all elements not in the set A.)

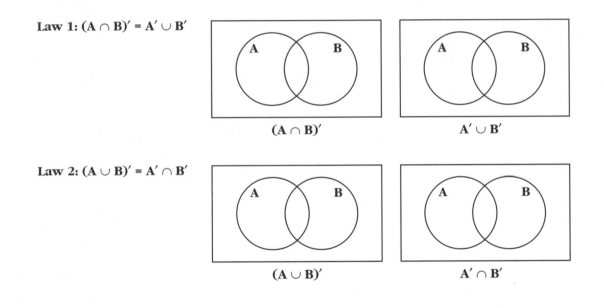

Law 1: $(A \cap B)' = A' \cup B'$

$(A \cap B)'$ $A' \cup B'$

Law 2: $(A \cup B)' = A' \cap B'$

$(A \cup B)'$ $A' \cap B'$

Related Reading

Boyer, Carl. *A History of Mathematics,* 2nd ed rev. Uta C. Merzbach. New York: John Wiley, 1991.

Cundy, H. Martyn, and A.P. Rollette. *Mathematical Models.* London: Oxford University Press, 1974.

De Morgan, Augustus. *A Budget of Paradoxes.* D.E. Smith (ed). Chicago: Open Court Publishing, 1915.

Eves, Howard. *An Introduction to the History of Mathematics.* **New York: Holt, Rinehart and Winston, 1990.**

Hollingdale, Stuart. *Makers of Mathematics.* **New York: Penguin Books, 1989.**

Kline, Morris. *Mathematics: The Loss of Certainty.* **New York: Oxford University Press, 1980.**

Kolpas, Sidney J. "Augustus De Morgan." *California Mathematics Council ComMuniCator* (June 1990) 24.

The Short Career of Galois

Born in a small village near Paris, **Evariste Galois** (1811–1832) established his mark in mathematics history as a highly original mathematician. One of his many accomplishments was to found the modern branch of mathematics known as group theory. His discoveries in this field resulted from his work with algebraic equations. For hundreds of years, mathematicians before Galois had sought to find algebraic methods to solve fifth-, sixth-, and higher-degree equations. Formulas and methods to solve equations of lesser degree had already been discovered—high school algebra students know that the second-degree equation $ax^2 + bx + c = 0$ can be solved using the well-known quadratic formula. Galois was the first to realize and to demonstrate that general polynomials with degree higher than four cannot be solved by algebraic means.

Galois is remembered not only for his many mathematical contributions, but also for his troubled and frustrating life.

Portrait of Evariste Galois from the first edition of Leopold Infeld's **Whom the Gods Love: The Story of Evariste Galois** *(New York, 1995).*

- His well-educated parents had little aptitude for mathematics, and so were not able to nurture his ability. However, Galois did acquire from them an implacable hatred of tyranny.

- As a boy, Galois's routine, mediocre classwork failed to challenge him, but he read and understood some of the works of such mathematicians as Niels Henrick Abel, Joseph Louis Lagrange, and Adrien-Marie Legendre. His teachers regarded him as eccentric.

- When he was 16 years old, Galois knew he had special mathematical abilities, but he was twice rejected at the École Polytechnique, a school that had nurtured many celebrated mathematicians.

- When he was 17 years old, a paper Galois wrote for the École Polytechnique in hopes of gaining admission was apparently lost by highly respected mathematician Augustin-Louis Cauchy.

- Galois entered the École Normale to prepare for teaching, but he was expelled as a result of a highly critical letter he wrote to the director.

- In frustration and disillusionment, he entered the National Guard—and was twice arrested for allegedly threatening the life of King Louis-Philippe.

- On May 30, 1832, at the age of 20, Galois was killed in a duel.

- Legend has it that Galois recorded the bulk of his life's work in an almost unintelligible 31-page document, scribbled during the night before his fatal duel.

Don't the events of Galois's twenty years of life make him sound like a fictional literary character? We can only wonder what he might have accomplished with some encouragement. ★

Activities

1. A group is one of the simplest, yet one of the most important, of mathematical systems. A group has just one operation—such as multiplication or addition—and four postulates. What are the four group postulates?

2. Show that the set of integers is a group under the operation of addition but not under the operation of multiplication.

3. There are many interesting groups that do not involve sets of numbers. Find some examples of such groups.

4. What is a Galois field?

Related Reading

Bell, E.T. *Men of Mathematics.* New York: Simon and Schuster, 1986.

———. *The Development of Mathematics.* Mineola, NY: Dover, 1992.

Daintith, John, and R.D. Nelson (eds). *Dictionary of Mathematics.* New York: Penguin Books, 1989.

Edwards, H.M. *Galois Theory.* New York: Springer Publications, 1984.

Infeld, Leopold. *Whom the Gods Love: The Story of Evariste Galois.* Reston, VA: National Council of Teachers of Mathematics, 1978.

Johnson, Art. *Classical Math: History Topics for the Classroom.* Palo Alto, CA: Dale Seymour, 1994.

Peterson, Ivars. *Islands of Truth: A Mathematical Mystery Cruise.* New York: W.H. Freeman, 1990.

ADA LOVELACE: FIRST COMPUTER PROGRAMMER

Today, computer technology influences many cutting-edge developments in such fields as medicine, education, and the arts. In the nineteenth century, **Ada Byron Lovelace** (1815–1852) rode the wave of innovation with her computer programming ideas—ideas that are still used today.

Ada Byron was raised by her mother's family, who encouraged her to study mathematics, hiring respected tutors for her. Despite severe headaches that affected her eyesight and paralysis in her legs that made movement difficult, Ada Byron was a gifted musician and liked constructing mechanical playthings. She enjoyed mathematics and spent considerable time reading about and working with algebra and geometry. She developed tremendous admiration for one of her mathematics tutors, **Mary Fairfax Somerville** (1780–1872), the "first lady of British mathematics." Eventually, the two became friends, the older woman supportive of the younger's mathematical interests. (For more on Mary Fairfax Somerville, see vignette 65.)

In 1833, Somerville introduced Ada Byron Lovelace (by then married to William King, Earl of Lovelace) to **Charles Babbage**, who invited her to view his Difference Engine, a calculating machine meant to run on steam power. Lovelace was enthralled by his invention and the two became close friends. Because Babbage's device was badly needed in England's shipping industry, the government granted him money to continue his work. Unfortunately the money ran out, but another of his machines interested Lovelace, and she encouraged Babbage to devote his attention to it. It was called the Analytical Engine—and its logical structure is used today in electronic digital computers. Lovelace developed the "logic" that made the Analytical Engine run and programmed the engine with this logic. Additionally, she observed that there were frequent situations where repeated calculations of a certain type were needed, so she conceived of the concept of a subroutine with a loop. Looping and recursion, another important programming technique recognized by Lovelace, is used to this day.

Ada Byron Lovelace. Illustration courtesy of Stock Montage, Chicago, Illinois.

A highlight of her career was the publication of a paper she had written with a colleague of Babbage's, describing the Analytical Engine, its potential, and its limitations. In addition to developing the subject of programming in the paper, Lovelace suggested the possibility of the computer being used to compose music. However, the paper was published without any mention of her involvement, and it was many years before it was widely known that she had authored most of it.

In honor of Lovelace's contributions to the development of the computer, the Department of Defense named the computer programming language ADA after her in 1979.

For more on computation, see vignettes 39, 83, 84, and 88. ★

ACTIVITIES

1. What association did mathematician **Augustus De Morgan** have with Lovelace? How did he influence her mathematical interests?

2. The binary system (base 2) was considered as a numerical system for the Analytical Engine.

   a. Fill in the missing conversions from base 10 to base 2.

   $0 = (0)_2$ $1 = (1)_2$ $2 = (10)_2$ $3 = (11)_2$ $4 =$ ____ $5 =$ ____

   $6 = (110)_2$ $7 =$ ____ $8 =$ ____ $9 =$ ____ $10 = (1010)_2$

   $11 =$ ____ $12 =$ ____

   b. Convert the following binary numbers to base 10.

   $(1011)_2 =$ ____ $(10001)_2 =$ ____ $(110110)_2 =$ ____

   $(1000000)_2 =$ ____

   c. Why is the binary system particularly suited for use in electronics and in computer programming?

3. Many modern computers and graphing calculators use the octal system (base 8). Perform some computations in this system. Other computers and graphing calculators use the hexadecimal system (base 16). The digits in this system are {0, 1, 2, 3, 4, 5, 6, 7, 8, 9, A, B, C, D, E, F}. Perform some computations in this system.

RELATED READING

Alic, Margaret. *Hypatia's Heritage*. Boston: Beacon Press, 1986.

Baum, Joan. *The Calculating Passion of Ada Byron*. Hamden, CT: Archeon Books, 1986.

Crowley, Mary L. "The 'Difference' in Babbage's Difference Engine." *Mathematics Teacher* (May 1985) 366–372, 354.

Johnson, Art. *Classical Math: History Topics for the Classroom*. Palo Alto, CA: Dale Seymour, 1994.

Logdson, Tom. *Computers and Social Controversy*. Rockville, MD: Computer Science Press, 1980.

Pappas, Theoni. *More Joy of Mathematics*. San Carlos, CA: Wide World/Tetra, 1991.

Perl, Teri. *Women and Numbers: Lives of Women Mathematicians plus Discovery Activities*. San Carlos, CA: Wide World/Tetra, 1993.

Schiebinger, Linda. *The Mind Has No Sex? Women in the Origins of Modern Science*. Cambridge, MA: Harvard University Press, 1989.

Toole, Betty Alexandra. *Ada, the Enchantress of Numbers*. Mill Valley, CA: Strawberry Press, 1992.

Pythagoras and President Garfield

James Abram Garfield (1831–1881) was sworn in as the twentieth United States president on March 4, 1881. The last president to be born in a log cabin, he was also the first in some respects: He was the first president to have his mother present during his inauguration ceremonies, the first to view an inaugural parade from a stand in front of the White House, and the first to be left-handed. In fact, he was ambidextrous and would entertain friends by simultaneously writing a statement in Greek with one hand and in Latin with the other.

Another of Garfield's firsts was that he has been the only United States president to develop a proof for the Pythagorean theorem, which he wrote in 1876 while still a member of the House of Representatives. Although the theorem is named after **Pythagoras** (ca 572–497 B.C.), historical records suggest that it was known to the Chinese and the Babylonians centuries before Pythagoras. Several hundred different proofs of the Pythagorean theorem have been recorded, so Garfield's proof doesn't rank among the greatest of mathematical accomplishments. Still, it is historically interesting and quite eloquent. It makes use of the fact that the area of a trapezoid is half the product of its altitude multiplied by the sum of the lengths of its parallel bases.

Garfield used three right triangles to form a trapezoid, as shown at right. The area of the trapezoid is the sum of the areas of the triangles. Hence:

$$\tfrac{1}{2}(a + b)(a + b) = \tfrac{1}{2}ab + \tfrac{1}{2}ab + \tfrac{1}{2}c^2$$
$$(a + b)(a + b) = ab + ab + c^2$$
$$a^2 + 2ab + b^2 = 2ab + c^2$$
$$a^2 + b^2 = c^2$$

His proof was published in the *New England Journal of Education* on April 1, 1876.

Garfield's time in office was brief. As he was leaving Washington on July 2, 1881, to attend the twenty-fifth reunion of his class at Williams College in Massachusetts, he was shot in the back by a disappointed office seeker, Charles J. Guiteau. Surgeons could not locate the bullet—Alexander Graham Bell even made an unsuccessful attempt to locate it with an electrical device. Lacking modern-day x-ray equipment and antibiotics, Garfield succumbed to infection and died on September 19, 1881. ★

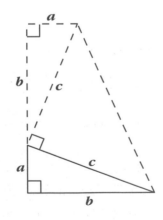

Activities

1. History records over 100 different proofs of the Pythagorean theorem. Research some of these proofs.

2. Use interactive geometry software to make a model of Garfield's proof of the Pythagorean theorem.

3. Chinese mathematicians were familiar with the Pythagorean theorem hundreds of years before Pythagoras. One of the oldest known proofs of the theorem is suggested in an ancient Chinese figure known as the *xian tu.* The figure shown at left is based on the *xian tu,* and it displays a large square made up of four congruent right triangles and a small square. The sides of one of the right triangles are labeled a, b, and c. The area of the large square is c^2 square units. Copy the figure (it may be easier to work with if you enlarge it), cut along the dotted lines, and rearrange the four triangles and the small square to demonstrate that $a^2 + b^2 = c^2$.

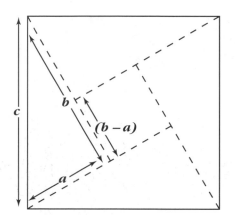

Related Reading

Bennett, Dan. *Pythagoras Plugged In: Proofs and Problems for The Geometer's Sketchpad.* Berkeley, CA: Key Curriculum Press, 1995.

Jeffries, Ona Griffin. *In and Out of the White House.* New York: Wilfred Funk, 1960.

Kane, Joseph Nathan. *Facts About the Presidents.* New York: W.H. Wilson, 1974.

Kolpas, Sidney J. *The Pythagorean Theorem: Eight Classic Proofs.* Palo Alto, CA: Dale Seymour, 1992.

Loomis, Elisha S. *The Pythagorean Proposition.* Washington, DC: National Council of Teachers of Mathematics, 1968.

Pappas, Theoni. *The Joy of Mathematics*. San Carlos, CA: Wide World/Tetra, 1989.

Swetz, Frank, and T.I. Kao. *Was Pythagoras Chinese? An Examination of Right Triangle Theory in Ancient China.* Reston, VA: National Council of Teachers of Mathematics, 1977.

HISTORY OF MATH

72

Lewis Carroll: Mathematician of Fantasy

Charles Lutwidge Dodgson (1832–1898) was a mathematics teacher at Oxford University in England. Under the pseudonym **Lewis Carroll**, he authored the famous children's classics *Alice's Adventures in Wonderland* and *Through the Looking-Glass.* Less well known are his books and pamphlets on mathematical subjects, including *Enunciations of Euclid* (1863), *Guide to the Mathematical Student* (1864), *Euclid and His Modern Rivals* (1879), and *Euclid I and II* (1882).

Carroll enjoyed inverting things—he wrote letters that had to be read from the last word to the first word, for instance. This principle of inversion also appears in many of his stories. In *Looking-Glass,* after running very fast for a period of time:

Alice and the Red Queen, illustrated by John Tenniel.

> *Alice looked around her in great surprise. "Why I do believe we've been under this tree the whole time! Everything's just as it was!"*
>
> *"Of course it is," said the Queen. "What would you have it?"*
>
> *"Well, in our country," said Alice, still panting a little, "you'd generally get to somewhere else—if you ran very fast for a long time as we've been doing."*
>
> *"A very slow sort of country!" said the Queen. "Now, here, you see, it takes all the running you can do, to keep in the same place."*

In the real world, speed = $^{distance}/_{time}$. If time is a constant, then the higher the speed, the greater the distance covered. However, in *Looking-Glass* we see the inversion process: speed = $^{time}/_{distance}$. In this mixed-up place, if time is constant, then the higher the speed, the *smaller* the distance covered. Another logical contradiction arises when Alice says, "I am so hot and thirsty," and the Queen replies, "I know what you'd like! Have a biscuit?" Offering a biscuit to a thirsty person doesn't make any sense to us, but it is certainly appropriate in the world of humorous contradictions and reality inversions described in *Alice's Adventures* and *Looking-Glass.*

__The Cheshire Cat,__
__illustrated by John Tenniel.__

Perhaps you've read this famous exchange between Alice and the Cheshire Cat:

> *"But I don't want to go among mad people," Alice remarked.*
>
> *"Oh, you can't help that," said the Cat: "we're all mad here. I'm mad. You're mad."*
>
> *"How do you know I'm mad?" said Alice.*
>
> *"You must be," said the Cat, "or you wouldn't have come here."*
>
> *Alice didn't think he proved it at all.*

The Cat justifies a statement equivalent to "If you're here, you must be mad" by merely reversing the premise and conclusion, saying, "If you're mad, you must be here." Alice doesn't buy the Cat's argument. Smart girl! If the Cat's inversion technique represented a valid argument process, then in geometry one could prove the statement "If a quadrilateral is a rectangle, then it is a square" (a false statement) by merely stating "If a quadrilateral is a square, then it is a rectangle" (a true statement). Alice would probably have been a good geometry student.

Lewis Carroll was truly a master of the art of nonsense—the fact that he was also a clever mathematician makes his literary works all the more interesting.

For more on logic, see vignettes 13, 67, 68, and 77. ★

Activities

1. Carroll's *Pillow Problems* is a collection of 72 mathematical problems involving arithmetic, algebra, geometry, trigonometry, calculus, and probability. Read this book and solve some of its problems. Why is it titled *Pillow Problems*?

2. Alice frequently gets entangled in a verbal jungle. For example, the White Knight tells Alice he has written a song, and "...either it will bring tears into their eyes or else—." Somewhat perplexed, Alice asks "Or else what?" How does the Knight respond?

3. Lewis Carroll loved puzzles, and he created one called a doublet. To solve this puzzle, you start with a word and transform it into another word by changing one letter at a time. The only catch is that each change you make must result in a new word. An example, changing PIG into STY, is given below.

   PIG → PIT → PAT → SAT → SAY → STY

   Why don't you try to solve some doublets? Change (a) CAT into DOG, (b) CAR into JET, (c) COOL into BELT, (d) GRASS into GREEN, (e) ONE into TWO, and (f) WINTER into SUMMER.

4. Create some of your own doublets.

Related Reading

Bergamini, David (ed). *Mathematics: Life Science Library.* **New York: Time-Life Books, 1972.**

Carroll, Lewis. *Pillow Problems and A Tangled Tale.* Mineola, NY: Dover, 1958.

Gardner, Martin. *More Annotated Alice.* New York: Random House, 1990.

Kelly, Richard. *Lewis Carroll.* Boston: G.K. Hall, 1977.

Pappas, Theoni. *More Joy of Mathematics.* **San Carlos, CA: Wide World/Tetra, 1991.**

THREE ANCIENT UNSOLVABLE PROBLEMS

73

I n the nineteenth century, it was proved that the three geometric constructions presented in this vignette can't be accomplished with Euclidean tools (a compass and an unmarked straightedge).* Yet, for 2,000 years mathematicians believed these constructions were possible! Ancient Greek mathematicians were the first to attempt to unlock the secret to these constructions, and in the process they developed vast amounts of useful mathematics—including the discovery and development of the conic sections.
(For more on conic sections, see vignette 16.)

Problem 1: Trisect an angle.

It's possible to trisect specific angles, such as a right angle, but this problem asks us to trisect *any* angle. It's possible, of course, to "eyeball in" two rays that approximate the rays of trisection.

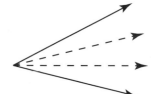

Problem 2: Construct the edge of a cube having twice the volume of a given cube.

If c is an edge of the given cube and x is the segment to be constructed, then the relation between c and x is given by $2c^3 = x^3$. According to legend, this problem originated with the mythical King Minos, who was dissatisfied with the size of a tomb constructed for his son. Minos wanted the volume of the tomb doubled.

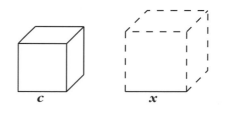

Problem 3: Construct a square having an area equal to that of a given circle.

If r is the radius of the given circle and x is a side of the desired square, then $\pi r^2 = x^2$. Greek mathematician **Anaxagoras** (ca 450 B.C.) was the first to work on this problem. ★

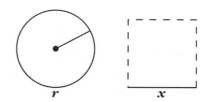

*A very thorough discussion of the three problems in this vignette can be found in Howard Eve's *An Introduction to the History of Mathematics*—see Related Reading.

ACTIVITIES

1. List the measures of some specific angles that can be trisected with a compass and a straightedge.

2. The proof that it is impossible to trisect a general angle with Euclidean tools uses the trigonometry identity $\cos ß = 4 \cos^3 \frac{ß}{3} - 3 \cos \frac{ß}{3}$. Prove this identity. [Hint: Start with $\cos ß = \cos(\frac{2ß}{3} + \frac{ß}{3})$.]

3. Research the Greek mathematician **Hippocrates of Chios** (ca 440 B.C.). What was the theory of lunes that he discovered while attempting to square the circle?

4. A method for constructing a circle with the same area as a given square is described in the ancient Indian mathematical works called the *Sulvasutras*. Research this method to see if it actually works. (You can find a description of this construction process in Frank Swetz's *Learning Activities from the History of Mathematics*—see Related Reading.)

RELATED READING

Bold, Benjamin. *Famous Problems of Geometry.* Mineola, NY: Dover, 1969.

Eves, Howard. *An Introduction to the History of Mathematics*. New York: Holt, Rinehart and Winston, 1990.

Hobson, E. W. "Squaring the Circle." *A History of the Problem.* New York: Chelsea Publishing, 1953.

Jacobs, Harold. *Mathematics: A Human Endeavor*. San Francisco: W.H. Freeman, 1987.

Kostovskii, A. N. *Geometrical Constructions Using Compasses Only.* Halina Moss (trans). New York: Blaisdell Publishing, 1961.

Lamb, John F. "Trisecting an Angle—Almost." *Mathematics Teacher* (Mar 1988) 220-222.

Swetz, Frank. *Learning Activities from the History of Mathematics*. Portland, ME: J. Weston Walch, 1994.

———. "Using Problems from the History of Mathematics in Classroom Instruction." *Mathematics Teacher* (May 1989) 370-377.

Yates, R.C. *The Trisection Problem.* Ann Arbor, MI: Edwards Bros., 1947.

Famous Twisted One-Sided Surfaces

74

German mathematician and astronomer **August Ferdinand Möbius** (1790–1868) created an object that has fascinated mathematicians and nonmathematicians alike: the **Möbius strip**. You can create an ordinary loop like the one shown below at top left by joining the two ends of a strip of paper. This loop has the basic geometry of a cylinder. It has two edges and two sides—an inside and an outside. If you wanted, you could paint the inside red and the outside green. To create a Möbius strip, give the paper a single twist before you join the ends, as shown below at top right. The topology of the Möbius strip is considerably different from the cylindrical loop. It only has one edge and one side—it can be painted one color without ever crossing an edge.

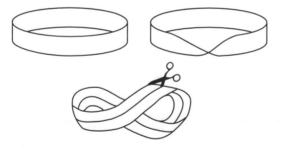

Engraved portrait of August Möbius from the frontispiece of his **Gesammelte Werke** *(Leipzig, 1889).*

You can get some interesting results by cutting the Möbius strip. When you cut around the middle of the strip, as shown above, the surprising result is revealed in this limerick by an anonymous author: "A mathematician confided/That a Möbius band is one-sided,/And you'll get quite a laugh/If you cut one in half,/For it stays in one piece when divided."

Another German mathematician, **Felix Klein** (1849–1925), devised a topological model of a one-sided surface known as the **Klein bottle**. In this unique bottle, the neck goes through the side of the bottle, as shown at right. The neck and base join, making the inside of the neck continuous with the outside of the base. Thus, the Klein bottle has no inside, just an outside!

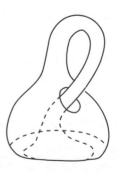

There is a connection between the Möbius strip and the Klein bottle: If the bottle were cut in half lengthwise, it would fall into two Möbius strips. This connection is described in another anonymous verse: "A mathematician named Klein/Thought the Möbius band was divine./Said he 'If you glue/The edges of two,/You'll get a weird bottle like mine.'" (For more on Felix Klein, see vignette 63.) ★

©1996 by Key Curriculum Press

Activities

1. Draw a line down the middle of each side of a strip of paper, as shown.

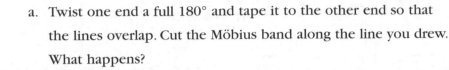

   a. Twist one end a full 180° and tape it to the other end so that the lines overlap. Cut the Möbius band along the line you drew. What happens?

   b. With another strip, twist one end 360° before taping. Again, cut along the line. What do you observe?

2. Draw two lines down the middle of each side of a strip of paper, as shown.

   a. Twist one end 180° and tape it to the other end so that the lines overlap. Cut along the lines. What do you observe?

   b. With another strip, twist one end 360° before taping. Can you guess what will happen when you cut along the lines?

3. Felix Klein led a protest against what he saw to be a disturbing trend in mathematics. What was this trend? What form did Klein's protest take?

Related Reading

Bergamini, David (ed). *Mathematics: Life Science Library*. **New York: Time-Life Books, 1972.**

Cundy, H. Martyn, and A.P. Rollette. *Mathematical Models.* London: Oxford University Press, 1974.

Davies, Paul. *The Edge of Infinity*. **New York: Simon and Schuster, 1982.**

Fauvel, John, et al. *Möbius and His Band: Mathematics and Astronomy in Nineteenth-Century Germany.* New York: Oxford University Press, 1993.

Guillen, Michael. *Bridges to Infinity: The Human Side of Mathematics*. **New York: St. Martin's Press, 1983.**

Jacobs, Harold. *Mathematics: A Human Endeavor*. **San Francisco: W.H. Freeman, 1987.**

Pappas, Theoni. *The Magic of Mathematics.* San Carlos, CA: Wide World/Tetra, 1994.

DETERMINING SIZE FOR INFINITE SETS

75

Russian-born mathematician **Georg Cantor** (1845–1918), intrigued by set theory and the theory of the infinite, defined what we mean by one infinite set being larger than another: "If set P can be put into a one-to-one correspondence with a subset of set Q, but set Q cannot be put into a one-to-one correspondence with P or a subset of P, then set Q is larger than set P."

This definition is obvious for finite sets. For instance, if $P = \{1, 2, 3\}$ and $Q = \{1, 2, 3, 4, 5\}$, then Q is larger than P. What may surprise you is that an infinite set can have the same size as a seemingly smaller subset of itself. For instance, if $A = \{1, 4, 9, 16, 25, 36, 49, \ldots\}$ and $B = \{1, 2, 3, 4, 5, 6, 7, \ldots\}$, then a one-to-one correspondence can be established, as shown below.

$$1^2 \leftrightarrow 1, \quad 2^2 \leftrightarrow 2, \quad 3^2 \leftrightarrow 3, \quad 4^2 \leftrightarrow 4, \quad 5^2 \leftrightarrow 5, \quad \text{etc.}$$

Cantor described the cardinality of the set of natural numbers $B = \{1, 2, 3, 4, 5, \ldots\}$ as $\aleph_0$ (aleph-null). Any infinite set that can be "paired up" with set B has the same cardinality, or cardinal number. Loosely speaking, $\aleph_0$ is a transfinite number—not a real number—that describes an infinite amount. Cantor developed a system of transfinite numbers to describe sizes of infinite sets, and he actually ordered these transfinite numbers, making $\aleph_0$ the smallest. The set of real numbers cannot be put into a one-to-one correspondence with $\{1, 2, 3, 4, 5, \ldots\}$ because the real numbers are a "larger" set and thus have a cardinal number greater than $\aleph_0$.

> *I am so in favor of the actual infinite that instead of admitting that Nature abhors it, as is commonly said, I hold that Nature makes frequent use of it everywhere, in order to show more effectively the perfections of its Author. Thus I believe that there is no part of matter which is not ... actually divisible; and consequently the least particle ought to be considered as a world full of an infinity of different creatures.*
>
> —Georg Cantor

Perhaps surprisingly, the set of positive rational numbers—numbers that can be written as the ratio of two positive integers—has cardinality $\aleph_0$. The chart at right shows how the rational numbers can be arranged so that they fall into a one-to-one correspondence with the positive integers shown below.

$$\{ \ 1, \quad 2, \quad 3, \quad 4, \quad 5, \quad 6, \quad 7, \quad 8, \quad \ldots\}$$
$$\updownarrow \quad \updownarrow \quad \updownarrow \quad \updownarrow \quad \updownarrow \quad \updownarrow \quad \updownarrow \quad \updownarrow$$
$$\{ \ ^1/_1, \quad ^2/_1, \quad ^1/_2, \quad ^1/_3, \quad ^2/_2, \quad ^3/_1, \quad ^4/_1, \quad ^3/_2, \quad \ldots\}$$

$$
\begin{array}{ccccc}
^1/_1 & ^1/_2 \to & ^1/_3 & ^1/_4 \to & ^1/_5 \quad \cdots \\
\downarrow \quad \nearrow & \swarrow & \nearrow & \swarrow & \\
^2/_1 & ^2/_2 & ^2/_3 & ^2/_4 & ^2/_5 \quad \cdots \\
& \swarrow & \nearrow & \swarrow & \\
^3/_1 & ^3/_2 & ^3/_3 & ^3/_4 & ^3/_5 \quad \cdots \\
\downarrow \quad \nearrow & \swarrow & & & \\
^4/_1 & ^4/_2 & ^4/_3 & ^4/_4 & ^4/_5 \quad \cdots \\
\swarrow & & & & \\
^5/_1 & ^5/_2 & ^5/_3 & ^5/_4 & ^5/_5 \quad \cdots \\
\end{array}
$$

$\cdots$

Cantor's revolutionary views on the nature of the infinite caused considerable controversy. Despite logical difficulties and the appearances of paradoxes, his work and thoughts on sets and the infinite created a whole new field of mathematical research that has penetrated almost every branch of mathematics.

For more on infinity, see vignettes 13, 14, 51, and 79. ★

©1996 by Key Curriculum Press

ACTIVITIES

1. Show that the set of whole numbers has the same cardinality as the set {1, 8, 27, 64, 125, 216, . . .}.

2. a. Show that the set $F = \{1, \frac{1}{2}, \frac{1}{3}, \frac{1}{4}, \frac{1}{5}, \ldots\}$ has the same cardinality as the set of whole numbers.

   b. How could you establish that set F has the same cardinality as the set of all positive rational numbers? Refer to the vignette to answer this question.

3. How did Cantor show that the cardinality of the set of whole numbers differs from that of the set of real numbers?

4. In set theory, what is Cantor's paradox?

5. Cantor's theory of infinite sets was both highly praised and heavily criticized. **David Hilbert** and **Bertrand Russell** were among his supporters, and **Leopold Kronecker** and **Henri Poincaré** protested his theory. Research this controversy.

RELATED READING

Beckmann, Petr. *A History of* π. New York: St. Martin's Press, 1976.

Daintith, John, and R.D. Nelson (eds). *Dictionary of Mathematics*. New York: Penguin Books, 1989.

Dash, Joan. *The Triumph of Discovery*. Westwood, NJ: Silver Burdett and Ginn, 1991.

Dauben, Joseph. *Georg Cantor: His Mathematics and Philosophy of the Infinite*. Cambridge, MA: Harvard University Press, 1979.

Kanigel, Robert. *The Man Who Knew Infinity: A Life of the Genius Ramanujan*. New York: Macmillan, 1991.

Kline, Morris. *Mathematics: The Loss of Certainty*. New York: Oxford University Press, 1980.

Pappas, Theoni. *The Joy of Mathematics*. San Carlos, CA: Wide World/Tetra, 1989.

Resnikoff, H.L., and R.O. Wells. *Mathematics in Civilization*. Mineola, NY: Dover, 1985.

Rucker, Rudolf. *Infinity and the Mind*. New York: Bantam Books, 1982.

76

Renaissance Woman: Sofia Kovalevskaya

Russian-born **Sofia Kovalevskaya** (1850–1891) was born into a relatively wealthy family, but educational opportunities for Russian girls of her time were scarce. However, her well-educated parents appreciated her intellectual talents and secured a tutor for her. Her ability in mathematics became apparent in a rather unique way: Because her childhood bedroom walls had been papered with Russian mathematician Mikhail Ostrogradsky's lecture notes, she had spent hours trying to decipher the text and the formulas. As a result, by the time she received formal training in calculus, she was already familiar with advanced mathematical notation.

Because higher education for women was not available in Russia and single women could only travel abroad with their parents' permission, she entered into a marriage of convenience with paleontologist Vladimir Kovalevsky in 1868 in order to accompany him to Heidelberg, Germany, where he planned to work. However, the university at Heidelberg didn't accept women as students, so she was unable to enroll. Fortunately, she became acquainted with mathematician **Karl Weierstrass** (1815–1897), who recognized her intellectual abilities and her enthusiasm for mathematics. He tutored Kovalevskaya privately for four years, and during this time she received the equivalent of a university education in mathematics and wrote several important mathematical papers. In 1874, having been awarded a Ph.D. in absentia and summa cum laude by Göttingen University for her thesis on partial differential equations, Kovalevskaya became the first European woman since the Renaissance to receive a doctorate in mathematics.

Despite many prejudices against women, Kovalevskaya's mathematical ability was recognized by the European mathematical community. She received a professorship in mathematics at the University of Stockholm, where she was a popular lecturer and conducted valuable research in mathematics and science. In 1888, she was awarded the

More Than Mathematics

In addition to being one of the nineteenth century's most important mathematicians, Kovalevskaya made significant contributions to the fields of science, poetry, and literature. Her autobiography, *Recollections of a Childhood* (1890), brought her great acclaim, and her story of a young revolutionary, *A Nihilist Girl* (published posthumously in 1892), was translated into seven languages.

Sofia Kovalevskaya: "It is impossible to be a mathematician without being a poet in soul."

Prix Bordin from the French Academy of Science for her paper entitled "On the Problem of the Rotation of a Solid Body About a Fixed Point." The award alone represented a high honor, but the Academy was so impressed with her paper that they substantially increased the amount of prize money given with the award.

An intelligent, talented woman who contributed to her era's atmosphere of change, Sofia Kovalevskaya will long be remembered for her contributions to mathematics and for her commitment to the advancement of women. ★

Activities

1. Read about Kovalevskaya's work regarding the rings of the planet Saturn.

2. In the latter part of the nineteenth century, there was a women's movement in Russia not unlike the recent women's movement in the United States. Study this movement and Kovalevskaya's role in it.

3. Kovalevskaya once said: "Say what you know, do what you must, come what may." How does this quote relate to the way she conducted her life?

4. Weierstrass initially had little interest in Kovalevskaya and found her to be a nuisance. Read about the development of the relationship between these two mathematicians.

5. How did Kovalevskaya develop a friendship with Russian novelist **Fyodor Mikhailovich Dostoevsky** (1821–1881)?

Related Reading

Alic, Margaret. *Hypatia's Heritage*. Boston: Beacon Press, 1986.

Greenes, Carole. *Sonya Kovalevsky*. Dedham, MA: Janson Publications, 1989.

Grinstein, Louise S., and Paul Campbell. *Women of Mathematics: A Bibliographic Sourcebook*. Westport, CT: Greenwood Press, 1987.

Kennedy, Donald. *Little Sparrow: A Portrait of Sophie Kovalesky*. Athens, OH: Ohio University Press, 1983.

Koblitz, Ann Hibner. *A Convergence of Lives: Sofia Kovalevskaia: Scientist, Writer, Revolutionary*. New Brunswick, NY: Rutgers University Press, 1993.

Osen, Lynn. *Women in Mathematics*. Cambridge, MA: MIT Press, 1984.

Perl, Teri. *Women and Numbers: Lives of Women Mathematicians plus Discovery Activities*. San Carlos, CA: Wide World/Tetra, 1993.

"Profiles and Contributions of Three Notable Women Mathematicians." *California Mathematics Council ComMuniCator* (Mar 1993) 38–39.

Swetz, Frank. *Learning Activities from the History of Mathematics*. Portland, ME: J. Weston Walch, 1994.

©1996 by Key Curriculum Press

77

Schools of Mathematical Thought

We humans rely in part on mathematics to effectively describe the world around us. Questions such as "What is mathematics?" "Where does mathematics come from?" and "How should mathematics be developed?" have existed for centuries. In early twentieth-century Europe, three important schools of mathematical philosophy emerged that attempted to answer these questions.

The Intuitionist School

Dutch mathematician **Luitzen Brouwer** (1881-1966) emerged as the leader of this school. Building upon the philosophies of **Immanuel Kant** (1724–1804), the intuitionists believe that mathematics is a human activity that originates and thrives within the mind—that it is independent of the real world. That is, mathematical knowledge comes purely from the mind, as do the concepts of space and time. While knowledge and understanding may begin with experiences, they do not originate from experience. So, for example, to the intuitionist, a logical construction of the real number system is not acceptable.

The Logistic School

English mathematicians and philosophers **Bertrand Russell** (1872-1970) and **Alfred North Whitehead** (1861-1947) cofounded the logistic school. The logistic philosophy holds that everything in mathematics is derivable from principles of logic. Unlike the intuitionists, the logicians viewed mathematics as an activity to be developed, not something that is inherent in the human mind. The logicians attempted to resolve paradoxes of the newly developing set theory through the development of sound logical principles, and they attempted a logical construction of the real number system. Whitehead and Russell's *Principia Mathematica* outlines the school's position.

The Formalist School

German mathematician **David Hilbert** (1862–1943) headed the formalists, who believed that mathematics should be developed through axiomatic systems. Hilbert argued against the logistic approach by asserting that in the development of logic, the whole numbers were inherently involved. Therefore, to build the number system on logic employed circular reasoning. Unlike the logicians, the formalists claimed that mathematics cannot be deduced from logic alone. There must be appropriate axioms—statements accepted without proof—before a systematic development of mathematics can begin. For the most part, modern mathematics education uses the formalist approach in the learning process.

> *The nineteenth century which prides itself upon the invention of steam and evolution, might have derived a more legitimate title to fame from the discovery of pure mathematics.*
>
> —Bertrand Russell

> *Mathematical science is in my opinion an indivisible whole, an organism whose vitality is conditioned upon the connection of its parts. For with all the variety of mathematical knowledge, we are still clearly conscious of the similarity of the logical devices, the relationship of the ideas in mathematics as a whole and the numerous analogies in its different departments.*
>
> —David Hilbert

Needless to say, all three schools have been subject to criticism, and they have fought intensely among themselves. However, all have exerted a healthy influence on modern mathematical thought.

For more on Immanuel Kant, see vignette 56. For more on David Hilbert, see vignette 79. For more on logic, see vignettes 13, 67, 68, and 72. ★

Activities

1. Research Hilbert's influence on three of his well-known students, scientists and mathematicians **Enrico Fermi** (1901–1954), **J. Robert Oppenheimer** (1904–1967), and **John von Neumann** (1903–1957).

2. Here is a simple paradox.

   Let *S* be the following statement: This statement is false.
   If *S* is true, then what it says is true. Hence *S* is false.
   If *S* is false, then this is exactly what the statement says, so *S* is true.

   Around 1900, paradoxes similar to this were discovered in mathematical structure. Research the logistic school's efforts to resolve these paradoxes.

3. Research the influence of Kant and of **David Hume** (1711–1776) on the intuitionist school.

4. What were some of the fundamental differences between the logistic school and the formalist school about the nature of mathematics?

Related Reading

Dummett, Michael. *Elements of Intuitionism.* New York: Clarendon Press, 1977.

Eves, Howard. *Great Moments in Mathematics After 1650.* Washington, DC: Mathematical Association of America, 1982.

Guillen, Michael. *Bridges to Infinity: The Human Side of Mathematics.* New York: St. Martin's Press, 1983.

Hilbert, David. *The Foundations of Geometry.* Chicago: Open Court Publishing, 1902.

Kline, Morris. *Mathematics: The Loss of Certainty.* New York: Oxford University Press, 1980.

Paulos, John Allen. *Beyond Numeracy: Ruminations of a Numbers Man.* New York: Alfred A. Knopf, 1991.

Reid, George. *Hilbert.* New York: Springer-Verlag, 1970.

Smith, Sanderson. *Great Ideas for Teaching Math.* Portland, ME: J. Weston Walch, 1990.

©1996 by Key Curriculum Press

Grace Chisholm Young: Versatile and Prolific

Grace Chisholm Young with her infant son Frank. Photo courtesy of Professor Sylvia Wiegand, University of Nebraska.

Like other women of her time, **Grace Chisholm Young** (1868–1944) faced considerable obstacles in her quest to obtain a quality education. In her native England, education was available for every child, but because the offerings for girls were very restricted, Young was educated primarily at home. Her mother and her father, the government's chief of the Division of Weights and Measures, made their home an enjoyable learning environment and encouraged their daughter to excel. Excel she did, learning six languages and becoming knowledgeable in music, medicine, and mathematics.

As an adult, Young set out to lead a life of her own, and her desire for intellectual freedom was well known. Having received a university education at Girton College in Cambridge, she traveled to Germany to attend Göttingen University so that she could earn an advanced degree. Despite the fact that many members of Göttingen's faculty were opposed to the idea of women attending the university, Young excelled in her studies. In 1895, she graduated magna cum laude with a Ph.D. in mathematics, the first woman in Germany to earn a doctorate in that field. In appreciation of her father's support, she dedicated her doctoral dissertation to him.

In 1896, Grace Chisholm married English mathematician **William Young** (1863–1942), and in the forty-four years that they were married, they collaborated on more than 200 articles and books. Most of them were published in William's name, but he made it clear that Grace was heavily involved in their production. Additionally, in 1905, she published a geometry book that included many paper-folding patterns for three-dimensional models, and in 1906, both published *The Theory of Sets of Points,* the first book to thoroughly demonstrate applications of set theory to problems in mathematical analysis. Perhaps her most distinguished work appears in a group of papers published from 1914 to 1916 in which she presented and developed theories and concepts in differential calculus.

Various stories about Grace Chisholm Young suggest that she was a well-loved, generous woman with a variety of talents and tremendous energy. ★

Activities

1. Elaborate on the personal qualities that made Young so highly respected and admired by those who knew her.

2. Research Young's contributions to the development of differential calculus.

3. What were some of the paper-folding activities described in Young's geometry book? Can they be used in mathematics classes today?

4. A piece of paper is approximately 0.008 inches thick. Assuming you could fold it in half as many times as you wanted, how high would the folded piece of paper be if you made the given number of folds?

   a. 1   b. 2   c. 3   d. 4
   e. 10   f. 20   g. 40   h. 64

5. Cut a piece of paper measuring 8½″ × 11″ in such a way that you end up with a continuous ring through which you can pass your entire body.

Related Reading

Bell, E.T. *The Last Problem*. Washington, DC: Mathematical Association of America, 1990.

Chenal-Ducey, Michelle. "Grace Chisholm Young." *California Mathematics Council ComMuniCator* (Mar 1993) 28–29.

Grattan-Guinness, I. "William Henry and Grace Chisholm Young: A Mathematical Union." *Annals of Science* 29 (1972) 105–186.

Grinstein, Louise S., and Paul Campbell. *Women of Mathematics: A Bibliographic Sourcebook*. Westport, CT: Greenwood Press, 1987.

Kline, Morris. *Mathematical Thought from Ancient to Modern Times*. New York: Oxford University Press, 1990.

Osen, Lynn. *Women in Mathematics*. Cambridge, MA: MIT Press, 1984.

Perl, Teri. *Math Equals: Biographies of Women Mathematicians and Related Activities*. Menlo Park, CA: Addison-Wesley, 1978.

An Inconceivable Inn

79

The concept of infinite sets has long puzzled mathematicians. However, mathematicians *have* known that a one-to-one correspondence could not be established between two finite sets of unequal size. Yet, that seems to be just what is happening in this puzzle to the right!

Did the landlord establish a one-to-one correspondence between nine rooms and ten travelers? Think about it!

German mathematician **David Hilbert** (1862–1943) once posed a similar problem. In Hilbert's version, the landlord told a traveler there were no vacancies. However, upon reflection, the landlord said, "I know how to get you a room." He knocked on the door of Room 1 and asked its occupant to move to Room 2. The occupant of Room 2 was then moved to Room 3, and so on, until each occupant had moved one room over. To the amazement of the late-arriving visitor, each guest had a new room and she was able to move into the vacated Room 1! She went right to bed, but she lay awake for hours wondering how everyone, including herself, had gotten a room when all the rooms had been occupied when she'd arrived. It finally occurred to her that she must be in Hilbert's Hotel, the only hotel in the world known to have an infinite number of rooms. By shifting each guest one room over, Room 1 was vacated, as shown below.

1   2   3   4   5   6   7   . . .

1   2   3   4   5   6   7   . . .

For more on infinity, see vignettes 13, 14, 51, and 75. ★

Ten weary, footsore travelers,
All in a woeful plight,
Sought shelter at a wayside inn
One dark and stormy night.
"Nine rooms, no more," the landlord said,
"Have I to offer you.
To each of you a single bed,
But the ninth must serve for two!"
A din arose. The troubled host
Could only scratch his head,
For of those tired men no two
Would occupy one bed.
The puzzled host was soon at ease—
He was a clever man—
And so to please his guests devised
This most ingenious plan.
In room marked A, two men were placed,
The third was lodged in B,
The fourth to C was then assigned,
The fifth retired to D.
In E the sixth he tucked away,
In F the seventh man,
The eighth and ninth in G and H,
And then to A he ran,
Wherein the host, as I have said,
Had laid two travelers by;
Then taking one—the tenth and last—
He lodged him safe in I.
Nine single rooms—a room for each—
Were made to serve for ten;
And this it is that puzzles me
And many wiser men.

—Anonymous

Activities

1. Resolve the puzzle of the ten travelers.

2. How does the concept of number cardinality put forth by **Georg Cantor** relate to Hilbert's Hotel?

3. **Galileo Galilei** believed that the whole is always greater than any of its parts, even with infinite sets. How does Hilbert's Hotel demonstrate that this is not true?

4. In his work *Sand Reckoner,* **Archimedes** wrote about large numbers and struggled with the concept of infinity. However, he didn't accept that there were an infinite number of grains of sand on a beach. Research his method for determining the number of grains of sand on all the beaches of the earth.

Related Reading

Davies, Paul. *The Edge of Infinity*. New York: Simon and Schuster, 1982.

Ellis, Keith. *Number Power in Nature and in Everyday Life*. New York: St. Martin's Press, 1978.

Guillen, Michael. *Bridges to Infinity: The Human Side of Mathematics*. New York: St. Martin's Press, 1983.

Kasner, Edward, and James R. Newman. *Mathematics and the Imagination*. Redmond, WA: Tempus Books, 1989.

Love, William P. "Infinity: The Twilight Zone of Mathematics." *Mathematics Teacher* (Apr 1989) 284-292.

Maor, Eli. *To Infinity and Beyond: A Cultural History of the Infinite*. Boston: Birkhauser Boston, 1987.

Rucker, Rudolf. *Infinity and the Mind*. New York: Bantam Books, 1982.

BRIEF PI TALES

80

Various values for the number pi (π) have been used throughout history. In ancient Asia, the value of π was frequently considered to be 3. In the Egyptian *Rhind Papyrus* (1650 B.C.) π = (⁴⁄₃)⁴, or approximately 3.1604. Greek mathematician **Archimedes** (ca 287–212 B.C.) used the fact that the circumference of a circle lies between the perimeter of any inscribed polygon and the perimeter of any circumscribed polygon to determine that π is between ²²³⁄₇₁ and ²²⁄₇. Rounded to two decimal places, his value for π equals 3.14. China's **Zu Chongzhi** (ca A.D. 480) came up with ³⁵⁵⁄₁₁₃, or 3.1415929 . . . , which is accurate to six decimal places. Hindu mathematicians **Aryabhata** (ca A.D. 530) and **Bhaskara** (1114–1185) obtained values of ⁶²,⁸⁴³⁄₂₀,₀₀₀ and ⁷⁵⁴⁄₂₄₀, respectively.

These mathematicians are just a few of the many who studied the approximations for π. Some produced amazingly accurate approximations long before the modern age of computers. In 1853, England's William Rutherford computed π accurate to 400 decimal places!

There are various mnemonic devices that can help us remember π to many decimal places. In 1914, the *Scientific American* published this mnemonic statement:

> *See, I have a rhyme assisting my fee-*
> *ble brain, its tasks ofttimes resisting.*

Replacing each word by the number of letters it contains yields π correct to 12 decimal places.

In 1906, A. C. Orr had written a similar but more detailed mnemonic that appeared in the *Literary Digest*. It helps us remember π to 30 decimal places.

> *Now I, even I, would celebrate*
> *In rhymes unapt, the great*
> *Immortal Syracusan, rivaled nevermore,*
> *Who in his wondrous lore,*
> *Passed on before,*
> *Left men his guidance*
> *How to circles mensurate.*

Would you want to memorize that?

So important is the number π that some have actually attempted to legislate its value.

Chinese mathematician Liu Hui's method for finding the approximate value of π (A.D. 264).

In 1897, the Indiana State Legislature came up with House Bill Number 246. Section I of the bill starts like this: "Be it enacted by the General Assembly of the State of Indiana: It has been found that the circular area is to the quadrant of the circumference, as the area of an equilateral rectangle is to the square on one side."

Apparently, the House believed this was an important issue, because they passed the bill with a vote of 67 to 0. However—for reasons that become obvious when you carefully read what is written in the bill— it became the subject of newspaper ridicule and was shelved by the Senate.

Concerning all the ill-fated attempts to supply a specific value for π, mathematics historian Howard Eves wrote: "These contributions, often amusing, and at times almost unbelievable, would require a publication all to themselves." According to him, the authors of the numerous documents claiming to yield an exact value for π suffer from morbus cyclometricus—the circle-squaring disease.

For more on pi, see vignette 2. ★

ACTIVITIES

1. Research the clever method used by Germany's **Ludolph van Cuelen** in 1610 to compute π to 35 decimal places. The number was engraved on his tombstone, and to this day in Germany, π is sometimes called "the Ludolphine number."

2. In 1760, **Comte de Buffon** (1707–1788) used probability and his famous needle method to determine π. What was his method?

3. Historically, a number of infinite series have been used to compute π. Use a calculator or a computer to check out these series to twenty places.

   a. **Gottfried Leibniz** used $\pi = 4(1 - \frac{1}{3} + \frac{1}{5} - \frac{1}{7} + \frac{1}{9} - \frac{1}{11} + \ldots)$.

   b. **Leonhard Euler** used $\pi^2 = 6[(\frac{1}{1})^2 + (\frac{1}{2})^2 + (\frac{1}{3})^2 + \ldots]$.

4. a. Research the complete 1897 Indiana State House Bill Number 246. Find within it statements that contradict both one another and elementary geometry.

   b. The bill makes the assumption that a circle and a square have equal areas if they have equal perimeters. Show that this is incorrect. The isoperimetric problem asks for the figure of largest area with fixed perimeter. Investigate the history of this problem.

RELATED READING

Beckmann, Petr. *A History of π.* New York: St. Martin's Press, 1976.

Castellanos, Dario. "The Ubiquitous π." *Mathematics Magazine* (Apr 1988) 67–98.

Davis, Philip, and Reuben Hersh. *The Mathematical Experience.* Boston: Birkhauser Boston, 1981.

Edgar, G.A. "Pi: Difficult or Easy?" *Mathematics Magazine* (June 1987) 141–150.

Edington, E. House Bill No. 246, Indiana State Legislature, 1897. *Proceedings of the Indiana Academy of Sciences* 45 (1935) 206–210.

Eves, Howard. *An Introduction to the History of Mathematics.* New York: Holt, Rinehart and Winston, 1990.

Lotspeich, Richard. "Archimedes' Pi—An Introduction to Iteration." *Mathematics Teacher* (Dec 1988) 208–210.

Peterson, Ivars. *Islands of Truth: A Mathematical Mystery Cruise.* New York: W.H. Freeman, 1990.

Shilgalis, Thomas W. "Archimedes and Pi." *Mathematics Teacher* (Mar 1989) 204–206.

HISTORY OF MATH

Emmy Noether: A Modern Mathematics Pioneer

81

In the judgment of the most competent living mathematicians, Fräulein Noether was the most significant creative mathematical genius thus far produced since the higher education of women began. In the realm of algebra, in which the most gifted mathematicians have been busy for centuries, she discovered methods which have proved of enormous importance in the development of the present-day generation of mathematicians.

—Albert Einstein

German-born **Emmy Noether** (1882–1935) was the daughter of **Max Noether**, a mathematics professor at the University of Erlangen who loved his subject and transferred this love to his daughter. Her parents' support of her and her own determination were such that Noether overcame the prejudice prevalent at that time against women seeking a higher education. This prejudice was reflected in a statement issued in 1898 by the Academic Senate at Erlangen, asserting that the admission of women students would "overthrow all academic order." She, along with only one other woman in a sizeable student body, began her studies at Erlangen auditing mathematics classes—the university did not allow women to officially register. In 1904, the school changed this policy, and she was able to continue her studies as a regular student, receiving her Ph.D. in mathematics in 1907.

Noether's mathematical strength was her ability to operate abstractly with difficult concepts. Instrumental in developing the axiomatic method as a powerful tool in mathematical research, she is primarily known for her significant contributions to the development of modern algebraic ideas. For example, in suggesting that algebra be linked with topology, she influenced the creation of a whole new field of mathematical study. (Topology is the study of properties of geometric forms that do not change under transformations such as bending or stretching.) The importance of this and her other contributions inspired mathematician Hermann Weyl (1885–1955) to remark at her memorial: "She originated above all a new and epoch-making style of thinking in algebra." Noether was also a highly successful and popular teacher at both Erlangen and the University of Göttingen, despite the fact that she continually encountered opposition from many male faculty members

Emmy Noether. Photo courtesy of Stock Montage, Chicago, Illinois.

©1996 by Key Curriculum Press

who felt that women should not be lecturers in higher education. She was genuinely concerned for her students, and her almost exclusively male students at Göttingen were known as "the Noether boys."

In 1933, Adolf Hitler came to power in Germany, and Noether and other Jewish intellectuals were prohibited from participating in all academic activities. She emigrated to the United States and secured teaching positions at Bryn Mawr College and at the Institute of Advanced Study at Princeton. Although she spent less than two years in the United States, she found great respect and friendship among her peers and her students. In 1935, she died unexpectedly as the result of an operation to remove a tumor, and her death shocked and saddened her many friends around the world. At the Moscow Mathematical Society, her friend Pavel Sergeevich Aleksandrov (1896–1982) remembered her with this tribute: "Emmy Noether was the greatest of women mathematicians, a great scientist, an amazing teacher, and an unforgettable person." ★

Activities

1. In what ways did Noether influence another prominent twentieth-century female mathematician, **Olga Taussky-Todd** (b 1906)?

2. Noether worked with abstract algebra, where operations frequently yield different results from those of traditional algebra. In clock algebra, for instance, $9 + 5 = 2$. If it's 9:00, and you plan to meet someone in 5 hours, you will meet them at 2:00. Use clock algebra to solve the equations given below.

a. $4 + 7 = z$

b. $8 + 7 = y$

c. $12 + 7 = x$

d. $12 + 12 = w$

e. $3 + 11 + 5 + 8 = t$

f. $5 - 3 + 7 = s$

g. $11 - 3 + 9 = r$

3. Consider the equation $x + 11 = 1$. What is the solution in regular algebra? In clock algebra? Consider the equation $x + y = 6$. How many pairs of whole numbers satisfy this equation in regular algebra? In clock algebra?

Related Reading

Alic, Margaret. *Hypatia's Heritage.* Boston: Beacon Press, 1986.

Brewer, James, and Martha Smith. *Emmy Noether: A Tribute to Her Life and Work.* New York: Marcel Dekken, 1981.

Dick, Auguste. *Emmy Noether, 1882–1935.* Basel, Switzerland: Birkhauser Verlag, 1970.

Perl, Teri. *Women and Numbers: Lives of Women Mathematicians plus Discovery Activities.* San Carlos, CA: Wide World/Tetra, 1993.

Rosser, Sue. *Female Friendly Science.* New York, NY: Pergamon Press, 1990.

Ramanujan's Formulas

82

Srinivasa Ramanujan (1887–1920) was raised in the town of Kumbakonam in southern India. Primarily self-educated, he developed a fascination for the study of mathematics. Between 1903 and 1914, he filled three notebooks with mathematical formulas and relationships. Because Ramanujan couldn't afford to buy much paper, he did his computations and experimentation on a slate, erasing all his intermediate work and recording only his final results on paper. It is questionable if any of Ramanujan's voluminous formulas and notes would have survived had he not sent some of his ideas to the English mathematician **G. H. Hardy** (1877–1947). Regarding Ramanujan's theorems, Hardy wrote: "I have never seen anything like them before. A single look at them is enough to show that they could only be written down by a mathematician of the highest class. They must be true because, if they were not, no one would have had the imagination to invent them."

In 1913, Hardy invited Ramanujan to Cambridge University in England. Unfamiliar with European developments in mathematics, Ramanujan supplemented his knowledge during the five years he spent in England, publishing numerous papers and achieving worldwide fame. Unfortunately, he was also unfamiliar with British winters, and he didn't dress properly to protect himself from the cold and the wet. In addition, because he had difficulty finding the appropriate fruits and vegetables to follow the eating customs of his religion, he wasn't well nourished. As a result, he became ill and returned to India in 1917.

Ramanujan died in 1920, and fortunately for mathematicians today, his wife kept track of the sheets of paper he filled with mathematical formulas. His work was not well known until 1976, when 130 pages of his scribbled material were discovered in a box of letters and bills in the library of Trinity College at Cambridge. Since then, mathematicians have been carefully studying these notes, known as the Lost Notebook, and hundreds of other pages of Ramanujan's notes found after his death. Ramanujan's notes were personal records in which he jotted down thousands of formulas, almost always without proof or even a hint of where they came from. Many of the intriguing assertions he made

Srinivasa Ramanujan

during the final year of his life have yet to be proved. As modern mathematicians have worked toward uncovering the processes leading to his perceptive statements of theorems, they have discovered new and useful mathematical methods and techniques.

Ramanujan's favorite topic was infinite series. One of his series formulas has been used in computer computations of π to millions of decimal places. He also worked with continued fractions and partition theory. Modern physicists have used Ramanujan's partition discoveries to solve problems in statistical mechanics. What would Ramanujan have been able to accomplish had he lived to have access to modern computers? It is generally acknowledged that his thinking was many decades ahead of his time. His legacy will keep today's mathematicians busy for many years to come.

For more information on the mathematics of India, see vignettes 2, 19, 24, and 28. ★

©1996 by Key Curriculum Press

Activities

1. Ramanujan believed that the complicated-looking number $e^{\pi\sqrt{163}}$ was an integer, and he actually computed its value. In 1974, John Brillo of the University of Arizona established that Ramanujan was correct. How did Brillo justify Ramanujan's assertion? What is the value of $e^{\pi\sqrt{163}}$?

2. Research the life and contributions of G. H. Hardy. Expand upon his relationship with Ramanujan.

3. In a conversation with Ramanujan, Hardy stated that the number 1729—the number of the taxi he had just ridden in—was a dull number. Ramanujan disagreed, asserting that the number 1729 was very interesting. Why is this number interesting?

4. Research the text of Ramanujan's first letter to Hardy, dated January 16, 1913.

Related Reading

Hardy, G. H. A. *A Mathematician's Apology*. Cambridge, MA: Cambridge University Press, 1992.

———. *Ramanujan*. New York: Chelsea Publications, 1959.

Kanigel, Robert. *The Man Who Knew Infinity: A Life of the Genius Ramanujan*. New York: Macmillan, 1991.

Newman, James R. *The World of Mathematics,* Vol I. New York: Simon and Schuster, 1956.

Pappas, Theoni. *More Joy of Mathematics*. **San Carlos, CA: Wide World/Tetra, 1991.**

Peterson, Ivars. *Islands of Truth: A Mathematical Mystery Cruise*. New York: W.H. Freeman, 1990.

Stewart, Ian. "The Formula Man." *New Scientist* (Dec 1987) 24–28.

Swetz, Frank. *Learning Activities from the History of Mathematics*. **Portland, ME: J. Weston Walch, 1994**.

COUNTING AND COMPUTING DEVICES

83

Throughout history, many people have used many devices—organic and mechanical—to perform the intricate processes of counting and computing.

Human fingers: Many cultures throughout human history have devised clever methods to use these ever-available counting and computing devices. Our fingers and toes total 20, accounting for some early 20-base number systems.

Abacus: Dating back perhaps 5,000 years, this simple yet effective device has assumed a variety of forms and was used by the ancient Chinese, Greeks, and Romans. It is still used in some parts of the world today.

Greek mechanical computer: In 1900, Greek fishermen found a corroded mechanism, approximately 2,000 years old, at the bottom of the Aegean Sea. It appeared to be part of a geared computer device. Were there computers in ancient Greece?

Quipus: The Inca empire of fifteenth- and sixteenth-century South America used knotted and colored strings to keep complex records of everything from the empire's population to the amount of food a village had in store for lean seasons.

Napier's bones: Invented by Scotland's John Napier (1550–1617), this simple device consisted of a series of rods containing the digits 1 to 9. Rotating the rods facilitated multiplication.

Slide rule: Napier's discovery of logarithms led to the invention of this device by William Oughtred (1574–1660). Really a compact set of logarithm tables, the slide rule was widely used well into the twentieth century.

Pascal's adding machine: Invented in 1642 by Frenchman Blaise Pascal (1623–1662), this machine helped Pascal add up figures for his father, a tax collector. In 1673, German Gottfried Leibniz (1646–1716) improved upon Pascal's device by constructing a calculator for multiplication and division.

Babbage's Difference Engine: In the early 1800s, Englishman Charles Babbage built an elaborate machine that could be programmed to process data. However, the existing technology wasn't advanced enough to allow

A counting dial from Hollerith's data processing machine.

Illustration from the patent application for Hollerith's data processing machine.

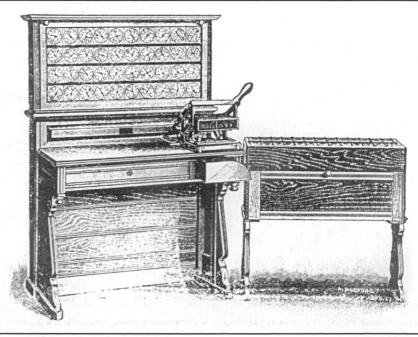

©1996 by Key Curriculum Press

engineers to produce the precision parts needed to make it run effectively. Babbage and English mathematician Ada Byron Lovelace (1815–1852) established the foundations for modern computer development.

Hollerith's data processing machine: In the late 1800s, American engineer Herman Hollerith (1860–1929) perfected a data processor that used punched cards. Until a nine-hole card puncher was created in 1916, the holes on the cards had to be punched one by one.

For more on counting and computing devices, see vignettes 1, 21, 32, 39, 59, 70, 84, and 88. ★

ACTIVITIES

1. How did ancient societies perform arithmetic with fingers? Research Chisonbop, a system of finger counting popular in the United States a few years ago.

2. In the Japanese abacus, called a *soroban,* the upper part of the rods contains one bead, and the lower part contains four beads.

   a. The figures at left indicate where to place the beads to represent various numbers. Draw the appropriate arrangements of beads on the incomplete figures.

   b. Indicate the number represented by each figure.

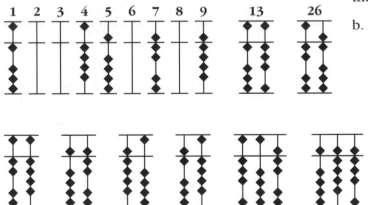

RELATED READING

Crowley, Mary L. "The 'Difference' in Babbage's Difference Engine." *Mathematics Teacher* (May 1985) 366–372, 354.

Goldstine, Herman. *The Computer from Pascal to Von Neumann.* Princeton: Princeton University Press, 1972.

Hyman, Anthony. *Charles Babbage, Pioneer of the Computer.* Princeton, NJ: Princeton University Press, 1982.

Papert, Seymour. *Mindstorms.* New York: Basic Books, 1980.

Pappas, Theoni. *The Joy of Mathematics.* San Carlos, CA: Wide World/Tetra, 1989.

Zaslavsky, Claudia. *Multicultural Mathematics.* Portland, ME: J. Weston Walch, 1993.

Zeintarn, M. *A History of Computing.* Framingham, MA: C.W. Communications, 1981.

The Computer's
Development

84

I n today's technology-rich world, it's easy to forget that the first digital (counting) computer was the human hand! This basic counting device was quickly extended with the use of implements such as notched sticks, containers of pebbles, and abacuses.

There is evidence that the ancient Greeks used gears to compute mechanically, but the first calculating machine of record was constructed by Blaise Pascal in the mid-seventeenth century. His invention preceded the adding machines that were commonly used for the next 200 years. These machines used a set of wheels with ten teeth that represented the digits 0 through 9. When a wheel passed from position 9 to position 0, it moved the neighboring wheel by one tooth, just as we "carry the 1" in addition. In the early nineteenth century, Charles Babbage invented a more complex calculating machine, called the Difference Engine. Together with Ada Byron Lovelace, Babbage programmed punched cards with patterns of holes corresponding to mathematical quantities, using the cards to evaluate mathematical functions.

The first electronic high-speed computer was designed by the United States Army to compute tables showing the flight trajectories of military projectiles. Called the ENIAC (Electronic Numerical Integrator and Calculator), it used the binary addition system {0, 1}. The creation of computers able to store the directions for their operation represented another important step in their development. Computers that could rely on memory to automatically lead them through their computing tasks saved people a tremendous amount of time and work. In the 1940s, the UNIVAC (Universal Automatic Computer) became the first commercial stored-memory machine.

Used primarily by government and industry, there were about one thousand computers in use in 1955, six thousand in 1960, and sixty thousand in 1970. Today millions of computers are used in homes, schools, and businesses for everything from solving complex mathematical problems to playing games. This increased use results from the invention of the microchip, which supplies a speed and a memory far exceeding that of older computers. A microchip is a chip of silicon with an integrated electrical circuit that can store millions of pieces, or bits, of binary infor-

Technocracy, the movement advocating that government and social systems be controlled by technological experts, flourished just before the beginning of the computer age. From the New York Times Magazine, *8 January 1932.*

mation and that can be used as the heart of the computer's operating system. Although people often use them to perform nonmathematical functions, computers still rely on mathematical principles for their operation. Data is stored and retrieved according to methods of mathematical logic, and electronic words and images, in electronic and hard-copy form, are converted from binary codes.

One of the latest developments in computer technology is the Internet, which has served to bring together millions of people throughout the world. Started in 1969 to link research sites working for the United States Department of Defense, the Internet can now be used by anyone interested in information and communication. Publications such as Louis Rosetto and Jane Metcalf's *Wired* and its on-line version, Hotwired,

cater to a subculture fascinated with the capabilities of this new medium, which features on-line text, sound, photos, video, and discussion for the twenty-first century.
For more on computation, see vignettes 39, 70, 83, and 88. ★

Activities

1. The binary system has the values 1, 2, 3, 4, 8, 16, ...

   a. On a balance scale, show how you can use weights of 1, 2, 3, 4, 8, and 16 grams to weigh objects from 1 to 31 grams. What additional weights would you need to be able to weigh objects up to 1 kilogram (1,000 grams)?

   b. Construct an alphabet that translates binary numerals into letters. (This is the principle used by computer word processors.)

2. The elementary programming languages BASIC and LOGO were developed in the mid-1960s. Investigate these and other computer languages. Do they have any interesting features or stories associated with them? What is the potential value to someone who learns how to program?

3. Use a computer in a way that interests you and share your experience with your class. Here are some ideas: Create a multimedia presentation. Write a simple computer program and explain how you did it and how it can be used. Write a story and use the computer to put it into book form. Create a spreadsheet that contains interesting information and explain why spreadsheets are useful for record keeping. Use a drawing program to create a piece of art. Compose a song.

Related Reading

Dewdney, A. K. *The Armchair Universe: An Exploration of Computer Worlds.* New York: W. H. Freeman, 1988.

Engle, Arthur. *Exploring Mathematics with Your Computer.* Washington, DC: Mathematical Association of America, 1993.

Kantrowitz, Barbara. "A Computer Cover Story." *Newsweek* (16 May 1994) 48.

Penrose, Roger. *The Emperor's New Mind.* New York: Oxford University Press, 1989.

Williams, Michael R. *A History of Computing Technology.* Englewood, NJ: Prentice Hall, 1993.

Bees as Mathematicians?

85

Honeybees construct their honeycombs in almost perfect hexagons joined together to form a continuous matrix. Let's explore why this is the best shape bees could use in their construction.

If bees constructed circular cells, there wouldn't be a common wall for an adjacent cell—the gaps between cells would be wasted storage space. Additionally, cells of five, seven, and eight sides wouldn't form a continuous matrix with common walls and no gaps. However, cells in the shape of equilateral triangles or squares *would* form a continuous matrix.

Now consider a cell with perimeter p. If this perimeter encloses a square, the square has side length $x = \frac{1}{4}p$ and area $A = x^2 = (\frac{1}{4}p)^2 = 0.0625p^2$.

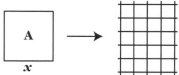

The area of an equilateral triangle with side length y is given by the equation $A = \frac{1}{2}y \times \frac{\sqrt{3}}{2}y$. (The height of the triangle is $\frac{\sqrt{3}}{2}y$.) If the triangle has perimeter p, we can substitute $\frac{1}{3}p$ for y, giving us $A = \frac{1}{2} \times \frac{1}{3}p \times \frac{\sqrt{3}}{2} \times \frac{1}{3}p \approx 0.048p^2$. So, an equilateral triangle encloses even less area than a square of the same perimeter.

The area of a regular hexagon can be given by the formula $A = \frac{1}{2}ap$, where a stands for apothem and p stands for perimeter. (The apothem is the height of one of the triangles within the hexagon, as shown at right.) If the side length is z, the apothem is $\frac{\sqrt{3}}{2}z$ and the hexagon has area $A = \frac{1}{2} \times \frac{\sqrt{3}}{2}z \times p$. Substituting $\frac{1}{6}p$ for z yields $A = \frac{1}{2} \times \frac{\sqrt{3}}{2} \times \frac{1}{6}p \times p \approx 0.072p^2$.

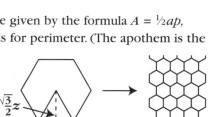

Because $0.072p^2 > 0.0625p^2 > 0.048p^2$, a given perimeter—and thus a given amount of hive-building material—will enclose considerably more area if the shape is hexagonal. Beekeepers who want to assist bees in building honeycombs provide them with a hexagonal framework—the bees won't use any other type. Do you think they instinctively know that the hexagon represents the most economical storage structure for their popular product? ★

> *Bees ... by virtue of a certain geometrical forethought ... know that the hexagon is greater than the square and the triangle, and will hold more honey for the same expenditure of material.*
> —Pappus (ca A.D. 300)

Activities

1. What is the average amount of wax bees use to construct a honeycomb? How much honey can be stored in a honeycomb? What are other interesting features of a hive?

2. When bees build a new honeycomb, why do they orient it in the same direction as the old hive?

3. Consider a piece of wire 12 inches long.

    12"

    a. If you had to bend the wire into a rectangle, what dimensions would maximize the enclosed area?

    b. If you had the choice of bending the wire into a square or a circle, which figure would have the greatest area?

Related Reading

Ellis, Keith. *Number Power in Nature and in Everyday Life.* New York: St. Martin's Press, 1978.

Gardner, Martin. *The Scientific Book of Mathematical Puzzles and Diversions.* New York: Simon and Schuster, 1959.

Kappraff, Jay. *Connections: The Geometric Bridge Between Art and Science.* New York: McGraw-Hill, 1991.

Pappas, Theoni. *The Magic of Mathematics.* San Carlos, CA: Wide World/Tetra, 1994.

Peterson, Ivars. *Islands of Truth: A Mathematical Mystery Cruise.* New York: W.H. Freeman, 1990.

von Neumann: Mathematics as Experience

86

Not greatly influenced by formal schools of mathematical thought, Hungarian-born **John von Neumann** (1903–1957), was a freewheeling spirit who believed that mathematics developed through experience. Recognized early, von Neumann's mathematical talents were such that he was able to obtain a Ph.D. in mathematics from Budapest while spending most of his time in Zurich earning a degree in chemical engineering. He began a teaching career in Germany, but like many other mathematicians and scientists of Jewish background, he emigrated to the United States to escape political unrest in Europe. In 1933, he became a member of the Institute for Advanced Study at Princeton, New Jersey, where he made considerable contributions to the development of mathematical physics (especially quantum theory), analysis, lattice theory, abstract algebra, and computer technology.

One of von Neumann's contributions to mathematics was the creation of game theory, which has been one of the more practical mathematical developments of modern times. Game theory—the analysis of models of strategic competition to determine the best strategy—is now used in a variety of situations, including economic planning and social science research. During the Cold War, his ideas were used by both the capitalist and communist sides to project minimum loss strategies.

In addition to his ability to solve extremely difficult problems in his head, von Neumann was noted for his sense of humor. Upon emerging from his wrecked car after an automobile crash, he said:"The trees on the right were passing me in orderly fashion at sixty miles per hour. Suddenly one of them stepped out in my path." ★

> *Much of the best mathematical inspiration comes from experience. It is hardly possible to believe in the existence of an absolute immutable concept of mathematical rigor dissociated from all human experience.*
>
> —John von Neumann

THEORY OF GAMES AND ECONOMIC BEHAVIOR

BY JOHN VON NEUMANN, and

OSKAR MORGENSTERN

PRINCETON
PRINCETON UNIVERSITY PRESS
1947

Title page of John von Neumann and Oskar Morgenstern's influential Theory of Games and Economic Behavior (*Princeton University Press, 1947*).

Activities

1. Mathematical folklore has von Neumann solving this problem very quickly: A bird flies back and forth between two trains approaching each other on the same track. The trains, initially 510 miles apart, travel toward each other at 80 and 40 miles per hour, respectively. The bird flies at 150 miles per hour. How far does the bird fly before it's caught between the trains? Can you solve this problem quickly?

2. Research von Neumann's comparisons between computing machines and living organisms.

3. A very valuable prize is behind one of three doors. There is nothing behind the other two doors. You choose a door—this door will not be opened, but one of the other doors will be opened to show you that the prize is not behind it. You will once again be allowed to choose a door and you will get what is behind it. What should you do to maximize your chances of getting the prize? Should you choose the door you initially chose, or should you switch to the other door that hasn't been opened?

Related Reading

Bergamini, David (ed). *Mathematics: Life Science Library.* New York: Time-Life Books, 1972.

Boyer, Carl. *A History of Mathematics.* 2nd ed rev. Uta C. Merzbach. New York: John Wiley, 1991.

Davis, Philip, and Reuben Hersh. *The Mathematical Experience.* Boston: Birkhauser Boston, 1981.

Goldstine, Herman. *The Computer from Pascal to Von Neumann.* Princeton: Princeton University Press, 1972.

Neumann, J. von. *The Computer and the Brain.* New Haven: Yale University Press, 1959.

Newman, James R. *The World of Mathematics,* Vol IV. New York: Simon and Schuster, 1956.

Paulos, John Allen. *Beyond Numeracy: Ruminations of a Numbers Man.* New York: Alfred A. Knopf, 1991.

Smith, Sanderson. *Great Ideas for Teaching Math.* Portland, ME: J. Weston Walch, 1990.

The Inquisitive Einstein

87

Twinkle, twinkle, little star.
How I wonder what you are.
—Children's rhyme

T he discoveries and assertions of physicist **Albert Einstein** (1879–1955) shook the world within the memory of many who are alive today. Once an obscure clerk, Einstein often relaxed after work at a Swiss patent office by playing Mozart on his violin—and working out his theory of relativity.

Einstein believed that the universe was not acting precisely in the manner suggested by Isaac Newton's long-accepted laws. Believing that time, length, and mass are not absolutes but vary according to speed, he also asserted that the speed of light was a constant— and totally independent of how fast a light source or an observer moved with respect to a beam. He put these ideas together in his theory of relativity. In the process, he developed his famous equation, $E = mc^2$, which states that energy (E) is equal to mass (m) multiplied by the square of the speed of light ($c = 186{,}000$ miles per second). This result was confirmed when uranium atoms were split and some of their mass was converted to energy.

Drawing heavily on the ideas of German mathematicians **Carl Friedrich Gauss** (1777–1855) and **Georg Friedrich Bernhard Riemann** (1826–1866), Einstein suggested a curved universe of four dimensions: height, width, breadth, and time. (For more on Carl Friedrich Gauss and Georg Friedrich Bernhard Riemann, see vignettes 61 and 66.) Even while scientists struggled with Einstein's theories, they looked on them with fascination because his theories held possible answers to some of our universe's mysteries.

Einstein once said: "We never cease to stand like curious children before the great mystery into which we are born." While he believed there are mathematical laws that rule the universe, he couldn't say whether we're now using the correct laws. However, in using them, we can hope to come closer and closer to the true universal laws. Relating mathematics to the physical world, he said: "It is certain that mathematics in general and geometry in particular owe their existence to our need to learn something about the properties of real objects." Many people consider Einstein to have been a brilliant man, yet he said of himself: "I have no particular talent. I am only inquisitive." ★

891

3. *Zur Elektrodynamik bewegter Körper; von A. Einstein.*

Daß die Elektrodynamik Maxwells — wie dieselbe gegenwärtig aufgefaßt zu werden pflegt — in ihrer Anwendung auf bewegte Körper zu Asymmetrien führt, welche den Phänomenen nicht anzuhaften scheinen, ist bekannt. Man denke z. B. an die elektrodynamische Wechselwirkung zwischen einem Magneten und einem Leiter. Das beobachtbare Phänomen hangt hier nur ab von der Relativbewegung von Leiter und Magnet, während nach der üblichen Auffassung die beiden Fälle, daß der eine oder der andere dieser Körper der bewegte sei, streng voneinander zu trennen sind. Bewegt sich nämlich der Magnet und ruht der Leiter, so entsteht in der Umgebung des Magneten ein elektrisches Feld von gewissem Energiewerte, welches an den Orten, wo sich Teile des Leiters befinden, einen Strom erzeugt. Ruht aber der Magnet und bewegt sich der Leiter, so entsteht in der Umgebung des Magneten kein elektrisches Feld, dagegen im Leiter eine elektromotorische Kraft, welcher an sich keine Energie entspricht, die aber — Gleichheit der Relativbewegung bei den beiden ins Auge gefaßten Fällen vorausgesetzt — zu elektrischen Strömen von derselben Größe und demselben Verlaufe Veranlassung gibt, wie im ersten Falle die elektrischen Kräfte.

Beispiele ähnlicher Art, sowie die mißlungenen Versuche, eine Bewegung der Erde relativ zum „Lichtmedium" zu konstatieren, führen zu der Vermutung, daß dem Begriffe der absoluten Ruhe nicht nur in der Mechanik, sondern auch in der Elektrodynamik keine Eigenschaften der Erscheinungen entsprechen, sondern daß vielmehr für alle Koordinatensysteme, für welche die mechanischen Gleichungen gelten, auch die gleichen elektrodynamischen und optischen Gesetze gelten, wie dies für die Größen erster Ordnung bereits erwiesen ist. Wir wollen diese Vermutung (deren Inhalt im folgenden „Prinzip der Relativität" genannt werden wird) zur Voraussetzung erheben und außerdem die mit ihm nur scheinbar unverträgliche

At age twenty-four, Einstein contributed the paper shown above to a scientific journal. The paper presents the theory of special relativity, expressing the concept that matter is one form of energy and that a quantity of energy equals the product of mass multiplied by the square of the speed of light ($E = mc^2$).

Activities

1. **Mileva Einstein-Maric**, who had a marvelous scientific mind, married Einstein in 1903. Some people, including Senta Tromel-Ploetz, author of *In the Shadow of Albert Einstein: The Tragic Life of Mileva Einstein-Maric,* argue that she should receive considerable recognition for accomplishments credited to Einstein. Research this claim.

2. Why did European scientists persuade Einstein to send a letter to President Franklin D. Roosevelt in 1939? What was the content of his letter?

3. What is einsteinium?

Related Reading

Barnett, Lincoln. *The Universe and Dr. Einstein.* New York: Signet Science Library Books, 1964.

Hawking, Stephen. *A Brief History of Time.* New York: Bantam Books, 1988.

Hoffman, Banesh. *Albert Einstein: Creator and Rebel.* New York: Viking Press, 1972.

Hollingdale, Stuart. *Makers of Mathematics.* New York: Penguin Books, 1989.

Infeld, Leopold. *Albert Einstein: His Work and Its Influence on Our Lives.* New York: Charles Scribner, 1950.

Johnson, Art. *Classical Math: History Topics for the Classroom.* Palo Alto, CA: Dale Seymour, 1994.

Kline, Morris. *Mathematics: The Loss of Certainty.* New York: Oxford University Press, 1980.

Pappas, Theoni. *More Joy of Mathematics.* San Carlos, CA: Wide World/Tetra, 1991.

Ross, Hugh. *The Fingerprint of God.* Orange, CA: Promise Publishing, 1989.

Grace Murray Hopper: Ever Confident

88

> *It is easier to gain forgiveness than to get permission.*
> —Grace Murray Hopper

Grace **Murray Hopper** (1906–1992) knew what she wanted: to immerse herself in the study of mathematics. Having graduated from Vassar College with degrees in mathematics and physics, she went on to receive her graduate degree and a Ph.D. in mathematics from Yale. Returning to Vassar, she taught mathematics for ten years before entering the Naval Reserve in 1943. Because of her mathematical ability she was assigned to intelligence operations, where she became involved with computers and computer programming.

One of the first computers Hopper worked with was the Mark I, the world's first large-scale automatically sequenced digital computer. Over 50 feet long with bulky mechanical relays that opened and closed noisily, it wasn't long before Hopper knew the ins and outs of this computer's operation. Her colleagues marveled at her programming efficiency, and ever-confident in her own abilities, she said, "I could make a computer do anything which I could completely define." In the late 1950s, to make computer programming language more user-friendly, Hopper developed a computer language written in English rather than in alienating symbols. She then developed a program that translated the English words into code. This led to the creation of the programming language COBOL (COmmon Business Oriented Language), which is still used today.

During her almost fifty years with the navy, Hopper rose to the rank of rear admiral. The recipient of many honors for distinguished service and for computer work, her awards included being named both Computer Science Man-of-the-Year by the Data Processing Management Association, and Distinguished Fellow of the British Computer Society. When she retired at age seventy-nine, she was the oldest commissioned officer and the only woman admiral in the navy. During her career, she had given over 200 lectures, in which she often displayed an 11.5-inch piece of wire to demonstrate how far a computer's electronic information travels in one billionth of a second.

For more on computation, see vignettes 39, 70, 83, and 84. ★

*Grace Murray Hopper.
Photo courtesy of Digital
Equipment Corporation.*

©1996 by Key Curriculum Press

Activities

1. Here are two lines from a hypothetical COBOL program.

   MULTIPLY RATE_OF_PAY BY HOURS_WORKED GIVING

   GROSS_PAY ROUNDED.

   COMPUTER EXCESS = (HOURS_WORKED – 40)*1.5

   What operations would be performed by a computer executing these program lines?

2. Research the computer terms given.

   a. Machine language

   b. Assembly language

   c. Compiler

3. How long would it take electronic computer information to travel (a) 1 mile, (b) 100 miles, and (c) 1,000 miles? Use the information given in this vignette to answer this question.

4. Two popular computer languages developed for computers are BASIC (Beginner's All-Purpose Symbolic Instruction Code) and FORTRAN (FORmula TRANslation). How do these languages differ from COBOL?

5. How was Grace Murray Hopper involved in the adoption of the word *bug* in computer jargon?

Related Reading

Dorf, Richard. *Computers and Man*. San Francisco: Boyd and Fraser, 1974.

Feigenbaum, Edward, and Pamela McCorduck. *The Fifth Generation*. Reading, MA: Addison-Wesley, 1983.

Graham, Neill. *The Mind Tool: Computers and Their Impact on Society*. St. Paul, MN: West Publishing, 1980.

Johnson, Art. *Classical Math: History Topics for the Classroom*. Palo Alto, CA: Dale Seymour, 1994.

National Women's History Project. *Outstanding Women in Mathematics and Science*. Windsor, CA: National Women's History Project, 1991.

"Numbers Count . . . to Everyone." Poster highlighting the lives of Maria Goeppert Mayer, Cecilia Payne-Gaposchkin, Grace Murray Hopper, Maggie Lena Walker, and Mary Dolciani Halloran. Boston: Houghton Mifflin, 1987.

SHIING-SHEN CHERN: A LEADER IN GEOMETRY

89

Shiing-shen Chern

C hinese mathematician **Shiing-shen Chern** (b 1911) has long devoted himself to the study and the advancement of both classical and modern geometry. In particular, his research in differential geometry has influenced many areas of mathematics and mathematical physics.

When he was a young child, Chern learned about numbers and the four arithmetic operations from his father. His interest sparked, he went on to teach himself more arithmetic, thus meeting the first of many challenges he was to encounter in his long-time quest for quality training in mathematics. When he became an adult, these challenges became more, well, *challenging*. Upon graduating from Nan Kai University in 1930, it seemed to Chern that many teachers who could offer him advanced training in mathematics did not encourage much originality or creative thinking in their students, but instead had them work on routine problems. To avoid this potentially stifling situation, he decided he would have to leave China to continue his studies. Because his family could not cover the expense this entailed, he applied and was accepted to Qing Hua graduate school, where he had a chance at earning a government fellowship that would allow him to study abroad. He graduated in 1934, indeed earning a two-year fellowship to study in the United States. However, his interest in the theory of curves and surfaces took him instead to Hamburg, Germany, then to Paris, France.

Chern loved the intensive work and research he was accomplishing abroad, but when Qing Hua offered him an appointment as a mathematics professor in 1937, he returned to China—just as the Sino-Japanese War was starting. Although the war created much hardship and hampered communication with the outside world, Chern was able to continue much important research, and he soon earned a reputation as one of the most talented mathematicians of China. His reputation did not go unnoticed in other parts of the world, and in 1943, he accepted a membership with the Institute for Advanced Study at Princeton, New Jersey. The two years he spent at Princeton proved to be very fruitful, and there Chern completed some of his most influential work.

In 1946, China beckoned once again, and Chern returned to organize the creation of China's Institute of Mathematics. However, within the next two years China was engulfed by civil war, and in 1949, Chern moved his family to the United States. For the next thirty years, he taught mathematics, first at the University of Chicago in Illinois, then at the University of California in Berkeley. In addition to his influential work as a professor, Chern has long dedicated efforts to creating an atmosphere in China conducive to that country's becoming a world leader in mathematics. To this end, he founded the Nan Kai Mathematical Research Institute in 1985, which provides mathematicians and students from China and around the world with an inspiring place in which to exchange ideas and concentrate on research.

His important work in differential geometry and his commitment to the sharing of research and ideas among many countries has earned Chern a place in history as an inspired and inspiring leader in mathematics.

For more on Chinese mathematics, see vignettes 4, 8, 22, 26, 48, and 71. ★

ACTIVITIES

1. What is the Chern-Pontryagin number?

2. Chern was instrumental in establishing the Mathematical Sciences Research Institute at the University of California at Berkeley in 1981. Why was this institute established? What research is conducted there now?

3. What kind of mathematical education did Chern receive during his teenage years in China? Does it differ from the education you receive now?

RELATED READING

Albers, Donald J., et al (eds). *More Mathematical People.* Boston: Harcourt Brace Jovanovich, 1990.

Chern, Shiing-shen. "What is Geometry?" *American Mathematical Monthly* 97, #8 (Oct 1990) 679–86.

Li, Yan, and Du Shiran. *Chinese Mathematics: A Concise History*. **New York: Oxford University Press, 1987.**

McGraw-Hill Encyclopedia of Science and Technology, 9th ed, Vol 9.

Mikami, Yoshio. *The Development of Mathematics in China and Japan.* New York: Chelsea Publishing, 1961.

Yau, Shing-Tung (ed). *Chern—A Great Geometer of the Twentieth Century.* Hong Kong: International Press, 1992.

90

M. C. Escher: Artist and Geometer

Dutch-born **Maurits Cornelis Escher** (1898–1972) was not particularly interested in mathematics or science as a child. However, he had a methodical personality, and in the lessons he received in carpentry and woodcarving, he developed a controlled approach to craftsmanship. These attributes are evident in the intricate and intriguing graphic works he created as an adult.

In his early work, Escher had experimented with drawings that depended on what he referred to as "a regular division of the plane," or symmetry. However, he didn't begin working in earnest with this motif until several years after he'd returned from a trip to Spain in 1922. Influenced by the geometric patterns that decorate the Alhambra, a thirteenth-century Moorish palace in Granada, Spain, Escher's work contains a major difference: He used recognizable life forms, such as animals, people, and plants. Following the dictates of their Islamic faith, the Moors had worked solely with abstract geometric designs that represented a beautiful, ordered, and reasoned universe.

For many years, Escher studied geometry to gain a greater understanding of symmetry and of the transformations called translation, rotation, and reflection. By using these transformations on grids of equilateral triangles and certain regular polygons, he created tessellations, or tilings. Tessellations are arrangements of closed shapes that completely fill a surface without overlapping or leaving gaps. Frequently, Escher extended his tessellations to create mysterious and dislocated drawings. In his lithograph titled *Reptiles* (1943), small salamander-like creatures leave the two-dimensional world of a drawing to become three-dimensional. After crawling over some objects on a desk, they re-enter the drawing, once again becoming two-dimensional.

Some of Escher's works contain surprising paradoxes—in certain imaginative situations, it's hard to believe what you see. For example, his *Waterfall* (1961) depicts a stream of water that appears to fall from a height, then flow upward toward its source. Thus the stream flows in perpetual, circular motion. In other works, staircases connect floors within a building—or do they lead outside?—and windows become part of the village they look upon.

For more on paradoxes and contradictions, see vignettes 13 and 72. For more on art and mathematics, see vignettes 34, 35, 50, 59, 100, 101, and 107. ★

> *By having confronted the enigmas that surround us, and by considering and analyzing the observations that I had made, I ended up in the domain of mathematics.*
>
> —M. C. Escher

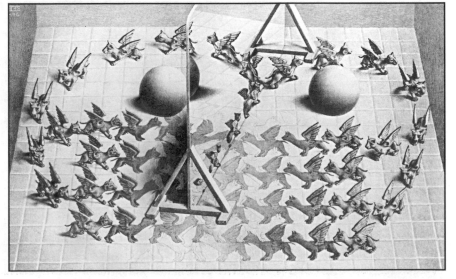

©1996 by Key Curriculum Press

Activities

1. A regular polygon is a polygon with all sides equal in length and all angles equal in measure. Examine regular polygons with three, four, five, six, and eight sides. Which of these can be used to tile a surface with no gaps or overlaps?

2. Define the terms *transformation, translation, rotation,* and *reflection.* In what ways are these concepts used in other works of art and architecture around the world?

3. A paradox is defined as a self-contradictory and false idea or situation. It is also defined as a seemingly absurd idea or situation that expresses a possible truth. Can you find paradoxical images in any Escher drawings? Describe the paradoxes you find. Do you think any of his paradoxes contain an element of truth? Explain.

4. Use interactive geometry software to create a tiling design.

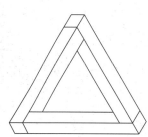

5. The Penrose triangle shown at left demonstrates the paradox of seeing a drawing of an object that cannot be constructed in three dimensions. Draw your own picture of the triangle. Explain why it is an impossible construction.

Related Reading

Edwards, Lois, and Kevin Lee. *TesselMania! Math Connection.* Berkeley, CA: Key Curriculum Press, 1995.

Escher, M.C. *Escher on Escher: Exploring the Infinite.* New York: Harry N. Abrams, 1986.

———. *The Graphic Work of M. C. Escher.* New York: Ballantine Books, 1960.

Schattschneider, Doris. *Visions of Symmetry: Notebooks, Periodic Drawings, and Related Works of M. C. Escher.* New York: W.H. Freeman, 1990.

Serra, Michael. "Geometric Art" and "Transformations and Tessellations." *Discovering Geometry: An Inductive Approach.* Berkeley, CA: Key Curriculum Press, 1989.

Seymour, Dale, and Jill Britton. *Introduction to Tessellations.* Palo Alto, CA: Dale Seymour, 1989.

Moon Flights

91

How far is far? How high is high? You'll never know until you try.

—Slogan from the Special Olympics

On July 16, 1969, United States astronaut **Neil Alden Armstrong** became the first human being to set foot on the moon. Modern mathematics, science, and human ingenuity had led to an event that had been the subject of dreams and fantasies for centuries.

The moon has inspired many imaginative people to write stories about traveling to this bright world. Early writers knew very little about earth's neighbor and so didn't depict it realistically. Many thought it was just another far-off land too difficult to reach using the existing methods of travel. Stories about going to the moon were simply fantasies written to amuse the reader. Greek writer **Lucian** (ca A.D. 120–180) wrote tales about heroes who flew to the moon with bird wings or who were carried to the moon by a whirlwind. In his epic poem *Orlando Furioso* (1516), Italian poet **Ludovico Ariosto** (1474–1533) created a hero who reached the moon by riding the chariot that had appeared before Elijah in the Bible.

Even the serious astronomer **Johannes Kepler** (1571–1630) indulged in fantasy. He wrote a story in which the hero reaches the moon in a dream. Interestingly, this is the first known story to give the moon "real" properties, although on Kepler's moon, days and nights were two weeks long.

When **Galileo Galilei** (1564–1642) established that the moon was indeed a real body in space, stories about journeys to the moon became even more popular. In *Man in the Moon,* a book by English writer **Francis Godwin** (1562–1633), the hero travels to the moon in a vehicle pulled by large birds. These many stories assumed that the space between earth and the moon was filled with air—humans had never reached the airless heights above the earth.

We now know that the space beyond the earth is a vacuum and that birdlike flight to the moon is impossible. French writer **Cyrano de Bergerac** (1619–1655) described seven different ways to reach the moon in 1650. Six were fantasy methods, but the seventh involved rocketry—almost 40 years before **Isaac Newton** established the basic principles of rocketry and over 300 years before developments in space travel would lead to the 1969 moon landing! ★

The life and the work of author, playwright, soldier, and adventurer Cyrano de Bergerac included far more than that written about him in Edmund Rostand's 1897 play. Pictured above is a page from de Bergerac's The Comical History of the States and Empires of the World of the Moon and Sun *(London, 1687), which touches on the possibility of space travel.*

©1996 by Key Curriculum Press

Activities

1. What are the dimensions of the moon and how do they compare with those of the earth? What is the average distance of the moon from the earth? What is the minimum distance? The maximum distance?

2. Find some fictional stories about the moon. What physical properties have been attributed to the moon? What assumptions have been made about travel to the moon?

3. Comment on these thoughts presented by Timothy Ferris in his book *The Universe and Eye*.

   a. If we seek to colonize the moon and other planets to escape ecological disaster at home, this effort will most certainly be doomed.

   b. If we take care of our own planet, we might be able to seed the moon and other planets with earthly life.

4. American physician **Lewis Thomas** realized that the earth is but a tiny island in the boundless and mysterious ocean of our universe. Comment on his statement: "The greatest of all accomplishments of twentieth-century science is the discovery of human ignorance."

Related Reading

Asimov, Isaac. *Guide to Earth and Space*. New York: Ballantine Books, 1991.

Eddington, Sir Arthur. *The Expanding Universe*. Cambridge, MA: Cambridge University Press, 1933.

Ferris, Timothy. *The Universe and Eye*. **San Francisco: Chronicle Books, 1993.**

French, Bevan M. *The Moon Book*. New York: Penguin Books, 1977.

Kaufmann, William J. *Planets and Moons*. New York: W.H. Freeman, 1979.

Pearce, David. "Is the Public Ready to Pay the Price?" *London Times* (26 Sept 1990).

Percentages and Statistics: What Do They Tell Us?

92

H istorically, statistics originated as "state-istics"—data collected by states to determine how many taxable farms or military-age men were in specific land regions. Now, statistical data is a common reality in many aspects of our lives. While statistics can provide us with much useful information, it's important that we learn to interpret what they actually tell us—and what they don't.

In August 1977, the Bureau of Labor Statistics stated that the unemployment rate was 6.1 percent for white workers and 14.5 percent for African American workers. In relation to these figures, the *New York Times* (3 September 1977) reported the following:

> *The bureau also reported that the ratio of black to white jobless rates "continued its recent updrift to the unusually high level of 2.4 to 1 in August," meaning that 2.4 black workers were without jobs for every unemployed white worker.*

While it's true that the ratio $14.5\%_1$ equals approximately 2.4, it is also true that there are far fewer African Americans than whites in the labor force. As an example, assume that the labor force consists of 1,000 whites and 100 African Americans. Using the Bureau of Labor Statistics figures, the number of unemployed whites would be $1,000 \times 6.1\%$, or approximately 60. The number of unemployed African Americans would be $100 \times 14.5\%$, or about 15. So, in fact, four white workers were unemployed for every one unemployed African American worker. The *Times'* conclusion provides a classic example of how someone compiling statistical data may confuse percentages with actual counts.

Because statisticians sometimes fail to take into account all the factors that contribute to a situation, their data may be misleading or incorrect. Statistics often influence public opinion about an issue, so inaccurate data can have far-reaching implications. For example, say a new police commissioner takes office in a large city. During the first year of his or her tenure, the number of petty larcenies reported in the city more than doubles. Can we conclude that the new commissioner is ineffective? Say we look carefully at all the related information and find that the statistic results from the establishment of a much-improved reporting system. We then see that what actually rose was the number of *reported* crimes. However, what do we know about the number of *actual* crimes committed compared with those committed in the year before the commissioner took office?

For more on statistics, see vignette 104. ★

> *Conclusions that are wrong or just incomprehensible are often the result of plain old-fashioned blunders. Rates and percentages are the most common cause of crooked arithmetic. Sometimes the matter can be straightened out by some numerical detective work.*
>
> —David S. Moore, *Statistics: Concepts and Controversies*

> *If a man stood with one foot in a hot oven and the other foot in a freezer, statisticians would say that on the average he was comfortable.*
>
> —*Quote Magazine* (29 June 1975)

Activities

1. A university offers only two degrees, one in math and one in science. Admission to these programs is very competitive. Admission data are given below.

	Male	Female
Admit	35	20
Deny	45	40

a. What is the percentage of male applicants admitted? Of female applicants admitted?

b. Is there a suggestion of possible discrimination against women? Data showing admission by program are given below.

MATH

	Male	Female
Admit	30	10
Deny	30	10

SCIENCE

	Male	Female
Admit	5	10
Deny	15	30

c. Is this data consistent with the original admission data?

d. What is the percentage of male applicants admitted to the math program? Of female applicants?

e. Is there a suggestion of possible discrimination against women in the math program?

f. What is the percentage of male applicants admitted to the science program? Of female applicants?

g. Is there a suggestion of possible discrimination against women in the science program?

h. Does the university discriminate against women in its admissions policy?

2. Comment on this statement that appears on the wrapper of a well-known brand of sugarless gum: "4 out of 5 dentists surveyed recommended sugarless gum for their patients who chew gum."

3. Comment on the quotes given below.

It is now proved beyond a shadow of a doubt that smoking is one of the leading causes of statistics.

—Fletcher Knebel

Statistical thinking will one day be as necessary for efficient citizenship as the ability to read and write.

—H. G. Wells

Each of us is a statistical impossibility around which hover a million other lives that were never destined to be born.

—Leslie Eiseley

Related Reading

Battista, Michael. "Mathematics in Baseball." *Mathematics Teacher* (Apr 1993) 336–342.

Dewdney, A.K. ***200% of Nothing***. **New York: John Wiley, 1993**.

Gross, Fred E., et al. *The Power of Numbers: A Teacher's Guide to Mathematics in a Social Studies Context.* Cambridge, MA: Educators for Social Responsibility, 1993.

Huff, Darrell. *How to Lie with Statistics.* New York: W.W. Norton, 1982.

Kline, Morris. *Mathematics and the Physical World.* New York: Thomas Y. Crowell, 1959.

————. ***Mathematics for the Nonmathematician***. **Mineola, NY: Dover, 1967**.

Lightner, James. "A Brief Look at the History of Probability and Statistics." *Mathematics Teacher* (Nov 1991) 623–630.

Moore, David S. ***Statistics: Concepts and Controversies***. **New York: W.H. Freeman, 1991**.

Paulos, John Allen. ***Innumeracy: Mathematical Illiteracy and Its Consequences***. **New York: Hill and Wang, 1988**.

Smith, Sanderson. ***Great Ideas for Teaching Math***. **Portland, ME: J. Weston Walch, 1990**.

WHEN A LOSS COULD HAVE BEEN A WIN

93

Can you imagine reading this headline on the sports page of a newspaper: "Braves Must Lose Final Two Games to Qualify for Playoffs." Believe it or not, in 1981 a situation like this was quite possible in major league baseball. Because of a players' strike and the loss of scheduled games, major league administrators decided that each of the four existing divisions would have a split season. The teams leading their respective divisions at the beginning of the strike were declared champions of the first half of the season. When play resumed after the strike, the second half-season would begin. The following playoff guidelines were established for each division.

1. If two different teams won a half-season, they would have a playoff for the division pennant.

2. If the same team won both half-seasons, then it would have a playoff for the division pennant with the team having the best overall winning percentage over both half-seasons. (This ensured a money-generating playoff for each division pennant.)

These guidelines were accepted and published by the proper authorities. They certainly seemed reasonable—until a hypothetical situation like that shown below was presented to league officials.

Assume two games remain in the second half-season.

FIRST HALF Final standings				SECOND HALF Two games remaining		
	Won	**Lost**			**Won**	**Lost**
Dodgers	50	20		**Dodgers**	48	20
Braves	49	21		**Astros**	47	21
Astros	40	30		**Braves**	45	23
Padres	32	38		**Reds**	25	43
Giants	20	50		**Giants**	21	47
Reds	19	51		**Padres**	18	50

Assume that the Braves are scheduled to play their final two games against the Dodgers. As the second-half standings indicate, the Braves have no chance of being champions of the second half-season because only two games remain to be played. If the Astros win the second half-season, they will play the Dodgers for the division championship and the Braves will be out of the championship. However, if the Dodgers win the second half-season, they will play for the championship against the team with the best overall record for the entire season.

Even if the Braves lose their last two games, their overall record of 96 wins and 44 losses will be superior to the 89 wins and 51 losses of the Astros if they win their last two games. The Braves would then face this unique situation: If they were to lose their last two games, they would automatically qualify for the division championship playoff. If they were to win one or two games against the Dodgers, they might be eliminated from the championship playoff. A winning strategy for the Braves would be to simply forfeit the two games to the Dodgers. Fortunately, this potentially troublesome situation did not arise during the 1981 split season. ★

ACTIVITIES

1. Why do many minor leagues in baseball use a split season schedule?

2. In recent years, major sports leagues have instituted a playoff system allowing as many as 16 teams to participate in playoffs at the end of a regular sports season. This lets teams with relatively poor won/lost records compete for a championship. Answer the questions below for your favorite major league baseball, basketball, hockey, and football teams.

   a. What is the worst won/lost record for a team that has won a championship?

   b. Show that it would be possible for a team to win a championship by losing more games than it wins during a regular season and playoffs.

3. A tennis tournament has eight players who are placed randomly in the first-round rung of the tournament ladders, as shown. The loser of the finals gets the Runner-up Cup. If the players are ranked, and if a player always defeats a player with a lower ranking, what is the probability that the second-best player will be the recipient of the Runner-up Cup?

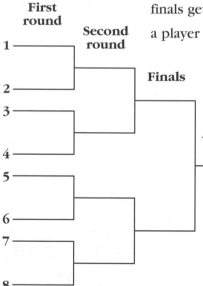

RELATED READING

Battista, Michael. "Mathematics in Baseball." *Mathematics Teacher* (Apr 1993) 336–342.

Boehm, David A. (ed). *Guinness Sports Record Book.* New York: Sterling Publications, 1990.

Hopkins, Nigel, et al. *Go Figure: The Numbers You Need for Everyday Life.* Detroit: Visible Ink Press, 1992.

Lineberry, W.P. (ed). *The Business of Sports.* New York: H.W. Wilson, 1973.

Smith, Sanderson. "It Could Have Happened! Sports Headline: Braves Must Lose Final Two Games to Qualify for Playoffs." *California Mathematics Council ComMuniCator* (Dec 1991).

Townsend, M.S. *Mathematics in Sport.* New York: John Wiley, 1984.

Voices from the Well 94

I t is only in recent years that women's achievements in mathematics and science have been given adequate acknowledgment. As you may have already discovered, the names that most frequently appear in the history of mathematics are those of men. Many women who have gained recognition in the quantitative fields did so by overcoming societal prejudices and the tremendous handicap of not being allowed to participate in university mathematics and science programs.

In 1982, dramatist **Terre Ouwehand** wrote *Voices from the Well*, a play showcasing extraordinary women from history, myth, literature, and art. Presented in Greek chorus style, the historical figures portrayed deliver monologues from their own time periods. One of the featured women is **Caroline Herschel** (1750–1848), who along with her brother William Herschel founded modern astronomy. Although Caroline was an equal partner in their many accomplishments—such as discovering a number of comets and nebulae—William received the lion's share of the credit, including being appointed England's Royal Astronomer for the discovery of the planet Uranus.

Although she was trained in concert singing and dressmaking, Caroline Herschel found she was more interested in the sciences. She pursued a career in astronomy for more than fifty years.

In *Voices from the Well*, Ouwehand reflects Caroline Herschel's frustration.

> *(seated before a telescope; notebook on lap)*
> *(muttering to self) . . . the mean sidereal oscillation . . . bisected by the fixed elliptical quotient . . . conjuncted at the point of annual stellar parallax—*
>
> *(responding to someone off-stage) Yes . . . yes, William, I have everything ready. Yes, both telescopes are set precisely at the angle and degree that we determined over dinner . . . as always. Yes, dear brother, it is now past time—Sirius is already at sixty degrees . . .*
> *(to self; writing in notebook) Note to self: tomorrow: have William's timepiece sent out for repair.*
>
> *(off-stage) Yes, the extra chair is here next to your station with log book already upon it . . . (to self/audience) so that I can, at your bidding—at the drop of a sidereal second— leap up, leave my own observations and come to your side to write down your observations . . . as always.*
> *(writing in her notebook) Note to self: tomorrow: have extra chair sent out for re-covering: tell upholsterer no hurry.*
>
> *(off-stage) No, William, I do not know where your new fifty magnitude lens is—it was certainly in its case last night, for so I replaced it myself after you had retired . . . (to self/audience) after I had cleaned it and reground it and cleaned it again and polished it, for*

Terre Ouwehand.
Photo by Kathleen Weir.

HISTORY OF MATH   ©1996 by Key Curriculum Press   193

*so I do with all your lenses, and all your glasses, all your mir-
rors, all your reflectors, your refractors, and detectors . . .*

*That is, of course, after I have copied out, in longhand, your
evening's observations, verified them with minute mathematical
calculations, and entered everything neatly and precisely in your
voluminous journal that will surely be published, surely be
hailed as the definitive text of modern astronomy—*

Eventually Caroline Herschel received recognition for her many contributions.
In 1835, she and **Mary Somerville** became the first women to be named as honorary members of the Royal Astronomical Society. (For more on Mary Somerville,
see vignette 65.) ★

Activities

1. Who are the other women included in *Voices from the Well*?

2. Research the life and the contributions of Caroline Herschel. Compare
her intellectual relationship with her brother William to that of **Albert
Einstein** and **Mileva Einstein-Maric**.

3. Two women in mathematics who experienced frustrations similar
to those of Herschel are **Charlotte Angas Scott** (1858-1931) and
Mary Francis Winston Newson (1869-1959). Research their lives
and contributions.

Related Reading

Dash, Joan. *The Triumph of Discovery*. **Westwood,
NJ: Silver Burdett and Ginn, 1991.**

McGrayne, S.B. *Nobel Prize Women in Science—Their
Lives, Struggles, and Momentous Discoveries*. New York:
Birch Lane Press, 1993.

National Women's History Project. *Outstanding
Women in Mathematics and Science*. **Windsor, CA:
National Women's History Project, 1991.**

Ogilvie, Marilyn Bailey. *Woman in Science*. Cambridge,
MA: MIT Press, 1991.

Osen, Lynn. *Women in Mathematics*. Cambridge, MA:
MIT Press, 1974.

Ouwehand, Terre. *Voices from the Well: Extraordinary
Women of History, Myth, Literature, and Art*. San Luis
Obispo, CA: Padre Productions, 1986.

Gender Equity in Mathematics

95

In the eighteenth century *The Ladies Diary* was one of the few sources of mathematical material readily available to women. Then, as in previous centuries, even educated women were taught little more than basic arithmetic unless they were assisted by a family member or friend who provided them with books or a tutor.

> *Our goal is to make people comfortable with mathematics. Math should be something that people aren't afraid of. After all, math is everywhere around us if we know how to recognize it.*
>
> —Theoni Pappas

Although girls and women have had freer access to a mathematics education in the twentieth century, this field of study is still considered by many to be a "male domain." However, despite little encouragement—or overt discouragement—many women have earned advanced degrees in mathematics and science and have gone on to make noteworthy contributions to these fields. For example, in 1983, **Dr. Julia Robinson** was elected president of the American Mathematical Society, the first woman officer to be elected in the history of the organization. Dr. Robinson was highly respected for her more than twenty year's mathematical research, and a few years earlier she had been elected to the prestigious National Academy of Sciences.

Many organizations have been formed to directly confront discrimination in the math and science fields. In 1971, Professor Mary Gray of American University issued a newsletter calling upon colleagues to formally address gender issues. Thus the organization **Women and Mathematics** was born. Around the same time, sociologist Dr. Lucy Sells completed research showing that mathematics was a "critical filter," keeping many young women from entering careers that had high salary potential and great social and economic usefulness. In 1973, after reviewing the implications of this research, a group of women educators and scientists in Berkeley, California, formed the **Math/Science Network**. Soon after, the Network organized the first Expanding Your Horizons conference, in which women from business, industry, and education invited high school girls to a day of activities and talks illustrating the value of an education in math and science. By 1995, the Network had coordinated conferences with thousands of adult volunteers, reaching more than 350,000 middle- and high-school girls all across the country.

Today there are several organizations that focus on women in the quantitative fields, such as **Women in Mathematics Education** and the **International Organization of Women and Mathematics Education**. Some of these organizations, notably **EQUALS** and **Family Math at the Lawrence Hall of**

The Ladies Diary, *"containing many delightful and entertaining particulars, peculiarly adapted for the use and diversion of the fair sex." Photo courtesy of the Department of Special Collections, Stanford University Libraries.*

©1996 by Key Curriculum Press

Science, organize workshops to educate teachers about how they can prevent gender discrimination in the classroom. Additionally, individuals from government, business, and research contribute to a better understanding of the importance of mathematics education.

Thanks to the efforts of women and men concerned with equity in education, women's participation and success in the fields of mathematics and science is rapidly growing. ★

Activities

1. Interview one or more women mathematicians. (The mathematics department of a local college or university can help you obtain a potential list to meet your interests.) In your interview, discuss the mathematics for which she is best known and the obstacles she may have faced in her career. Present to the class what you learned in your interview.

2. Women all around the world have long struggled for equity in education and in the work force. Study the advances or the setbacks to women's rights in these areas, both historic and current, in a country of your choosing.

Related Reading

Chipman, S.F., L.R. Brush, and D.M. Wilson (eds). *Women in Mathematics: Balancing the Equation*. Hillsdale, NJ: Lawrence Erlbaum, 1985.

Downey, Diane, T. Slesnick, and J. Stenmark. *Math for Girls and Other Problem Solvers*. Berkeley, CA: EQUALS/Lawrence Hall of Science, 1981.

Fennema, Elizabeth, and G.C. Leder (eds). *Mathematics and Gender*. New York: Teachers College Press, 1990.

National Women's History Project. *Outstanding Women in Mathematics and Science*. Windsor, CA: National Women's History Project, 1991.

Perl, Teri. *Women and Numbers: Lives of Women Mathematicians plus Discovery Activities*. San Carlos, CA: Wide World/Tetra, 1993.

Rózsa Péter and Recursion

96

Rózsa Péter (1905–1977) was a leading contributor to the theory of recursive functions. The Hungarian mathematician was also the first person to propose that recursive functions be studied in their own right. Today, recursion plays a vital role in computer programming and is used to define number processes and geometric objects such as fractals. The Sierpiński gasket and the Koch snowflake, shown below, are examples of fractals defined recursively. (For more on fractals, see vignettes 35, 101, 103, and 107.)

In 1927, Péter graduated from Budapest's Eötvös Loránd University, then went on to become a world-famous logician. Committed to sharing her mathematical knowledge with nonmathematicians, she wrote *Playing with Infinity: Mathematical Explorations and Excursions* (1961), a popular book that has been translated into twelve languages. Her *Recursive Functions in Computer Theory,* which describes the connections between recursive functions and computer languages, represents the culmination of her mathematical research.

Péter defined recursion as follows: "[T]he Latin technical term recursion refers to a certain kind of stepping backwards in the sequence of natural numbers, which necessarily ends after a finite number of steps. With the use of such recursions, the values of even the most complicated functions used in number theory can be calculated in a finite number of steps. The emphasis is on the finite number of steps."

Are you having a hard time visualizing recursion? You're not alone. Because it is an abstract concept that is not apparent in everyday life, some find it difficult to understand. **Molly Lynn Watt** of the Education Development Center in Newton, Massachusetts, has created what she calls plays to help teachers and students understand recursion. In these plays, students (players) use dramatic techniques to "act out" recursion. Watt discusses this concept as it relates to the LOGO programming language. When LOGO solves a complicated problem by "calling" a copy of itself to act as its helper, it is breaking the problem into Péter's "finite number of steps," thus utilizing the concept of recursion.

One play involves washing birthday party dishes. If LOGO were a person, it wouldn't wash all the party dishes after everyone had gone home; it would use a recursive procedure to get the job done. First, a procedure to follow is created.

```
TO DO.BIRTHDAY.PARTY.DISHES
    If your placemat is empty
        STOP
        Otherwise: clear dishes from placement
    Wash dishes
    Dry dishes
    Put dishes away
    DO.BIRTHDAY.PARTY.DISHES
END
```

> *I myself work in a field that was created for purposes internal to mathematics. This is the theory of the so-called recursive functions— I would not have dreamed that this theory could also be applied practically. And today? My book on recursive functions was the second Hungarian mathematical book to be published in the Soviet Union, and precisely on the practical grounds that its subject matter has become indispensable to the theory of computers. And so it goes, sooner or later, for all branches of so-called pure mathematics ... one never has to worry that one is working on something useless.*
>
> —Rózsa Péter

Sierpiński gasket

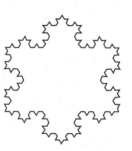

Koch snowflake

The first player follows the first line of the procedure, DO.BIRTHDAY.PARTY.DISHES, which directs the player to see if the placemat is empty. If it is empty, there are no dishes to do and the play is over. If there are dishes on the placemat, the player continues to follow the procedure line by line. He or she clears, washes, dries, and puts away his or her dishes, then calls the next player to follow another copy of the procedure. That player follows the same instructions, then calls the next player, who follows the instructions, and so on. Eventually, a player is called who has an empty placemat, so the procedure stops and the play ends. Thus, recursion was used to turn a big job into many little ones, which made the job easier to complete.

Here is an example of how recursion can be used to define number processes. The function $n!$ is called n factorial and equals $1 \times 2 \times 3 \times \ldots \times (n - 1) \times n$, when $n \geq 0$.

Recursively the factorial function can be defined like this:

$$f(n) = \begin{cases} 1 & \text{if } n = 0 \\ n \times f(n - 1) & \text{if } n > 0 \end{cases}$$

Both definitions are equivalent. For example, $4! = 1 \times 2 \times 3 \times 4 = 24$, and

$$\begin{aligned} f(4) &= 4 \times f(3) \\ &= 4 \times 3 \times f(2) \\ &= 4 \times 3 \times 2 \times f(1) \\ &= 4 \times 3 \times 2 \times 1 \times f(0) \\ &= 4 \times 3 \times 2 \times 1 \times 1 \\ &= 24. \ \star \end{aligned}$$

Activities

1. The Tower of Hanoi is a classic puzzle that was created in 1883. Learn how to solve this puzzle, then describe a solution in terms of recursion.

2. Write a LOGO program that uses recursion.

3. BASIC, LOGO, and PASCAL are three computer languages that are taught in schools. Compare the ways in which each language handles recursion.

Related Reading

Morris, Edie, and Leon Harkleroad. "Rózsa Péter: Recursive Function Theory's Founding Mother." *The Mathematical Intelligencer* 12(1) (1990) 59-64.

Péter, Rózsa. *Playing with Infinity: Mathematical Explorations and Excursions.* Mineola, NY: Dover, 1961.

Poundstone, William. *The Recursive Universe.* New York: William Morrow, 1985.

Tamássy, István. "Interview with Rózsa Péter," trans Leon Harkleroad. *Modern Logic* 4(3) (1994) 277–280.

Watt, Molly and Daniel Watt. *Teaching with Logo.* Menlo Park, CA: Addison-Wesley, 1985.

Triskaidekaphobia

97

T he word is indeed a mouthful, but **triskaidekaphobia**—fear of the number 13—affects many people in our society, even if they can't pronounce the term for their affliction. We can prove mathematically that every year must have a Friday the 13th, and when that day comes, it's been estimated that United States businesses lose millions of dollars because of canceled appointments, absenteeism, and the like. This problem is compounded by the media's "unlucky 13" stories that attract the public's attention prior to a Friday the 13th.

> *Number was born in superstition and reared in mystery, ... numbers were once made the foundations of religion and philosophy, and the tricks of figures have had a marvelous effect on credulous people.*
> —F. W. Parker

Triskaidekaphobia has influenced many historical figures and events. Industrialist Henry Ford wouldn't do business on Friday the 13th. Multimillionaire Paul Getty once stated: "I wouldn't care to be one of thirteen at a table." Many guests at hotels refuse to stay in Room 13, so rooms are frequently numbered 12, 12A, and 14, avoiding the number 13 altogether. In 1965, noticing that the queen of England, Elizabeth II, was scheduled to leave from Platform 13 at a German railway station, railway officials changed the platform's number to 12A. Some speculate that a fear of the number 13 is the reason we recognize only 12 constellations in the zodiac, omitting a thirteenth—Ophiuchus, the Serpent Holder—that, by its location, could be included.

Incredibly, there is no satisfactory explanation for the genesis of triskaidekaphobia. The ancient Hebrews thought 13 was unlucky because the thirteenth letter in the Hebrew alphabet is the letter *M,* which is the first letter in the word *mavet,* meaning "death." Some believe that 13 is unlucky because it follows 12, which in ancient Babylonia, China, and Rome was considered a lucky number associated with completion and perfection. Still others suggest that a fear of the number 13 stems from the fact that, in the biblical tradition, there were thirteen diners at the fateful Last Supper. A very practical source of today's triskaidekaphobia may be that years ago London bakers were subject to harsh penalties if they were caught selling bread in short weight. They would add an extra loaf to each dozen sold to be sure the sale met the minimum weight requirement. They avoided the word *thirteen* by calling their sales baker's dozens or long dozens.

Rationalists argue that many fear the number 13 simply because they have been raised to believe it's unlucky. There may be more accidents on Friday the 13th because some people are jittery with worry. Additionally, triskaidekaphobics (another mouthful!) may magnify the bad things that happen on that day while overlooking the many good things that take place. These self-fulfilling prophecies are not uncommon in human affairs.

For more on the significance of numbers, see vignettes 12, 21, 31, 33, 34, 44, 54, and 59. ★

Activities

1. Prove that every year must have a Friday the 13th. (Hint: Start by considering January 1. In any year, it must be one of seven days of the week.)

2. Find some of the many historical examples in which 12 is considered to be a lucky number or is associated with "good."

3. Why was the number 13 significant in the ancient Mayan calendar?

4. Historically, the number 14 has usually been considered a "good" number. Why is this so? (Maybe it's because anything looks good after 13!)

5. What is the Thirteenth Amendment to the Constitution of the United States? What are some other United States connections to the number 13?

Related Reading

Ellis, Keith. *Number Power in Nature and in Everyday Life*. New York: St. Martin's Press, 1978.

Friend, J. Newton. *Numbers: Fun and Facts*. New York: Charles Scribner, 1954.

Room, Adrian. *The Guinness Book of Numbers*. Middlesex, England: Guinness Publishing, 1989.

Schimmel, Annemarie. *The Mystery of Numbers*. New York: Oxford University Press, 1993.

Sitomer, Mindel, and Harry Sitomer. *How Did Numbers Begin?* New York: Thomas Y. Crowell, 1980.

Stokes, William T. *Notable Numbers*. Los Altos, CA: Stokes Publishing, 1986.

The Four-Color Problem

98

Map coloring has long fascinated mathematicians, especially those who work in topology. A question that many have struggled to answer is: How many different colors does a map need to differentiate every region from its immediate neighbor? The hitch is that no two bordering regions can share the same color. This problem is known as the **four-color problem**.

If a map consists entirely of straight lines that begin and end at an edge, only two colors are needed, as shown in the figure at top right. Two colors will do the job no matter how many lines are drawn. What about maps in which the borders between regions don't consist solely of straight lines? It's easy to show that at least four colors are necessary. Look at the circular diagram shown at mid-right. Its regions clearly need four colors; it could not be colored with only three. The detail of the map of the United States at bottom right further illustrates this fact. If the color scheme shown were used, the state indicated by "?" would have to be colored with a color other than red, green, or blue.

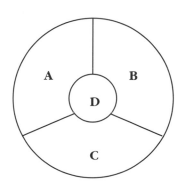

The four-color problem was formulated in 1852 by Frederick Guthrie, a student of mathematics educator **Augustus De Morgan** (1806–1871). (For more on Augustus De Morgan, see vignette 68.) It soon caught the interest of other mathematicians, and although many were convinced that only four colors were needed to color a map, they could not find a proof. For the next several decades, a variety of proofs were put forward, and a couple were even accepted as correct. However, all were found to be defective.

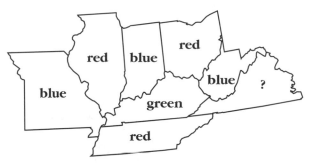

In 1976, **Kenneth Appel** (b 1932) and **Wolfgang Haken** (b 1928) of the University of Illinois presented a computer-assisted proof of the four-color theorem to a mathematical congress in Toronto. The proof had required more than 1,000 hours of computer time to check over 100,000 different situations, a job that would have taken a human years to accomplish. Besides representing the culmination of a century's worth of effort, the proof of the four-color theorem is significant in that it was the first to have been constructed primarily with a computer. It has caused much controversy in the mathematics community because many mathematicians feel a proof that relies on an exhaustion of possibilities cannot be as valid as one that results from a person's keen insight. ★

Activities

1. The four-color map problem applies to maps drawn on a flat surface. Draw some maps on a Möbius strip and color their regions. Can you create a situation for which you need more than four colors? (For information on the Möbius strip, see vignette 74.)

2. A torus is a three-dimensional surface that looks like an inner tube or a donut. Can you create a map on a torus that would require more than four colors?

3. There is only one state in the United States that has this property: It is bordered by six other states, and you can enter each of the bordering states by traveling directly south from some point in this particular state. Identify the state.

4. The map shown displays a large portion of the United States. Use four colors to color all the states.

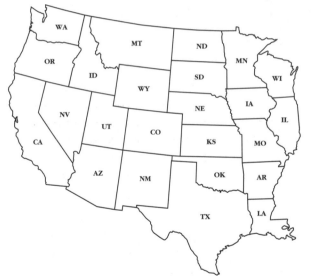

Related Reading

Appel, Kenneth, and Wolfgang Haken. "The Four Color Proof Suffices." *The Mathematical Intelligencer* 8, #1 (1986) 10–20.

Barnette, David. *Map-Coloring, Polyhedra, and the Four-Color Problem*. Washington, DC: Mathematical Association of America, 1983.

Bergamini, David (ed). *Mathematics: Life Science Library*. **New York: Time-Life Books, 1972.**

Hollingdale, Stuart. *Makers of Mathematics*. **New York: Penguin Books, 1989.**

Jacobs, Harold. *Mathematics: A Human Endeavor*. **San Francisco: W.H. Freeman, 1987**.

Lénárt, István. *Non-Euclidean Adventures on the Lénárt Sphere*. Berkeley, CA: Key Curriculum Press, 1996.

Paulos, John Allen. *Beyond Numeracy: Ruminations of a Numbers Man*. **New York: Alfred A. Knopf, 1991**.

Peterson, Ivars. *Islands of Truth: A Mathematical Mystery Cruise*. New York: W.H. Freeman, 1990.

Saaty, T., and P. Kainen. *The Four Color Problem: Assaults and Conquests*. New York: McGraw-Hill, 1977.

PROBLEMS IN PROBABILISTIC REASONING

99

There is general agreement among mathematics educators that modern mathematics education should include a study of probability. Two University of Saskatchewan mathematics instructors, **Jack A. Hope** and **Ivan W. Kelly**, have identified five problems in probabilistic reasoning commonly encountered.

1. **We are frequently unaware that everyday expressions of probability are highly ambiguous**. The ambiguity of everyday expressions can be demonstrated by estimating probability values (from 0 to 100 percent) for each of the commonly used expressions given below.

doubtful	perhaps	it could be	nearly certain
small chance	high chance	one can expect	chances are not great
reasonable chance	most likely	likely	unlikely

   If you were to compare your estimates with those of others in your class, you'd probably find that you all interpreted these expressions quite differently.

2. **We sometimes believe that the prediction of an independent event cannot be detached from the outcomes of similar events in the past**. Say you tossed a coin five times, and you got heads four times and tails once. If you asked, "What is the probability that heads will turn up on the next toss?" most people would probably give you an answer other than the correct one: 50 percent. This type of reasoning error is known as the "gambler's fallacy," well-known to the famous seventeenth-century gambler **Chevalier de Méré**. (In asking his friend Blaise Pascal to analyze his gambling methods, de Méré paved the way for the beginning of probability theory.)

3. **All too often, we have undue confidence in small samples**. Consider a city with two hospitals. Hospital A averages 45 births per day, and Hospital B averages 15 births per day. In which hospital would there be a greater number of days on which 60 percent of the children born were of the same sex? Would you expect both hospitals to have about the same number of such days? The correct response to the first question is B because small samples are more variable than large samples.

4. **We sometimes confuse *unusual* events with *low-probability* events**. Just because an event is unusual does not imply that it has a lower probability of occurring than less noticeable events. Which is more likely in a four-card hand dealt from a shuffled deck: an ace of hearts, an ace of spades, an ace of clubs, and an ace of diamonds; *or* a two of hearts, a queen of spades, a seven of hearts, and a ten of clubs? You answered correctly if you said that both are equally likely hands.

5. **It is often difficult to estimate the frequency of conspicuous or memorable events**. For example, you may think that deaths by homicide are more prevalent than deaths by stroke. Homicide death rates are certainly reported in the media more than death by natural causes, so there is a tendency for some people to greatly overestimate homicide death rates and underestimate stroke death rates.

For more on probability, see vignettes 44, 46, and 49. ★

©1996 by Key Curriculum Press

ACTIVITIES

1. Comment on this statement about an actual national newscast: "Later that evening we were watching the news . . . the TV weathercaster announced that there was a 50 percent chance of rain for Saturday and a 50 percent chance for Sunday, [concluding] that there was a 100 percent chance of rain that weekend."

2. Comment on this claim made in a utility company's advertisement: If you installed a certain energy-saving device, you would "get a $50 rebate and a savings of 200 percent on energy."

3. Analyze and comment on the distinction between the problems stated below.

   Problem 1: If a coin is flipped ten times, which of the given three sequences is most likely to occur? Least likely to occur?

   a. H H H H H H H H H H

   b. HT H HT H T H H T

   c. T T T T T H H H H H

   Problem 2: If a coin is flipped ten times, which of the given outcome's is most likely and least likely?

   a. The total number of heads = 10, and the total number of tails = 0.

   b. The total number of heads = 6, and the total number of tails = 4.

   c. The total number of heads = 5, and the total number of tails = 5.

RELATED READING

Campbell, Stephen K. *Flaws and Fallacies in Statistical Reasoning*. Englewood Cliffs, NJ: Prentice-Hall, 1974.

Ekeland, Ivar. *Mathematics and the Unexpected*. Chicago: University of Chicago Press, 1988.

Ellis, Keith. *Number Power in Nature and in Everyday Life*. New York: St. Martin's Press, 1978.

Huff, Darrell. *How to Lie with Statistics*. New York: W.W. Norton, 1982.

Kosko, Bart. *Fuzzy Thinking: The New Science of Fuzzy Logic*. New York: Hyperion, 1993.

Moore, David S. *Statistics: Concepts and Controversies*. New York: W.H. Freeman, 1991.

Paulos, John Allen. *Innumeracy: Mathematical Illiteracy and Its Consequences*. New York: Hill and Wang, 1988.

Ethnomathematics 100

The mathematical skills used in everyday activities go unrecognized. They are so embedded in other activities that [people who use these skills] deny having [them]. We often came across comments like this one by a woman who fished for oysters: "I don't know these things; I didn't go to school. I know about the oysters because we fish; the price of oysters we have to know. If they're selling five oysters at 750, then they're selling each one at 150." Similar denials of knowledge have been observed in other cultures .... However, these denials should not discourage us from looking further into people's mathematical knowledge.

—Street Mathematics and School Mathematics

I f you study the mathematical experiences of someone from another country, from a different ethnic or social background, or of a different gender, you are likely to find that these experiences differ significantly from your own. The professional study of the diverse ways in which people of different cultures experience mathematical knowledge is known as **ethnomathematics**.

In academic situations, students are generally taught that mathematics is universal; everyone considers mathematics to be a certain body of knowledge that includes a specific set of problems, computations, and symbols. This view tends to exclude the occupational mathematics that people around the world use in their everyday lives. For example, Brazilian child street vendors and adult construction workers often use mathematics in their work, but they may not call what they're doing mathematics because they didn't learn it in school. The aesthetic and the tradition of weaving requires that weavers understand complex mathematical concepts, even if they don't consider those concepts in a formal way. Geometric principles such as symmetry and tiling are inherent in the art of quiltmaking, an art that has played an important social and economic role in communities around the world.

Language often highlights cultural differences in mathematical understanding. Children of the traditional Quechua culture in Ecuador understand the mathematics they use for practical purposes, but they may have to simply memorize math in Spanish language schools because number names are not clearly related. For example, they know the number 222 in the Quechua language as *ishcai patsac ishcai chuna ishcai,* meaning "two hundreds, two tens, two." However, the Spanish equivalent, *doscientos veintidos,* means "two hundreds twenty-two" and doesn't have any direct reference to the tens place.

In 1985, the **International Study Group on Ethnomathematics** (ISGEm) was formed at the suggestion of Ubiratan D'Ambrosio of Brazil. This group actively promotes programs that improve conditions for mathematics study by groups not usually encouraged in this field, including girls, immigrants, rural students, and children living in poverty. With the continued work of ISGEm, mathematics educators around the world are finding that informal mathematics education is pervasive, that the social context of education has a great influence on student performance, and that quality education depends upon an understanding of culture.

For more on nonacademic mathematics, see vignettes 21, 25, 35, 50, 54, and 59. ★

Activities

1. Interview someone who has a different cultural background from yours. (Remember, a person's cultural background involves gender, country of origin, ethnicity, economic status, and so on.) Ask your interview subject to discuss her or his experience of mathematics from a cultural (not a personal) standpoint. Does her or his experience differ from your own? In what ways?

2. Interview two people who work in an occupation that you think requires little math skill. Ask them to consider their work from a broad mathematical standpoint, taking into account logic, probability, special reasoning, measurement, computation, and data analysis. Do they find that they were unaware of the mathematics in their job? Do their answers surprise you? Discuss what you learned in small groups.

3. Some people interested in mathematics choose not to go into a traditionally math-related field, yet they consciously use mathematics in their work. Such people include weavers, sculptors, printers, and musicians. Read about someone who works with mathematics in a unique way and present what you learn to the class.

Related Reading

Ascher, Marcia. *Ethnomathematics: A Multicultural View of Mathematical Ideas*. Pacific Grove, CA: Brooks/Cole Publishing, 1991.

Closs, M.P. (ed). *Native American Mathematics*. Austin, TX: University of Texas Press, 1986.

Gerdes, Paulus. "How to Recognize Hidden Geometrical Thinking: A Contribution to the Development of Anthropological Mathematics." *For the Learning of Mathematics* 6 (2) (1986) 10–12, 17.

McDowell, Ruth. *Symmetry: A Design System for Quiltmakers*. Lafayette, CA: C and T Publishing, 1994.

Nunes, Terezinha, et al. *Street Mathematics and School Mathematics*. New York: Cambridge University Press, 1993.

Washburn, Dorothy K., and Donald W. Crowe. *Symmetries of Culture: Theory and Practice of Plan Pattern Analyses*. Seattle: University of Washington Press, 1988.

Zaslavsky, Claudia. *Africa Counts: Number and Pattern in African Culture*. New York: Lawrence Hill Books, 1979.

———. *Math Comes Alive: Activities from Many Cultures*. Portland, ME: J. Weston Walch, 1987.

Fascinating Fractals

101

I n recent years Polish-born mathematician **Benoit Mandelbrot** (b 1924) has captured the fancy of the mathematical world by focusing attention on a class of self-similar curves known as fractals. ("Self-similar" means that a shape's details resemble the shape's big picture.) Two classical fractals are shown here.

The Sierpiński Gasket

In 1916, Polish mathematician **Waclaw Sierpiński** (1882–1969) introduced the gasket (sometimes called the Sierpiński triangle). To create it, begin with a triangle (like the black one shown), join the midpoints of its sides, then remove the middle triangle (white). This will leave three smaller black triangles—repeat this process on each of them. Then repeat it again with the new smaller black triangles. A few steps in the process are shown below.

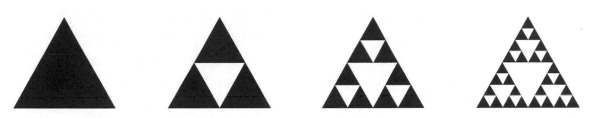

The Sierpiński gasket is the set of points in the plane that will result if you repeat this process infinitely. Interestingly, as you proceed infinitely, the gasket's area (total areas of the black triangles) approaches zero because you remove more and more of the area with each step. However, its perimeter (the sum of the perimeters of all the black triangles) becomes infinitely large.

The Koch Snowflake

The snowflake curve was created in 1904 by Swedish mathematician **Helge von Koch** (1870–1924). To construct it, divide a line segment into three equal parts. Then, remove the middle part of the segment and replace it with an equilateral triangle, removing the triangle's base. Repeat this procedure with the four new segments, then again with the sixteen new segments, and so on. A few steps are shown below.

Now, if you carry out these steps infinitely with the three sides of an equilateral triangle, you will generate the Koch snowflake. A later step in the construction process is shown below.

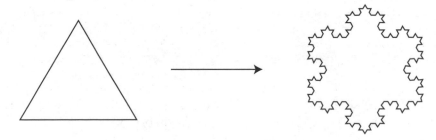

©1996 by Key Curriculum Press

As with the Sierpiński gasket, the snowflake's perimeter increases infinitely. The area is finite, but, unlike the gasket's area, does not approach zero. An intuitive argument that the area remains finite might involve convincing yourself that the snowflake's area will always be less than the area of the paper on which you draw your original (generating) triangle.

For more on fractals, see vignettes 35, 96, 103, and 107. ★

Activities

1. Consider the Sierpiński gasket. If the perimeter of the original triangle is one unit, what is the perimeter of the figure after the first step (when the "middle" triangle is removed)? After the second step? The third step? The tenth step?

2. If the area of the Koch snowflake's generating triangle is one square unit, what is the area after the first step? The second step? The tenth step? What is the limiting value of the area as the number of steps approaches infinity?

3. Mandelbrot coined the word *fractal* to describe objects with fractional dimension. For example, while a line segment is a one-dimensional object and a square is a two-dimensional object, a Sierpiński gasket is something in between. It's composed of infinitely many line segments, but it doesn't have any area. Do some research and write a report on how fractional dimensions are calculated.

Related Reading

Barnsley, Michael. *Fractals Everywhere*. Boston: Academic Press, 1988.

Barton, Ray. "Chaos and Fractals." *Mathematics Teacher* (Oct 1990) 524–529.

Briggs, John. *Fractals: The Patterns of Chaos*. New York: Simon and Schuster, 1992.

Camp, Dane R. "A Fractal Excursion." *Mathematics Teacher* (Apr 1991) 265–275.

Cibes, Margaret. "The Sierpiński Triangle: Deterministic Versus Random Models." *Mathematics Teacher* (Nov 1990) 617–621.

Feder, Jens. *Fractals*. New York: Plenum Press, 1988.

Mandelbrot, Benoit B. *The Fractal Geometry of Nature*. New York: W.H. Freeman, 1983.

Peitgen, Heinz-Otto, Hartmut Jurgens, and Dietmar Saupe. *Fractals for the Classroom*. New York: Springer-Verlag, 1992.

REATHA CLARK KING: WOMAN OF SCIENCE

102

*Reatha Clark King.
Photo courtesy of the
General Mills Foundation.*

During prehistoric times, women gathered food for their communities, learning by experimentation to distinguish among hundreds of edible and medicinal plants. As seasons cycled, these women observed the effect that heat and rain had on certain plants, under what conditions those plants thrived, and when they were available for use. These early botanists were the first women scientists. Today, women continue to make significant contributions in every branch of science.

Mathematics plays a very important role in science, as it does in many other quantitative fields. (*Quantitative* means "capable of being measured by quantity.") In their work, scientists frequently rely on such mathematical concepts as logic, deductive reasoning, probability, measurement, computation, and data analysis.

One woman who has used her mathematical ability to successfully pursue a career in science is **Dr. Reatha Clark King** (b 1938). Raised in rural Georgia, where she worked long hours in cotton fields and on landlords' farms, she originally considered becoming a teacher at her local high school. However, she fell in love with chemistry at Clark College and went on to earn a Ph.D. in chemistry at the University of Chicago. Although King had more educational opportunities as a woman than her predecessors, she was sometimes lonely being one of the few women in the university's graduate chemistry program.

Upon completing her studies, King did research work in fluorine flame colorimetry for six years at the National Bureau of Standards. She returned to academia to become a professor of chemistry and associate dean at York College, and then moved on to earn her third graduate degree, this time in business. The president of Metropolitan State University in Minnesota for eleven years, she worked to promote opportunities for minorities and women in higher education. Currently, King is the president and executive director of the General Mills Foundation, a contributer to the areas of education, health and social action, the arts, and cultural affairs.

King's belief in quality education for all is summarized by her observation: "I realized early in life that education is our best enabling resource, that technical skills are important, and that my stamina for championing educational opportunity for all people is inexhaustible." ★

©1996 by Key Curriculum Press

This arresting cover of a 1957 publication on the launching of Sputnik shows the new Soviet science crashing through a stale text of science. Many young women, fascinated by this and subsequent space exploration, have been motivated to excel in mathematics and science.

ACTIVITIES

1. Read about a woman who is making or has made significant contributions to the field of science. Prepare a visual presentation of what you learn and share it with your class.

2. Research the life and work of eighteenth-century mathematician and scientist **Émilie du Châtelet** (1706–1749).

3. In 1994, a comet named Shoemaker-Levy 9 collided with the planet Jupiter. Named after the team who discovered it, Carolyn and Eugene Shoemaker and David Levy, the comet's course and impact was observed by a team of astronomers that included many women. How did the collision affect the scientific community? The public? What was the importance of this event? Look up magazine and newspaper articles about this topic and write a report about what you discover.

RELATED READING

Alic, Margaret. *Hypatia's Heritage*. **Boston: Beacon Press, 1986.**

Dash, Joan. *The Triumph of Discovery*. **Westwood, NJ: Silver Burdett and Ginn, 1991.**

Jackson, G. Black *Women—Makers of History—A Portrait.* Oakland, CA: GRT Printing, 1975.

McGrayne, S.B. *Nobel Prize Women in Science—Their Lives, Struggles, and Momentous Discoveries.* New York: Birch Lane Press, 1993.

Phillips, Patricia. *The Scientific Lady: A Social History of Women's Scientific Interests 1520–1918.* New York: St. Martin's Press, 1990.

Schiebinger, Londa. *The Mind Has No Sex?: Women in the Origins of Modern Science.* Cambridge, MA: Harvard University Press, 1989.

©1996 by Key Curriculum Press

How Long Is a Coastline?

103

How long is the Atlantic coastline of the United States? The recent interest in fractals and chaos theory has made people realize that this type of question is considerably more complex than once thought. On a typical globe, the Atlantic coastline appears to be a fairly smooth line, as shown at top right. However, it looks somewhat ragged on a map showing only the United States, and it looks even *more* ragged on a map depicting only the eastern states. The eastern coastline contains many capes, bays, coves, and other irregularities, so a measurement of the coastline's length could vary considerably, depending on the scale used to find it. Even a very small piece of a coastline has within itself a variety of irregularities!

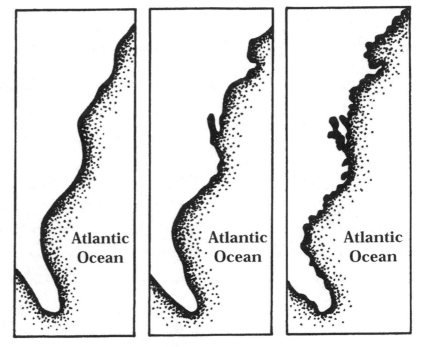

We can use the Koch snowflake fractal construction process to demonstrate the complexities of coastline measurement. Clearly, a coastline is not so uniform as the snowflake, but the model at bottom right shows the variety of possible responses to a question such as: How long is a coastline? The drawings model the same stretch of coastline, and each successive drawing shows more detail.

So, let's get back to our original question: How long is the Atlantic coastline of the United States?

For more on fractals, see vignettes 35, 96, 101, and 107. ★

Coastline length = 100 miles

A cove is represented.
Coastline length = 133 miles

Smaller coves are introduced, some within coves.
Coastline length = 178 miles

Even smaller coves are shown, some within coves.
Coastline length = 237 miles

Activities

1. Research these fractal-related topics.

   a. A Peano curve

   b. The devil's staircase

   c. Self-similarity

   d. Space-filling curve

2. How is the concept of fractals applied in modern cartography?

3. Find a map of Great Britain or another country with an irregular boundary. Make sure the map has a scale so that you can estimate the distance.

   a. Choose a sequence of points along the country's boundary. Join consecutive points with line segments to form a polygon. Estimate the length of the boundary by finding the perimeter of the polygon (measure the polygon's sides, then total them).

   b. Now double the number of points and repeat the instructions in 2a.

   c. How does your estimate in 2b compare to the estimate you made in 2a? How could you obtain a more accurate estimate of the boundary length?

Related Reading

Briggs, John. *Fractals: The Patterns of Chaos*. New York: Simon and Schuster, 1992.

Maor, Eli. *To Infinity and Beyond: A Cultural History of the Infinite*. Boston: Birkhauser Boston, 1987.

Pappas, Theoni. *More Joy of Mathematics*. San Carlos, CA: Wide World/Tetra, 1991.

Paulos, John Allen. *Beyond Numeracy: Ruminations of a Numbers Man*. New York: Alfred A. Knopf, 1991.

Peitgen, Heinz-Otto, Harmut Jurgens, and Dietmar Saupe. *Chaos and Fractals: New Frontiers of Science*. New York: Springer-Verlag, 1992.

Peterson, Ivars. *The Mathematical Tourist: Snapshots of Modern Mathematics*. New York: W.H. Freeman, 1988.

Pickover, Clifford. *Computers, Pattern, Chaos and Beauty*. New York: St. Martin's Press, 1990.

Edna Paisano: Using Statistics to Aid Communities

104

W hen Edna Lee Paisano (b 1948) was growing up on the Nez Percé Indian Reservation in Sweetwater, Idaho, she learned to preserve her family's cultural traditions and make them a part of her daily life. For example, her grandmother taught her how to make moccasins and beaded purses, which they sold to help support the family. Additionally, owning the fishing, hunting, and mineral rights to the land in the Nez Percé area made it easier for the tribe to be self-sufficient, and in the tipi in the backyard of Paisano's home, the family regularly prepared, dried, and smoked the meat of deer, elk, and moose.

> *...I need to study more statistics so I can continue to do things which are really important for my people.*
>
> —Edna Paisano

Although she loved her community and the wilderness areas of the reservation, Paisano decided she had to leave them to successfully work for the betterment of her community. (In this endeavor, she followed in her mother's footsteps. When Paisano was a child, her mother, Frances, earned first a teaching degree, then a graduate degree in special educational. In 1980, Frances was awarded the Leo Reano Memorial Award from the National Educational Association for her education efforts on behalf of American Indians.) A talented mathematics and science student, Paisano attended the University of Washington and earned a graduate degree in social work, studying statistics in the process. During her time at the university, she worked with the American Indian community in Seattle, Washington, and was heavily involved in an eventually successful effort to establish a cultural center for American Indians at Seattle's Fort Lawton.

Edna Paisano

As a program specialist, Paisano visited reservations, spending time with tribal governments to provide assistance and suggestions for the betterment of living standards and education. However, because she experiences arthritis, traveling was difficult and painful. Paisano decided she could work more effectively if she took a job that didn't require traveling. In 1976, she was hired by the United States Census Bureau to work on issues regarding American Indians and Alaskan Natives, becoming the first American Indian to become a full-time employee of the bureau.

As a result of visiting tribal areas and of examining the data from both a questionnaire she developed and the 1980 census, Paisano discovered that American

Indians in some locations were undercounted. Because the allocation of important federal funds to tribal units is based on census figures, Paisano used modern statistical techniques to improve the accuracy of the census. By encouraging education in relevant mathematics-related fields such as computer programming, demography, and statistics, and by coordinating a public information campaign, she and her colleagues alerted American Indian communities to the importance of the census.

Did Paisano's efforts prove effective? There is reason to believe they did, because the 1990 census revealed a 38 percent increase in the number of United States residents counted as American Indians.

For more on American Indian mathematics, see vignettes 3, 6, 24, 25, 32, 40, and 59. For more on statistics, see vignette 92. ★

Activities

1. Paisano was jailed as a result of her efforts to persuade the United States government to give Fort Lawton, which legally was Indian property, to the American Indians. Research the Fort Lawton story.

2. When carelessly used, statistics can be misleading.

    a. Find some historical examples of the misuse of statistics.

    b. Find examples of the misuse of statistics in current magazine, newspaper, and television promotions and advertisements. Discuss in groups some of the ramifications of the misuse of statistics.

    c. Many people don't know the distinction between three statistical averages: mean, median, and mode. Define these statistical averages.

3. Read about the life of **Fanya Montalvo** (b 1948). How has she contributed to the field of mathematics?

Related Reading

Alcoze, Thom, et al. *Multiculturalism in Mathematics, Science, and Technology: Readings and Activities.* Menlo Park, CA: Addison-Wesley, 1993.

Alic, Margaret. *Hypatia's Heritage.* **Boston: Beacon Press, 1986.**

Castillo, Toby T. *Apache Mathematics, Past and Present.* Whitewater, AZ: Whitewater Middle School Press, 1994.

Closs, M.P. (ed). *Native American Mathematics.* **Austin, TX: University of Texas Press, 1986.**

Moore, David S. *Statistics: Concepts and Controversies.* **New York: W.H. Freeman, 1991.**

Perl, Teri. *Women and Numbers: Lives of Women Mathematicians plus Discovery Activities.* **San Carlos, CA: Wide World/Tetra, 1993.**

Escalante: Stand and Delíver

105

> *I have not been in the country very long, but I do know this. For a 16-year-old, low-income Hispanic kid growing up in East Los Angeles, there are a lot of things that are dangerous. Calculus is not one of them.*
>
> —Jaime Escalante,
> *Stand and Deliver*

In the 1980s, **Jaime Escalante** was concerned that each year only a few of the predominantly Hispanic students at Los Angeles's Garfield High School went on to college. To remedy this situation, he started a personal crusade in an effort to better prepare his students for the challenges of higher education and the working world. Because his class had not been encouraged to explore the many options education had to offer them, convincing them that their studies were worthwhile wasn't easy. Escalante told them: "The money is in computers and physics and chemistry and biology. And they want you out there, but you have to speak their language first—and the language is math."

Thanks to the movie *Stand and Deliver,* a chronicle of Escalante's success as a mathematics teacher, his motto, *ganas,* Spanish for "desire," is now well known across the nation. It was *ganas* that pushed Escalante to implement an advanced placement calculus program at Garfield, a program that eventually produced one of the country's highest number of students with passing rates. Initially, the first class to participate in the program thought it was a waste of their time to study calculus and prepare for the challenging Advanced Placement (AP) Calculus Examination. However, with Escalante's encouragement and drive, they worked hard and supported one another—even after school and on weekends—to achieve what they thought they couldn't. When they finally took the AP exam, the Educational Testing Service (ETS) at first suspected them of cheating. The students were retested under ETS supervision and performed as well as they had on the first test, demonstrating a remarkable triumph for the qualities of spirit, determination, and *ganas.*

In addition to President Ronald Reagan recognizing Escalante as one of the country's outstanding educators, California State Superintendent of Public Instruction Bill Honig presented a National Educator Award to Escalante in 1988, citing him as one who is "not afraid to try new approaches in efforts to inspire students and make learning come alive."

Jackie Joyner-Kersee visits Escalante and students on the FUTURES set to share how important math was in reaching her goal of the gold medal at the Seoul Olympics.

To reach more students, Escalante became the host of an instructional television series, *FUTURES with Jaime Escalante*. The series was produced by the Foundation for Advancements in Science and Education (FASE) and is distributed by the Public Broadcasting System (PBS). *FUTURES* introduces students to the excitement and the variety of math- and science-based careers. The most popular classroom program in the history of PBS, it received more than fifty awards, including the highest honor in the broadcasting field, the George Foster Peabody Award. Escalante also appeared in two FASE family specials for PBS: *Math...Who Needs It?!* and *Living and Working in Space: The Countdown Has Begun.* ★

Activities

1. With your class, watch the movie *Stand and Deliver*. How did Escalante overcome the many obstacles he faced in the process of changing his students' attitudes about learning and mathematics? What message do you think the film conveys?

2. Who sponsors the National Educator Award program? What is its purpose?

3. Write about a teacher who has helped you attain a personal goal. Present an account of your experience to your class.

4. What are your plans for the future? How do you think you could positively impact the lives of those you come into contact with?

Related Reading

Dreyfous, Tommy, and Theodore Eisenberg. "On the Aesthetics of Mathematical Thought." *For the Learning of Mathematics* 6 (Feb 1986) 2–10.

Ferrina-Mundy, Joan, and Darien Lauten. "Learning About Calculus Learning." *Mathematics Teacher* (Feb 1994) 115–121.

Hogben, Lancelot. *Mathematics for the Millions*. **New York: W.W. Norton, 1967.**

Underwood, Dudley (ed). *Readings for Calculus*. Washington, DC: Mathematical Association of America, 1992.

Winkel, Brian J. "Ant, Tunnels, and Calculus: An Exercise in Mathematical Modeling." *Mathematics Teacher* (Apr 1994) 284–287.

CHAOS IN JURASSIC PARK

106

There is always more to learn in our never-ending search to understand the world we inhabit. In the 1970s, mathematicians and scientists began to explore with computers the irregular, discontinuous, and erratic side of nature. They discovered a surprising order in situations that had previously been classifed as chaotic, such as the shapes of clouds, the intertwining of blood vessels, and the galactic clustering of stars. Michael Crichton's science fiction thriller *Jurassic Park* provides fascinating insights into **chaos theory** through the eyes and the mind of fictional mathematician Ian Malcolm.

On a remote island off Costa Rica we find Jurassic Park, a secret theme park created by the Hammond Foundation. As a result of the foundation's scientists implementing an astonishing technique for recovering and cloning dinosaur DNA, creatures extinct for eons roam Jurassic Park. John Hammond plans to soon unveil his secret to the world and allow the public to visit his awesome creation. Malcolm is one of a small party of people who know Hammond's secret—and he is convinced from the beginning that Jurassic Park is doomed.

Tyrannosaur

> *"I have always maintained this island would be unworkable,"* Malcolm said. *"I predicted it from the beginning. You're going to have to shut the thing down."*
>
> *"Shut it down!" Hammond stood angrily. "This is ridiculous."*
>
> *. . . [Hammond's lawyer asks,] "Your paper concludes that Hammond's island is bound to fail?"*
>
> *"Correct."*
>
> *"Because of chaos theory?"*
>
> *"Correct."*
>
> *. . . "But hadn't you better see the island, to see what he's actually done?"*
>
> *"No. That is quite unnecessary. The details don't matter. Chaos theory tells me that the island will quickly proceed to behave in unpredictable fashion."*
>
> *"And you're confident of your theory."*
>
> *"Oh, yes," Malcolm said. "Totally confident." He sat back in the chair. "There is a problem with that island. It is an accident waiting to happen."*

The persistent Malcolm informs a small and not-so-receptive audience that chaos theory asserts we cannot predict certain phenomena—such as the weather—more than a few days ahead. By the logic of Dr. Wu, the scientist who cloned the dinosaurs, it was totally predictable that because they were all female, they couldn't reproduce. But Malcolm found otherwise.

> *...Malcolm said ... "Your compys are breeding."*

> *Wu shook his head. "I don't see how."*

> *"They're breeding, and so are the othnielia, the maiasaurs, the hypsys—and the velociraptors."*

But if the dinosaurs were breeding, why weren't their offspring picked up by the park's computer, which counted and tracked each of the park's dinosaurs? Malcolm examined the computer program and found the human flaw built into the program structure.

> *"Now you see the flaw in your procedures," Malcolm said. "You only tracked the expected number of animals. You were worried about losing animals, and your procedures were designed to advise you instantly if you had less than the expected number. But that wasn't the problem.*
> *The problem was that you had more than the expected number."*

Chaos theory asserts that in certain systems there is sensitive dependence on that system's initial conditions—the smallest of differences can lead to unpredictable behavior. Unchecked, flaws in a system can become severe, and, according to Malcolm, "system recovery may prove impossible." In *Jurassic Park,* humans tried to duplicate conditions that existed millions of years ago—and a peaceful, seemingly controllable island fell victim to chaos theory.

> *Malcolm sighed. "Do you have any idea," he said, "how unlikely it is that you, or any of us, will get off this island alive?"*

For more on chaos theory, see vignettes 35, 101, 103, and 107. ★

Velociraptor

ACTIVITIES

1. Chaos theory asserts that small changes in initial conditions can lead to unpredictable behavior in the future. Most people would probably agree that in many situations the difference between 1 and 1.001 is relatively insignificant. We know that 1 raised to any power is always 1. Use a calculator to check the degree to which the following indicated powers of 1.001 differ from powers of 1.

    a. 1.001^{100}

    b. 1.001^{1000}

    c. $1.001^{20,000}$

    d. $1.001^{100,000}$

2. What was it that allowed the female dinosaurs in Jurassic Park to breed?

3. By studying a graph that showed their heights, mathematician Ian Malcolm concluded that the dinosaurs of Jurassic Park were breeding. How did he come to his conclusion? (The graph is shown in the book, but it is not visually presented in the movie.)

4. What message do you think *Jurassic Park* means to convey?

RELATED READING

Crichton, Michael. *Jurassic Park*. New York: Ballantine Books, 1990.

Devaney, R.L. *Chaos, Fractals, and Dynamics*. Menlo Park, CA: Addison-Wesley, 1990.

Gleick, James. *Chaos: Making a New Science*. New York: Viking Penguin, 1987.

Naeye, Robert. "Chaos Squared." *Discover* (Mar 1994) 28.

Peitgen, Heinz-Otto, Hartmut Jurgens, and Dietmar Saupe. *Chaos and Fractals: New Frontiers of Science*. New York: Springer-Verlag, 1992.

————. *Fractals for the Classroom*. **New York: Springer-Verlag, 1992**.

Prigogine, Ilya, and I. Stenger. *Order Out of Chaos*. New York: Bantam Books, 1984.

Schroeder, Manfred. *Fractals, Chaos, Power Laws*. New York: W.H. Freeman, 1990.

Names in Chaos and Fractals

107

Gaston Julia

Julia's work in modern dynamical systems theory is a source of many of the most beautiful fractals known today. They are appropriately called Julia sets. Without the benefit of a computer to generate images, Julia and his colleague Pierre Fatou studied the possibilities of geometric equations that produced not simply circles and conic sections, but whorls, branches, and sparks. As a French soldier in World War I, Julia was severely wounded and lost his nose. As a result, he had several painful operations and did much of his creative mathematical research in a hospital bed.

Benoit Mandelbrot

Born in Warsaw, Poland, Mandelbrot developed fractal geometry to analyze certain irregularities in nature that classical geometry cannot, such as the whorls and crags of coastlines, mountain ranges, and snowflakes. What makes these natural phenomena significant to fractal geometry is that they are statistically self-similar; that is, the details look like the whole. Additionally, Mandelbrot "discovered" the beautiful and amazingly complex Mandelbrot set, shown at right, and was one of the first to notice strange attractors that have surfaced in a variety of seemingly unrelated fields in the modern chaos theory.

Edward Lorenz

In 1960, while playing with a computer model of simple weather systems, Lorenz discovered that two almost identical initial weather conditions can, with the passage of time, diverge into two completely different weather

> *Clouds are not spheres, mountains are not cones, coastlines are not circles, and bark is not smooth, nor does lightning travel in a straight line .... many patterns of Nature are so irregular and fragmented .... The existence of these patterns challenge us to study those forms that Euclid leaves aside as being "formless," to investigate the morphology of the "amorphous."*
> —Benoit Mandelbrot

patterns with no dicernible relation to each other. This is a manifestation of what is known as the butterfly effect. Lorenz's observation marked the beginning of chaos theory.

Mitchell Feigenbaum

Working as a physicist at Los Alamos National Laboratory in New Mexico, Feigenbaum studied dynamic systems, finding that chaos poses problems that dcfy acccptcd ways of working in science. For example, he demonstrated that systems can often behave quite normally and smoothly for a wide range of initial conditions, then suddenly become chaotic when a parameter of the system obtains a critical value. In the 1970s, Feigenbaum began searching for connections between different types of irregularity, and he came to see that buried in chaos is a surprising order.

Heinz-Otto Peitgen

To Peitgen, the world is an art form, filled with beautiful images that are the result of complex iterative processes. He says, "What is the true aspect of the natural object? The tree, let's say—what is important? Is it the straight line, or is it the fractal object?" Unafraid of experimentation and new technology, his work in mathematics has centered around the universe of the Mandelbrot set. Peitgen has been instrumental in educating the public about the beauty of fractals and chaos.

Robert L. Devaney

Professor Devaney's area of expertise in dynamical systems seems very appropriate given the dynamic way in which he works. His career has taken him to six continents

The Mandelbrot set

and to forty-six of the fifty states, he has written over fifty research papers in the fields of complex analytic dynamics and computer experiments in dynamics, and he has produced several short films about chaos. Additionally, he is Director of the Dynamical Systems and Technology Project, whose goal it is to educate teachers about how to effectively use technology and the concepts of chaos, fractals, and dynamics in the classroom.

For more on fractals and chaos, see vignettes 35, 96, 101, 103, and 106. ★

Activities

1. Find some examples of Julia sets. How are they generated? How are they related to collections of points called escape sets and prisoner sets?

2. In the context of chaos theory, elaborate on the concept of a strange attractor.

3. How are numbers in the complex number plane "trapped" in the Mandelbrot set?

4. The diagram below shows the first four steps in the construction of a Pythagorean tree. Continue the construction through ten steps. Start by constructing a much larger square on a separate piece of paper.

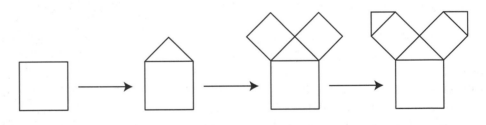

Related Reading

Briggs, John. ***Fractals: The Patterns of Chaos.*** **New York: Simon and Schuster, 1992.**

Devaney, R.L. *Chaos, Fractals, and Dynamics: Computer Experiments in Mathematics.* Menlo Park, CA: Addison-Wesley, 1989.

———. *Professor Devaney Explains the Fractal Geometry of the Mandelbrot Set* (video). Berkeley, CA: Key Curriculum Press, 1996.

Dewdney, A.K. "Computer Recreations: A Tour of the Mandelbrot Set Aboard the Mandelbus." *Scientific American* (Feb 1989) 108–111.

Gleick, James. ***Chaos: Making a New Science.*** **New York: Viking Penguin, 1987.**

Hofstadter, Douglas R. "Strange Attractors: Mathematical Patterns Delicately Poised Between Order and Chaos." *Scientific American* (May 1992) 16–29.

Peterson, Ivars. *The Mathematical Tourist: Snapshots of Modern Mathematics.* New York: W.H. Freeman, 1988.

Geometric Shapes and Politics

108

Some refer to the shape on the map of North Carolina at right as "a string of pearls"—we certainly can't describe it with common geometric words like *circle, rectangle,* or *triangle.* This particular shape is pretty complex—it's 160 miles long and, at some points, as narrow as a one-lane highway. Believe it or not, this shape represents North Carolina's Twelfth Congressional District.

In July 1993, the United States Supreme Court decided by a 5–4 vote that this district may be unconstitutional. Revisions made in 1982 to the 1965 Voting Rights Act required that states with histories of considerable racial discrimination draw up political districts that would give minority candidates a better chance of being elected. As a result, North Carolina's Twelfth Congressional District was redrawn so that 53 percent of the area's voting population consisted of African Americans (as reported in *Time,* 12 July 1993). However, the selective shape of the district offended the court's majority, who feared that the racially based construction of such districts could lead to political factionalism in the United States.

The 1993 Supreme Court decision reflects ambivalence about whether constructing political districts along racial lines is an effective way to ensure representation for underrepresented voting populations.

North Carolina isn't the only state that has had a bizzare-shaped voting district. In 1992, Louisiana's Fourth Congressional District was 400 miles long and only 80 feet wide at its narrowest point. It edged the state's northeastern border, sending several fingers south to include minority voters. Since then, this district has been redrawn twice and currently consists of a large, contained area in northwestern Louisiana. ★

North Carolina 12th District
Source: U.S. Census Bureau

Eligible voters
412,000
Black **53.3%**
White **46.7%**

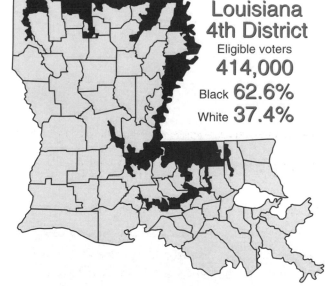

Louisiana 4th District
Eligible voters
414,000
Black **62.6%**
White **37.4%**

Illustrations ©1993 Time Inc.
Reprinted with permission.

Activities

1. Research the political districts in your state. Have they changed during the last few years? If so, why? Are there any unusual geometric shapes among the districts in your state?

2. Some parts of the political districts shown in this vignette are simply narrow bands that are considerably less in width than the length of a football field. If you lived in one of these bands, most of your neighbors would be in another political district. What community implications could this have for you and your family?

3. If you knew the number of square miles in the area of the state of North Carolina, what methods could you use to approximate the area of that state's Twelfth Congressional District?

4. Discuss in groups whether you think political districts should be constructed to ensure adequate representation for underrepresented voting groups.

Related Reading

Greenhouse, Linda. "Court Accepts a Crucial Redistricting Case." *New York Times* (10 Dec 1994) 8.

Moore, David S. *Statistics: Concepts and Controversies*. New York: W.H. Freeman, 1991.

Tufte, Edward R. *The Visual Display of Quantitative Information*. Cheshire, CT: Graphics Press, 1983.

Van Biema, David. "Snakes or Ladders." *Time* (12 July 1993) 30–31.

Witkowski, Joseph C. "Mathematical Modeling and the Presidential Election." *Mathematics Teacher* (Oct 1992) 520–521.

Appendix: Outstanding Educators I Know

Today's events will be tomorrow's history. During my teaching career and my work with national mathematics education organizations, I have been fortunate to gain the acquaintance of many dedicated educators who are making supreme efforts to promote quality quantitative education for all students. These individuals are both promoting history and making history. They possess the qualities necessary to help students become productive, efficient, caring, and strong citizens. They are truly people who "make things happen."

These individuals serve as representatives of the hundreds of educators I personally know who exemplify the best in quantitative education. And, of course, they represent only a very small sample of the many teachers within all academic disciplines who inspire students by promoting the realization that the future belongs to the educated.

Willie Amos

Willie Amos

As principal of Simmons High School in Hollandale, Mississippi, Mr. Amos has initiated such programs as the Jobs for Mississippi's Graduates and the Rural Entrepreneurship Program. Emphasizing open communication, high achievement, and mutual respect, he has expanded the curriculum at Simmons to include a daily reading program and higher-level courses in mathematics and science. In 1992, Mr. Amos received the National Educator Award for his efforts to promote quality education for all students.

G. Asenath Andrews

Ms. Andrews is the principal of the Catherine Ferguson Academy in Detroit, Michigan, an institute that provides educational opportunities for middle and high school students who are pregnant or are parents. Created in response to studies showing that a majority of teenage mothers drop out of school because they lack child-care assistance, the Academy provides both on-site child care and nursery units that serve over 200 children. The efforts of Ms. Andrews have provided many young mothers and fathers a chance at obtaining the education necessary to better their lives.

Roy L. Barnes

Roy L. Barnes

When he was a mathematics teacher at Dollarway Junior High School in Pine Bluff, Arkansas, Mr. Barnes made his mathematics classroom a place of action. Everyday he encouraged his students to get involved in hands-on group work, computer activities, and oral presentations. His classroom was described as "a bustling workshop that reflects his own enthusiasm for mathematics."

Willard H. Blaskopf, Jr.

Jewel Boutté

Iris M. Carl

Pamela Watkins Coffield

Christine Comins

He believes that teachers are responsible to adjust to the changing needs of new generations of students, so he promotes efforts that allow teachers to keep abreast of the latest advances in their fields. Mr. Barnes is currently a mathematics specialist and Curriculum Research and Design Team member at the Arkansas Department of Education, and he is a recipient of the 1993 National Educator Award.

Willard H. Blaskopf, Jr.

Mr. Blaskopf is the innovative Chairman of the Newark Academy Mathematics Department in Livingston, New Jersey, and a member of the New Jersey Coalition of Mathematics Education. A frequent speaker at National Council of Teachers of Mathematics (NCTM) meetings, his topics include mathematics history, women in mathematics, multicultural mathematics, standardized testing, and reading and writing as part of the mathematics curriculum. In fact, he developed a required mathematics reading list for all grades at the Newark Academy. Additionally, Mr. Blaskopf works in the Newark High Achievers program, which provides educational opportunities to academically talented inner city students.

Jewel Boutté

Within her first three years as principal of Crenshaw High School in Los Angeles, California, Ms. Boutté successfully implemented programs that transformed the school to one where students excell not only in athletics but also in academics. Her initiative to strengthen the curriculum for college preparation resulted in over ninety percent of the school's graduates going on to college. Perhaps her most noteworthy accomplishment was the establishment of a nationally-recognized teacher training academy at Crenshaw, the first such academy in California and the second in the nation. Ms. Boutté attributes her success at Crenshaw to the strong support and efforts of the school's teachers, students, parents, and of the Los Angles Unified School District. Having served eight years as principal, Ms. Boutté left Crenshaw in 1992 to become program manager at the Center for Applied Cultural Studies and Academic Achievement at San Francisco State University.

Iris M. Carl

After many years of teaching mathematics at the elementary, secondary, and graduate levels—and after receiving a variety of honors for her work in mathematics education—Ms. Carl served as instructional supervisor and as Director of Mathematics (K–12) for the Independent School District in Houston, Texas. She has served on the NCTM Board of Directors, and in 1989, Ms. Carl's outstanding work and dedication to mathematics education resulted in her election to the office of President of the NCTM. In 1993, she testified at the United States House of Representatives Subcommittee Hearing on Mathematics and Science Education, and on several occasions between 1982 and 1994, she has been a witness, providing congressional testimony.

Pamela Watkins Coffield

For twenty-five years, teacher Pamela Coffield has successfully motivated students to learn mathematics with her innovative and entertaining method of instruction, which includes real-life, often humorous, applications of statistical methods. Ms. Coffield is Mathematics Department Chair at Brookstone School in Columbus, Georgia, and is a co-director of quantitative literacy workshops for teachers, sponsored by the American Statistical Association and the Woodrow Wilson National Fellowship Foundation. Her awards include the Edyth May Sliffe Award for Distinguished Teaching and the 1987 Georgia Presidential Award for Mathematics Teaching.

Christine Comins

In addition to her duties as a teacher at Pueblo County High School, Ms. Comins has volunteered in an academic program for at-risk ninth graders and has sponsored a math/science club in which students run a math/science fair and a math bowl for middle grade students. Regarded by students and peers as a master teacher, Ms. Comins is the recipient of a Presidential Award in Mathematics and a National Educator Award. Her accomplishments are reflected by the fact that award-winning elementary and secondary mathematics teachers around the country elected her president of the Council of Presidential Awardees in Mathematics (CPAM).

Margarita Cotto-Hernandez

Margarita Cotto-Hernandez

Principal at Burton Elementary School in Grand Rapids, Michigan, Ms. Cotto-Hernandez is credited with expanding and improving the educational process for her city's large, culturally-diverse population. During the school's "Role-Model/Careers Day," she invited members of Grand Rapids' many communities into classrooms to provide students with first-hand education about various cultures and careers. Ms. Cotto-Hernandez uses her experience as a bilingual teacher's aide, a community liaison, a special education teacher, and a migrant program director to enlighten and educate the students, the parents, and the staff of Burton.

Gretchen Davis

Ms. Davis is the Mathematics Department Chair at California's Santa Monica High School. Her current and former students give her high praise for opening their eyes to the relevance of math in their lives. In encouraging open-ended questions and stressing the importance of writing—such as keeping a mathematics journal—she successfully implements the NCTM *Standards* in her teaching. Ms. Davis has received numerous honors, including District Teacher of the Year, Mentor Teacher, Woodrow Wilson and GTE/GIFT fellowships, and PTA Honorary Service Awards. In their February 1990 issue, the *Mathematics Teacher* magazine featured two of her articles about the classroom use of statistics and data analysis.

Gretchen Davis

Teresa de Garcia

Emphasizing the need to respect cultural diversity among her colleagues, Ms. de Garcia teaches bilingual and family mathematics at Boulder University Hill Elementary, an alternative school in Colorado. She regularly invites parents of students to participate in her classroom, and she introduces them to various community resources that can aid their children's educational process. A 1989 recipient of the National Educator Award, Ms. de Garcia has been described as one who "personifies all that is positive and relevant about bilingual and alternative education."

Jenlane Gee Matt

Jenlane Gee Matt

Named the 1989 California Teacher of the Year, Mrs. Matt is a third grade teacher at Christine Sipherd Elementary School in Modesto. While serving as a mentor teacher, Mrs. Matt developed a highly successful drug education program that served as a model for other schools in Stanislaus County. Working with a literature-based curriculum, she promotes student self-esteem and discipline by encouraging cooperative learning and peer coaching. Mrs. Matt gains strong support and commitment from the parents of her students by keeping open lines of communication with them.

Frank W. Griffin

As head of the mathematics department at Cate School in Carpinteria, California, Mr. Griffin has actively implemented the use of graphing calculators and software applications at all levels of the mathematics curriculum. He is a

Frank W. Griffin

David S. Heckman

Seiichi and JoAnn Kaida

Winnie R. Miller

Tamiko Jobe Miyagi

participant in California's Tri-County Mathematics Project and, as a recipient of a Woodrow Wilson Foundation fellowship, has led numerous summer workshops in the Foundation's Teacher Outreach (TORCH) program. Mr. Griffin holds a Teaching Chair at Cate, has coauthored two calculus books, and is the 1994 Tandy Technology Scholar.

Mario J. Guerrero

A sixth grade teacher at Jackson Elementary School in Selma, California, and the recipient of a National Educator Award, Mr. Guerrero has developed a number of innovative programs that enhance the learning process for young children. For example, he developed an outdoor program at the Yosemite Institute that stresses mathematics, science, reading, and writing. Mr. Guerrero encourages his students to research topics, conduct interviews, and report stories for the local radio show he produces, "From a Shorter Point of View."

David S. Heckman

As Chair of the Mathematics/Computer Department at Monmouth Academy in Maine, Mr. Heckman was involved in the development of current certification standards for mathematics teachers and of Maine's Common Core of Learning, a framework for learning outcomes. A driving force behind the integration of technology into the mathematics curriculum, he is a past president of the Association of Teachers of Mathematics in Maine, a Woodrow Wilson Teacher, a Milken National Educator, a Tandy Technology Scholar, and a recipient of Maine's Presidential Award in Mathematics.

Seiichi and JoAnn Kaida

Mr. and Mrs. Kaida work together at St. Andrew's Priory School in Honolulu, Hawaii, where Mrs. Kaida is a mathematics teacher and Mr. Kaida is the school's computer head. (He also teaches math at Honolulu's Hawaii Pacific University.) In 1986, Mrs. Kaida received the South Dakota Presidential Award for Excellence in the Teaching of Mathematics. She currently serves on the NCTM C-ME Committee, which fosters equity in mathematics as it relates to NCTM activities and to the general teaching of mathematics. While he was living in Tokyo, Japan, Mr. Kaida was the math department chair at the International School of the Sacred Heart and taught students from over sixty countries. He has published a number of books in Japan that teach English through the use of math and science.

Gene McCallum

As principal at Audubon Junior High School in Los Angeles, Mr. McCallum has successfully generated widespread parental and community involvement in the educational process. For instance, members of the Black Engineers Support Group visit classes and work directly with students. Concerned about at-risk youth, he coordinated the "Adopt-a-Kid" program, which fosters a mentor relationship between students and teachers. Due in part to Mr. McCallum's efforts, Audubon has earned recognition as a state and federal Distinguished School.

Winnie R. Miller

Mathematics teacher Winnie Miller advocates cross-curriculum instruction at Hillsboro High School in Oregon, using materials such as journals and math poetry to stimulate her students. Active in professional associations, Ms. Miller shares her enthusiasm and teaching strategies with her colleagues by speaking at workshops and conferences. She was the 1991 recipient of the Award for Excellence in Teaching Science and Mathematics from the Oregon Museum of Science and Industry and the Tektronix Foundation, and has been nominated for a Presidential Award.

Tamiko Jobe Miyagi

Ms. Miyagi teaches mathematics at the Academy of Math and Science in Las Vegas, Nevada. She has served on many school district task forces to study curriculum improvement and development, and she has contributed to teacher training by conducting district and statewide in-services in mathematics. Born in Okinawa, Japan, and fluent in Japanese, she spends her summers in Michigan as a speaker in the Global Multicultural Education Summer Institute. Past president of the Southern Nevada Mathematics Council, Ms. Miyagi is the recipient of both a National Educator Award and a Presidential Award for Excellence in Science and Mathematics Teaching.

Larry Moye

A mathematics teacher for the North Slope Borough School District in Barrow, Alaska, Mr. Moye has served as president of the Alaska Council of Mathematics Teachers, has co-led the Alaska Mathematics Consortium summer institutes, and has served on both the Mathematics Standards and Frameworks committees for the State of Alaska 2000 Project. Reaching students at six remote North Slope villages via satellite and compressed video, he weaves cross-cultural teaching techniques into his mathematics classes, balancing creativity, tradition, cultural heritage, and contemporary needs.

Larry Moye

Francis Kemba Mustapha

Born in a village in West Africa, Mr. Mustapha now teaches biology at South Side High School in Fort Wayne, Indiana. When he was a young student, there was no school in his village, so he was sent to a school in a nearby town. Of his teachers, Mr. Mustapha states: "Those teachers, though imperfect, opened up the world for me." It is through his efforts that his home village now has its own school. Now an inspiring teacher who is active in DNA research, Mr. Mustapha is the recipient of a 1993 National Educator Award.

Francis Kemba Mustapha

Lorna Mae Nagata

While she was a fourth-grade teacher at Fremont Elementary School in Alhambra, California, Ms. Nagata promoted writing in all school subjects—including mathematics—by coordinating a publishing project in which teams of her students wrote, illustrated, and bound their own books. Additionally, she worked with the parents of Fremont students, local community members, and the PTA to develop fund-raising projects, such as a walk-a-thon, that enabled her school to purchase computers. As a result of her innovative and creative teaching methods, she was awarded the 1988 National Educator Award. Currently the principal of Mulberry Elementary School in Whittier, California, Ms. Nagata works with her staff to implement the recommendations of the California Mathematics Framework.

Lorna Mae Nagata

Phillip Pérez

Within two years of Dr. Pérez becoming principal, the turnaround at Revere Elementary School in Anaheim, California, was dramatic. With its predominantly Hispanic student population, he strove to overcome difficulties in meeting the needs of bilingual students. Working with parents, staff, and students as "partners," he turned Revere into a school where "students like to be." He initiated parent-education programs on topics such as homework, discipline, and tutoring. As a result of his efforts, Revere was presented with a California Distinguished School Award. Dr. Pérez is currently serving as the deputy superintendent in Riverside, California.

Phillip Pérez

John Pingayak

A teacher and cultural heritage coordinator for the Kashunamiut School District in Chevak, Alaska, Mr. Pingayak is committed to teaching students about

Cheryl H. Powers

Lucie T. Refsland

Diann Resnick

Thomas Ridgeway

their Native Alaskan heritage. He has developed and participated in a variety of cultural programs aimed at increasing cultural pride, such as the Tanqik Theater Group and Native Alaskan language workshops. In accepting a National Educator Award, Mr. Pingayak said: "I have been teaching in my hometown, Chevak, because I made the commitment to myself that I would come back and help my own people."

Cheryl H. Powers

A science teacher at Cate School in Carpinteria, Ms. Powers is a frequent speaker, workshop leader, and organizer for professional educational organizations. She devotes her summers to improving her skills and knowledge as a teacher by participating in programs at research centers such as Lawrence Berkeley Laboratories and Brookhaven National Laboratories. Ms. Powers has served on the Board of Directors of the California Science Teachers Association, has received fellowships from the GTE/GIFT program and the Woodrow Wilson National Fellowship Foundation, and was a 1993 Tandy Technology Scholar.

Lucie T. Refsland

A recipient of the West Virginia Secondary Mathematics Teacher of the Year award, an exchange professor with the People's Republic of China, and a Woodrow Wilson National Foundation fellowship, Dr. Refsland is currently an associate professor of mathematics at Bluefield State College. For ten years she served as head coach and coordinator of the West Virginia State High School Mathematics team, which successfully participated in the American Regions Mathematics League (ARML). Dr. Refsland is presently a member of the Board of Governors of the West Virginia Mathematics Coalition and is involved in training elementary school mathematics teachers.

Diann Resnick

Ms. Resnick, an innovative educator, teaches mathematics at Houston's Bellaire High School. She is recognized for her efforts to bring technology into the classroom and for her work on the Board of Directors of the Rice University School Mathematics Project, a program for teacher training. In her teacher-training capacity, Ms. Resnick has led workshops for the American Statistical Association and the Woodrow Wilson National Fellowship Foundation. A Texas Presidential Award recipient, she has been a member of the College Board Achievement Level Mathematics Committee and the Task Force and Advanced Placement Committees in Statistics. Ms. Resnick is a 1995 Tandy Technology Scholar.

Thomas Ridgeway

For over twenty years, Mr. Ridgeway has taught mathematics and music to students at the Georgia Academy for the Blind. He is blind himself, and as a former student of the Academy, he used voice output technology and braille displays to learn computer programming. Currently, he composes band scores and writes music and dialogue for original musicals. By his own example, he has inspired his students to excel. Mr. Ridgeway is the recipient of a National Educator Award and the 1988 Georgia Handicapped Employee of the Year.

Lucia D. Rivera

In her role as principal of Bradford Elementary School in Pueblo, Colorado, Dr. Martinez emphasizes the importance of lifelong learning. So that the parents of Bradford students can further their education as their children are doing, she provides them with facilities to prepare for the Graduate Equivalency Degree examination. Dr. Martinez developed all-volunteer after-school tutorials that encourage individual achievement and, to increase her students' involvement in the community, she instituted a mentor program with the Latino Chamber of Commerce. In 1989, Dr. Martinez received a Colorado National Educator Award.

Milton S. Shishido

In an effort to curb racial tensions and youth gang conflicts, Mr. Shishido, principal of Waipahu High School in Hawaii, promoted a partnership between his school staff and the surrounding multicultural community. He empowered his staff to create programs such as the Business and Computer Technology Learning Center, Project WIMP (Writing in Math Problems, which integrates writing and mathematics skills), and SMILE, a drug-abuse prevention program for elementary and intermediate schools.

W. Cecil Short

Principal at Oxon High School in Maryland, Mr. Short is recognized for his efforts to ensure that uniformly high standards in education apply to all students. He develops programs that "motivate African American students to achieve educational excellence with an emphasis on positive self-esteem." Among many other achievements, Mr. Short has established a comprehensive volunteer committee of parents that supports the total operation of the school. Their motto is "Do It Now," and they provide such amenities as a chaperone service for all extracurricular activities.

Charmaine Tinker

Ms. Tinker is the principal of Sherwood Regional Alternative Middle School in Columbus, Ohio, which focuses on the mathematics, science, and fine arts disciplines. She developed S.O.S.—a "science on Saturdays" program—and a Saturday school for remediation and proficiency practice testing. Her major objective is to build confidence in students so that they can obtain the education necessary to lead successful and productive lives. Ms. Tinker was a recipient of a 1992 National Educator Award.

José Luis Valderas

A former director of a teacher training program for Hispanic students, Dr. Valderas is now director of compensatory education programs for public schools in Bay City, Michigan. He emphasizes the value of mentoring, tutoring, and conducting "how-to" workshops as a way for students to give back to their communities the education they've received. The son of migrant workers, Dr. Valderas sets examples for others by serving in community agencies, school district study committees, and on the boards of directors of the United Way, Bay Arts Council, and the Hispanic Ministry and Cultural Center, Diocese of Saginaw. He is the 1991 Michigan recipient of a National Educator Award.

Edward J. Wong

The 1987 Mississippi Teacher of the Year, Mr. Wong teaches social studies at Vicksburg High School. His teaching ability and rapport with students have been featured on the local television series "Education: The Way Up" and in the book *I Am a Teacher: A Tribute to America's Teachers* by Robin Sachs. As part of Mississippi's "Be a Hero: Teach" campaign, he appeared in a television public service announcement to promote teaching. Mr. Wong is the recipient of WLBT-TV's Spirit of Mississippi Award.

Lucia D. Rivera

W. Cecil Short

José Luis Valderas

Edward J. Wong

Selected Answers

Activities for which answers will vary are not included.

2 Ancient References to Pi

1. $62,832/20,000 \approx 3.1416$

2. Circumference = 30 cubits
   Diameter = 10 cubits

3. 12,000 gallons
   Height = 9 feet 1 inch

4. 3.1605

3 The Pyramids of Egypt and the Americas

1. 2366 centimeters, 41°

4 Chinese Mathematical Activities

1. First (horizontal) row = 2, 7, 6
   Second row = 9, 5, 1
   Third row = 4, 3, 8

3. The pond is 12 feet deep. The break is $4^{11}/_{20}$ feet above the ground.

5 *The Rhind Mathematical Papyrus* and the St. Ives Puzzle

1. 3.160493827 . . .

6 Early Astronomy

1. One light year equals the distance light can travel in one year
   $= 9.46 \times 10^{15}$ meters
   $= 9,460,000,000,000$ kilometers
   $= 5,878,000,000,000$ miles
   $= 5.878 \times 10^{12}$ miles

   The magnitude of a star equals the measure of the star's relative brightness as seen from Earth. A star of magnitude x is 2.51 times as bright as a star of magnitude $x + 1$.

   One astronomical unit (AU) equals the radius of Earth's orbit
   $= 1.49 \times 10^{11}$ meters
   $= 1.49 \times 10^{8}$ kilometers
   $= 9.26 \times 10^{7}$ miles

   Sirius is 5.00×10^{13} miles from Earth.

9 Thales: A Man of Legend

2.a. He measured the length of the shadow cast by the pole.

  b. He measured the base of the pyramid and divided by two.

  c. Triangle *EBD* ~ triangle *BCA*

d. $AC = {}^{(DB \times CB)}\!/_{BE}$

4.a. 90°

  b. There are eight possible pairs: $(x, y) = (\pm 3, \pm 4)$ or $(\pm 4, \pm 3)$.

10 The Golden Age of Greece

1.a. 15, 21

  b. 25, 36

2. The triangular numbers are in the third diagonal of Pascal's triangle. The square numbers don't have any obvious pattern.

13 The Paradoxes of Zeno

2.a. $x > 1111\tfrac{1}{9}$ meters

  b. $x < 1111\tfrac{1}{9}$ meters

  c. $x = 1111\tfrac{1}{9}$ meters

3.a. Twice as fast

  b. 5 seconds

  c. $2D$ meters

14 Infinitude of Primes

4. $f(1) = 43, f(2) = 47, f(3) = 53, f(4) = 61, f(5) = 71$

5. Prime up to $N = 80$; that is, $f(79) = 1601$ is a prime, $f(80) = 1681 = 41 \times 41$ is not a prime.

6. The first number in this sequence that is not prime is $2 \times 3 \times 5 \times 7 \times 11 \times 13 + 1 = 30,031$ (equal to 59×509).

15 The Elements of Euclid

1. A line is itself a set of points. Hence the definition is circular, basically defining a concept in terms of itself.

3.a. 12

  b. 7

16 Appolonius and Conic Sections

1.a. Distance from point P to directrix $= 50, PF = 50$

  b. Yes

  c. Yes

2.a. 20

19 The Formulas of Heron and Brahmagupta

2. Area of quadrilateral $= 48$ square units

20 Diophantus of Alexandria

Vignette riddle: Diophantus died at age 84.

2.a. 4, 7, 9, 11

  b. $AB = 100$, $AD = 35$, $AC = 28$, $BD = 75$, $DC = 21$

24 The Concept of Zero

2. A line with slope zero is a horizontal line. A line with no slope (undefined slope) is a vertical line.

25 Mathematics in Play: The Throw Sticks Game

1.c. p^3, $(1 - p)^3$, $3p(1 - p)^2$, $3p^2(1 - p)$

26 Mathematicians of the Middle Ages

3. $\angle A = 90°$; $\angle B = 63°$; $\angle C = 27°$; $a : b : c = 1.12 : 1 : 0.51$

27 Islamic Mathematics

1. Answers may vary. One possible solution is that the son inherited twice as much as the wife and the wife inherited twice as much as the daughter. Thus the son received $\frac{4}{7}$ of the inheritance, the wife received $\frac{2}{7}$, and the daughter received $\frac{1}{7}$.

30 The Poet Mathematicians

5. 120 water lilies

31 The Fibonacci Sequence

Vignette riddle: 377 pairs of rabbits (the sequence is 1, 1, 2, 3, 5, 8, 13, 21, 34, 55, 89, 144, 233, 377).

34 The Golden Ratio and Rectangle

4. 10

41 Changing Universe: Ptolemy, Copernicus, Kepler

3.a. $\frac{1}{2}\pi$ feet = 0.159 feet, or about 1.9 inches

  b. $\frac{1}{2}\pi$ feet = 0.159 feet, or about 1.9 inches

  c. Given a circle of any size, an increase in the circumference of 1 foot will result in a radius increase of 1.9 inches.

44 Pascal's Useful Triangle

1.a. 3%

  b. 16%

  c. 31%

  d. 31%

e. 16%

f. 3%

5. 252 routes

46 Gambling Initiates Probability Study

1. 67%

3. a. 16%, b. 36%, c. 48%

49 The Bernoulli Family

4. The Bernoulli numbers are related to the power series expansion of $x/(e^x - 1)$.

52 Euler and the Number *e*

1.a. $68,484.75

b. $73,401.76

c. $73,874.38

d. $73,890.56

2. Making $3/(n + 1)! < 0.005$ gives $n = 5$.
Then $1 + 1 + 1/2! + 1/3! + 1/4! + 1/5! = 2.7167$, accurate to two places.

Making $3/(n + 1)! < 0.0005$ gives $n = 8$.
Then $1 + 1 + 1/2! + 1/3! + 1/4! + 1/5! + 1/6! + 1/7! + 1/8! = 2.7183$, accurate to three places.

53 The Seven Bridges of Königsberg

2.a. Four, no

b. Answers may vary.

c. Answers may vary.

57 Benjamin Banneker: Problem Solver

3. 19 bullocks, 1 cow, 80 sheep

61 Carl Friedrich Gauss: Mathematician of Influence

1.a. 5,000,050,000

b. 210,559

c. $n/2(n + 1)$

62 Mathematics and the Electoral College

3.a. Chin (18 votes)

b. Vallejo (37 votes)

c. Ionesco (191 points)

d. Yager (28 to 27 against Ionesco, 37 to 18 against Chin, 33 to 22 against Vallejo, and 36 to 19 against Pak)

68 De Morgan: Caring Teacher

1. $x = 43$

70   Ada Lovelace: First Computer Programmer

2.a. $4 = (100)_2$; $5 = (101)_2$; $7 = (111)_2$; $8 = (1000)_2$; $9 = (1001)_2$; $11 = (1011)_2$; $12 = (1100)_2$

   b. $(1011)_2 = 11$; $(10001)_2 = 17$; $(110110)_2 = 54$; $(1000000)_2 = 64$

81   Emmy Noether: A Modern Mathematics Pioneer

2.a. $z = 11$

   b. $y = 3$

   c. $x = 7$

   d. $w = 12$

   e. $t = 3$

   f. $s = 9$

   g. $r = 5$

3. $-10, 2, 7, 7$

85   Bees as Mathematicians?

3.a. A $3'' \times 3''$ square

   b. The circle

86   von Neumann: Mathematics as Experience

1. Distance bird flies = 637.5 miles

3. You should switch doors. This yields a probability of ⅔ that you will get the prize.

88   Grace Murray Hopper: Ever Confident

3.a. 5.5096×10^{-6} seconds

   b. 5.5096×10^{-4} seconds

   c. 0.0055096 seconds

92   Percentages and Statistics: What Do They Tell Us?

1.a. Males 44%, females 33%

   b. Answers will vary.

   c. Answers will vary.

   d. Males 50%, females 50%

   e. Answers will vary.

   f. Males 25%, females 25%

   g. Answers will vary.

   h. Answers will vary.

93   When a Loss Could Have Been a Win

3. 57%

99   Problems in Probabilistic Reasoning

3.   Problem 1: All have the same probability (0.001)

Problem 2: (a) 0.001; (b) 0.205; (c) 0.246

106 Chaos in Jurassic Park

1.a. 1.105115698

b. 2.716923932

c. 480,340,920.9

d. 2.5571013×10^{43}

Bibliography

References in **bold type** are recommended for school libraries.

Abbreviations: National Council of Teachers of Mathematics (NCTM); Mathematical Association of America (MAA); Consortium for Mathematics and its Applications (COMAP)

Aaboe, Asger. *Episodes from the Early History of Mathematics.* Washington, DC: MAA, 1978.

Abbott, Edwin. *Flatland.* New York: Barnes and Noble, 1963.

Abraham, R.H., and C.D. Shaw. *Dynamics, The Geometry of Behavior.* Palo Alto, CA: Addison-Wesley, 1992.

Adamczeivski, Jan. *Nicholas Copernicus and His Epoch.* Philadelphia: Copernicus Society of America, 1973.

Adams, William J. *The Life and Times of the Central Limit Theorem.* New York: Kademon Publishing, 1974.

Adele, Gail. "When did Euclid Live? An Answer Plus a Short History of Geometry." *Mathematics Teacher* (Sept 1989) 460–463.

Adler, Alfred. "Mathematics and Creativity." *New Yorker Magazine* (19 Feb 1972) 39–40.

Aero, Rita. *Things Chinese.* New York: Doubleday, 1980.

Agostini, Granco. *Math and Logic Games.* New York: Harper and Row, 1980.

Albers, Donald, and G.L. Alexanderson (eds). *Courant in Göttingen and New York.* New York: Springer-Verlag, 1976.

———. *Mathematical People: Profiles and Interviews.* Chicago: Contemporary Books, 1986.

———, et al (eds). *More Mathematical People.* Boston: Harcourt Brace Jovanovich, 1990.

Alcoze, Thom, et al. *Multiculturalism in Mathematics, Science and Technology: Readings and Activities.* Menlo Park, CA: Addison-Wesley, 1993.

Al-Daffa, Ali A. *The Muslim Contributions to Mathematics.* Atlantic Heights, NJ: Humanities Press, 1977.

Alexanderson, Gerald (ed). *The Pólya Picture Album: Encounters of a Mathematician.* New York: Birkhauser Boston, 1987.

Alexandroff, A.D., et al. *Mathematics: Its Content, Methods, and Meaning.* Cambridge, MA: MIT Press, 1963.

Alic, Margaret. *Hypatia's Heritage.* Boston: Beacon Press, 1986.

Allen, R.H. *Star Names: Their Lore and Meaning.* Mineola, NY: Dover, 1963.

Allman, G.J. *Greek Geometry from Thales to Euclid.* New York: Arno Press, 1976.

Apler, J.L. *Groups and Symmetry.* New York: Springer-Verlag, 1978.

Amir-Moez, Ali R. "Mathematics of Music." *Recreational Mathematics Magazine* 3 (1961) 31–36.

Anderson, Bill D., and John F. Lamb, Jr. "The Mathematical Aspects of a Lunar Shuttle Landing." *Mathematics Teacher* (Oct 1981) 549–553.

Anderson, Bill D., Dennis P. Grantham, and John F. Lamb. "Mathematical Aspects of a Lunar Shuttle Landing Revisited." *Mathematics Teacher* (Sept 1984) 460–464.

Andrade, E.N. *Sir Isaac Newton.* New York: Doubleday, 1958.

Andrews, G.E. "An Introduction to Ramanujan's Lost Notebook." *American Mathematical Monthly* 86 (1979) 89–108.

Andrews, William S. *Magic Squares and Cubes.* Mineola, NY: Dover, 1960.

Apostol, Tom. *The Story of Pi* (Computer-animated videotape). Reston, VA: NCTM, 1989.

———, et al. *A Century of Calculus.* Washington, DC: MAA, 1992.

Appel, Kenneth, and Wolfgang Haken. "The Four Color Proof Suffices." *The Mathematical Intelligencer* 8, #1 (1986) 10–20.

———. "The Solution of the Four-Color-Map Problem," *Scientific American* (Oct 1977) 108–121.

Archambeau, Sister Mary Leona. "Pythagorean Triples Grouped into Families." *Mathematics Teacher* (Mar 1968) 251–252.

———. "Outline of the History of Mathematics, Part II." *American Mathematical Monthly* LVI (Jan 1949) 21–26.

Arndt, A. B. "Al-Khwarizmi." *Mathematics Teacher* (Dec 1983) 668–670.

Arpaia, Pasquale J. "Discoveries in Mathematics." *Mathematics Teacher* (May 1972) 463–465.

Ascher, Marcia. *Ethnomathematics: A Multicultural View of Mathematical Ideas*. Pacific Grove, CA: Brooks/Cole Publishing, 1991.

———, and Robert Ascher. *Code of the Quipu: A Study in Media, Mathematics, and Culture.* Ann Arbor, MI: The University of Michigan Press, 1981.

Asimov, Isaac. *Guide to Earth and Space.* New York: Ballantine Books, 1991.

———. *In the Beginning ....* New York: Crown Publishers, 1981.

————. *Only a Trillion.* New York: Ace Books, 1980.

————. *Realm of Numbers.* Boston: Houghton Mifflin, 1959.

————. *Today and Tomorrow and ....* New York: Dell Publishing, 1975.

Atneosen, Gail H. "The Schwartz Paradox: An Interesting Problem for the First-Year Calculus Student." *Mathematics Teacher* (Mar 1972) 281-284.

Aubrey, John. *Brief Lives.* Ann Arbor, MI: Ann Arbor Paperbacks, 1962.

Aviv, Cherie, and Sid Rachlin. "Magic Cubes: A Total Experience." *Mathematics Teacher* (Sept 1981) 464-472.

Ayton, Joseph. "A Visit to a Mathematical Shrine." *Mathematics Teacher* (Oct 1969) 479-480.

Bailey, William T. "Friday the Thirteenth." *Mathematics Teacher* (May 1969) 363-364.

Baker, G.J., and J.P. Gollub. *Chaotic Dynamics, An Introduction.* New York: Cambridge University Press, 1990.

Bakst, Aaron. *Mathematics: Its Magic and Mastery.* New York: D. Van Nostrand, 1952.

Ball, W.W.R. *A Short Account of the History of Mathematics.* Mineola, NY: Dover, 1960.

————, and Coxeter, H.S.M. *Mathematical Recreations and Essays.* Mineola, NY: Dover, 1987.

Ballew, David W. "The Wheel of Aristotle." *Mathematics Teacher* (Oct 1972) 507-509.

Banchoff, Thomas F. *Beyond the Third Dimension.* New York: W.H. Freeman, 1990.

Bankoff, Leon. "Are the Twin Circles of Archimedes Really Twins?" *Mathematics Magazine* (Sept/Oct 1974) 214-218.

Bardis, Panos D. "Evolution of Pi: An Essay in Mathematical Progress from the Great Pyramid to ENIAC." *School Science and Mathematics* (Jan 1960) 73-78.

Barit, Julian. "The Lore of Number." *Mathematics Teacher* (Dec 1968) 779-783.

Barker, Stephen F. *Philosophy of Mathematics.* Englewood Cliffs, NJ: Prentice-Hall, 1964.

Barnard, Douglas. *It's All Done by Numbers.* New York: Hawthorn Books, 1968.

Barnett, I.A. "Mathematics as an Art: The Higher Arithmetic." *Mathematics Teacher* (Apr 1968) 424-434.

Barnett, Lincoln. *The Universe and Dr. Einstein.* New York: Signet Science Library Books, 1964.

Barnette, David. *Map-Coloring, Polyhedra, and the Four-Color Problem.* Washington, DC: Mathematical Association of America, 1983.

Barnsley, Michael. *Fractals Everywhere.* Boston: Academic Press, 1988.

Barrow, John D. *Pi in the Sky: Counting, Thinking, and Being.* New York: Oxford University Press, 1992.

————. "The Mathematical Universe." *World and I Magazine* (May 1989) 306-311.

Baron, M. *The Origins of the Infinite Calculus.* Mineola, NY: Dover, 1987.

Barton, Ray. "Chaos and Fractals." *Mathematics Teacher* (Oct 1990) 524-529.

Bates, Nathaniel, and Sanderson Smith. *101 Puzzle Problems.* Concord, MA: Bates Publishing, 1980.

Battista, Michael. "Mathematics in Baseball." *Mathematics Teacher* (Apr 1993) 336-342.

Baum, Joan. *The Calculating Passion of Ada Byron.* Hamden, CT: Archeon Books, 1986.

Baum, Robert J. (ed). *Philosophy and Mathematics from Plato to the Present.* San Francisco: W.H. Freeman, 1973.

Baumgardt, Carola. *Johannes Kepler: Life and Letters.* New York: Philosophical Library, 1952.

Becker, Jerry P. "Notes on the First International Congress on Mathematics Education." *Mathematics Teacher* (Apr 1970) 318-319.

Beckmann, Petr. *A History of π.* New York: St. Martin's Press, 1976.

Beiler, Albert H. *Recreations in the Theory of Numbers: The Queen of Mathematics Entertains.* Mineola, NY: Dover, 1964.

Bell, E.T. "Buddha's Advice to Students and Teachers of Mathematics." *Mathematics Teacher* (May 1969) 373-383.

————. *Mathematics: Queen and Servant of Science.* Washington, DC: MAA, 1987.

————. *Men of Mathematics.* New York: Simon and Schuster, 1986.

————. *The Development of Mathematics.* Mineola, NY: Dover, 1992.

————. *The Last Problem.* Washington, DC: MAA, 1990.

————. *The Magic of Numbers.* New York: McGraw-Hill, 1946.

Bell, R.C. *Board and Table Games from Many Civilizations.* Mineola, NY: Dover, 1979.

Bellman, Richard. *A Collection of Modern Mathematical Classics: Analysis.* Mineola, NY: Dover, 1961.

Benacerraf, Paul. "God, the Devil and Gödel." *The Monist* 51 (1967) 9-32.

————, and Hilary Putnam (eds). *Philosophy of Mathematics.* New York: Prentice-Hall, 1964.

Benedict, Betty, and Sanderson Smith. *FUNctional Geography of the United States.* Carpinteria, CA: Cate School Press, 1993.

Benjamin Banneker (poster). Burlington, NC: Cabisco Mathematics, Carolina Biological Supply, 1991.

Bennett, Charles H. *On Random and Hard-to-Describe Numbers.* IBM Thomas J. Watson Research Center Research Report RC 7483, 1979.

Bennett, Dan. *Pythagoras Plugged In: Proofs and Problems for The Geometer's Sketchpad.* Berkeley, CA: Key Curriculum Press, 1995.

Bergamini, David (ed). *Mathematics: Life Science Library.* New York: Time-Life Books, 1972.

Berggren, J. *Episodes in the Mathematics of Medieval Islam.* New York: Springer-Verlag, 1986.

Bezuszka, Stanley J., and Margaret Kenney. *Number Treasury.* Palo Alto, CA: Dale Seymour, 1982.

Bibby, John. *Quotes, Damned Quotes, And . . . .* Edinburgh, Scotland: Liberton Brae, 1986.

Bidwell, James K., and Bernard K. Lange. "Girolamo Cardano: A Defense of His Character." *Mathematics Teacher* (Jan 1971) 25-31.

———. "Humanize Your Classroom with the History of Mathematics." *Mathematics Teacher* (Sept 1993) 461-464.

———. "Mayan Arithmetic." *Mathematics Teacher* (Nov 1967) 762-768.

———. "The Teaching of Arithmetic in England from 1550 until 1800 as Influenced by Social Change." *Mathematics Teacher* (Oct 1969) 484-490.

Billstein, Rick, and Johnny Lott. "Golden Rectangles and Ratios." *Student Mathematics Notes* (Sept 1986).

Bishop, Alan J. *Mathematics Education and Culture.* Dordrecht, the Netherlands: Kluwer Academic Publishers Group, 1988.

Bishop, E. "The Crisis in Contemporary Mathematics." *Historia Mathematica* 2 (1975) 507-517.

Blackwell, William. *Geometry and Architecture.* Berkeley, CA: Key Curriculum Press, 1994.

Blenkinsopp, Joseph. *The Pentateuch.* New York: Doubleday, 1992.

Blumenthal, Leonard M. *A Modern View of Geometry.* San Francisco: W.H. Freeman, 1961.

Boag, Tom, Charles Boberg, and Lyn Hughes. "On Archimedian Solids." *Mathematics Teacher* (May 1979) 371-376.

Bochenski, I.M. *A History of Formal Logic.* South Bend, IN: Notre Dame University Press, 1961.

Bocher, Salomon. *The Role of Mathematics in the Rise of Science.* Princeton, NJ: Princeton University Press, 1966.

———. *Mathematics in Cultural History.* New York: Charles Scribner's, 1973.

Boehm, David A. (ed). *Guiness Sports Record Book.* New York: Sterling Publications, 1990.

Bold, Benjamin. *Famous Problems of Geometry.* Mineola, NY: Dover, 1969.

Bolzano, B. *Paradoxes of the Infinite.* London: Routledge and Kegan Paul, 1950.

Bonola, Roberto. *Non-Euclidean Geometry.* Mineola, NY: Dover, 1955.

Bool, F.H., et al. *M.C. Escher, His Life and Complete Works.* New York: Harry N. Abrams, 1982.

Bowles, Martha, and Rochelle Newman. *The Golden Relationship.* Bradford, MA: Pythagorean Press, 1987.

———, and Rochelle Newman. *Universal Patterns.* Bradford, MA: Pythagorean Press, 1987.

Boltyansky, Vladimir. "Beyond Euclid: Turning the Incredible into the Obvious." *Quantum* (Sept/Oct 1992) 19-23.

Boslough, John. *Stephen Hawking's Universe.* New York: Avon Books, 1989.

Botts, Truman. "More on the Mathematics of Musical Scales." *Mathematics Teacher* (Jan 1974) 75-84.

Bouleau, *The Painter's Secret Geometry: A Study of Composition in Art.* New York: Hacker, 1963.

Boulez, Piene, and Andrew Gerzso. "Computers in Music." *Scientific American* (Apr 1988) 44-51.

Boulger, William. "Pythagoras Meets Fibonacci." *Mathematics Teacher* (Apr 1989) 277-282.

Bourgoin, J. *Arabic Geometrical Pattern and Design.* Mineola, NY: Dover, 1973.

Boyd, James N. *Professor Bear's Mathematical World.* Salem, VA: Virginia Council of Teachers of Mathematics, 1987.

Boyer, Carl. *A History of Mathematics,* 2nd ed rev. Uta C. Merzbach. New York: John Wiley, 1991.

———. *History of Analytic Geometry.* New York: John Wiley, 1956.

———. *The History of Mathematics and Its Conceptual Development.* Mineola, NY: Dover, 1959.

Bradley, A. Day. "Al-Biruni's Table of Chords." *Mathematics Teacher* (Nov 1970) 615-617.

———. "The Three-Point Problem." *Mathematics Teacher* (Dec 1972) 703-706.

Brainerd, C.J. "The Origins of Number Concepts." *Scientific American* (Mar 1973) 101-109.

Brandon, W. *The American Heritage Book of Indians.* New York: Dell Publishing, 1964.

Braumbagh, R.S. *Plato's Mathematical Imagination; the Mathematical Passages in the Dialogues and Their Interpretation.* Bloomington, IN: Indiana University Press, 1954.

Brewer, James, and Martha Smith. *Emmy Noether: A Tribute to Her Life and Work.* New York: Marcel Dekken, 1981.

Brewster, Sir David. *Life of Newton.* London: John Murray, 1831.

Briggs, John. *Fractals: The Patterns of Chaos.* New York: Simon and Schuster, 1992.

———, and David Peat. *Turbulent Mirror.* New York: Harper and Row, 1989.

Briggs, William L. "Lessons from the Greeks and Computers." *Mathematics Magazine* (Jan 1982) 19-25.

Brinton, D.G. "The Origin of Sacred Numbers." *American Anthropologist* 7 (1894) 168-173.

Brizio, A.M., et al. *Leonardo the Artist.* New York: McGraw-Hill, 1980.

Broughton, Peter. "Halley's Comet in the Classroom." *Mathematics Teacher* (Feb 1986) 85-89.

Brown, J.D. "Music and Mathematicians Since the Seventeenth Century." *Mathematics Teacher* (Dec 1968) 783-787.

Brown, Lloyd A. *The Story of Maps.* Boston: Little, Brown and Bonanza Books, 1949.

Brown, R. Gene, and K. Johnston. *Paciolo on Accounting.* New York: McGraw Hill Book, 1963.

Brown, Stephen I. "From the Golden Rectangle and Fibonacci to Pedagogy and Problem Solving." *Mathematics Teacher* (Feb 1976) 180-188.

Bruins, E. M. "Egyptian Arithmetic." *Janus* 68 (1981) 33-52.

———. "On the History of Logarithms: Burgi, Napier, Briggs, de Decker, Vlacq, Huygens." *Janus* 67 (1980) 241-260.

———. "The Division of the Circle and Ancient Arts and Sciences." *Janus* 63 (1976) 61-84.

Budden, F.J. *The Fascination of Groups.* New York: Cambridge University Press, 1972.

Buhler, W.K. *Gauss: A Bibliographical Study.* New York: Springer-Verlag, 1981.

Bunch, Bryan H. *Mathematical Fallacies and Paradoxes.* New York: Van Nostrand Reinhold, 1982.

Bunt, Lucas, Phillip S. Jones, and Jack Bedient. *The Historical Roots of Elementary Mathematics.* Mineola, NY: Dover, 1988.

Burdick, David L. "The Empirical Foundations of Probability Theory." *Mathematics Teacher* (Apr 1973) 316-318.

Burkert, W. *Lore and Science in Ancient Pythagoreanism.* Cambridge, MA: Harvard University Press, 1972.

Burton, David L. *Elementary Number Theory.* Boston: Allyn and Bacon, 1976.

———. *The History of Mathematics: An Introduction.* Boston: Allyn and Bacon, 1985.

Bushwich, N. *Understanding the Jewish Calendar.* Brooklyn, NY: Moznaim, 1989.

Buxton, Laurie. *Do You Panic About Maths?* Suffolk, England: Heinemann Educational Books, 1981.

Cajori, Florian. *A History of Mathematics.* New York: Chelsea Publishing, 1991.

Calinger, Ronald (ed). *Classics of Mathematics.* Oak Park, IL: Moore Publishing, 1982.

Camp, Dane R. "A Fractal Excursion." *Mathematics Teacher* (Apr 1991) 265-275.

———. "The Legend of SOH CAH TOA." *Mathematics Teacher* (Apr 1990) 286-287.

Campbell, Douglas, and John Higgins. *Mathematics, People, Problems, Results.* Belmont, CA: Wadsworth International, 1984.

Campbell, Stephen K. *Flaws and Fallacies in Statistical Reasoning.* Englewood Cliffs, NJ: Prentice-Hall, 1974.

Campbell, William. "An Application from the History of Mathematics." *Mathematics Teacher* (Sept 1977) 538-540.

Cardano, Girolamo. *The Great Art, or the Rules of Algebra,* trans Richard Witmer. Cambridge, MA: MIT Press, 1968.

Carnap, R. *Logical Foundations of Probability.* Chicago: University of Chicago Press, 1950.

Carroll, Lewis. *Pillow Problems and A Tangled Tale.* Mineola, NY: Dover, 1958.

Carter, Jack. "Discrete Mathematics: Women in Mathematics." *California Mathematics Council ComMuniCator* (Mar 1993) 10-12.

Casson, Lionel (ed). *Ancient Egypt.* New York: Time-Life Books, 1965.

Castellanos, Dario. "The Ubiquitous π." *Mathematics Magazine* (Apr 1988) 67-98.

Castillo, Toby T. *Apache Mathematics, Past and Present.* Whiteriver, AZ: Whiteriver Middle School Press, 1994.

Chace, Arnold B. *The Rhind Mathematical Papyrus.* Reston, VA: NCTM, 1979.

Chaitin, G. "Randomness in Arithmetic." *Scientific American* (July 1988) 80-85.

Chenal-Ducey, Michelle. "Grace Chisholm Young." *California Mathematics Council ComMuniCator* (Mar 1993) 28-29.

Cheney, William Fitch. "Can We Outdo Mascheroni?" *Mathematics Teacher* 46 (1953) 152-156.

Chern, Shiing-shen. "What is Geometry?" *American Mathematical Monthly* 97, #8 (Oct 1990) 679-86.

Chipman, S.F., L.R. Brush, and D.M. Wilson (eds). *Women in Mathematics: Balancing the Equation.* Hillsdale, NJ: Lawrence Erlbaum, 1985.

Christiansen, Bent. "A Description of the Department of Mathematics, The Royal Danish School of Educational Studies." *Mathematics Teacher* (Mar 1970) 271-279.

Christianson, Gale E. *In the Presence of the Creator: Isaac Newton and His Times.* New York: Cambridge University Press, 1984.

Cibes, Margaret. "The Sierpiński Triangle: Deterministic versus Random Models." *Mathematics Teacher* (Nov 1990) 617-621.

Clason, Robert. "Problem Solving and Multiplication of Rational Numbers: Three Old Devices." *Mathematics Teacher* (May 1973) 414-419.

Cleminshaw, C.H. *The Beginner's Guide to the Stars.* New York: Thomas Y. Crowell, 1977.

Closs, Michael P. *Native American Mathematics*. Austin, TX: University of Texas Press, 1986.

Cohen, I. Bernard. "Newton's Discovery of Gravity." *Scientific American* (Mar 1981) 166-179.

Cohen, Patricia Cline. *A Calculating People: The Spread of Numeracy in Early America.* Chicago: University of Chicago Press, 1982.

Cole, Alison. *Perspective.* New York: Dorling Kindersley, 1992.

Coleman, Donald B. "The Silver Ratio: A Vehicle for Generalization." *Mathematics Teacher* (Jan 1989) 54-59.

Collier, J. *Indians of the Americas.* New York: Mentor Books, 1948.

Colman, Weaver. "Figurate Numbers." *Mathematics Teacher* (Nov 1974) 661-666.

Connelly, Owen (ed). *The Historical Dictionary of Napoleonic France, 1799-1815.* Westport, CT: Greenwood Press, 1985.

Contino, Mike. "The Question Box: Watch Out For Zero." *California Mathematics Council ComMuniCator* (June 1993) 22.

Cook, Theodore A. *The Curves of Life.* Mineola, NY: Dover, 1979.

Coolidge, J.L. *A History of Geometrical Methods.* Mineola, NY: Dover, 1963.

———. *The Mathematics of Great Amateurs.* New York: Oxford University Press, 1949.

Costabel, Pierre. "The Wheel of Aristotle and French Consideration of Galileo's Arguments." *Mathematics Teacher* (May 1968) 527-534.

Coughlin, Raymond, and David E. Zitarelli. *The Ascent of Mathematics.* New York: McGraw Hill Book, 1984.

Courant, Richard, and Herbert Robins. *What Is Mathematics?* New York: Oxford University Press, 1948.

Court, N.A. "Notes on Inversion." *Mathematics Teacher* 55 (1962) 655-657.

Coxeter, H.S.M. "Music and Mathematics." *Mathematics Teacher* (Mar 1968) 312-320.

———. *Non-Euclidean Geometry.* Toronto: University of Toronto Press, 1947.

———, and Samuel L. Greitzer. *Geometry Revisited.* Washington, DC: MAA, 1967.

Crawford, John A., and Calvin T. Long. "Guessing, Mathematical Induction, and a Remarkable Fibonacci Result." *Mathematics Teacher* (Nov 1979) 613-616.

Critchlow, K. *Islamic Patterns: An Analytical Approach.* London: Thames Hudson, 1984.

Crossley, Jon N., et al. *What is Mathematical Logic?* New York: Oxford University Press, 1972.

Crowe, M.J. "Ten 'Laws' Concerning Patterns of Change in the History of Mathematics." *Historia Mathematica* 2 (1975) 161-166.

Crowley, Mary L., and Kenneth Dunn. "On Multiplying Negative Numbers." *Mathematics Teacher* (Apr 1985) 252-256.

Crowley, Mary L. "The 'Difference' in Babbage's Difference Engine." *Mathematics Teacher* (May 1985) 366-372, 354.

Crichton, Michael. *Jurassic Park.* New York: Ballantine Books, 1990.

Cuban, Larry. *Teachers and Machines: The Classroom Use of Technology Since 1920.* New York: Teachers College Press, Columbia University, 1985.

Cundy, H. Martyn, and A.P. Rollette. *Mathematical Models.* London: Oxford University Press, 1974.

Cunningham, Helen. "I 'Found Well'." *Mathematics Teacher* (Nov 1975) 594-597.

———. "1776." *Mathematics Teacher* (Apr 1976) 310-311.

Czepiel, James, and Edward Esty. "Mathematics in the Newspaper." *Mathematics Teacher* (Nov 1980) 582-586.

Daintith, John, and R.D. Nelson (eds). *Dictionary of Mathematics.* New York: Penguin Books, 1989.

Dalton, LeRoy. *Algebra in the Real World.* Palo Alto, CA: Dale Seymour, 1983.

Damarin, Suzanne. "Mathematics: A Feminist Perspective." *NCTM Yearbook.* Reston, VA: NCTM, 1990.

Dantzig, T. *Number: The Language of Science.* New York: Macmillan, 1967.

———. *The Bequest of the Greeks.* New York: Charles Scribner's, 1955.

Dash, Joan. *The Triumph of Discovery.* Westwood, NJ: Silver Burdett and Ginn, 1991.

Datta, B., and A.N. Singh. *History of Hindu Mathematics.* Bombay, India: Asia Publishing House, 1962.

Daubin, Joseph W. *Georg Cantor: His Mathematics and Philosophy of the Infinite.* Cambridge, MA: Harvard University Press, 1979.

———. *The History of Mathematics from Antiquity to the Present.* New York: Garland, 1985.

David, F.N. *Games, Gods and Gambling.* New York: Hafner Publishing, 1962.

Davies, Paul. *The Edge of Infinity.* New York: Simon and Schuster, 1982.

Davies, W.V. *Reading the Past: Egyptian Hieroglyphs.* Berkeley, CA: University of California Press, 1987.

Davis, H.T. *Alexandria, the Golden City.* Evanston, IL: Principia Press of Illinois, 1957.

Davis, James. "An Evening with Pi." *Journal of Recreational Mathematics* (Mar 1981) 197-203.

Davis, Kenneth C. *Don't Know Much About History.* New York: Avon Books, 1990.

Davis, Martin, and Reuben Hersh. "Hilbert's Tenth Problem." *Scientific American* (Nov 1973) 84-91.

Davis, Philip. "Fidelity in Mathematical Discourse: Is 1 + 1 Really 2?" *American Mathematical Monthly* 78 (1972) 252-263.

———. "Mathematics by Fiat?" *The Two Year College Mathematics Journal* (June 1980).

———. *The Lore of Large Numbers.* Washington, DC: MAA, 1961.

———, and William Chinn. *3.14156 and All That.* Boston: Birkhauser Boston, 1985.

———, and Reuben Hersh. *Descartes' Dream.* New York: Harcourt Brace Jovanovich, 1986.

———, and Reuben Hersh. *The Mathematical Experience.* Boston: Birkhauser Boston, 1981.

Dawes, Robin M. *Rational Choice in an Uncertain World.* San Diego, CA: Harcourt Brace Jovanovich, 1988.

De Camp, L.S. *The Ancient Engineers.* Garden City, NY: Doubleday, 1963.

Dedron, P., and J. Itard. *Mathematics and Mathematicians.* London: Transworld Publications, 1973.

Del Grande, John. "The Method of Archimedes." *Mathematics Teacher* (Mar 1993) 240-243.

Delman, Morton. "Counterpoint as an Equivalence Relation." *Mathematics Teacher* (Feb 1967) 137.

DeLong, Howard. "Unsolved Problems in Arithmetic." *Scientific American* (Mar 1971) 50-60.

Dembart, Lee. "Scientists Buzzing: Fermat's Last Theorem May Have Been Proved." *Los Angeles Times* (8 Mar 1988) 3, 23.

Denson, Philinda Stern. "Mathematics History Time Line." *Mathematics Teacher* (Nov 1987) 640-642.

DeTemple, Duane, and Jack M. Robertson. "The Equivalence of Euler's and Pick's Theorems." *Mathematics Teacher* (Mar 1974) 222-226.

Devaney, R.L. *Chaos, Fractals, and Dynamics.* Menlo Park, CA: Addison-Wesley, 1990.

———. *Chaos, Fractals, and Dynamics: Computer Experiments in Mathematics.* Menlo Park, CA: Addison-Wesley, 1989.

———. *Professor Devaney Explains the Fractal Geometry of the Mandelbrot Set* (video). Berkeley, CA: Key Curriculum Press, 1996.

Devlin, Keith. *Mathematics: The New Golden Age.* New York: Penguin Books, 1988.

Dewdney, A.K. *200% of Nothing.* New York: John Wiley, 1993.

———. *The Magic Machine.* New York: W.H. Freeman, 1990.

———. "Computer Recreations: A Tour of the Mandelbrot Set Aboard the Mandelbus." *Scientific American* (Feb 1989) 108-111.

Diana, Lind Mae. "The Peruvian Quipu." *Mathematics Teacher* (Oct 1967) 623-628.

Dibble, W.E. "A Possible Pythagorean Triangle at Stonehenge." *Journal for the History of Astronomy* 17 (1976) 141-142.

Dick, Auguste. *Emmy Noether, 1882-1935.* Basel, Switzerland: Birkhauser Verlag, 1970.

DiDomenico, Angelo S. "Eureka! Pythagorean Triples from the Addition Table." *Mathematics Teacher* (May 1985) 336-38.

Dieudonne, J. "The Work of Nicholas Bourbaki." *American Mathematical Monthly* 77 (1970) 134-145.

Dijksterhuis, E.J. *Archimedes.* Princeton, NJ: Princeton University Press, 1987.

Dilke, O.A.W. *Reading the Past: Mathematics and Measurement.* Berkeley, CA: University of California Press, 1987.

Dittrich, Alan. "An Experiment in Teaching the History of Mathematics." *Mathematics Teacher* (Jan 1973) 35-38.

Dobler, Sam. *From Recreation to Computation Around the World.* San Carlos, CA: Math Products Plus, 1980.

Dodge, Clayton. "Guido Fubini." *Mathematics Teacher* (Jan 1969) 44-47.

Donahue, Richard. "Estimating Pi by Microcomputer." *Mathematics Teacher* (Mar 1988) 203-206, 226.

Dorf, Richard. *Computers and Man.* San Francisco: Boyd and Fraser Publishing, 1974.

Dorman, Janet et al. "Fields and Near-Fields of Order Pairs of Reals." *Mathematics Teacher* (Apr 1966) 335-341.

Dorris, H. *100 Great Problems of Elementary Mathematics: Their History and Solution.* Mineola, NY: Dover, 1965.

Downey, Diane, T. Slesnick, and J. Stenmark. *Math for Girls and Other Problem Solvers.* Berkeley, CA: EQUALS/Lawrence Hall of Science, 1981.

Drake, Stillman. *Discoveries and Opinions of Galileo.* Garden City, NY: Doubleday, 1957.

———. *Galileo at Work: His Scientific Biography.* Chicago: University of Chicago Press, 1978.

Dresselhaus, Mildred et al. "Interventions to Increase the Participation of Women in Physics." *Science* 263 (11 Mar 1994) 1392-1393.

Dreyer, J.L.E. *A History of Astronomy.* Mineola, NY: Dover, 1953.

Dreyfous, Tommy, and Theodore Eisenberg. "On the Aesthetics of Mathematical Thought." *For the Learning of Mathematics* 6 (Feb 1986) 2-10.

Dubbey, J.M. *The Mathematical Work of Charles Babbage.* New York: Cambridge University Press, 1978.

Dummett, Michael. *Elements of Intuitionism.* New York: Clarendon Press, 1977.

Dunham, William. "An 'Ancient/Modern' Proof of Heron's Formula." *Mathematics Teacher* (Apr 1985) 258-259.

———. "Euclid and the Infinitude of Primes." *Mathematics Teacher* (Jan 1987) 16-17.

———. *Journey through Genius: The Great Theorems of Mathematics.* Somerset, NJ: John Wiley, 1990.

———. "The Bernoullis and the Harmonic Series." *The College Mathematics Journal* (Jan 1987) 18-23.

———. ***The Mathematical Universe: An Alphabetical Journey Through the Great Proofs, Problems, and Personalities*. New York: John Wiley, 1994.**

Dunmore, Paul. "The Uses of Fallacy." *New Zealand Mathematics Magazine* (1970).

Dunningham, G.W. *Carl Friedrich Gauss: Titan of Science.* New York: Hafner Publications, 1955.

Easton, Job B. "The Rule of Double False Position." *Mathematics Teacher* (Jan 1967) 56-58.

Edeen, J., and S., V. Slachman. *Portraits for Classroom Bulletin Boards: Women Mathematicians.* Palo Alto, CA: Dale Seymour Publications, 1990.

Edgar, G.A. "Pi: Difficult or Easy?" *Mathematics Magazine* (June 1987) 141-150.

Edwards, Charles H. *The Historical Development of the Calculus.* New York: Springer-Verlag, 1979.

Edwards, Harold. *Fermat's Last Theorem.* New York: Springer-Verlag, 1977.

Edwards, I. E. S. *The Pyramids of Egypt.* New York: Penguin Books, 1961.

Edwards, H.M. *Galois Theory.* New York: Springer Publications, 1984.

Edwards, Lois, and Kevin Lee. *TesselMania! Math Connection.* Berkeley, CA: Key Curriculum Press, 1995.

Ehrman, Ester. *Mme. du Chalelet: Scientist, Philosopher, and Feminist of the Enlightenment.* Leamington Spa, United Kingdom: Berg, 1986.

Einhorn, Erwin. "A Method for Approximating the Value of Pi with a Computer Application." *Mathematics Teacher* (May 1973) 427-430.

Ekeland, Ivar. *Mathematics and the Unexpected.* Chicago: University of Chicago Press, 1988.

Ellis, Keith. *Number Power in Nature and in Everyday Life.* New York: St. Martin's Press, 1978.

Ercolano, Joseph L. "Remarks on the Neglected Mean." *Mathematics Teacher* (Mar 1973) 253-255.

Ernst, Bruno. *The Magic Mirror of M.C. Escher.* New York: Ballantine Books, 1976.

Escher, M.C. *Escher on Escher: Exploring the Infinite.* New York: Harry N.Abrams, 1986.

———. *The Graphic Work of M. C. Escher.* New York: Ballantine Books, 1960.

Espenshade, Pamela H. "A Text on Trigonometry by Levi Ben Gerson (1288-1344)." *Mathematics Teacher* (Oct 1967) 628-637.

Evans, George W. "Some of Euclid's Algebra." *Mathematics Teacher* (Apr 1968) 405-414.

Eves, Howard. "A Geometric Capsule Concerning the Five Platonic Solids." *Mathematics Teacher* (Jan 1969) 42-44.

———. ***An Introduction to the History of Mathematics.* New York: Holt, Rinehart and Winston, 1990.**

———. *Great Moments in Mathematics After 1650.* Washington, DC: MAA, 1982.

———. *In Mathematical Circles.* Boston: Prindle, Weber and Schmidt, 1969.

———. *Mathematical Circles Revisited.* Boston: Prindle, Weber and Schmidt, 1971.

———. *Mathematical Circles Squared.* Boston: Prindle, Weber and Schmidt, 1972.

———. *Mathematical Circles Adieu.* Boston: Prindle, Weber and Schmidt, 1977.

———. *Return to Mathematical Circles.* Boston: Prindle, Weber and Schmidt, 1982.

———. "The Bernoulli Family." *Mathematics Teacher* (Mar 1966) 276-278.

———. "The Latest About Pi." *Mathematics Teacher* (Feb 1962) 129-130.

Fabricant, Mona, and Sylvia Svitak. "Why Women Succeed in Mathematics." *Mathematics Teacher* (Feb 1990) 150-154.

Fadiman, Clifton. *Fantasia Mathematica.* New York: Simon and Schuster, 1958.

Fakhry, Ahmed. *The Pyramids.* Chicago: University of Chicago Press, 1974.

Fang, J. *Bourbaki.* New York: Paideia Press, 1970.

———. "Kant and Modern Mathematics." *Philosophica Mathematica* 2 (1955) 47-68.

Fant, Alfred B. "Half Man, Half Myth." *Mathematics Teacher* (Mar 1969) 225-228.

Faul, Henry. *Ages of Rocks, Planets, and Stars.* New York: McGraw-Hill, 1966.

Fauvel, John. *History in the Mathematics Classroom: The IREM Papers.* Leicester, England: The Mathematical Association, 1990.

———, et al. *Möbius and His Band: Mathematics and Astronomy in Nineteenth-Century Germany.* New York: Oxford University Press, 1993.

———, and Jeremy Gray. *The History of Mathematics, A Reader.* Dobbs Ferry, NY: Sheridan House, 1987.

Feder, Jens. *Fractals.* New York: Plenum Press, 1988.

Fehr, Howard F. "Some Remarks on Japanese Mathematics Education." *Mathematics Teacher* (Jan 1970) 73-77.

———. "The Education of Mathematics Teachers in Other Countries." *Mathematics Teacher* (Jan 1969) 48-56.

———. "The Present Year-Long Course in Euclidean Geometry Must Go." *Mathematics Teacher* (Feb 1972) 102, 151-154.

Feigenbaum, Edward, and Pamela McCorduck. *The Fifth Generation.* Reading, MA: Addison-Wesley, 1983.

Feldman, Richard. "Benjamin Franklin and Mathematics." *Mathematics Teacher* (Feb 1959) 125-127.

———. "History of Elementary Matrix Theory." *Mathematics Teacher* 55 (1962) 482-484, 589-590, 657-659.

———. "The Cardano-Tartaglia Dispute." *Mathematics Teacher* (Mar 1961) 160-163.

Fennema, Elizabeth, and G.C. Leder (eds). *Mathematics and Gender.* New York: Teachers College Press, 1990.

Ferrina-Mundy, Joan, and Darien Lauten. "Learning About Calculus Learning." *Mathematics Teacher* (Feb 1994) 115-121.

Ferris, Timothy. *The Universe and Eye.* San Francisco: Chronicle Books, 1993.

Fine, Terrance L. *Theories of Probability: An Examination of Foundations.* New York: Academic Press, 1973.

Firl, Donald H. "The Move to Metric: Some Considerations." *Mathematics Teacher* (Nov 1974) 581-584.

Fischer, Irene. "The Shape and Size of the Earth." *Mathematics Teacher* (May 1967) 508–516.

Herz-Fischler, Roger. "How to Find the 'Golden Number' Without Really Trying." *Fibonacci Quarterly* 19 (1971) 406–410.

———. *A Mathematical History of Division in Extreme and Mean Ratio.* Waterloo, Canada: Wilfrid Laurier University Press, 1987.

Fitzgerald, Edward. *The Rubaiyat of Omar Khayyam.* Mt. Vernon, New York: Peter Pauper Press, 1946.

Fitzpatrick, Sister Mary Mercy and Sister Antonietta Fitzpatrick. "Robert Joseph Boscovich: Forerunner of Modern Atomic Theory." *Mathematics Teacher* (Feb 1968) 167–176.

Flegg, Graham, et al. *Nicolas Chuquet: Renaissance Mathematician.* Boston: D. Redel Publishing, 1985.

———. *Numbers: Their History and Meaning.* New York: Schocken Books, 1983.

———. *Numbers Through the Ages.* Dobbs Ferry, NY: Sheridan House, 1989.

Flusser, Peter. "An Ancient Problem." *Mathematics Teacher* (May 1981) 389–390.

———. "Bertrand's Box Paradox." *Mathematics Teacher* (Dec 1984) 700–704.

———. "Euler's Amazing Way to Solve Equations." *Mathematics Teacher* (Mar 1992) 224–227.

Fokio, Catherine. "Bring Non-Euclidean Geometry Down to Earth." *Mathematics Teacher* (Sept 1985) 430–431.

Fowler, D.H. "A Generalization of the Golden Section." *Fibonacci Quarterly* 20 (1982) 146–158.

———. *The Mathematics of Plato's Academy.* Cary, NC: Oxford University Press, 1990.

Fraenkel, A.A. "The Recent Controversies About the Foundations of Mathematics." *Scripta Mathematica* 13 (1947) 17–36.

Francis, George K. *A Topological Picturebook.* New York: Springer-Verlag, 1987.

Francis, Richard L. "A Note on Perfect Numbers." *Mathematics Teacher* (Nov 1975) 606–607.

———. "Did Gauss Discover That, Too?" *Mathematics Teacher* (Apr 1986) 288–293.

———. "From None to Infinity." *College Mathematics Journal* (May 1986) 226–230.

———. "Mathematical Haystacks: Another Look at Repunit Numbers." *College Mathematics Journal* (May 1988) 240–246.

———. *Mathematical Look at the Calendar.* Arlington, MA: COMAP, 1988.

———. "Star Numbers and Constellations." *Mathematics Teacher* (Jan 1993) 88–89.

Frantz, Marny, and Sylvia Lazarnick. "The Mandelbrot Set in the Classroom." *Mathematics Teacher* (Mar 1991) 173–177

Freebury, H.A. *A History of Mathematics.* New York: Macmillan, 1961.

Freitag, Herta, and Arthur H. Freitag. "The Magic of a Square." *Mathematics Teacher* (Jan 1970) 5–14.

———. *The Number Story.* Reston, VA: NCTM, 1960.

French, Bevan M. *The Moon Book.* New York: Penguin Books, 1977.

Friberg, J. "Numbers and Measures in the Earliest Written Records." *Scientific American* (Feb 1984) 78–85.

Friend, J. Newton. *Numbers: Fun and Facts.* New York: Charles Scribner's, 1954.

Frisinger, H. Howard. "Mathematics and Our Founding Fathers." *Mathematics Teacher* (Apr 1976) 301–307.

Fults, J.L. *Magic Squares.* La Salle, IL: Open Court Publishing, 1974.

Gade, J.A. *The Life and Times of Tycho Brahe.* Princeton, NJ: Princeton University Press, 1947.

Gallencamp, C. *Maya: The Riddle and Rediscovery of a Lost Civilization.* New York: David McKay, 1959.

Gamow, George. *1,2,3, … Infinity.* New York: The Viking Press, 1947.

Gans, David. *An Introduction to Non-Euclidean Geometry.* New York: Academic Press, 1973.

Garcia, Linda. *The Fractal Explorer.* Santa Cruz, CA: Dynamic Press, 1991.

Garder, Arthur O. "The History of Mathematics as a Part of the History of Mankind." *Mathematics Teacher* (May 1968) 524–527.

Gardner, Martin. *Aha! Insight.* San Francisco: W.H. Freeman, 1978.

———. *Fractal Music, Hypercards, and More.* New York: W.H. Freeman, 1992.

———. *More Annotated Alice.* New York: Random House, 1990.

———. *The New Ambidextrous Universe.* New York: W.H. Freeman, 1990.

———. "The Remarkable Lore of the Prime Numbers." *Scientific American* (Mar 1964) 120–128.

———. *The Scientific Book of Mathematical Puzzles and Diversions.* New York: Simon and Schuster, 1959.

———. *Time, Travel, and Other Mathematical Bewilderments.* New York: W.H. Freeman, 1988.

———. *Wheels, Life, and Other Mathematical Amusements.* New York: W.H. Freeman, 1983.

Garland, Trudi H. *Fascinating Fibonaccis: Mystery and Magic in Numbers.* Palo Alto, CA: Dale Seymour, 1987.

———, and Charity Kahn. *Math and Music: Harmonic Connections.* Palo Alto, CA: Dale Seymour, 1994.

Garman, Brian. "Applying a Linear Function to Schedule Tennis." *Mathematics Teacher* (Oct 1984) 544–547.

Gaughan, Edward D. "An 'Almost' Diophantine Equation." *Mathematics Teacher* (May 1980) 374–376.

Gay, J., and M. Cole. *The New Mathematics in an Old Culture. A Study of Learning among the Kpelle of Liberia.* New York: Holt, Rinehard and Winston, 1976.

Gemignani, M.C. "On the Geometry of Euclid." *Mathematics Teacher* (Feb 1967) 160–164.

Ghyka, Matila. *The Geometry of Art and Life.* Mineola, NY: Dover, 1977.

Gies, Joseph, and Francis Gies. *Leonardo of Pisa and the New Mathematics of the Middle Ages.* New York: Thomas Y. Crowell, 1969.

Gillespie, Charles C. "The Scientific Importance of Napolean's Egyptian Campaign." *Scientific American* (Sept 1994).

Gillings, Richard J. *Mathematics in the Time of the Pharaohs.* Mineola, NY: Dover, 1982.

Gillings, Richard J. "The Remarkable Mental Arithmetic of the Egyptian Scribes, II." *Mathematics Teacher* (May 1966) 476–484.

Gindikin, Seymon. *Tales of Physicists and Mathematicians.* Cambridge, MA: Birkhauser Boston, 1988.

Gittleman, Arthur. *History of Mathematics.* Columbus, Ohio: Charles E. Merrill Publishing, 1975.

Glavas, C.B. "High School Mathematics Reform in Greece." *Mathematics Teacher* (Nov 1966) 671–674.

Gleick, James. *Chaos: Making a New Science.* New York: Viking Penguin, 1987.

Glenn, James (ed). *The Tree of Mathematics.* Pacoima, CA: The Digest Press, 1957.

Glenn, William, and Donovan Johnson. *Invitation to Mathematics.* Garden City, NY: Doubleday, 1961.

Goldberg, Dorothy. "In Celebration: Newton's *Principia,* 1687–1987." *Mathematics Teacher* (Dec 1987) 711–714.

Goldstine, Herman. *The Computer from Pascal to Von Neumann.* Princeton, NJ: Princeton University Press, 1972.

———. *A History of Numerical Analysis.* New York: Springer-Verlag, 1977.

Golos, Ellery B. *Foundations of Euclidean and Non-Euclidean Geometry.* New York: Holt, Rinehart and Winston, 1968.

Goodwin, Grenville. *The Social Organization of the Western Apache.* Tucson: University of Arizona Press, 1969.

Gorman, P. *Pythagoras: A Life.* Boston: Rutledge and Keegan, 1979.

Gornick, Vivian. *Women in Science: Portraits From a World in Transition.* New York: Simon and Schuster, 1983.

Grabiner, Judith V. "The Centrality of Mathematics in the History of Western Thought." *Mathematics Magazine* (Oct 1988) 220–230.

———. "Is Mathematical Truth Time-Dependent?" *American Mathematical Monthly* 81 (1974) 354–365.

———. *The Origins of Cauchy's Rigorous Calculus.* Cambridge, MA: MIT Press, 1981.

Grace, Sister Mary. "Poland's Contributions to Mathematics." *Mathematics Teacher* (Apr 1967) 383–386.

Graham, L.A. *Ingenious Mathematical Problems and Methods.* Mineola, NY: Dover, 1959.

Graham, Malcolm. "President Garfield and the Pythagorean Theorem." *Mathematics Teacher* (Dec 1976) 686–687.

Graham, Neill. *The Mind Tool: Computers and Their Impact on Society.* St, Paul, MN: West Publishing, 1980.

Grattan-Guinness, I. *The Development of the Foundations of Mathematical Analysis from Euler To Riemann.* Cambridge, MA: MIT Press, 1970.

———. "William Henry and Grace Chisholm Young: A Mathematical Union." *Annals of Science* 29 (1972) 105–186.

Gray, Jeremy. *Ideas of Space.* New York: Oxford University Press, 1989.

Green, Thomas M., and Charles Hamberg. *Pascal's Triangle.* Palo Alto, CA: Dale Seymour Publications, 1986.

Greenblatt, M.H. "Pi-Three vs. Pi-Four." *Mathematics Teacher* (Mar 1969) 223–225.

———. "The 'Legal' Value of π and Some Related Mathematical Anomalies." *American Scientist* (Dec 1965) 427A–432A.

Greenburg, Marvin Jay. *Euclidean and Non-Euclidean Geometries: Development and History.* San Francisco: W.H. Freeman, 1980.

Greenes, Carole. *Sonya Kovalevsky.* Dedham, MA: Janson Publications, 1989.

Greenhouse, Linda. "Court Accepts a Crucial Redistricting Case." *New York Times* (10 Dec 1994) 8.

Greitzer, Samuel L. "Credit Where Credit is Due." *Mathematics Teacher* (Feb 1967) 155–157.

Grinstein, Louise S. "A Note on the Greatest Integer Function." *Mathematics Teacher* (Jan 1970) 71–72.

———, and Paul Campbell. *Women of Mathematics: A Biblio-graphic Sourcebook.* Westport, CT: Greenwood Press, 1987.

Gross, Fred E., et al. *The Power of Numbers: A Teacher's Guide to Mathematics in a Social Studies Context.* Cambridge, MA: Educators for Social Responsibility, 1993.

Groza, Vivian Shaw. *A Survey of Mathematics: Elementary Concepts and Their Historical Development.* New York: Holt, Rinehart and Winston, 1968.

Grunbaum, Branko, and G.C. Shephard. *Tilings and Patterns.* New York: W.H. Freeman, 1987.

Grunfeld, Frederic (ed)., *Games of the World.* New York: Ballantine Books, 1977.

Gudden, Stanley. *A Mathematical Journey.* New York: McGraw-Hill, 1976.

Guillen, Michael. Bridges to Infinity: *The Human Side of Mathematics.* New York: St. Martin's Press, 1983.

Guy, Richard K. "The Strong Law of Small Numbers." *American Mathematical Monthly* (Oct 1988) 697–712.

Haak, Sheila. "Using the Monocord: A Classroom Demonstration of the Mathematics of Musical Scales." *Mathematics Teacher* (Mar 1982) 238–244.

Hacker, Sidney G. "Identification of Napier's Inequalities." *Mathematics Teacher* (Jan 1970) 67–71.

Hald, Anders. *A History of Probability and Statistics and Their Applications Before 1750.* Somerset, NJ: John Wiley, 1990.

Haldane, Elizabeth. *Descartes: His Life and Times.* New York: American Scholar Publications, 1966.

Hall, A.R. *Philosophers at War: The Quarrel Between Newton and Leibniz.* New York: Cambridge University Press, 1980.

Hall, Rupert. *From Galileo to Newton.* Mineola, NY: Dover, 1981.

Hall, Tord. *Carl Friedrich Gauss.* Cambridge, MA: MIT Press, 1970.

Halmos, Paul. *I Want to be a Mathematician.* New York: Springer-Verlag, 1985.

———. "Mathematics as a Creative Art." *American Scientist* 56 (1968) 375–389.

Hamilton, M. "Egyptian Geometry in the Elementary Classroom." *Arithmetic Teacher* 23 (1976) 436–438.

Hamming, R.W. "The Unreasonable Effectiveness of Mathematics." *American Mathematical Monthly* 87 (1980) 81–90.

Hanawalt, Kenneth. "The End of a Perfect Number." *Mathematics Teacher* (Nov 1965) 621–622.

Hankins, T.L. *Jean d'Alembert: Science and the Enlightenment.* New York: Clarendon Press, 1970.

———. *Sir William Rowan Hamilton.* Baltimore: John Hopkins University Press, 1980.

Hansen, David W. "The Dependence of Mathematics on Reality." *Mathematics Teacher* (Dec 1971) 715–719.

Hardy, G. H. *A Mathematician's Apology.* New York: Cambridge University Press, 1992.

———. *Ramanujan.* New York: Chelsea Publications, 1959.

Hart, Ivor. *Makers of Science: Mathematics, Physics, and Astronomy.* Freeport, NY: Books for Libraries Press, 1968.

Harvey, Margaret, and Bonnie Litwiller. "Polygonal Numbers: A Study of Patterns." *Arithmetic Teacher* (Jan 1970) 33–38.

Hatcher, Robert S. "Some Little-Known Recipes for Pi." *Mathematics Teacher* (May 1973) 470–474.

Hawking, Stephen. *A Brief History of Time.* New York: Bantam Books, 1988.

Hawkins, Gerald S. *Mindsteps to the Cosmos.* New York: Harper and Row, 1983.

———. *Stonehenge Decoded.* New York: Doubleday, 1965.

———. *History of Greek Mathematics,* Vol I and II. Mineola, NY: Dover, 1981.

———. *Mathematics in Aristotle.* New York: Oxford University Press, 1949.

Heath, T.L. *13 Books of Euclid's Elements.* Mineola, NY: Dover, 1956.

Heims, Steve. *John Von Neumann and Norbert Wiener.* Cambridge, MA: MIT Press, 1980.

Hellman, Morton J., and Madeleine J. Long. "Mathematics and the American Flag." *Mathematics Teacher* (May 1993) 418–419.

Hemmings, Ray, and Dick Tanta. *Images of Infinity.* United Kingdom: Leapfrogs, 1984.

Henbest, Nigel. *Mysteries of the Universe.* New York: Van Nostrand Reinhold, 1981.

Henderson, George L., and Mary Van Beck. "Mathematics Educators Must Help Face the Environmental Pollution Problem." *Mathematics Teacher* (Jan 1971) 33–36.

Henkin, Leon A. "Are Logic and Mathematics Identical?" *The Chauvenet Papers,* Vol. II. Washington, DC: The MAA, 1978.

Herivel, J. *Joseph Fourier, the Man and the Physicist.* New York: Clarendon Press, 1975.

Herold, J. Cristopher. *Bonaparte in Egypt.* New York: Harper and Row, 1962.

Heydenreich, L.H. et al. *Leonardo the Inventor.* New York: McGraw-Hill, 1980.

Hiber, Ann. *A Convergence of Lives: Sofia Kovalevskaia: Scientist, Writer, Revolutionary.* New Brunswick, NJ: Rutgers University Press, 1993.

Hilton, Peter. "Cryptanalysis in World War II and Mathematics Education." *Mathematics Teacher* (Oct 1984) 548–558, 562.

Hirsch, Christian R. "Pick's Rule." *Mathematics Teacher* (May 1974) 431.

Historical Topics for the Mathematics Classroom. Reston, VA: NCTM, 1989.

History of Pi (posters and cartoons). Burlington, NC: Cabisco Mathematics, Carolina Biological Supply, 1988.

Hlavaty, Julius H. "The First International Congress on Mathematics Education." *Mathematics Teacher* (Apr 1970) 319–321.

Hobson, E.W. *"Squaring the Circle," a History of the Problem.* New York: Chelsea Publishing, 1953.

Hodgers, Andrew. *Alan Turing: The Enigma.* New York: Simon and Schuster, 1983.

Hoffer, Alan R. "What You Always Wanted to Know About Six but Have Been Afraid to Ask." *Arithmetic Teacher* (Mar 1973) 173–180.

Hoffman, Banesh. *Albert Einstein: Creator and Rebel.* New York: Viking Press, 1972.

Hoffman, Paul. *Archimedes Revenge: The Challenge of the Unknown.* New York: W.W. Norton, 1988.

———. "Fermat Still Has Last Laugh." *Discover* (Jan 1989) 48–50.

Hofmann, J.E. *The History of Mathematics.* New York: Philosophical Library, 1957.

———. *Classical Mathematics, a Concise History of the Classical Era in Mathematics.* New York: Philosophical Library, 1959.

Hofstadter, Douglas R. *Gödel, Escher, Bach: An Eternal Golden Braid.* New York: Vintage Books, 1980.

———. "Strange Attractors: Mathematical Patterns Delicately Poised Between Order and Chaos." *Scientific American* 245 (May 1992) 16–29.

Hogben, Lancelot. *Mathematics for the Millions*. New York: W.W. Norton, 1967.

———. *The Wonderful World of Mathematics*. New York: Doubleday, 1968.

Hoggatt, Vernon E. *Fibonacci and Lucas Numbers*. Boston: Houghton Mifflin, 1968.

Hohlfeld, Joe, and Lynn Schwandt. "Six Is a Fascinating Number." *Arithmetic Teacher* (Apr 1975) 269-270.

Hollingdale, Stuart. *Makers of Mathematics*. New York: Penguin Books, 1989.

Holmes, Thomas B. *Electronic and Experimental Music*. New York: Charles Scribner, 1985.

Holten, G. *Thematic Origins of Scientific Thought, Kepler to Einstein*. Cambridge, MA: Harvard University Press, 1973.

Honsberger, R. *Mathematical Gems II*. Washington, DC: MAA, 1973.

Hooper, Alfred. *Makers of Mathematics*. New York: Vintage Books, 1948.

Hope, Jack A., and Ivan W. Kelly. "Common Difficulties with Probabilistic Reasoning." *Mathematics Teacher* (Nov 1983) 565-569.

Hopkins, Nigel, et al. *Go Figure: The Numbers You Need for Everyday Life*. Detroit, MI: Visible Ink Press, 1992.

Hopley, Ronald B. "Nested Platonic Solids: A Class Project in Solid Geometry." *Mathematics Teacher* (May 1994) 312-318.

Howell, John. *Laurie Anderson*. New York: Thunder's Mouth Press, 1992.

Huff, Darrell. *How to Lie With Statistics*. New York: W.W. Norton, 1982.

Hughes, Barnabas. "Hawaiian Number Systems." *Mathematics Teacher* (Mar 1982) 253-256.

———. "Rhetoric, Anyone?" *Mathematics Teacher* (Mar 1970) 267-270.

Hughes, P., and G. Brecht. *Vicious Circles and Infinity*. London: Penguin Books, 1978.

Huntley, H.E. *The Divine Proportion: A Study in Mathematical Beauty*. Mineola, NY: Dover, 1970.

Hurd, Stephen. "Egyptian Fractions: Ahmes to Fibonacci to Today." *Mathematics Teacher* (Oct 1991) 561-568.

Hurley, James F. "An Application of Newton's Law of Cooling." *Mathematics Teacher* (Feb 1974) 141-142.

Hutchinson, J. "Fractals and Self-similarity." *Indiana University Journal of Mathematics* 30 (1981) 713-747.

Iacobacci, Rora F. "Women of Mathematics." *Mathematics Teacher* (Apr 1970) 329-337.

Id, Yusif. "An Analemma Construction for Right and Oblique Ascensions." *Mathematics Teacher* (Dec 1969) 669-678.

———, and E.S. Kennedy. "A Medieval Proof of Heron's Formula." *Mathematics Teacher* (Nov 1969) 585-587.

Ifrah, George. *From One to Zero: A Universal History of Numbers*. New York: Viking Penguin, 1985.

Infeld, Leopold. *Albert Einstein: His Work and Its Influence on Our Lives*. New York: Charles Scribner's, 1950.

———. *Quest: An Autobiography*. New York: Chelsea Publishing, 1980.

———. *Whom the Gods Love: The Story of Evariste Galois*. Reston, VA: NCTM, 1978

Ingalls, Edmund E. "George Washington and Mathematics Education." *Mathematics Teacher* (Oct 1954) 409-410.

Jackson, G. *Black Women Makers of History: A Portrait*. Oakland, CA: GRT Printing, 1975.

Jacobs, Harold. *Mathematics: A Human Endeavor*. San Francisco: W.H. Freeman, 1987.

Jaffe, A.J., and Herbert F. Spirer. *Misused Statistics: Straight Talk for Twisted Numbers*. New York: Marcel Dekker, 1987.

Jaki, Stanley L. *Cosmos and Creator*. Edinburgh: Scottish Academic Press, 1980.

Jeffrey, Neil I. "Mathematics in Photography." *Mathematics Teacher* (Dec 1980) 657-662.

Jeffries, Ona Griffin. *In and Out of The White House*. New York: Wilfred Funk, 1960.

Jensen, Roderick V. "Classical Chaos." *American Scientist* (Mar–Apr 1987) 168-181.

Johnson, Art. *Classical Math: History Topics for the Classroom*. Palo Alto, CA: Dale Seymour, 1994.

Johnson, Phillip E. "The Early Beginnings of Set Theory." *Mathematics Teacher* (Dec 1970) 690-692.

Jones, Arthur et al. *Abstract Algebra and Famous Impossibilities*. New York: Springer-Verlag, 1991.

Jones, John D.S. "Mysteries of Four Dimensions." *Nature* (Apr 1988) 488-489.

Jones, Lesley. *Teaching Mathematics and Art*. Gloucester, England: Stanley Thornes, 1991.

Jones, Phillip S. "Discovery Teaching: From Socrates to Modernity." *Mathematics Teacher* (Oct 1970) 501-508.

———. "1876 Plus or Minus 10." *Mathematics Teacher* (Nov 1976) 586-593.

Jones, Richard Foster. *Ancient and Moderns*. Mineola, NY: Dover, 1981.

Joseph, George G. *The Crest of the Peacock: Non-European Roots of Mathematics*. New York: Penguin Books, 1991.

Jung, C.G. *Man and His Symbols*. Garden City, NY: Doubleday, 1964.

Juster, Norton. *The Dot and the Line*. New York: Random House, 1961.

Kalmus, H. "Animals as Mathematicians." *Nature* 202 (1964) 1156-1160.

Kane, Joseph Nathan. *Facts About the Presidents*. New York: W.H. Wilson, 1974.

Kanigel, Robert. *The Man Who Knew Infinity: A Life of the Genius Ramanujan*. New York: Macmillan, 1991.

Kaplan, James, and Aaron Strauss. "Dynamical Systems: Birkhoff and Smale." *Mathematics Teacher* (Oct 1976) 495-501.

Kappraff, Jay. *Connections: The Geometric Bridge Between Art and Science.* New York: McGraw-Hill, 1991.

Kasner, Edward, and James R. Newman. *Mathematics and the Imagination.* Redmond, WA: Tempus Books, 1989.

Kass-Simon, G., and P. Farnes. *Women of Science: Righting the Record.* Bloomington, IN: Indiana University Press, 1990.

Katz, Victor. *A History of Mathematics: An Introduction*. New York: HarperCollins, 1993.

Kaufmann, William J. *Planets and Moons.* New York: W.H. Freeman, 1979.

Kavett, Hyman, and Phyllis F. Kavett. "The Eye of Horus is Upon You." *Mathematics Teacher* (May 1975) 390-394.

Keese, Earl F. "'The Pit and the Pendulum': Source for a Creative Activity." *Mathematics Teacher* (Nov 1975) 602-604.

Kelly, Richard. *Lewis Carroll.* Boston: G.K. Hall, 1977.

Kemeny, J.G. "Mathematics Without Numbers." *Daedalus* 88 (1959) 577-591.

Kennedy, Donald. *Little Sparrow: A Portrait of Sophie Kovalesky.* Athens, OH: Ohio University Press, 1983.

Kennedy, Hubert C. "Giuseppe Peano at the University of Turin." *Mathematics Teacher* (Nov 1968) 703-706.

Kenner, H. *Geodesic Math and How to Use It.* Berkeley, CA: University of California Press, 1976.

Kenschaft, Patricia. "Charlotte Angas Scott, 1858-1931." *The College Mathematics Journal* 18 (1987) 98-110.

———. *Winning Women into Mathematics.* Washington, DC: MAA, 1991.

———, and Kaila Katz. "Sylvester and Scott." *Mathematics Teacher* (Sept 1982) 490-494.

Kern, Jane F., and Cherry C. Mauk. "Exploring Fractals: A Problem-Solving Adventure Using Mathematics and Logo." *Mathematics Teacher* (Mar 1990) 179-185, 244.

Kershner, R.B., and L.R. Wilcox. *The Anatomy of Mathematics.* New York: Ronald Press, 1950.

Kimberling, Clark. "Complex Roots: The Bairstow-Hitchcock Method." *Mathematics Teacher* (Apr 1986) 278-282.

———. "Emmy Noether, Greatest Woman Mathematician." *Mathematics Teacher* (Mar 1982) 246-249.

Kitcher, P. *The Nature of Mathematical Knowledge.* New York: Oxford University Press, 1984.

Kleiner, Israel. "Thinking the Unthinkable: The Story of Complex Numbers (with a Moral)." *Mathematics Teacher* (Oct 1988) 583-592.

———, and Shmuel Avital. "The Relativity of Mathematics." *Mathematics Teacher* (Oct 1984) 554-558.

Kline, Morris. *Mathematical Thought from Ancient to Modern Times.* New York: Oxford University Press, 1990.

———. *Mathematics and the Physical World.* New York: Thomas Y. Crowell, 1959.

———. *Mathematics: A Cultural Approach.* Reading, MA: Addison-Wesley, 1962.

———. *Mathematics: An Introduction to Its Spirit and Use.* San Francisco: W.H. Freeman, 1979.

———. *Mathematics for the Nonmathematician*. Mineola, NY: Dover, 1967.

———. *Mathematics in Western Culture.* New York: Oxford University Press, 1964.

———. *Mathematics: The Loss of Certainty*. New York: Oxford University Press, 1980.

———. *Why Johnny Can't Add: The Failure of the New Math.* New York: St. Martin's Press, 1973.

Knorr, W.R. *The Evolution of the Euclidean Elements.* Boston: D. Reidel Publishing, 1975.

Koblitz, Ann Hibner. *A Convergence of Lives: Sofia Kovalevskaia: Scientist, Writer, Revolutionary.* Cambridge, MA: Birkhauser Boston, 1983.

Koehler, O. "The Ability of Birds to Count." *Bulletin of Animal Behavior* 9 (Mar 1951)

Koestler, Arthur. *The Watershed: A Life of Kepler.* New York: Doubleday, 1960.

Kogelman, Stanley, and Joseph Warren. *Mind over Math.* New York: McGraw-Hill, 1978.

Kohn, Judith B. "A Physical Model for Operations with Integers." *Mathematics Teacher* (Dec 1978) 734-736.

Kolata, Gina. "Progress on Fermat's Famous Math Problem." *Science* (Mar 1987) 1572-1573.

Kolpas, Sidney J. "Augustus De Morgan." *California Mathematics Council ComMuniCator* (June 1990) 24.

———. *The Pythagorean Theorem: Eight Classic Proofs.* Palo Alto, CA: Dale Seymour, 1992.

Korner, S. *The Philosophy of Mathematics: An Introduction.* New York: Harper and Row, 1962.

Kosko, Bart. *Fuzzy Thinking: The New Science of Fuzzy Logic.* New York: Hyperion, 1993.

Kost, Franklin. "Two Solutions to a Problem of Huygens." *Mathematics Teacher* (Feb 1985) 144-145.

Kostovskii, A.N. *Geometrical Constructions Using Compasses Only,* trans Halina Moss. New York: Blaisdell Publishing, 1961.

Kramer, Edna. *The Mainstream of Mathematics.* Princeton Junction, NJ: Scholars Bookshelf, 1988.

———. *The Nature and Growth of Modern Mathematics.* Princeton, NJ: Princeton University Press, 1981.

Kuhn, Stephen W. "The Number Phoenix: A Summer Awakening." *Mathematics Teacher* (Apr 1988) 315-321.

Kuhn, Thomas S. *The Copernican Revolution.* New York: Modern Library, 1957.

Kulczycki, Stefan. *Non-Euclidean Geometry.* New York: Pergamon Press, 1961.

Lamb, John F. "Trisecting an Angle—Almost." *Mathematics Teacher* (Mar 1988) 220-222.

———. "Two Egyptian Construction Tools." *Mathematics Teacher* (Feb 1993) 166-167.

Lamb, Sydney. *Mathematical Games, Puzzles, and Fallacies.* New York: Raco Publishing, 1977.

Lassere, F. *The Birth of Mathematics in the Age of Plato.* London: Hutchinson, 1964.

Lauber, Murray. "Casting Out Nines: An Explanation and Extensions." *Mathematics Teacher* (Nov 1990) 661-665.

Lawlis, Frank. "The Basis of Music: Mathematics." *Mathematics Teacher* (Oct 1967) 593-596.

Lénárt, István. *Non-Euclidean Adventures on the Lénárt Sphere.* Berkeley, CA: Key Curriculum Press, 1996.

Lenz, Gerald E. "Kurt Gödel, Mathematician and Logician." *Mathematics Teacher* (Nov 1980) 612-614.

Lewis, Thomas. "Debating the Unknowable." *The Atlantic Monthly* (July 1981).

Li, Yan, and Du Shiran. *Chinese Mathematics: A Concise History*. New York: Oxford University Press, 1987.

Libbrecht, Ulrich. *Chinese Mathematics in The Thirteenth Century: The Shy-shu Chiu-Chang of Ch'in Chiu-shoa.* Cambridge, MA: MIT Press, 1973.

Lick, Dale W. "The Remarkable Bernoulli Family." *Mathematics Teacher* (May 1969) 401-409.

Lightner, James. "A Brief Look at the History of Probability and Statistics." *Mathematics Teacher* (Nov 1991) 623-630.

———. "A Chain of Influence in the Development of Geometry." *Mathematics Teacher* (Jan 1991) 15-19.

Lineberry, W.P. (ed). *The Business of Sports (The Reference Shelf Series).* New York: H.W. Wilson, 1973.

Linn, Charles, (ed). *The Ages of Mathematics.* New York: Doubleday, 1977.

———. *The Golden Mean.* New York: Doubleday, 1974.

Lipsey, Sally I. "Adam Smith in the Mathematics Classroom." *Mathematics Teacher* (Mar 1975) 189-194.

Littlewood, J.E. *A Mathematician's Miscellany.* London: Methuen, 1953.

Lloyd, Daniel B. "Further Evidences of Primeval Mathematics." *Mathematics Teacher* (Nov 1966) 668-670.

Locher, J.L. *The World of M.C. Escher.* New York: Harry N. Abrams, 1971.

Lockwood, James R., and Garth E. Runion. *Deductive Systems: Finite and Non-Euclidean Geometries.* Reston, VA: NCTM, 1978.

Lodge, Sir Oliver. *Pioneers of Science.* Mineola, NY: Dover, 1960.

Logdson, Tom. *Computers and Social Controversy.* Rockville, MD: Computer Science Press, 1980.

Longfellow, Henry Wadsworth. *Kavanaugh: A Tale.* New Haven, CT: College and University Press, 1965.

Loomis, Elisha S. *The Pythagorean Proposition.* Washington, DC: NCTM, 1968.

Lotspeich, Richard. "Archimedes' Pi: An Introduction to Iteration." *Mathematics Teacher* (Dec 1988) 208-210.

Love, William P. "Infinity: The Twilight Zone of Mathematics." *Mathematics Teacher* (Apr 1989) 284-292.

Loyd, Samuel. *The Eighth Book of Tan.* Mineola, NY: Dover, 1968.

Lucas, J. "Minds, Machines and Gödel." *Philosophy* 36 (1961) 112.

Lumpkin, Beatrice. "A Mathematics Club Project from Omar Khayyam." *Mathematics Teacher* (Dec 1978) 740-744.

MacHale, Desmond. *George Boole: His Life and Work.* Dublin, Ireland: Dun Laoghaire, 1985.

Mahoney, Michael. *The Mathematical Career of Pierre de Fermat (1601-1655).* Princeton, NJ: Princeton Univesity Press, 1973.

Malcolm, Paul S. "Mathematics of Musical Scales." *Mathematics Teacher* (Nov 1972) 611-615.

Maletsky, Evan. "Ancient Babylonian Mathematics." *Mathematics Teacher* (Apr 1976) 295-298.

Mandelbrot, Benoit B. *The Fractal Geometry of Nature.* New York: W.H. Freeman, 1983.

Manheim, Jerome H. "The Genesis of Point Set Topology: From Newton to Hausdorff." *Mathematics Teacher* (Jan 1966) 36-41.

Manning, H.P. *Non-Euclidean Geometry.* Mineola, NY: Dover, 1963.

Manning, Kenneth R. "A History of Extraneous Solutions." *Mathematics Teacher* (Feb 1970) 165-175.

Manuel, Frank. *A Portrait of Isaac Newton.* Cambridge, MA: Harvard University Press, 1968.

Maor, Eli. "The History of Pi on the Pocket Calculator." *Journal of College Science Teaching* (Nov 1976) 97-99.

———. ***To Infinity and Beyond: A Cultural History of the Infinite.* Boston: Birkhauser Boston, 1987.**

———. "What is There So Mathematical About Music?" *Mathematics Teacher* (Sept 1979) 415-422.

Markowsky, George. "Misconceptions About the Golden Ratio." *The College Mathematics Journal* (Jan 1992) 2-19.

Marks, Robert. *The Growth of Mathematics: From Counting to Calculus.* New York: Bantam Books, 1964.

Martin, George E. *The Foundations of Geometry and the Non-Euclidean Plane.* New York: Springer-Verlag, 1982.

Martin, J. Susan. "Activities: The Fibonacci Sequence." *Mathematics Teacher* (Jan 1981) 39-42.

Maslova, G.G., and A.I. Markushevitz. "Mathematics in the Schools of the U.S.S.R." *Mathematics Teacher* (Mar 1969) 231-239.

Maxfield, Margaret. "Mixture Problems by Some 'Old Math.'" *Mathematics Teacher* (May 1974) 426-427.

May, Kenneth O. "Mathematics and Art." *Mathematics Teacher* (Oct 1967) 568-572.

Maynard, Jacquelyn. "Napoleon's Waterloo Wasn't Mathematics." *Mathematics Teacher* (Nov 1989) 648-653.

Maziarz, Edward, and Thomas Greenwood. *Greek Mathematical Philosophy.* New York: Ungar, 1968.

McGervey, John D. *Probabilities in Everyday Life.* New York: Ballantine Books, 1986.

McGinty, Robert, William Mutch, and John Van Beynen. "A Brief Historical Dictionary of Mathematical Terms." *Mathematics Teacher* (Nov 1985) 638-640.

McGrayne, S.B. *Nobel Prize Women in Science: Their Lives, Struggles and Momentous Discoveries.* New York: Birch Lane Press, 1993.

McLeish, John. *The Story of Numbers: How Mathematics Has Shaped Civilization.* New York: Fawcett Columbine, 1991.

McMillan, Robert. "Babylonian Quadratics." *Mathematics Teacher* (Jan 1984) 63-65.

McMullin, Ernan (ed). *Galileo: Man of Science.* New York: Basic Books, 1967.

Medonick, Henrietta (ed). *The Treasury of Mathematics: A Collection of Source Material.* New York: Philosophical Library, 1965.

Mendelssohn, Kurt. *The Riddle of the Pyramids.* New York: Praeger Publications, 1974.

Menke, Frank G. *The Encyclopedia of Sports.* South Brunswick, NJ: Barnes, 1975.

Menninger, K.W. *Mathematics in Your World.* New York: Viking Press, 1962.

———. *Number Words and Number Symbols: A Cultural History of Numbers.* Cambridge, MA: MIT Press, 1977.

Menzel, Donald H. *A Field Guide to the Stars and Planets.* Boston: Houghton Mifflin, 1964.

Merlan, Philip. *From Platonism to Neoplatonism.* The Hague, Holland: Martinus Nijhoff, 1960.

Merz, John. *Leibniz.* New York: Hacker Press, 1948.

Meschkowski, Herbert. *The Evolution of Mathematical Thought.* New York: Holden-Day Publishing, 1965.

———. *Ways of Thought of Great Mathematicians.* San Francisco: Holden-Day Publishing Publishing, 1964.

Meserve, Bruce. "Euclidean and Other Geometries." *Mathematics Teacher* (Jan 1967) 2-11.

Mesmard, Jean. *Pascal: His Life and Works.* New York: Philosophical Library, 1952.

Metz, James. "The Law of Cosines as Seen by Pythagoras." *Mathematics Teacher* (Feb 1985) 109-111.

———, and Joseph Canella. "MATH'E MA TISH'ANS." *Mathematics Teacher* (Dec 1978) 765-766.

Midonick, H.O. (ed). *The Treasury of Mathematics.* New York: Philosophical Library, 1965.

Mielke, Paul. "Rational Points on the Number Line." *Mathematics Teacher* (Oct 1970) 475-479.

Mikami, Yoshio. *The Development of Mathematics in China and Japan.* New York: Chelsea Publishing, 1961.

Miller, Charles, and Vern E. Heeren. *Mathematical Ideas.* Oakland, NJ: Scott Foresman, 1982.

Miller, William A., and Robert G. Clason. "Golden Triangles, Pentagons, and Pentagrams." *Mathematics Teacher* (May 1994) 338-344, 350-353.

Mills, C.N. "Mathematical Miscellanea." *Mathematics Teacher* (May 1953) 341-345.

———. "Radii of the Apollonius Contact Circles." *Mathematics Teacher* (Oct 1966) 574-576.

Minsky, M. *Computation: Finite and Infinite Machines.* Englewood Cliffs, NJ: Prentice-Hall, 1967.

Mitchell, Charles. "Henry Wadsworth Longfellow, Poet Extraordinaire." *Mathematics Teacher* (May 1989) 378-379.

———. "Real-World Mathematics." *Mathematics Teacher* (Jan 1990) 12-16.

Mitchell, Merle. *Mathematical History: Activities, Puzzles, Stories, and Games.* Reston, VA: NCTM, 1978.

Moakes, A.J. "The Calculation of Pi." *Mathematics Gazette* 54 (1970) 261-264.

Moeschl, Richard. *Exploring the Sky.* Chicago: Independent Publishers Group, 1989.

Moffatt, Michael (ed). *The Ages of Mathematics (4 vols).* New York: Doubleday, 1977.

Moise, Edwin, and Floyd Downs. *Geometry.* Menlo Park, CA: Addison-Wesley, 1982.

Monk, J.D. "On the Foundations of Set Theory." *American Mathematical Monthly* 77 (1970) 703-711.

Moore, A.W. *The Infinite.* New York: Routledge Press, 1990.

Moore, David S. *Statistics: Concepts and Controversies.* New York: W.H. Freeman, 1991.

Moore, Doris Langley. *Ada, Countess of Lovelace: Byron's Legitimate Daughter.* London: John Murray, 1977.

Moore, Patrick. *Watchers of the Stars: The Scientific Revolution.* New York: Michael Joseph, 1974.

Moran, Jim. *The Wonderous World of Magic Squares.* New York: Vintage Books, 1982.

More, Louis Trechnard. *Isaac Newton: A Biography.* New York: Charles Scribner's, 1962.

Morgan, Frank. "Soap Films and Problems without Unique Solutions." *American Scientist* (May-June 1986) 232-235.

Morgan, Virginia Moss. *Through the Ages.* New York: Vantage Press, 1990.

Moritz, Robert Edouard. *On Mathematics and Mathematicians.* Mineola, NY: Dover, 1958.

Morris, Edie, and Leon Harkleroad. "Rózsa Péter: Recursive Function Theory's Founding Mother." *The Mathematical Intelligencer* 12 #1, 59-64.

Morris, Janet. "Math Anxiety: Teaching to Avoid It." *Mathematics Teacher* (Sept 1981) 413-416.

Motz, Lloyd, and Jefferson Hane Weaver. *The Story of Mathematics.* New York: Plenum Publishing, 1993.

Mozans, H.J. *Woman in Science.* Cambridge, MA: MIT Press, 1974.

Murdock, George P. *Africa: Its People and Their Cultural History.* New York: McGraw-Hill, 1959.

Muir, Jane. *Of Men and Numbers, the Story of the Great Mathematicians.* New York: Dodd Mead, 1961.

Munitz, Milton K. *Theories of the Universe from Babylonian Myth to Modern Science.* Glencoe, IL: The Free Press, 1957.

Naeye, Robert. "Chaos Squared." *Discover* (Mar 1994) 28.

Nagel E., and J.R. Newman. *Gödel's Proof.* New York: New York University Press, 1958.

Nasr, S.H. *Science and Civilization in Islam.* Cambridge, MA: Harvard University Press, 1968.

National Women's History Project. *Outstanding Women in Mathematics and Science.* Windsor, CA: National Women's History Project, 1991.

Needham, M. *Science and Civilization in China,* Vol III. New York: Cambridge University Press, 1959.

Neitz, John A. "Evolution of Old Secondary-School Arithmetic Textbooks." *Mathematics Teacher* (Apr 1967) 387-393.

Nelson, David et al. *Multicultural Mathematics.* New York: Oxford University Press, 1993.

Neugebauer, Otto. "Mathematical Methods in Ancient Astronomy." *Bulletin of the American Mathematical Society* 54 (1948) 1013-1041.

———. *The Exact Sciences in Antiquity.* Mineola, NY: Dover, 1969.

Neuwirth, Lee. "The Theory of Knots." *Scientific American* (June 1979) 110-124.

Newell, Virginia K., and Joella Gipson. *Black Mathematicians and Their Works.* Ardmore, PA: Dorrance, 1980.

Newman, James R. *The World of Mathematics.* New York: Simon and Schuster, 1956.

Niemann, Chris. "Professor L. Carroll Teaches Alice How to Add." *Mathematics Teacher* (Mar 1972) 285-286.

Niven, I. *Numbers: Rational and Irrational.* New York: Random House, 1961.

North, John D. "Sylvester, James Joseph." *Dictionary of Scientific Biographies* 13 (1976) 216-222.

Numbers Count ... to Everyone. (poster highlighting lives of Maria Goeppert Mayer, Cecilia Payne-Gaposchkin, Grace Murray Hopper, Maggie Lena Walker, and Mary Dolciani Halloran) Boston: Houghton Mifflin, 1987.

Ogilvie, Marilyn Bailey. *Women in Science.* Cambridge, MA: MIT Press, 1991.

Ogilvy, C. Stanley. *Tomorrow's Math: Unsolved Problems for the Amateur.* New York: Oxford University Press, 1972.

———, and John T. Anderson. *Excursions in Number Theory.* Mineola, NY: Dover, 1966.

O'Keefe, Vincent. "Mathematics: Musical Relationships: A Bibliography." *Mathematics Teacher* (Apr 1972) 315-324.

Oliver, Bernard. "Heron's Remarkable Triangle Area Formula." *Mathematics Teacher* (Feb 1993) 161-163.

Oliver, Roland, and J.D. Fage. *A Short History of Africa.* New York: New York University Press, 1962.

Olson, Melfried, and Gerald Goff. "A Divisibility Test for Any Prime." *School Science and Mathematics* (Nov 1986) 578-581.

Oppenheim, Leo. *Ancient Mesopotamia.* Chicago: University of Chicago Press, 1964.

Ore, Oystein. *Cardano: The Gambling Scholar.* Mineola, NY: Dover, 1965.

———. *Graphs and Their Uses.* New York: Random House, 1963.

———. *Niels Henrik Abel: Mathematician Extraordinary.* New York: Chelsea Publishing, 1974.

———. *Number Theory and Its History.* Mineola, NY: Dover, 1988.

Osborn, Mary. "Status and Prospects of Women in Science in Europe." *Science* 263 (11 Mar 1994) 1389-1391.

Osen, Lynn. *Women in Mathematics.* Cambridge, MA: The MIT Press, 1984.

O'Shea, Thomas. "The Diary of Two Problem Solvers." *Mathematics Teacher* (Dec 1991) 748-753.

Ostler, Elliott, and Neal Grandgenett. "Fibonacci Strikes Again!" *Quantum* (July/Aug 1992) 15-17, 30.

Ouwehand, Terre. *Voices from the Well: Extraordinary Women of History, Myth, Literature, and Art.* San Luis Obispo, CA: Padre Productions, 1986.

Owen, G. *Game Theory.* New York: Academic Press, 1982.

Packel, Edward. *The Mathematics of Games and Gambling.* Washington, DC: MAA, 1981.

Pagels, Heinz R. *Perfect Symmetry.* New York: Simon and Schuster, 1985.

Papert, Seymour. *Mindstorms.* New York: Basic Books, 1980.

Pappas, Theoni. *The Joy of Mathematics.* San Carlos, CA: Wide World/Tetra, 1989.

———. *More Joy of Mathematics.* San Carlos, CA: Wide World/ Tetra, 1991.

————. *The Magic of Mathematics*. San Carlos, CA: Wide World/Tetra, 1994.

————. *Mathematics Appreciation*. San Carlos, CA: Wide World/Tetra, 1987.

————. *Math Talk*. San Carlos, CA: Wide World/Tetra, 1991.

Parker, R.A. *Demotic Mathematical Papyri*. Providence, RI: Brown University Press, 1972.

Paulos, John Allen. *Beyond Numeracy: Ruminations of a Numbers Man*. New York: Alfred A. Knopf, 1991.

————. *Innumeracy: Mathematical Illiteracy and Its Consequences*. New York: Hill and Wang, 1988.

Pawlikowski, George J. "The Men Responsible for the Development of Vectors." *Mathematics Teacher* (Apr 1967) 393-396.

Pazwash, Hormoz, and Gus Mavrigian. "The Contributions of Karaji, Successor to al-Khwarizmi." *Mathematics Teacher* (Oct 1986) 538-541.

Pearce, David. "Is the Public Ready to Pay the Price?" *The London Times* (26 Sept 1990).

Peat, David F. *Superstrings and the Search for the Theory of Everything*. Chicago: Contemporary Books, 1988.

Pedro, Daniel. *Geometry and the Visual Arts*. Mineola, NY: Dover, 1976.

Peeples, Susan Martin. "Activities: The Golden Ratio in Geometry." *Mathematics Teacher* (Nov 1982) 672-676.

Peitgen, Heinz-Otto, Hartmut Jurgens, and Dietmar Saupe. *Fractals for the Classroom*. New York: Springer-Verlag, 1992.

————, and P.H. Richter. *The Beauty of Fractals*. New York: Springer-Verlag, 1986.

————, et al. *Chaos and Fractals: New Frontiers of Science*. New York: Springer-Verlag, 1992.

Peressini, Anthony, and Donald Sherbert. *Topics in Modern Mathematics*. New York: Holt, Rinehart and Winston, 1971.

Perl, Teri. *Math Equals: Biographies of Women Mathematicians and Related Activities*. Menlo Park, CA: Addison-Wesley, 1978.

————. "The Ladies' Diary . . . Circa 1700." *Mathematics Teacher* (Apr 1977) 354-358.

————. *Women and Numbers: Lives of Women Mathematicians plus Discovery Activities*. San Carlos, CA: Wide World/Tetra, 1993.

Peterson, Ivars. *Islands of Truth: A Mathematical Mystery Cruise*. New York: W.H. Freeman, 1990.

————. *The Mathematical Tourist: Snapshots of Modern Mathematics*. New York: W.H. Freeman, 1988.

Philip, J.A. *Pythagoras*. Toronto: University of Toronto Press, 1966.

Phillips, Esther. *Studies in the History of Mathematics,* Vol 28. Washington, DC: MAA, 1987.

Phillips, J.P. "Brachistochrone, Tautochrone, Cycloid: Apple of Discord." *Mathematics Teacher* (May 1967) 506-508.

————. "Curves with Proper Names." *Mathematics Teacher* (Apr 1968) 432-433.

Phillips, Patricia. *The Scientific Lady: A Social History of Women's Scientific Interests 1520-1918*. New York: St Martin's Press, 1990.

Piaget, J. "How Children Form Mathematical Concepts." *Scientific American* 189 (1953) 74-79.

Pickover, Clifford. *Computers, Pattern, Chaos and Beauty*. New York: St. Martin's Press, 1990.

————. *Mazes of the Mind*. New York: St. Martin's Press, 1992.

Pierce, R.C. "Sixteenth-Century Astronomers Had Prosthaphaeresis." *Mathematics Teacher* (Oct 1977) 613-614.

Pnina, Abir-Am G., and Dorinda Outram (eds). *Uneasy Careers and Intimate Lives: Women in Science, 1789-1979*. New Brunswick, NJ: Rutgers University Press, 1987.

Poincare, Henri. "Intuition and Logic in Mathematics." *Mathematics Teacher* (Mar 1969) 205-212.

Pólya, George. *How To Solve It*. Garden City, NY: Doubleday, 1957.

————. *Patterns of Plausible Inference*. Princeton, NJ: Princeton University Press, 1954.

————. *Mathematical Discovery*. New York: John Wiley, 1962.

————. "Some Mathematicians I Have Known." *American Mathematical Monthly* 76 (1969) 746-752.

Popp, Walter. *History of Mathematics: Topics for Schools*. London: Open University Press, 1978.

Posamentier, Alfred, and Noam Gordan. "An Astounding Revelation on the History of π." *Mathematics Teacher* (Jan 1984) 52, 47.

Poundstone, William. *The Recursive Universe*. New York: William Morrow Publications, 1985.

Prenowitz, W., and M. Jordan. *Basic Concepts of Geometry*. New York: Blaisdell-Ginn, 1965.

Priclipp, Robert W. "Digital Sums of Perfect Numbers and Triangular Numbers." *Mathematics Teacher* (Mar 1969) 179-182.

————. "Nies Henrik Abel." *Mathematics Teacher* (Oct 1969) 482-484.

————. "Perfect Numbers, Abundant Numbers, and Deficient Numbers." *Mathematics Teacher* (Dec 1970) 692-696.

————. "Three Famous Mathematicians." *Mathematics Teacher* (Feb 1969) 125-127.

Prigogine, Ilya, and I. Stenger. *Order Out Of Chaos*. New York: Bantam Books, 1984.

"Profiles and Contributions of Three Notable Women Mathematicians." *California Mathematics Council ComMuniCator* (Mar 1993) 38-39.

Puritz, C.W. "An Elementary Method for Calculating Pi." *Mathematical Gazette* 58 (1974) 102-108.

Putnam, H. *Mathematics, Matter and Method*. New York: Cambridge University Press, 1975.

———. "Paradox." *Scientific American* 206 (1962) 84–96.

Raab, Joseph. "The Golden Rectangle and Fibonacci Sequence as Related to the Pascal Triangle." *Mathematics Teacher* (Nov 1962) 538–543.

Ransom, William R. *Can and Can't in Geometry.* Portland, ME: J. Weston Walch, 1960.

———. *Famous Geometries.* Portland, ME: J. Weston Walch, 1959.

Ranucci, Ernest. "The World of Buckminster Fuller." *Mathematics Teacher* (Oct 1978) 568–577.

Raphael, Brother L. "The Return of the Old Mathematics." *Mathematics Teacher* (Jan 1967) 14–17.

———. "The Shoemaker's Knife." *Mathematics Teacher* (Apr 1973) 319–323.

Read, Cecil B. "A Book Printed in the Year VII." *Mathematics Teacher* (Feb 1966) 138–140.

———. "Anomalous Mathematical Nomenclature." *Mathematics Teacher* (Feb 1969) 121–125.

———. "Debatable or Erroneous Statements Relating to the History of Mathematics." *Mathematics Teacher* (Jan 1968) 75–79.

———. "Historical Oddities Relating to the Number Pi." *School Science and Mathematics* (Apr 1960) 348–350.

———. "Shanks, Pi, and Coincidence." *Mathematics Teacher* (Nov 1967) 761–762.

Redondi, Pietro. *Galileo Heretic.* Princeton, NJ: Princeton University Press, 1989.

Reichenbach, H. *The Theory of Probability.* Berkeley, CA: University of California Press, 1949.

Reid, Constance. *A Long Way From Euclid.* New York: Thomas Y. Crowell, 1963.

———. *From Zero to Infinity.* Washington, DC: MAA, 1992.

———. "The Autobiography of Julia Robinson." *The College Mathematics Journal* 17 (1986) 3–21.

———. *The Search for E.T. Bell, Also Known as John Taine.* Washington, DC: MAA, 1993.

Reid, George. *Courant in Göttingen and New York: The Story of an Improbable Mathematician.* New York: Springer-Verlag, 1976.

———. *Hilbert.* New York: Springer-Verlag, 1970.

Reimer, Luetta, and Wilbert Reimer. *Mathematicians are People, Too: Stories from the Lives of Great Mathematicians.* Dale Seymour Publications, 1990.

Renn, J., and R. Schulmann. *Albert Einstein/Mileva Maric: The Love Letters.* Princeton, NJ: Princeton University Press, 1992.

Resnikoff, H.L., and R.O. Wells. *Mathematics in Civilization.* Mineola, NY: Dover, 1985.

Restivo, S., and R. Collins. "Mathematics and Civilization." *The Centennial Review* 26 (1982) 277–301.

Rey, H.A. *The Stars.* Boston: Houghton Mifflin, 1966.

Reyerson, Hardy C. "Anyone Can Trisect an Angle." *Mathematics Teacher* (Apr 1977) 319–321.

Ribenboim, Paulo. *Thirteen Lectures on Fermat's Last Theorem.* New York: Springer-Verlag, 1979.

Richter, Jean Paul. *The Notebooks of Leonardo da Vinci.* Mineola, NY: Dover, 1970.

Rickey, V.F. "Isaac Newton: Man, Myth, and Mathematics." *College Mathematics Journal* 18 (1987) 362–389.

Rigby, J.F. "Equilateral Triangles and the Golden Ratio." *The Mathematical Gazette* 72 (1988) 27–30.

Ringenberg, L.A. *A Portrait of 2.* Reston, VA: NCTM, 1956.

Robins, Gay, and Charles Shute. *The Rhind Mathematical Papyrus.* Mineola, NY: Dover, 1987.

Rodgers, James T. *Story of Mathematics for Young People.* New York: Pantheon Books, 1966.

Rolf, Howard L. "Friendly Numbers." *Mathematics Teacher* (Feb 1967) 157–160.

Rolwing, Raymond H., and Maita Levine. "The Parallel Postulate." *Mathematics Teacher* (Dec 1969) 665–669.

Room, Adrian. *The Guinness Book of Numbers.* Middlesex, England: Guinness Publishing, 1989.

Ropes, George H. "Cubic Equations for High School." *Mathematics Teacher* (Apr 1970) 356–359.

Rosenberg, Nancy. *How To Enjoy Mathematics With Your Child.* New York: Stein and Day, 1970.

Ross, Hugh. *The Fingerprint of God.* Orange, CA: Promise Publishing, 1989.

Rosser, Sue. *Female Friendly Science.* New York: Pergamon Press, 1990.

Rothman, Tony. *Science à la mode: Physical Fashions and Fictions.* Princeton, NJ: Princeton University Press, 1989.

Rucker, Rudolf. *Geometry, Relativity and the Fourth Dimension.* Mineola, NY: Dover, 1977.

———. *Infinity and the Mind.* New York: Bantam Books, 1982.

Ruelle, David. *Chance and Chaos.* Princeton, NJ: Princeton University Press, 1991.

Runion, Garth E. *The Golden Section and Related Curiosa.* Glenview, IL: Scott Foresman, 1972.

Russ, Laurence. *Mancala Games.* Algonac, MI: Reference Publications, 1984.

Saaty, T., and P. Kainen. *The Four Color Problem: Assaults and Conquests.* New York: McGraw-Hill, 1977.

Saccheri, Girolamo. *Euclides Vindicatus,* trans and ed George Bruce Halsted. New York: Chelsea Publishing, 1986.

Sacco, William, et al. *Graph Theory: Euler's Rich Legacy.* Providence, RI: Janson Publications, 1987. Sackett, Dudley. *The Discipline of Numbers.* Boston: Ginn, 1966.

Sagan, Carl. *Cosmos.* New York: Random House, 1980.

Saidan, A.S. "Finger Reckoning in an Algebraic Poem." *Mathematics Teacher* (Nov 1968) 707-708.

———. "A Recreational Problem in a Medieval Arithmetic." *Mathematics Teacher* (Nov 1966) 666-667.

Salem, Lionel, Frederic Testard, and Coralie Salem. *The Most Beautiful Mathematical Formulas.* Somerset, NJ: John Wiley, 1992.

Salisbury, Andrew John. "Some Strategy Games Using Desargues's Theorem." *Mathematics Teacher* (Nov 1962) 652-653.

Salmon, Wesley (ed). *Zeno's Paradoxes.* New York: Bobbs-Merrill Educational Publishing, 1970.

Sampson, R.V. *Progress in the Age of Reason: The Seventeenth Century to the Present Day.* Cambridge, MA: Harvard University Press, 1956.

Sandler, B.R., and E. Hoffman. *Teaching Faculty Members to Be Better Teachers: A Guide to Equitable and Effective Classroom Techniques.* Washington, DC: American Association of Colleges, 1992.

Sarton, George. *Ancient Science and Modern Civilization.* Lincoln, NE: University of Nebraska Press, 1954.

———. *Six Wings: Men of Science in the Renaissance.* Bloomington, IN: Indiana University Press, 1957.

———. *The Study of the History of Mathematics.* Mineola, NY: Dover, 1954.

Sastry, K.R.S. "Reader Reflections: Is Pythagoras Nasty?" *Mathematics Teacher* (May 1985) 332-333.

———. "The Quadratic Formula: A Historical Approach." *Mathematics Teacher* (Nov 1988) 670-672.

Sawyer, W.W. *What is Calculus About?* New York: Random House, 1961.

Scarre, Chris (ed). *Timelines of the Ancient World.* New York: Dorling Kindersley, 1993.

Schaaf, William L. *Carl Friedrich Gauss: Prince of Mathematics.* New York: Franklin Watts, 1964.

Schaff, William L. "Art and Mathematics: A Brief Guide to Source Materials." *American Mathematical Monthly* 58 (1951) 167-177.

———. *Carl Friedrich Gauss: Prince of Mathematics.* New York: Franklin Watts, 1964.

———. "Mathematics in Use, As Seen on Postage Stamps." *Mathematics Teacher* (Jan 1974) 16-24.

Schattschneider, Doris. *M.C. Escher: Visions of Symmetry.* New York: W.H. Freeman, 1990.

———. *Visions of Symmetry: Notebooks, Periodic Drawings, and Related Works of M. C. Escher.* New York: W.H. Freeman, 1990.

Schiebinger, Linda. *The Mind Has No Sex?: Women in the Origins of Modern Science.* Cambridge, MA: Harvard University Press, 1989.

Schielack, Vincent P. "The Fibonacci Sequence and the Golden Ratio." *Mathematics Teacher* (May 1987) 357-358.

Schiffer, M. M., and Leon Bowden. *The Role of Mathematics in Science.* Washington, DC: MAA, 1984.

Schimmel, Annemarie. *The Mystery of Numbers.* New York: Oxford University Press, 1993.

Schimmel, Judith. "A Celebration in Honor of Isaac Newton." *Mathematics Teacher* (Dec 1991) 727-730.

Schmaltz, Rosemary. *Out of the Mouths of Mathematicians: A Quotation Book for Philomaths.* Washington, DC: MAA, 1993.

Schofield, P.H. *The Theory of Proportion in Architecture.* New York: Cambridge University Press, 1958.

Schouweiler, Pat, and Diana Hestwood. *Famous Mathematicians.* Minneapolis, MN: The Math Group, 1977.

Schrader, Dorothy V. "De Arithmetica, Book I, of Boethius." *Mathematics Teacher* (Oct 1968) 615-628.

———. "The Arithmetic of Medieval Universities." *Mathematics Teacher* (Mar 1967) 264-275.

Schroeder, Lee L. "Buffon's Needle Problem: An Exciting Application of Many Mathematical Concepts." *Mathematics Teacher* (Feb 1974) 183-186.

Schroeder, Manfred. *Fractals, Chaos, Power Laws.* New York: W.H. Freeman, 1990.

Schwartz, Richard. *Mathematics and Global Survival.* Needham, MA: Silver Burdett and Ginn, 1990.

Schwartzman, Stephen. "Factoring Polynomials and Fibonacci." *Mathematics Teacher* (Jan 1986) 54-56, 65.

———. "Some Little-known Rules and Why They Work." *Mathematics Teacher* (Oct 1985) 554-558.

Scott, J.F. *A History of Mathematics: From Antiquity to the Beginning of the Nineteenth Century.* New York: Barnes and Noble, 1969.

Seidenberg, A. "On the Eastern Bantu Root for Six." *African Studies* 18 (1959) 28-34.

Seitz, Donald T. "A Geometric Figure Relating the Golden Ratio and Pi." *Mathematics Teacher* (May 1986) 340-341.

Serra, Michael. "Geometric Art" and "Transformations and Tessellations." *Discovering Geometry: An Inductive Approach.* Berkeley, CA: Key Curriculum Press, 1989.

Seymour, Dale. *Visual Patterns in Pascal's Triangle.* Palo Alto, CA: Dale Seymour Publications, 1986.

———, and Jill Britton. *Introduction to Tessellations.* Palo Alto, CA: Dale Seymour, 1989.

Shapiro, Max. S. (ed). *Mathematics Encyclopedia.* Garden City, NY: Doubleday, 1977.

Sharpe, Richard, and John Piggott (eds). *The Book of Games.* New York: Galahad Books, 1977.

Shilgalis, Thomas W. "Archimedes and Pi." *Mathematics Teacher* (Mar 1989) 204-206.

Shloming, Robert. "Thabit Ibn Qurra and the Pythagorean Theorem." *Mathematics Teacher* (Oct 1970) 519-528.

Shockley, James E. *Introduction to Number Theory.* New York: Holt, Rinehart and Winston, 1967.

Shoemaker, Richard W. *Perfect Numbers.* Reston, VA: NCTM, 1973.

Shouk, Mahmoud A. "Mathematics Education in the Arab States." *Mathematics Teacher* (Apr 1970) 321-325.

Siegel, Patricia Joan, and Kay Thomas Finley. *Women in the Scientific Search: An American Bibliography, 1724-1979.* Metuchen, NJ: Scarecrow Press, 1985.

Siemens, David F. "Of Bees and Mathematicians." *Mathematics Teacher* (Nov 1967) 758-761.

Singer, Charles. *A Short History of Scientific Ideas.* New York: Oxford University Press, 1959.

Sitomer, Mindel, and Harry Sitomer. *How Did Numbers Begin?* New York: Thomas Y. Crowell, 1980.

Sizer, Walter S. "Other Numeral Systems: Alive and Thriving." *Mathematics Teacher* (Jan 1990) 17-19.

Skolnick, Joan. *How to Encourage Girls in Math and Science.* Englewood Cliffs, NJ: Prentice Hall, 1982.

Slaught, H.E. "Romance of Mathematics." *Mathematics Teacher* (Dec 1966) 744-748.

Slawsky, Norman. "The Artist as a Mathematician." *Mathematics Teacher* (Apr 1977) 298-308.

Smart, James. "Catherine Beecher and Her Dream for Mathematics Education." *California Mathematics Council ComMuniCator* (Mar 1993) 34.

———. "Theorems for Finite Sets of Primes." *Mathematics Teacher* (Apr 1970) 307-310.

Smeltzer, Donald. *Man and Number.* New York: Collier Books, 1962.

Smith, Arthur. "Angles of Elevation of the Pyramids of Egypt." *Mathematics Teacher* (Feb 1982) 124-127.

———. *History of Mathematics.* Mineola, NY: Dover, 1958.

———. *Number Stories of Long Ago.* Reston, VA: NCTM, 1958.

———. "Unsettled Questions Concerning the Mathematics of China." *Scientific American* 33 (1931) 244-250.

———, and J. Ginsburg. *Numbers and Numerals.* Reston, VA: NCTM, 1958.

Smith, David E. *The Geometry of René Descartes.* Macia L. Latham (trans). Mineola, NY: Dover, 1954.

Smith, Norman Kemp. *Immanuel Kant's Critique of Pure Reason.* New York: St. Martin's Press, 1965.

Smith, Sanderson. *An Introduction to Investment Mathematics.* Englewood, NJ: Franklin Publishing, 1968.

———. *Great Ideas for Teaching Math.* Portland, ME: J. Weston Walch, 1990.

———. "It Could Have Happened! Sports Headline: Braves Must Lose Final Two Games to Qualify for Playoffs." *California Mathematics Council ComMuniCator* (Dec 1991).

———. "Two Unusual Representations for the Set of Real Numbers." *Mathematics Teacher* (Dec 1970) 665.

Smithson, Thomas W. "An Eulerian Development for Pi: A Research Project for High School Students." *Mathematics Teacher* (Nov 1970) 597-608.

Snapper, Ernst. "What is Mathematics?" *American Mathematical Monthly* 86 (1979) 551-557.

Sommons, G. *Calculus Gems: Brief Lives and Memorable Mathematics.* New York: McGraw-Hill, 1992.

Sondheimer, Ernest, and Alan Rogerson. *Numbers and Infinity: An Historical Account of Mathematical Concepts.* New York: Cambridge University Press, 1981.

Spaulding, Raymond E. "Pythagorean Puzzles." *Mathematics Teacher* (Feb 1974) 143-146.

———. "Sam Loyd, America's Greatest Puzzlist." *Mathematics Teacher* (Mar 1976) 201-211.

Spencer, Donald D. "Computers: Their Past, Present, and Future." *Mathematics Teacher* (Jan 1968) 65-75.

Spender, Dale. *Women of Ideas and What Men Have Done To Them.* London: HarperCollins, 1990.

Sprent, Peter. *Taking Risks: The Science of Uncertainity.* New York: Viking Penguin, 1988.

Srinevasan, P.K. "Sighting the Value of Pi." *Mathematics Teacher* (May 1981) 380-384.

Srinvasiengar, C.N. *The History of Ancient Indian Mathematics.* Calcutta, India: The World Press, 1967.

Stannard, W.A. "Applying the Technique of Archimedes to the 'Birdcage' Problem." *Mathematics Teacher* (Jan 1979) 58-60.

Stabler, E.R. *Introduction to Mathematical Thought.* Reading, MA: Addison-Wesley, 1948.

Steen, Lynn Arthur (ed). *Mathematics Today.* New York: Springer-Verlag, 1978.

——— (ed). *On the Shoulders of Giants: New Approaches to Numeracy.* Washington, DC: National Academy Press, 1990.

———. "Order from Chaos." *Science News* 107 (1975) 292-293,

———. "Unsolved Problems in Geometry." *Mathematics Teacher* (May 1980) 366-369.

Stein, Sharyn. "Young's Vision." *Mathematics Teacher* (Apr 1993) 331-333.

Stein, S.K. *Mathematics, The Man-Made Universe.* San Francisco: W.H. Freeman, 1963.

Steiner, George. *After Babel.* New York: Oxford University Press, 1975.

Steiner, Mark. *Mathematical Knowledge.* Ithaca, NY: Cornell University Press, 1975.

Steinhaus, Hugo. *Mathematical Snapshots.* New York: Oxford University Press, 1969.

Stevens, Peter S. *Patterns in Nature.* Boston: Little and Brown, 1974.

Stewart, Ian. *Another Fine Math You've Got Me Into ....* New York: W.H. Freeman, 1992.

———. *Does God Play Dice?* New York: Basil Blackwell, 1989.

———. "Gauss." *Scientific American* 237 (July 1977) 122-131.

———. "The Formula Man." *New Scientist* (Dec 1987) 24-28.

———. *The Problems of Mathematics.* New York: Oxford University Press, 1987.

———, and Martin Golubitsky. *Fearful Symmetry: Is God a Geometer?* Oxford: Blackwell Publishers, 1992.

Stigler, Stephen M. *History of Statistics: The Measurement of Uncertainty Before 1900.* Cambridge, MA: Harvard University Press, 1986.

———, "Who Discovered Baye's Theorem?" *American Statistician* (Nov 1983) 290-296.

Stokes, William T. *Notable Numbers.* Los Altos, CA: Stokes Publishing, 1986.

Strauss, Aaron. "ENIAC: The First Computer." *Mathematics Teacher* (Jan 1976) 66-72.

Straffin, Philip D. *Game Theory and Strategy.* Washington, DC: MAA, 1993.

Struik, Dirk J. *A Concise History of Mathematics*. Mineola, NY: Dover, 1987.

———. *A Source Book in Mathematics 1200-1800.* Princeton, NJ: Princeton University Press, 1969.

———. "Omar Khayyam as Mathematician." *Mathematics Teacher* (Apr 1958) 280-285.

———. "On Ancient Chinese Mathematics." *Mathematics Teacher* 56 (1963) 424-432.

Suess, Dr. *Sneetches.* New York: Random House, 1961.

Sullivan, Walter. *We Are Not Alone.* New York: McGraw-Hill, 1964.

Sutton, O.G. *Mathematics in Action.* Mineola, NY: Dover, 1957.

Swetz, Frank. "Back to the Present: Ruminations of an Old Arithmetic Text." *Mathematics Teacher* (Sept 1993) 491-494.

———. *Capitalism and Arithmetic: The New Math of the 15th Century.* La Salle, IL: Open Court Publishing, 1987.

———. "Chinese Mathematics Revision in Accordance with the Teachings of Mao Tse-Tung." *Mathematics Teacher* (Nov 1971) 615-619.

———. *From Five Fingers to Infinity: A Journey Throught the History of Mathematics.* Peru, IL: Open Court, 1994.

———. *Learning Activities from the History of Mathematics.* Portland, ME: J. Weston Walch, 1994.

———. "Mathematical Education in Malaysia." *Mathematics Teacher* (May 1969) 410-417.

———. "Mathematics Education: The People's Republic of China." *Mathematics Teacher* (Feb 1973) 113-120.

———. "Mysticism and Magic in the Number Squares of Old China." *Mathematics Teacher* (Jan 1978) 50-56.

———. *The Sea Island Mathematical Manual: Surveying and Mathematics in Ancient China.* University Park, PA: Pennsylvania State University Press, 1992.

———. "Seeking Relevance? Try the History of Mathematics." *Mathematics Teacher* (Jan 1984) 54-62.

———. "Using Problems from the History of Mathematics in Classroom Instruction." *Mathematics Teacher* (May 1989) 370-377.

———, and T.I. Kao. *Was Pythagoras Chinese? An Examination of Right Triangle Theory in Ancient China.* Reston, VA: NCTM, 1977.

Tarwater, Dalton (ed). *The Bicentennial Tribute to American Mathematics 1776-1976.* Washington, DC: MAA, 1977.

Tauber, Gerald E. *Man's View of the Universe.* New York: Crown Publishers, 1979.

Taviss, Irene (ed). *The Computer Impact.* Englewood Cliffs, NJ: Prentice-Hall, 1970.

Taylor, A.E. *Aristotle.* Mineola, NY: Dover, 1955.

Taylor, E.G.R. *The Mathematical Practitioners of Tudor and Stuart England.* New York: Cambridge University Press, 1954.

Taylor, Harold, and Loretta Taylor. *George Pólya: Master of Discovery.* Palo Alto, CA: Dale Seymour, 1993.

Taylor, Jerry D. "Euler, the Master Calculator." *Mathematics Teacher* (Sept 1983) 424-428.

Temple, Robert. *The Genius of China.* New York: Simon and Schuster, 1986.

Teppo, Anne. "Van Hiele Levels of Geometric Throught Revisited." *Mathematics Teacher* (Mar 1991) 210-221.

Thiel, Rudolf. *And There Was Light: The Discovery of the Universe.* New York: Alfred A. Knopf, 1957.

Tietze, H. *Famous Problems of Mathematics.* Baltimore, MD: Graylock Publications, 1965.

Tobias, Sheila. *Overcoming Math Anxiety.* New York: W.W. Norton, 1978.

Todhunter, Isaac. *A History of the Mathematical Theory of Probability, from the Time of Pascal to that of Laplace.* New York: Chelsea Publishing, 1949.

Tompkins, Peter. *Secrets of the Great Pyramid.* New York: Harper and Row, 1971.

Townsend, Charles Barry. *World's Hardest Puzzles.* New York: Sterling Publishing, 1993.

Townsend, M.S. *Mathematics in Sport.* New York: John Wiley, 1984.

Tranberg, Carl C., and Hussein Kayhan. "Mathematics Teaching in Afghanistan, 1964." *Mathematics Teacher* (Feb 1966) 143-146.

Tuana, Nancy (ed). *Feminism and Science*. Bloomington, IN: Indiana University Press, 1989.

Tuck, Bernard H. "Life and Times of Johann Kepler." *Mathematics Teacher* (Jan 1967) 58-65.

Tufte, Edward R. *The Visual Display of Quantitative Information*. Cheshire, CT: Graphics Press, 1983.

Tuller, Annita. *A Modern Introduction to Geometries*. New York: D. Van Nostrand, 1967.

Turnbull, H.W. *The Great Mathematicians*. New York: New York University Press, 1961.

Tymoczko, Thomas. *Making Room for Mathematicians in the Philosophy of Mathematics*. Northampton, MA: Smith College, 1981.

———. "The Four-Color Problem and its Philosophical Significance." *Journal of Philosophy* 76 (1979) 57-83.

Ulam, S.M. *Adventures of a Mathmatician*. New York: Charles Scribner's, 1976.

Underhill, W. Vance. "A Useful Old Theorem." *Mathematics Teacher* (Feb 1983) 98-100.

Underwood, Dudley. "π: 1832-1879." *Mathematics Magazine* (May 1962) 153-154.

———. *Readings for Calculus*. Washington, DC: Mathematical Association of America, 1992.

Usiskin, Zalman. "Transformations in High School Geometry Before 1970." *Mathematics Teacher* (Apr 1974) 353-360.

Van Biema, David. "Snakes or Ladders." *Time* (12 July 1993) 30-31.

Vanden Eynden, Charles. "Fermat's Last Theorem: 1637-1988." *Mathematics Teacher* (Nov 1989) 637-640.

Van der Waerden, B.L. *Geometry and Algebra in Ancient Civilizations*. New York: Springer-Verlag, 1983.

———. *Science Awakening*. New York: Oxford University Press, 1961.

Vare, Ethlie Ann, and Greg Ptacek. *Mothers of Invention, from the Bra to the Bomb: Forgotten Women and Their Unforgettable Ideas*. New York: Morrow, 1988.

Varnadore, James. "Pascal's Triangle and Fibonacci Numbers." *Mathematics Teacher* (Apr 1991) 314-316, 319.

Vergara, William C. *Mathematics in Everyday Things*. New York: Harper and Brothers, 1959.

Vilenkin, N. Ya. *Stories About Sets*. New York: Academic Press, 1972.

Vogel, Malvina (ed). *The 2nd Big Book of Amazing Facts*. New York: Waldman Publishing, 1982.

Von Neumann, J. *The Computer and the Brain*. New Haven, CT: Yale University Press, 1959.

Voreb'ev, N.N. *Fibonacci Numbers*. New York: Blaisdell, 1961.

Vrooman, J.R. *Rene Descartes: A Biography*. New York: Putnam, 1970.

Wagner, John, and Robert McGinty. "Superstitious?" *Mathematics Teacher* (Oct 1972) 503-505.

Waismann, Friedrich. *Introduction to Mathematical Thinking: The Formation of Concepts in Modern Mathematics*. New York: Torchbooks/The Science Library, 1959.

Walbesser, Henry. "Algorithms and the Bicentennial." *Mathematics Teacher* (May 1976) 414-418.

Waldrop, M. Mitchell. *Complexity*. New York: Simon and Schuster, 1992.

Wallace, Edward C., and Joseph Wiener. "A New Look at Some Old Formulas." *Mathematics Teacher* (Jan 1985) 56-58.

Walton, Karey Doyle. "Albrecht Dürer's Renaissance Connections between Mathematics and Art." *Mathematics Teacher* (Apr 1994) 278-282.

Walton, Karen Doyle. "Is Nicolas Bourbaki Alive?" *Mathematics Teacher* (Nov 1990) 666-668.

Wang, H. *Reflections on Kurt Gödel*. Cambridge, MA: MIT Press, 1988.

Watson, James D. "Pythagorean Triples: What Kind? How Many?" *Mathematics Teacher* (Feb 1976) 108-110.

Weaver, Warren. *Lady Luck*. Mineola, NY: Dover, 1982.

Wedberg, Anders. *Plato's Philosophy of Mathematics*. Westport, CT: Greenwood, 1977.

Weil, Andre. *Number Theory: An Approach Through History, from Hammurabi to Legendre*. Boston: Birkhauser Boston, 1983.

Weiner, Allan. "President Garfield's Configuration." *Mathematics Teacher* (Oct 1982) 567-570.

Wells, David. *The Penguin Dictionary of Curious and Interesting Numbers*. New York: Viking Penguin, 1986.

Wheeler, Michael. *Lies, Damn Lies, and Statistics. The Manipulation of Public Opinion in America*. New York: Dell, 1976.

Whitehead, Alfred North. *An Introduction to Mathematics*. New York: Oxford University Press, 1948.

Whitman, Betsy S. "Mary Frances Winston Newson: The First American Woman to Receive a Ph.D. in Mathematics from a European University." *Mathematics Teacher* (Nov 1983) 576-577.

Whittaker, Edmund. *From Euclid to Eddington*. Mineola, NY: Dover, 1958.

Wilder, Raymond. *The Evolution of Mathematical Concepts*. New York: John Wiley, 1968.

———. *The Foundations of Mathematics*. New York: John Wiley, 1965.

Williams, Gail A. "My Changing Perception of Mathematics." *Mathematics Teacher* (Mar 1983) 170-172.

Williams, Richard H., and Roy Mazagatti. "Mathematical Firsts: Who Done It?" *Mathematics Teacher* (May 1986) 387-391.

Williams, Robert. *The Geometrical Foundation of Natural Structure*. Mineola, NY: Dover, 1979.

Williams, Trevor. *A Biographical Dictionary of Scientists*. New York: John Wiley, 1974.

Wills, Herbert. *Leonardo's Dessert: No Pi*. Reston, VA: NCTM, 1985.

Willson, William Wynne. "The Uniqueness of the Field of Complex Numbers." *Mathematics Teacher* (May 1969) 369-372.

Winkel, Brian J. "Ant, Tunnels, and Calculus: An Exercise in Mathematical Modeling." *Mathematics Teacher* (Apr 1994) 284-287.

Witkowski, Joseph C. "Mathematical Modeling and the Presidential Election." *Mathematics Teacher* (Oct 1992) 520-521.

Wolf, Fred Allen. *Parallel Universes*. New York: Simon and Schuster, 1992.

Wolfe, Harold. *Introduction to Non-Euclidean Geometry*. New York: Holt, Rinehart and Winston, 1945. Wolfson, Harry. *Religious Philosophy*. Cambridge, MA: Harvard University Press, 1961.

Wollan, G.N. "Maclaurin and Taylor and Their Series." *Mathematics Teacher* (Mar 1968) 310-320.

Woodrow Wilson Gender Equity in Mathematics and Science Congress. Princeton, NJ: The Woodrow Wilson National Fellowship Foundation, 1993.

Wren, F. Lynwood. "The 'New Mathematics' in Historical Perspective." *Mathematics Teacher* (Nov 1969) 579-585.

Wrench, J.W., and David Taylor. "The Evolution of Extended Decimal Approximations to π." *Mathematics Teacher* (Dec 1960) 644-650.

Wursthorn, Peter A. "The Position of Thomas Carlyle in the History of Mathematics." *Mathematics Teacher* (Dec 1966) 755-770.

Yates, R.C. *Geometrical Tools*. St. Louis: Educational Publishers, 1949.

Yau, Shing-Tung (ed). *Chern—A Great Geometer of the Twentieth Century*. Hong Kong: International Press, 1992.

Yen, Clara. *Why Rat Comes First: A Story of the Chinese Zodiac*. San Francisco: Children's Book Press, 1991.

Young, Jeff, and Duncan Bell. "The Twentieth Fermat Number is Composite." *Mathematics of Computation* (Jan 1988) 261-263.

Young, Lawrence. *Mathematicians and Their Times*. Amsterdam, Holland: North-Holland, 1981.

Yushkevich, A. *A History of Mathematics in the Middle Ages*. New York: Cambridge University Press, 1985.

Zammatio, C. et al. *Leonardo the Scientist*. New York: McGraw-Hill, 1980.

Zaslavsky, Claudia. *Africa Counts: Number and Pattern in African Culture*. **New York: Lawrence Hill Books, 1979.**

———. "Black African Traditional Mathematics." *Mathematics Teacher* (Apr 1970) 345-356.

———. "Bringing the World Into the Math Class." *Curriculum Review* 24 (Jan-Feb 1985) 62-65.

———. ***Multicultural Mathematics*. Portland, ME: J. Weston Walch, 1993.**

———. "Multicultural Mathematics Education for the Middle Grades." *Arithmetic Teacher* (Feb 1991) 8-13.

———. "Networks: New York Subways, A Piece of String, and African Traditions." *Arithmetic Teacher* (Oct 1991) 42-47.

———. "People Who Live in Round Houses." *Arithmetic Teacher* (Sept 1989) 18-21.

———. "Symmetry and Other Mathematical Concepts in African Life." *NCTM Yearbook*. Reston, VA: NCTM, 1979.

———. "Symmetry in American Folk Art." *Arithmetic Teacher* (Sept 1990) 6-12.

Zatzkis, Henry. "On Fermat's Quadrature of the Parabola." *Mathematics Teacher* (Apr 1974) 333-334.

Zeintarn, M. *A History of Computing*. Framingham, MA: C.W. Communications, 1981.

Zepp, Raymond A. "Numbers and Codes in Ancient Peru: The Quipu." *Arithmetic Teacher* (May 1992) 42-44.

Zerger, Monte. "The Magic of Pi." *Journal of Recreational Mathematics* 12 (1979) 21-23.

Ziman, J. *Puzzles, Problems and Enigmas*. New York: Cambridge University Press, 1981.

Zwier, Paul J. "Multitudinous Kinds of Counting Numbers and Their Generating Functions." *Mathematics Teacher* (Nov 1970) 617-621.

Index

Page numbers in italics refer to illustrations.

A

A priori knowledge, 112

Abacus, *1, 2,* 43, 96, 169, 170

Abu Ali al-Hasan ibn al-Haytham, 53

Abu'l-Wafa, Muhammad, 54

Academy (Plato's), 21

Achilles, The (Zeno), 25, 26

ADA language, 141

Africa, *99*
    art of, 69, 100
    Benin (Nigeria), 100
    Bushoon (Zaire), 99
    cowrie shells, as currency, 41, 42
    drumming in, 107
    farming cycles in, 15
    geometric patterning, 99
    Great Enclosure at Musawwarat, 69
    Igbo (Nigeria), 99
    Kikuyu (Kenya), 100
    Kuba (Zaire), 100
    lusona, 99–100, *99*
    number history in, 41–42
    Oware (Ghana), 100
    sand drawings of, 99–100
    Taita (Kenya), 41
    Yoruba (Nigeria), 41, 42

Agnesi, Maria Gaetana, 109–110, *109*

Agnesi's curve, 110

Ahmes Papyrus, 9

Al-Bahir fi'l-hisab (al-Samaw'al), 57

d'Alembert, Jean le Rond, 57

Alexandria, 33, *33,* 35
    library of, 19, 33
    end of mathematics in, 45–46
    mathematics of, 19, 33, 35–37, 39, 45–46

Algebra
    (Bombelli), 73
    (Euler), 101

Algebra, 39, 55, 57, 61, 131, 137, 139, 166
    abstract, 135, 137, 166

Boolean, 135
Cardano-Tartaglia dispute, 71
clock, 166
fundamental theorem of, 123–124
notation in, 75
quaternion, 135
topology and, 165

Alhambra, the, 69, 183

Almagest (Ptolemy), 51–52

Almanac (Banneker), 113, *113,* 114

American Indian mathematics. *See* North American Indian mathematics.

American Mathematical Society, 129, 195

Analytic Engine, 141, 142

Analytical Institutions (Agnesi), 109

Anaxagoras, 101, 149

Anaximander, 21

Anderson, Laurie, 107–108

Angle, trisection of, 149, *149*

Apollonius, 31, 45, 53

Appel, Kenneth, 201

Archimedes, 3, 19, 21–22, 45, 121, 162, 163

Argand, Jean Robert, 73

Ariosto, Ludovico, 185

Aristotle, 19, 20

Arithmetica (Diophantus), 39–40, *39,* 45

Arithmetica integra (Stifel), 65

Armstrong, Neil Alden, 185

Arnauld, Antoine, 57

Ars Conjectandi (Bernoulli), *97*

Ars magna, sive de regulis algebraicis (Cardano), 71, 73

Art, mathematics and, 67, *67,* 69–70, *69,* 183–184, *183,* 205, 206, 221
    African, 99–100
    American Indian, 119–120, *119*
    Islamic, 69, 183

Aryabhata, 4, 55, 163

Aryabhatiya (Aryabhata), 4, *4*

Assyria, 11, 13
    astronomy in, 14

Astrolabe, 45, *45,* 46

Astrology, 55

Astronomy, 54, 113, 115, 131, 193, 194
    Anasazi, 119
    development of astrolabe, 45, 46
    early, 11–16, 17–18, 21
    Islamic, 54

Asymptote, 102

Atomic physics, 73

Augustus, Thomas, 130

Axiom, 19, 29

Axiomatic method, 165

Aztec cosmology, 120

B

Babbage, Charles, 141, 169, 171

Babylon, 15, *15*

Babylonia, 11
    astronomy in, 14, 17
    cosmology in, 13
    geometry in, 17
    lunisolar calendars, 15
    number system in, 1
    Pythagorean theorem in, 7
    prediction of eclipses, 12

Baghdad, 19, 53

Banneker, Benjamin, 113–114, *113*

Barrow, Isaac, 94

Barrow, John D., 112

Baseball, seasonal statistics in, 191–192

BASIC language, 172, 180, 198

Bath (liquid measure), 4

Bayt al-Hikma (House of Wisdom), 53

Beecher, Catherine, 132

Bees, hive-building of, 173–174

Bell, Alexander Graham, 143

Bergerac, Cyrano de, 185

Bernoulli, Daniel I, 97, 98

Bernoulli, Jacob, 93, 97, 98

Bernoulli, Johann, 93, 97, 98

Bernoulli, Johann II, 97, 98

Bernoulli, Johann III, 97, 98

Bernoulli, Nicholas I, 97, 98

Bernoulli numbers, 98

Bertrand's conjecture, 28

Bhaskara, 47, 55–56, 57, 73, 163

Bible, mathematics in, 3–4, 66

Bingen, Hildegard von, 14, 52

Binomial, powers of, 59, 87

Blanc, M. Le, 117, 121

Bolyai, János, 127

Bolyai-Lobachevsky geometry, 127

Bombelli, Rafael, 73

Bonaparte, Napoleon, 115, 116, 117

Boole, George, 135–136

Boole, Mary Everest, 133

Boswell, James, 2

Brachistochrone, 97

Brahmagupta, 37, *37*, 47

Brahmasphutasiddhanta (Brahmagupta), 37

Brillo, John, 168

Brouwer, Luitzen, 111

Bruno, Giordano, 84

Budget of Paradoxes, A (De Morgan), 137

Buffon, Comte de, 164

Bürgi, Jobst, 77

Butterfly effect, 221

Büttner, J. G., 123

C

Caesar, Julius, 79, *79*

Cajori, Florian, 55

Calculus, 75, 93, 94, 97, 133
    differential, 137, 160
    integral, 137
    notation of, 115
    of variations, 97

Calendar
    African, 15
    Aztec, 120
    Babylonian lunisolar, 15
    Chinese, 15
    development of, 11
    European bone, 15
    Gregorian, 79, 80
    Hebrew, 79, 80
    Julian, 79, *79*
    Khmer temple calendar, 16
    lunar, 16
    Mayan, 11, 80
    Muslim, 79, 80
    reform of, *43, 59, 59,* 79
    Roman, *16*
    of Troth, 12

Calendrical computer, 15–16

Calendrical mathematics, 15, 95

Cambodia, Khmer temple calendar of, 16

Cantor, Georg, 25, 101, 153–154, 162

Cantor, Moritz, 9

Cardano, Girolamo, 57, 71, *71, 73*

Cardinality, 153–154

Carroll, Lewis (Charles Lutwidge Dodgson), 145–147

Cartesian coordinate system, 85

Cartesian plane, 85

Cauchy, Augustin-Louis, 133, *134,* 139

Celestial mechanics, 115

Celestial spheres, 81, *81*

Chaos theory, 211, 217–219, 221–222

Châtelet, Émilie du, 210

Cheng Dawei, 43

Chern, Shiing-shen, 181–182

Cheshire Cat, 146

China
    calendars of, 15, 16
    discovery of pi in, 3
    mathematics of, 12, 43–44, 51, 57, 95–96, 144, 181–182
    number system in, 1
    Pascal's triangle in, 7, *7,* 8, 66
    Pythagorean theorem in, 7

Chisonbop, 170

Chong Zhen li shu, 95

Chuquet, Nicolas, 57

Circle, 17, 31, *31*
    circumference of, 82

Claudius Ptolemy. *See* Ptolemy.

Clavius, Christoph, 79

Coastlines, length of, 211, *211*

COBOL language, 179, 180

Coefficients, literal, 75

Cole, Frank Nelson, 129

Comets, 31, *31*

Complete Introduction to Algebra (Euler), 57

Computer programming, 141–142, 197–198

Computer proofs, 201

Computers, 4, 27, 77, 89, 167, 174, 214, 215, 217, 221, 222
    arts, in the, 70, 107–108
    calendrical, 15–16
    development of, 169–172, *169,* 179–180

conic sections, 31

Copernicus, Nicholas, 31, 51, 81, *82*

Cosmology, 13–14, *13,* 21, 23, 81–82, *81, 83, 119, 120*

Counting
    abacus, *1, 2,* 43, 96, 169, 170
    devices for, 169–170, *169*
    Difference Engine, 141, 169–170, *169*
    finger counting, 2, 41, 169
    Greek mechanical computer, 169
    origin of, 1–2
    Pascal's adding machine, 169
    Pomo methods of, 119
    quipus, 63–64, 169

Counting rods, 96

Cowrie shells, as currency, 41, 42

Cube, construction of, 149, *149*

Cubic equations, 43, 59, 62, 71–72, 110

Cubism, 69

Cubit, 3

Cuelen, Ludolph van, 164

Cuneiform, 1

Cunha, José Anastácio da, 133

Cyclic quadrilateral, 37, 82

Cyril, 46

D

Data processor, *169,* 170

Dedekind, Richard, 134

Deductive reasoning, 19, 29

De Morgan, Augustus, 137–138, 142, 201

De Morgan's laws, 137

Descartes, René, 57, 73, 75, 85–86, 94, 112
    folium of, 85
    rule of signs, 86

Description of the Wonderful Law of Logarithms, A (Napier), 77, *77*

Devaney, Robert L., 221–222

Dialogue on the Great World Systems (Galilei), 83

Dichotomy, The (Zeno), 25

Difference Engine, 141, 169–170, *169,* 171

Differential equations, 115
    Cauchy-Riemann, 134
    partial, 155

Diophantus, 39–40, 45, 53, 57

Directrix, 32

Discourse on the Method (Descartes), 85

Discussion of the Difficulties with Euclid (Khayyam), 59

Disquisitiones arithmeticae (Gauss), 121

Dissertatio (Kepler), 84, *84*

Dodgson, Charles Lutwidge (Lewis Carroll), 145–147

Dolciani, Mary, 134

Doublet puzzle, 147

Dürer, Albrecht, *53*

Dynamics, 221–222

E

e, 24, 103–104

$E = mc^2$, 177

Earth
  circumference of, 33, 34
  position of in solar system, 81, 83

Easter Island figures, 69

Egypt
  calculation of length of year, 11
  cosmology in, 13
  discovery of pi, 3, 4
  geometric concepts in, 17–18
  mathematical papyruses in, 9–10
  number system in, 1
  pyramids of, 5–6, 17

Einstein, Albert, 124, *165,* 177, 178, 194

Einstein-Maric, Mileva, 178, 194

Eisely, Leslie, 189

Electoral college, 125–126

Elements (Euclid), 29–30, 59, 95, 115, 127, 131

Elements of Geometry
  (Legendre), 115–116
  (Playfair), 127

Ellicot, George, 113

Ellipse, 31, *31, 32*

ENIAC (Electronic Numerical Integrator and Calculator), 171

Epicycloid, 132

EQUALS, 195

Equilateral triangle, 21, 123, 173, 183, 184, 207
  formula for area of, 38

Eratosthenes, 19, 33, 34

Escalante, Jaime, 71, 215–216, *215*

Escher, Maurits Cornelis, 183, *183*

Essay on Probabilities (De Morgan), 137

Ethnomathematics, 205–206

Eubulides, 26

Euclid, 19, 27, 29–30, 39, 53, 95, 115, 127, 129, 131

Euclides ab omni maevo vindicatus (Saccheri), 127

Euler, Leonhard, 25, 57, 73, 89, 90, 101, 103–104, *103,* 105, 115, 129, 136, 164

F

Factorial function, 198

Family Math at the Lawrence Hall of Science, 195

Fatou, Pierre, 221

Feigenbaum, Mitchell, 221

Fermat, Pierre de, 85, 89–90, *89,* 91

Fermat's Last Theorem, 89–90

Fermi, Enrico, 158

Ferris, Timothy, 186

Ferro, Scipione del, 71

Fibonacci (Leonardo of Pisa), 9, 61–62

Fibonacci sequence, 61–62, 67

Focus, 32

Formalist school of mathematics, 157, 158

FORTRAN language, 180

Four-color problem, 201–202

Fourier, Joseph, 107

Fractals, 70, 207–208, 211, 212, 221–222

Franciscus Aguilonius, 53

Franklin, Benjamin, 125

Fuller, Thomas, 114

G

Galilei, Galileo, 14, 83–84, *83,* 93, 162, 185

Galois, Evariste, 139–140, *139*

Game theory, 174

Garfield, James A., 143

Gauss, Carl Friedrich, *73,* 121–122, 177

Gender equity in mathematics, 195–196

Geodesy, 115

Geometric patterning, 99

Geometry
  algebra and, 75
  algebraic, 133
  analytic, 85
  Bolyai-Lobachevsky, 127–128
  coordinate, 75
  differential, 182
  Euclidean, 111, 149–150
  hyperbolic, 127–128
  non-Euclidean, 36, 112, 124, 127–128, 133
  Pasch's axiom, 29
  primitive terms, 29
  projective, 75
  spherical, 95, 128
  Thales' development of concepts in, 17–18
  unsolvable problems in, 149–150

Germain, Sophie, 120–121, *120*

God, relationship of to mathematics, 35

Godwin, Francis, 185

Goldbach, Christian, 28

Golden ratio, 67

Golden rectangle, 67–68

Golden triangle, 68

Graph theory, 99–100

Gravitation, laws of, 93

Greece
  calendrical computer, 15–16
  golden age of, 19–20
  mathematics of, 3, 17–23, 25, 27, 29, 31, 33
  role of women in, 23, 45–46

Gregory, Duncan Farquharson, 138

Gregory XII, Pope, 79

Group theory, 139–140

Guo Shoujing, 43

Gutenberg, Johannes, 82

H

Haidao suanjing, 43

Haken, Wolfgang, 201

Halley, Edmond, 31

Halley's Comet, 31

Hamilton, William Rowan, 135, *135,* 136

Hardy, G. H., 167, 168

Harmonices mundi (Kepler), 107

Heron of Alexandria, 37, 38

Heron's formula, 37–38

Herschel, Caroline, 131, 193, *193,* 194

Herschel, William, 193

Hexagon, 173

Hieratic form of records, 9

Hieroglyphics, 1, *1,* 9

Hijra year, 79, 80

Hilbert, David, 154, 157, 158, 161

Hilbert's Hotel, 161–162

Hindu-Arabic number system, 54, 61

Hippocrates of Chios, 150

Hollerith, Herman, 170

Hollerith's data processing machine, *169,* 170

Hopper, Grace Murray, 179, *179,* 180

Hrotswitha of Gandersheim, 51

Hudde, Jan, 75

Hume, David, 112, 158

Huygens, Christiaan, 94

Hydroscope, 45

Hydrostatics, first law of, 22

Hypatia of Alexandria, 39, 45-46, *45*

Hyperbola, 31

I

ibn Yahya al-Samaw'al, 54, 57

In artem analyticem isagoge (Viète), 75

Inca
    calendar of, 64
    quipus of, 63-64, *63, 169*

Indeterminant equations, 39, 56

India
    astronomy in, 60
    caste system in, 55
    cosmology in, 13, *14*
    discovery of pi in, 3
    introduction of negative numbers, 57
    kuttaka, 56
    mathematics of, 4, 37, 47-48, 55-56, 150, 167-168

Infinite series, 167

Infinite sets, 83, 101-102, 153-154, 161-162

Infinity, 25-26, 27, 101-102, 153, 161-162

Interest, compounded, 103

International Organization of Women and Mathematics Education, 195

International Study Group on Ethnomathematics (ISGEm), 205

Internet, 171-172

Intuitionist school of mathematics, 157

Inversion, Carroll's principle of, 145

Investigation of the Laws of Thought, An (Boole), 135

Islamic mathematics, 19, 53-54, 57, 59-60, 66, 69, 79, 128

Isosceles triangle, 17, 20, 21

J

Jiuzhang suanshu (Liu), 43, 44, 57

Joyner-Kersee, Jackie, *215*

Julia, Gaston, 70, 221

Julia sets, 221, 222

Jurassic Park (Crichton), 217-218, 219

K

Kant, Immanuel, 111-112, 157, 158

Kepler, Johannes, 31, 81, 84, 93, 107, 185

Khayyam, Omar, 59, *59,* 60

al-Khwarizmi, Muhammad ibn Musa, 53, 54, 128

King, Dr. Reatha Clark, 209, *209*

Klein bottle, 151, *151*

Klein, Felix, 127-128, 151, 152

Knebel, Fletcher, 189

Koch snowflake, 197, *197,* 207, *207,* 208, 211

Kovalevskaya, Sofia, 155-156, *155*

Kovalevsky, Vladimir, 155

Kronecker, Leopold, 154

L

Ladies Diary, The, 195, *195*

Lagrange, Joseph Louis, 115, *115,* 117, 121, 136, 139

Laplace, Pierre-Simon, 115, 131

Law of the excluded middle, 136

Leap year, 15, 79

Legendre, Adrien-Marie, 115-116, *115,* 122, 139

Leibniz, Gottfried, 93, 97, 109, 115, 164, 169

Leibniz's rule, 94

Lemniscate of Bernoulli, 98

Leonardo da Vinci, 67, *67*

Leonardo of Pisa. *See* Fibonacci.

Les cinq livres des zetetiques (Viète), 75

Levers, principle of, 21

Levy, David, 210

L'Hospital, Marquis de, 98

L'Hospital's rule, 98

Li Ye, 43

Liber abacci (Fibonacci), 9, 61

Lilavati (Bhaskara), 55, *55*

Line, 29

Liu Hui, 3, 43, 101

Lobachevsky, Nikolai, 127, *127*

Logarithmorum (Napier), 77

Logarithms, 65, 75, 77-78, 169

Logic, 135, 137, 145, 157

Logistic school of mathematics, 157, 158

LOGO language, 172, 197-198

Longfellow, Henry Wadsworth, 59, *59,* 60

Looping, 141

Lorenz, Edward, 221

Lost Notebook (Ramanujan), 167

Lovelace, Ada Byron, 132, 141, 170, 171

Lucas, Edouard Anatole, 27, 129

Lucian, 185

Ludolphine number, 164

Luo shu, 7, 8

Lusona, 99-100, *99*

M

Maclaurin series, 104

Magic Mirror (Escher), *183*

Magic squares, 7, 8

Mandelbrot, Benoit, 70, 207, 208, 221

Mandelbrot set, 221, *221*

Map coloring, 201-202

Mark I computer, 179

Marx, Karl, 93

Mascheroni, Lorenzo, 117

Math/Science Network, 195

Mathematical analysis, 121, 159

Mathematical physics, 174

Matrices, 136

Maya
    calendar of, 11, 80
    mathematics of, 47, *47,* 48, *48*
    pyramids, 5-6

Mechanism of the Heavens, The (Somerville), 131

Mei Jeu-cheng, 95

Mei shi congshu jiyao (Mei), 95

Mei Wending, 95-96

Memoir on the Vibrations of Elastic Plates (Germain), 122

Méré, Chevalier de, 91, 203

Mersenne, Marin, 129

Mersenne prime, 129

Mesopotamia, 1, 6

Metaphysical Foundations of Natural Science (Kant), 111

Method of least squares, 107

Microchip, 171

Minus (–) sign, *65*

Möbius, August Ferdinand, 151, *151*

Möbius strip, 151-152, *151,* 202

Molten sea, 3, *3,* 4

Montalvo, Fanya, 214

Morgenstern, Oskar, *174*

Müller, Johannes (Regiomontanus), 51-52

Music, mathematics and, 107-108, 141

Muslim calendar, 79, 80

N

Napier, John, 65, 77, 78, 169

Napier's bones, 78, *78,* 95, 169

Napoleon's theorem, 116, 117

Native American mathematics. *See* North American Indian mathematics.

Neoplatonists, 36

Networks, 105–106

Neumann, John von, 158, 174–176

Newton, Isaac, 51, 93, 109, 111, 115, 185

Noether, Emmy, 165–166, *165*

Noether, Max, 165

Non-Euclidean geometry, 36, 112, 124, 127–128, 133

North American Indian mathematics, 49–50, 119–120
  Anasazi, 119, 120
  Apache, 49
  art, 119–120
  astronomy, 119
  cosmology, *119*
  counting, 119, 120
  games, 49–50, *49*
  Hopi, 119, 120
  Navajo, 50, 119–120
  Nez Percé, 213
  Ojibwa, 120
  Pomo, 119
  Pueblo, 119–120
  Sioux, 120

Number patterns, 20

Number processes, 198

Number systems
  bases in, 1, 41, 142
  binary, 142, 172
  Hindu-Arabic, 54
  origins of, 1, 41

Number theory, 90, 116, 121–122, 124

Numbers
  abundant, 130
  complex, 73–74
  concept of zero, 47–48
  deficient, 130
  ideal, 23
  imaginary, 73, 74
  irrational, 23, 24, 65
  mysticism and, 65–66
  negative, *43*, 47, 57–58, 75
  perfect, 129–130
  prime, 27–28, 129
  rational, 108
  real, 73, 74
  symbolism of, 41, 42, 44, 120, 199, 200
  transfinite, 153

Numerical notation, 9

O

Oeuvres de Descartes (Descartes), *85*

On the Connexion of the Physical Sciences (Somerville), *132*

One-to-one correspondence, principle of, 1, 2, 41, 161–162

Oppenheimer, J. Robert, 158

Optics, 53

Oughtred, William, 169

Ouwehand, Terre, 193, *193,* 194

P

Paisano, Edna, 213–214, *213*

Parabola, 31, *31,* 32, 102

Paradoxes, 25, 158, 183, 184

Parallel lines, 127–128

Parallel postulate, 59, 127, 128

Partial differential equations, 155

Pascal, Blaise, 7, 57, 65, 87, 91, 169, 203

PASCAL language, 198

Pascal's adding machine, 169

Pascal's triangle, 7, *7,* 8, 43, 62, 66, 87–88, *87,* 91

Pasch's axiom, 29

Peacock, George, 138

Peitgen, Heinz-Otto, 221

Penrose triangle, 184, *184*

Percentages, 187

Péter, Rózsa, 197

Philo Judaeus, 35

Philosophiae naturalis principia mathematica (Newton), 93, 109

Pi (π), 3–4, 24, 43, 55, 163–164, 167

Pictographs, 120

Plato, 19, 20, 21

Platonism, 21

Platonists, 36

Playfair, John, 127

Plus (+) sign, *65*

Poincaré, Henri, 128, *133,* 154

Point, 29

Politics, mathematics and, 223–224

Polygons, 123, 183, 184

Polynomial equations, 86, 124, 139

Postulates, 19, 29, 127

Primitive terms, 29

Principios Mathematicos (Cunha), 133

Probability theory, 87, 91–92, *97,* 115, 137, 203–204

Ptolemy, Claudius, 45, 55, 81, *81*

Pyramids, 5–6, *5,* 17, 18, 44, 69

Pythagoras, 7, 19, 20, 23, *23,* 107, 129

Pythagorean theorem ($a^2 + b^2 = c^2$), 5, 7, 8, 89
  Bhaskara's proof of, 56
  Chinese proof of, 144, *144*
  Garfield's proof of, 143, *143, 144*

Pythagorean tree, 222, *222*

Pythagorean triple, 24

Pythagoreans, 21, 23

Q

Qin Jiushao, 51

Quadratic equations, 71

Quadratic formula, 139

Quantum theory, 174

Quaternion algebra, 135

Quaternions, 133, 135

Quipus, 63–64, *64,* 169

R

Radicals, multiplication law for, 73, 74

Ramanujan, Srinivasa, 167–168, *167*

Recursion, 141, 197–198

Reflection, 184

Regiomontanus. *See* Müller, Johannes.

Republic (Plato), 21

Rhind Mathematical Papyrus, 9, 10

Ricci, Mateo, 96

Riemann, Georg Friedrich Bernhard, 128, 133, 177

Right triangle
  area of, 38
  Pythagorean triple and, 24

Robinson, Dr. Julia, 195

Rocketry, 185

Rotation, 184

Rubaiyat (Khayyam), 59

Rule of signs, 86

Russell, Bertrand, 154, 157

S

Saccheri, Girolamo, 127

St. Ives Puzzle, 9

Scott, Charlotte Angas, 194

Set theory, 153–154, 159

Sets, 138
  cardinality of, 153–154
  finite, 101
  infinite, 83, 101–102, 153–154, *153*

Seven bridges of Königsberg problem, 105, 106

Shoemaker, Carolyn, 210

Shoemaker, Eugene, 210

Shoemaker-Levy 9, 210

Shushu jiuzhang (Qin), 51

Siddantasiromani (Bhaskara), 55

Siddhantas, 3

Sierpiński gasket, 197, *197,* 207, *207,* 208

Sieve of Eratosthenes, 34

Siyuan yujian (Zhu), 7

Slide rule, 169

Somerville, Mary Fairfax, 131-132, *131,* 141, 194

Somerville, William, 131

Soroban. See Abacus.

Statistics, 187-189, 213-214

Stifel, Michael, 57, 65-66, 77

Stonehenge, 16

Suan pan. See Abacus.

Sulvasutras, 150

Sun, 11
   as center of universe, 51

Symbolic logic, 137

Symmetry, 119-120, 183

T

Table of chords, 55, 82

Tartaglia, Niccolò, 71, *71*

Taussky-Todd, Olga, 166

Taylor, Richard, 89

Technocracy, *171*

Tetractys, 23

Thales of Miletus, 17, 18

Theon, 45, 46

Theorem, 29, 127

Theory of Games and Economic Behavior, (von Neumann) 174, *174*

Theory of Sets of Points, The, (Young) 159

Thirteen, fear of number, 199, 200

Thomas, Lewis, 186

Topology, 133, 151, 165, 201

Torus, 202

Tower of Hanoi, 198

Traité de mécanique céleste (Laplace), 115, 131

Transformations, 183, 184

Triangles
   congruence of, 17
   Plato's description of, 21
   types of. *See* individual names.

Trigonometric ratios, 43, 75

Trigonometry, 55, 137
   spherical, 43, 54

Trisection of an angle, 149, *149*

Triskaidekaphobia, 199, 200

Troth, 11

Twelfth Amendment, 125

U

UNIVAC (Universal Automatic Computer), 171

Universe, models of, 21, 23, 31, 51, 81-82, *81,* 83

V

Vector analysis, 124

Vector forces, 73

Venn diagrams, 138

Viète, François, 57, 75-76

Vija-Ganita (Bhaskara), 47, 55

Voices from the Well (Ouwehand), 193, 194

W

Walker, Maggie Lena, *133,* 134

Wallis, John, 94, 101

Wang Xiaotong, 43

Water clock, 55

Watt, Molly Lynn, 197

Weierstrass, Karl, 134, 155, 156

Wells, H. G., 189

Whitehead, Alfred North, 157

Wiles, Andrew, 89

Witch of Agnesi, 110

Women in mathematics, 23, 45-46, *45,* 51, 52, *69,* 70, 107-108, 109-110, *109,* 121-122, *121,* 131-132, *131,* 133-134, *133,* 141-142, *141,* 155-156, *155,* 159-160, *159,* 165-166, *165,* 170, 171, 178, 179-180, *179,* 193-194, *193,* 195-196, 197-198, 213-214, *213*

Women in science, 209-210, *210*

X

Xian tu, 144, *144*

Y

Yang Hui, 7

Yi Xing, 12

Young, Grace Chisholm, 159-160

Young, William, 159

Z

Zeno of Elea, 25, *25*

Zeno's paradoxes, 25

Zero, concept of, 47-48, *47, 48,* 57, 107-108

Zhu Shijie, 7, 43

Ziggurats, 6

Zu Chongzhi, 163